The Next Rural Economies

Constructing Rural Place in Global Economies

The Next Rural Economies

Constructing Rural Place in Global Economies

Edited by

Greg Halseth
University of Northern British Columbia

Sean Markey
Simon Fraser University

David Bruce
Mount Allison University

www.cabi.org

CABI Publishing is a trading name of CAB International

CABI Head Office
Nosworthy Way
Wallingford
Oxfordshire OX10 8DE
UK

Tel: +44 (0)1491 832111
Fax: +44 (0)1491 833508
E-mail: cabi@cabi.org
Website: www.cabi.org

CABI North American Office
875 Massachusetts Avenue
7th Floor
Cambridge, MA 02139
USA

Telf: +1 617 395 4056
Fax: +1 617 354 6875
Email: cabi-nao@cabi.org

A catalogue record for this book is available from the British Library, London, UK.

Library of Congress Cataloging-in-Publication Data

The next rural economies : constructing rural place in global economies / edited by Greg Halseth, Sean Markey, David Bruce.
    p. cm.
    Includes bibliographical references and index.
    ISBN 978-1-84593-581-8
1. Rural development. 2. Rural population. 3. Rural-urban relations. 4. Rural tourism. 5. New business enterprises. I. Halseth, Greg. II. Markey, Sean Patrick, 1970- III. Bruce, David, 1967- IV. Title.

HN49.C6N497 2010
307.1'412091722--dc22

2009029188

ISBN-13: 978 1 84593 581 8

Printed and bound in the UK from copy supplied by the authors by CPI Antony Rowe

Contents

Rural Policy and Governance

Rural–Urban Exchange

Renewal in Resource Peripheries

Closing

List of Contributors

Claire Aragau is a new scholar with a well developed track record in small and periurban towns research. She is an Assistant Professor at the Université de Paris Ouest Nanterre La Défense in France since September 2008. Dr. Aragau has participated in a number of international conferences and she is well known for her articles and chapter book about the fluctuations of land and property market on the urban fringe in the west region of France. She works with the Ile-de-France Region in a plan focusing on the social and environment durability of the Paris periurban fringes.
(claire.aragau@free.fr)

Neil Argent is Associate Professor in Human Geography in the Division of Geography and Planning at the University of New England, Armidale, New South Wales in Australia. Dr. Argent has conducted research into the geographical dimensions and regional development implications of rural bank branch closures, and is also investigating the impact of changing population densities upon the social and economic viability of rural settlement systems, and how rural people's perceptions of population densities (e.g. feelings of overcrowding or isolation) affect their social interaction patterns and the overall vitality of rural communities. With others he is currently investigating the dimensions and community-level and rural planning impacts of amenity-led-in-migration into rural Australian communities. The present paper draws upon recent research examining farmers' social and economic linkages with their 'local' town and community in Australia's agricultural heartlands. His widely published research contributes to questions of rural and small sustainability and opportunities for new economic development.
(nargent@une.edu.au)

David Bruce is Director of the Rural and Small Town Programme and Adjunct Professor of Geography and Environment at Mount Allison University in Canada. He was also co-investigator in the research "Building Capacity of Rural Communities in the New Economy" and a member of the Canadian Rural Revitalization Foundation. David has knowledge and expertise in the field of rural community development and associated topics of housing, information technology adoption, population mobility and migration, rural poverty, organizational growth and development, and community economic development. He works with municipalities and regional agencies in the development of community plans focusing on the intersection of labour force development, population issues, and migration.
(dwbruce@mta.ca)

Christopher Bryant is a Past-Chair (2000-2006) of the IGU Commission on the Sustainability of Rural Systems, Full Professor, and Director of the Laboratory on Sustainable Development and Territorial Dynamics, Geography, at the University of Montreal in Canada, the Editor of the *Canadian Journal of Regional Science*, and Co-director of Continuous Training for Rural Development Officers in Québec for Solidarité Rurale du Québec. He is a recognized world leader in rural and small town research, both in rural communities in the urban fringe and in peripheral rural regions. He has a lengthy record of SSHRC awards, the latest of which (2008–2011) involves an action research process aimed at working with local players in the urban fringe of Montreal and Paris to construct ways of re-dynamising degraded agricultural territories. Dr. Bryant has an extensive research and publications program which has focused upon studies in Ontario, Quebec, France, and other locations around the world. His research since the early 1990s on the adaptation of agriculture to climatic change was recognized in various ways, e.g. as lead author on a synthesis of Canadian research in the climatic change/agriculture field for a special issue of Climatic Change (2000) and through the award of several major research contracts by NRCan, (Climate Change and Adaptation Program) in this domain, the most recent of which focused on the co-construction of planning tools for adaptation, involving action research in this domain He also produced in 2007 a report for IDRC on the needs and possible configurations of an International Comparative Research Program on Adaptation to Climate Change, a report that also focused on the need for action research. He has been awarded a major research grant in the SSHRC's 2008 environmental competitions for a comparative study of adaptation of agriculture to climate change and variability in two agricultural areas characterised by water competition between agriculture and nearby cities, one in south-west Québec and the other in south-west Ontario. The focus is ultimately on the co-construction of public policy and collective intervention to enhance the adaptive capacity of the agricultural sector to climate change and variability.
(christopher.robin.bryant@gmail.com)

Mary Cawley is Senior Lecturer in Geography at the National University of Ireland in Galway, Ireland. Her research interests focus upon rural and small town economic development, with a strong interest in the role of tourism in creating additional economic value and local sustainability. Her research work has been focused primarily upon Ireland; however, international work has included collaborations in multi-country European projects and with colleagues in France in particular. Dr. Cawley is widely published in the international journal literature, and her work is recognized as including a critical perspective on the role of institutions, governance, and sustainability in rural and small town development debates. Mary's research interest is related to the geography of social and economic change in rural areas. Issues researched include impact of rural-urban commuting, population change and migration, the role of small and medium-sized enterprises in the rural economy, and rural tourism.
(mary.cawley@nuigalway.ie)

Jean-Paul Charvet is Professor at the Université of Paris Ouest Nanterre La Défense in the Department of Geography in France. He runs a research laboratory on the development of rural and suburban areas. Dr. Charvet is also a consultant to various agencies and organizations for agriculture. Jean Paul is an eminent international specialist in rural agriculture. He has researched the globalization of agriculture through topics such as: global food systems, food systems, green revolution, and global competitiveness. He asks the world to reflect about food safety. In rich countries where almost the entire population is assured of adequate food rations, the main question now is the quality of food and the techniques used for "food safety" and to prevent significant security and farmland losses from rural-urban sprawl.
(jean-paul.charvet@u-paris10.fr)

Deborah Che is an independent researcher who previously was at Kansas State University (USA). Her research interests include rural and community development, natural resource-based tourism (i.e., agritourism, ecotourism, hunting) development and marketing, cultural/heritage tourism, and arts-based economic development strategies. A common theme in her extensive rural and small town research in Appalachia and the U.S. Midwest involves the interconnection between economic restructuring and shifting land uses. As a result of her numerous publications and funded research projects, she has been invited to present in international rural geography and tourism conferences in the USA, Europe, Asia, and Canada. Dr. Che is on the editorial board of "Tourism Geographies" and has served as Chair of the Recreation, Tourism, and Sport specialty group of the Association of American Geographers.
(deborah.che@gmail.com)

Owen J. Furuseth is the Associate Provost for Metropolitan Studies and Extended Academic Programs and a Professor in the Department of Geography and Earth Sciences at the University of North Carolina at Charlotte in USA. He is an internationally recognized senior rural and small town scholar. Dr. Furuseth has a diverse set of research interests including change in the rural–urban fringe, economic transformations as a result of in-migration and economic restructuring, and the social and political consequences of new immigrant groups in rural and small town communities. Owen serves as a Series Editor for Ashgate Publishing's Perspectives on Rural Policy and Planning.
(ojfuruse@uncc.edu)

Hugh J. Gayler is a Full Professor in the Department of Geography at Brock University in Canada. His research has explored the evolution of land use, community development, and economic development within the Niagara Fruitbelt region of Ontario. With more than 35 years of publishing and research experience on this topic, Dr. Gayler is able to bring not only a well informed sense of context, but also a keen interest on how these trajectories of change are creating new rural and small town landscapes. He has been combining his academic position at the university with consulting activities, as well as acting as an assessor for SSHRC

Research Grant Competitions, and a reviewer for the University of Nebraska Press, the Nova Scotia Department of Agriculture, and Environment Canada. (hjgayler@brocku.ca)

Greg Halseth is the Canada Research Chair in Rural and Small Town Studies, Professor in the Geography Program at the University of Northern British Columbia, and Acting Director of the Community Development Institute at UNBC. His research interests centre on community (economic) development and the social geography of rural and small town community change. Current research projects include household and community strategies for coping with economic change in BC's resource-base towns, and the historical geography of sawmill towns along the upper Fraser River from Valemount to Prince George. Dr. Halseth is a member of various advisory councils both at federal, provincial and community levels. Greg is a member of the governing council of the Social Sciences and Humanities Research Council of Canada. His research focuses on the community economic development of rural and small town places like Mackenzie and Tumbler Ridge (British Columbia). (halseth@unbc.ca)

Lisa Mathis Butler Harrington is Professor in the Department of Geography at Kansas State University in USA, and Director of KSU Natural Resource and Environmental Studies, Regional Association of American Geographers Great Plains/Rocky Mountain Region. Dr. Harrington has contributed widely to national and international conferences on rural areas, natural resources, and land use. Her research is focused primarily upon the implications of farming and agricultural land use change in the High Plains area of the US. She has undertaken additional research around the implications of climate change and rural resource use in Kansas; shifts in agricultural commodity demands, such as for biofuel inputs, and other energy issues are significantly changing the future context of rural agricultural communities and economies. Lisa has also been very involved in professional service activities and a variety of research grants panels. (lbutlerh@ksu.edu)

Salma Loudiyi is a Research Fellow, AgroParisTech ENGREF, UMR Metafort (France) and a lecturer at ENITA (Ecole nationale des ingenieurs agricoles). She is member of the International Union of Geography, the Commission on Sustainability of Rural Systems, and member of the National Committee of Geography in France (CNFG). Her research interests are in the administration of land and local development, inter-communality, and peripheral spaces. Dr. Loudiyi is extensively published and well known in the international community. (sloudiyi@gmail.com)

Don Manson is the Coordinator of the University of Northern British Columbia's Community Development Institute. At UNBC he is an Adjunct Professor in the Geography Program and a Research Associate on the Research Chair's Rural and Small Town Studies Team, and with a Degree in Political Science, his research interests include citizen participation, sustainable communities, healthy community, and the economic history of Northern British Columbia. He has

served as Project Manager for UNBC's Rural and Remote Health Research Institute, the National Rural Health Research Summit, and the 2001 British Columbia Health Conference. For three years he served as the policy advisor to the Chair of the Ministerial Advisory Council on Rural Health to the Federal Minister of Health.
(manson@unbc.ca)

Sean Markey is an Assistant Professor with the Centre for Sustainable Community Development at Simon Fraser University. Dr. Markey's research interests include issues of local and regional development and rural sustainability. He is involved with municipalities, non-profit organizations, aboriginal communities, and the business community to promote and develop sustainable forms of local economic development. Dr. Markey is the principle author of *Second Growth: Community Development in Rural British Columbia* (UBC Press 2005).
(spmarkey@sfu.ca)

Masatoshi Ouchi is a Professor, Department of Agri-food and Environmental Policy, School of Agriculture, Meiji University, Japan. His book entitled Social Change in Post-War Rural Japan offers a new history of post-war Japanese rural society where the generation of farmers born between 1926 and 1934 played a central role in transforming rural society. They experienced land reform, modernized Japanese agriculture, coped with overproduction and, as they grew older, suffered the consequences of an aging rural society with decreasing numbers in the younger generations. Dr. Ouchi visited Canada in 2007 through the New Rural Economy Research Initiative. In Brandon Manitoba, he visited the Brandon Research Station at Brandon University, and also he visited Agriculture and Agri-Food Canada. In British Columbia, Masatoshi visited the University of Northern British Columbia and many communities along the Upper Fraser River.
(ouchi@isc.meiji.ac.jp)

Doug Ramsey is an Associate Professor, Department of Rural Development, at Brandon University in Canada. In 2005, he was a Visiting Professor, Universität des Saarlandes, Saarbrücken, Germany (funded by the Canadian Embassy, Berlin, and the Universität des Saarlandes). Dr. Ramsey is interested in understanding the conditions of communities and how they respond to change. Some of his work has included issues such as agricultural restructuring and diversification, rural tourism, and rural community condition. Doug is the founding Editor of the Journal of Rural and Community Development and is a Co-Editor of the Canadian Human Landscapes Examples Series in the Canadian Geographer. He has also acted as the Chair of the Neighbourhood Renewal Corporation, City of Brandon; and with the Rural Geography Study Group of the Canadian Association of Geographers. Doug is presently a Board Member with Travel Manitoba, a Crown Agency of the Province of Manitoba.
(ramsey@brandonu.ca)

Bill Reimer is an internationally recognized scholar in rural and small town issues at Concordia University in Montreal (Canada). For the last ten years, he has headed the research initiatives of the Canadian Rural Revitalization Foundation (CRRF), including more than $5 million in research contracts through SSHRC's Social Cohesion and Initiative on the New Economy Programs. Dr. Reimer has published extensively in academic journals, made important contributions to policy debates on social capital, social exclusion, rural and urban relations, and community and economic development. This includes the analysis of women's role in farm production, the informal economy, poverty in rural areas, the development of a theoretical framework for the analysis of exclusion, and its application to several types of vulnerable groups. Bill is involved with international research networks in the United States, Europe, Japan, and Australia. His research interests are with the capacity of rural and small town places to cope with change. Such capacity issues focus upon family, community, and governance mechanisms. (Bill.Reimer@concordia.ca)

Tony Sorensen is Adjunct Professor in the School of Behavioural Cognitive and Social Science at the University of New England, Armidale, New South Wales in Australia. He is a Fellow of the Institute of Australian Geographers, a Past President of the Australian and New Zealand Regional Science Association, and has published widely in Geography, Economics, Urban Planning, and Public Policy. Tony is currently working for the Cotton Cooperative Research Centre on innovative small businesses in cotton communities and researching the dynamics of rural community resilience. More generally, he works in the field of rural change and adaptation. The urban-centric models of research and development or creativity developed in Europe and North America fail to describe or explain much of Australia's highly effective innovation system, which is has a heavy rural bias and is spatially disconnected. (asorense@une.edu.au)

David Storey is a Senior Lecturer in Geography at the University of Worcester in England with research expertise on rural socio-economic change, rural development policies, and issues of place and identity. Dr. Storey has investigated the utilization of community-based partnership responses to developmental problems in rural areas in both Ireland and Britain, as well as the use of local heritage in rural place promotion. His work has been undertaken for a range of local authorities and voluntary bodies in the English West Midlands, as well as the Commission for Rural Communities; this recent work includes a survey of environmental issues in Cleobury Mortimer, work-life balance issues in Worcestershire and countryside access for under-represented groups. Storey's work is widely published. (d.storey@worc.ac.uk)

Kelly Vodden is an Assistant Professor in the Department of Geography at Memorial University in Newfoundland and Labrador (Canada). As a new scholar she has already established an impressive publication record. Kelly has extensive interests in rural and small town community economic development research and practice.

She has been part of several major collaborative research projects undertaken by SFU's Community Economic Development Centre and Memorial University and is currently engaged in research projects on regional governance and the use of local knowledge in coastal management.
(kvodden@mun.ca)

Nigel Walford is Professor at the School of Geography, Geology and the Environment at Kingston University in the UK. His research interests focus upon the application of geographical information systems to human geography issues. This includes a special interest upon rural and small town population dynamics and development issues. His work has focused upon southeast England and Wales. He has an extensive publication record in both national and international journals, books, and conferences. He is an internationally recognized scholar.
(N.Walford@kingston.ac.uk)

Jim Walmsley is Professor in the Division of Geography and Planning in the School of Behavioural, Cognitive and Social Sciences at the University of New England Armidale, New South Wales (Australia). He is a Fellow of the Academy of the Social Sciences in Australia and was President of the Institute of Australian Geographers 2006–2008. His major current research interest is on lifestyle and leisure in advanced western society. He has particular interests in lifestyle-led migration and the changing nature and role of leisure-based activity in both metropolitan and non-metropolitan areas of Australia.
(jim.walmsley@une.edu.au)

Michael Woods is Professor of Human Geography and Director of the Institute of Geography and Earth Sciences at Aberystwyth University in Wales, Co-Director of the Wales Rural Observatory, and a senior member of the Wales Institute of Social and Economic Research, Data and Methods (WISERD). His research interests include rural politics, rural conflicts, and rural social movements; community governance and participation; and globalization and rural localities. Michael's work is extensively published in top international journals, and he is author of *Contesting Rurality: Politics in the British Countryside* (Ashgate, 2005), *Rural Geography* (Sage, 2005) and *Rural* (Routledge, forthcoming 2010), co-author of *Key Concepts in Rural Geography* (Sage, forthcoming 2010, with Lewis Holloway and Ruth Panelli) and *An Introduction to Political Geography* (Routledge, 2004, with Martin Jones and Rhys Jones) and editor of *New Labour's Countryside: Rural Policy in Britain since 1997* (Policy Press, 2008). He is currently co-ordinating a major European Union Framework Programme 7 project on 'Developing Europe's Rural Regions in the Era of Globalization' (DERREG) (www.derreg.eu), and his recent research includes studies of grassroots rural protest, rural community governance, and migrant labour, particularly in England and Wales.
(m.woods@aber.ac.uk)

Acknowledgments

There are many people who contributed to the original workshop and to the production of this volume. We would like to pay particular thanks to the following organizations, programs, and individuals.

Funding support for the workshop was made available through the Social Sciences and Humanities Research Council's Aid to Research Workshops and Conferences in Canada program. We also appreciate the work of former UNBC President Don Cozzetto and senior staff on the President's Executive Council for supporting the workshop. Also of great assistance was Gerry Salembier, Assistant Deputy Minister, Western Economic Diversification Canada as well as Wendy Rogers, Senior Business Officer, Western Economic Diversification Canada – just when it looked as if we could not hold this important international workshop, a small grant from Western Economic Diversification gave us the hope and faith to move forward with our plans.

Production of the workshop required the assistance of many people. Kelly Giesbrecht helped put together our initial workshop plan and funding application. The UNBC Conference and Events Office did an outstanding job of organizing all of the basic logistics, services, and site facilities. The staff of UNBC's Community Development Institute, especially Ashley Kearns, Kyle Kusch, Laura Ryser, Michelle White, Alison Matte, and Chelan Hoffman, helped with all aspects of workshop planning and put in long hours during the course of the workshop itself to handle all the needed tasks and details. Rosemary Raygada Watanabe was our key workshop organizer and manager – she expertly looked after all facets of the workshop and its success is due in large part to the seamless event she orchestrated.

Funding support for the publication of this book was received from each of our institutions. This includes a UNBC publication grant from the Office of Research, a publication grant from Simon Fraser University, as well funding support from Dr. Stephen McClatchie, Provost and Vice-President (Academic and Research), Mount Allison University. This assistance is gratefully acknowledged.

While production of the book required a tremendous amount of work from the editorial team, we were ably assisted. West Coast Editorial Associates, members Audrey McClellan and Louise Oborne did an outstanding job of proofreading the chapters and providing constructive comments to the authors. Lesley King and Shankari Wilford at CABI assisted as we moved the book into production. We would especially like to thank Claire Parfitt, Commissioning Editor at CABI, for taking this project forward and providing support and encouragement. At UNBC, all of the production work for the book manuscript was done by Rosemary Raygada Watanabe. As with the workshop, Rosemary was an expert master on the computer and with all of the various production software as she created a marvellous final product.

The most important thank-yous, of course, go to each of the contributing authors in this book. When contacted to participate in the workshop, all were enthusiastic. Throughout the workshop and book preparation stages, they have been an academic dream team always working to tight time frames and high standards. Most importantly, when the workshop confronted a budget crisis, many of these authors worked with their own institutions to confirm travel and support funding to allow them to participate. The organizing committee of the workshop and the co-editors of this book thank them all most sincerely for their commitment to this project.

Finally, we also wish to thank the North Central Municipal Association and all of the community and local government representatives who attended the workshop. Their presence helped to ground conference discussions in the realities of place, and also helped to facilitate an early mobilization of the ideas and debates from around the world into practice and their application in northern BC.

We hope that readers find this book providing stimulation for thought, debate, and action.

Greg Halseth – Prince George
Sean Markey – Vancouver
David Bruce – Sackville

June 2009

Chapter 1

Introduction: The Next Rural Economies

Greg Halseth, Sean Markey, Bill Reimer, Don Manson

The Next Rural Economies brings together rural and small-town scholars from seven OECD countries to present essays on the possible future of rural development. Past approaches to rural development have tended to focus on the "space economy," implying attention to comparative advantages, natural-resource endowments, and development strategies that sought mainly to overcome the cost of distance. Through the cumulative efforts of rural development practitioners and researchers, this space-based approach is being challenged and complemented by a recognition of the growing importance of "place-based economies." A place-based approach to rural development means that the unique attributes and assets of individual communities and regions now underscore their attractiveness for particular and contextually appropriate types of activities and investments.

The dynamics and functional attributes of place provided the purpose and substance of a workshop held in the spring of 2008 at the University of Northern British Columbia, "Space to Place: The Next Rural Economies." The participants all shared a common focus in their work on rural community and regional development, and the workshop provided a framework for sharing and advancing our understanding of place-based approaches to rural development. The production of this volume was a key workshop objective from the outset, allowing us to identify core themes for participants to reference in their chapters (see below). This continuity of purpose and reflection facilitated a robust comparative treatment of the rural experience in each country setting.

The common themes that emerge in the following chapters do so despite the tremendous variety of rural places that are represented in the research. Defining "rural" is highly dependent on the variables one wishes to prioritize—population (Statistics Canada, 1999); density (Organization for Economic Co-operation and Development, 1994); economic features, ecological systems, or social characteristics (Hoggart and Buller, 1987). Given the diversity of rural places represented by the authors of this volume, we are drawn to the definitional continuum described by Cloke (1977) and its expression as "degrees of rurality," conceptualized by du Plessis *et al.* (2002), as a way of uniting these stories under the rural banner. The degrees of rurality encompass a wide range of rural characteristics (and urban influences) and also allow for the self-expression and identification of rural peoples, whose communities may lie outside the narrow indicator parameters of a particular definition of rural, but who still consider themselves to be rural residents.

Regardless of how the specific communities and regions are defined, the stories in this text combine to inform us of the continued relevance of rural areas. This relevance comes in many forms, including the production of *food*; connection to *resources* as factors of production, sources of economic dependency, or sites for conservation; places of *cultural* importance, contributing to broader regional or national identities; and also as important places for the overall trend toward *localization*, which is being driven by both cultural preference (e.g., local food production, buy-local campaigns, and resistance to the homogenization of globalization) and by factors of production (i.e., changes in the cost structures of distance as determined by the price of energy).

The authors of these chapters remind us that rural matters, but in ways that are in a state of almost constant flux. The 21st century is defined by fast-paced change. The implications for rural and small-town places are that any solution to current economic circumstances will soon need to be revisited or revitalized. In other words, if you create success today, you had better start planning for the next transition starting tomorrow. Attention in the global economy to flexibility and responsiveness requires continuous attention to our rural and small-town economic development processes. This attention signals a call for a return to intervention, albeit in different forms than in the past. New understandings of competitiveness and conceptualizations of a *new* rural economy have underlined the importance of making strategic investments in the physical and social infrastructure of a community—i.e., investments in *place*. These chapters teach us that doing things, at the local and regional level, matters and that not doing things has consequences. As a common theme, "place" has re-emerged as a fundamental ingredient within the rural economy, where territory matters more than sector and competitive advantage more than comparative advantage.

In the remainder of this chapter, we will expand upon our understanding of the differences between, and the significance of, space and place to rural development. We will identify and describe core themes and related issues that we use to bring conceptual coherence to the volume. Finally, we will provide brief chapter summaries to guide readers to specific articles of interest and also to provide a sense of the scope of the entire text.

Understanding Space and Place

Championing place over space is not new to research and analytical materials. It is a theme that has gained prominence in geography, sociology, and economics over the last few decades (Bradford, 2005; Harvey, 1990; Organization for Economic Co-operation and Development, 2006; Partridge and Rickman, 2008). What is relatively new, however, is an elaboration of the implications it may have for policy and local action. It is for this reason that we have grounded our discussion in rural futures and considered how a place-based focus will provide useful insights and suggestions for such action. Our first task, therefore, is to clarify the significance of a focus on place and its differentiation from a focus on space.

Space and place are largely metaphoric concepts. Places are located in space, and the tools we use for identifying spaces (height, width, breadth, latitude, and longitude) can also be used for identifying the characteristics of places. The differences emerge when we come to use them for analytical and policy objectives.

An analysis based on *space* emphasizes the ways in which distance, density, and physical obstacles organize economic or social relationships and the ways in which we manage the world around us (Cairncross, 1997; O'Brien, 1992). Classic economic and geographic location models that represent settlements as dots on an isotrophic plain, linked by transportation/communication corridors, are reductionist examples of space-based thinking and analysis. Researchers working from this perspective have tended to treat the units of analysis as relatively autonomous and then examined the relationships among their characteristics and the spatial features in which they exist. Analytically, these "autonomous" characteristics then become the venue of policy and programmatic decision making focuses on particular variables, roles, or sectors. Specific individuals and the environments in which they live are represented by particular conjunctions of characteristics, and decisions about the future are made with respect to regularities identified in these relationships. Using this perspective, we have been able to effectively separate general patterns and trends from the idiosyncrasies of unique cases and identify the processes and drivers underlying them. Important insights about settlement patterns, service delivery, communication, institutional structures, and migration, for example, have emerged from this approach.

Our forecasts for the future are heavily dependent on space-based types of analysis. In order to anticipate future trends, we identify characteristics of individuals or groups, their physical, economic, and social spaces, and then trace the changing relationships among them over time. By projecting these relationships into the future, we can create scenarios for planning and action.

These insights about space have also driven many of our policies regarding rural areas. Settlement, health policies, development of transportation infrastructure, social service delivery, and even political boundaries have been established and modified according to the conditions of, and research into, population density, communication and transportation costs, and commuting flows. Even when it comes to community and regional planning, the focus on space has provided useful insights. Based on this research, for example, communities have been encouraged to identify the characteristics that give them a relative advantage in comparison to other communities and to reduce the space-related barriers that keep them outside the centres of economic or social power.

However, there are significant limits to the way in which an emphasis on space in general can be used to interpret our activities and empower rural people. The accelerating pace and transformation of the global economy in regards to such issues as mobility (of people, capital, information, etc.), the service/creative sectors, and others, highlight how the limits of a space-based approach are becoming more significant. Space-based analyses tend to be transformed from their descriptive roots to proscriptive objectives, and in the process they come to represent these trends and relationships as inexorable (Markey *et al.*, 2008), driving us to futures we all must share and over which we have limited influence. In practical terms, they have de-emphasized the ways in which particular places with unique constellations of characteristics and histories have reorganized themselves in surprising and innovate ways, sometimes bucking the general trends. These situations have become the stuff of a more place-based focus.

Place-based analyses follow Massey's finding that general processes "never work themselves out in pure form. There are always specific circumstances, a particular history, a particular place or location. What is at issue is the articulation of the general *and* the local" (1984, p. 9). Such analyses also build from Bradford's (2004, 2005) observations that it is in "places" that today's major public policy issues play out, that "place" matters to both quality of life and economic prosperity, that spatially concentrated problems demand place-sensitive and holistic approaches, and thus today's policy challenges are resistant to simple sectoral interventions. In other words, place-based analyses emphasize the uniqueness of individuals, locations, or regions as a way to discern possibilities and options otherwise discounted or invisible to a space-based analysis. As a result, such analyses are usually more locally descriptive in nature, focusing on the particular conjunction of general characteristics in time and space, and the historical processes leading to that conjuncture. Historical and dispositional explanations predominate over demographic and functional ones (Stinchcombe, 1968), and the significance of perception, identity, representations, and social construction are highlighted over the structural focus emphasized in a space-based approach. Place-based approaches emphasize the agency of individual or group actors over the structures in which they operate.

The importance of a place-based analysis is readily apparent when we consider the natural endowments of particular places. The physical location of a mountain, river, mineral deposit, microclimate, or soil type can determine the impact and implications for settlement, opportunities, and challenges of these places. This effect is made even more complex when we consider how these assets are understood, valued, and reconciled with local aspirations and visions of rural development. That these place-unique arrangements modify the impacts of general policies is a well-recognized feature, influencing economic policies and the application of a wide variety of programs—from capital and financial development to insurance and regional development.

The importance of place is not as well recognized, however, when it comes to individual and social behaviour. Policy makers tend to adopt the neo-liberal perspective that sees human beings as relatively autonomous units, able to make choices independent from those around them and free to move so long as transportation and housing costs are adequately managed. This view of human action has been challenged by researchers investigating the significance of social networks, cohesion, and social capital in supporting functional and resilient communities, industries, and economies. Rather than seeing individuals as autonomous units, they view human beings as centres of action, well integrated into a network of ties and guided by norms and constraints that significantly guide the options and opportunities of each person. Mobility, therefore, is not just a matter of overcoming the costs of physical relocation, but also entails considerable challenges in the reorganization of the social ties that are integral to our welfare and identity.

From this point of view, place takes on an even more important role. For most people, the networks that influence our earliest socialization and identity are geographically close. As we age, these networks expand, but for the most part they remain most intense within our neighbourhood, city, or region (Wellman, 1999). From the viewpoint of an individual, therefore, a social network takes on the characteristics of a place. And like a river, mountain, or mineral deposit, it is difficult to take this social network with you when you move.

Our state agencies have recognized the importance of social networks—at least with respect to those required for health, education, justice, and welfare. By providing relatively standardized services in key institutions, we facilitate the movement of individuals in keeping with policies requiring labour mobility. To the extent that these policies are successful, we can expect that the support provided for educating our children, for example, is equivalent whether we live in one region of a country or another. In general terms this may be the case, but in fact we find that even these state services vary considerably, and once we include the many informal and personal ties required for health and vitality, we are again forced to recognize the unique characteristics of each person's social place. Place matters, therefore, not only for its physical characteristics, but also for the social and institutional characteristics it presents for those who are connected to it.

Both space and place approaches are useful for analysis and policy making. A space-based approach provides useful insights for identifying the general patterns of community change and separating the relative contributions of economic, social, and political factors to those changes. A place-based approach, on the other hand, helps us see and understand the local responses to those changes—emphasizing how the historically specific conjuncture of key factors and the particular perceptions and identities of local people and groups create new conditions that can significantly modify the general trends they share. Place-based approaches highlight local conditions, the roles of local actors, and the agency of individuals and groups. They are, therefore, particularly useful for strategic planning at the local level. If the new rural economy demands that communities approach economic development and renewal by reimagining and rebundling their assets and matching opportunities with aspirations, then a place-based analysis and approach is key to both identifying local actions and grounding supportive public policy (Apedaile, 2004; Halseth *et al.*, 2007; Markey *et al.*, 2006).

This book emphasizes place-based approaches. Our choice is strategic—for both analytical and pragmatic objectives. Analytically, place-based approaches have been underdeveloped and are, therefore, in greater need of attention to complement those using a space-focused approach. Pragmatically, they help us avoid the tendencies to homogenization, commoditization, and resignation that have been so prominent in our rural policies (Fluharty, 2006).

Integrative Themes and Emerging Issues

We selected four themes to provide a conceptual framework to guide each author in the book: rural restructuring, the next rural economy, governance, and rural investment. These themes provide insights into the structural dynamics of change in rural areas. They also challenge each author to bridge the gap between theory and reality, to illustrate the processes and practices that are actively constructing (or deconstructing) the next rural economies. The following section provides a brief summary of these core themes and a sampling of the many divergent issues stemming from them that are contained in the volume.

Rural Restructuring

First, the chapters that follow relay varying experiences with the processes and impacts of rural restructuring. This provides an opportunity to synthesize common patterns and critical differences in how restructuring expresses itself in various industrial and cultural settings. Restructuring may be understood as changes in economy, government, and environment that shift established patterns of economic development and political responsibility. This volume presents cases of restructuring as both crisis events that force a rapid adaptation and also as general processes of more gradual industrial, demographic, and political change (Bradbury, 1989; Lovering, 1991).

What is clearly evident from our time together at the workshop is that central to a place-based approach to rural development is a reorientation of the relationships that govern and shape rural areas. This involves new roles for governments at all levels, a shift in the dynamic relationship between rural industries and the places they do business, and increasing responsibilities for communities and regions to shape their futures. The chapters in this volume present a tremendous diversity of experiences and trajectories in how these new relationships are being constructed and maintained. While this is to be expected as we replace our general space-based perspective of rural development with a more magnified lens that allows the specificities of place to emerge into view, there remain striking commonalities in the "push" and "pull" forces that are driving change in the rural experience.

Push factors include the cumulative impacts of government and industry restructuring over the past three decades. Government withdrawal has been a steady trend under the influence of neo-liberalism and managerialism, dramatically reshaping the relationship between rural places and their traditional senior-government stewards. Similarly, the relationship between industry and the communities/regions where they operate, so prominent in the construction of rural places in the postwar period, has been all but severed down to the sinews of a flexible workforce—one that is sometimes not even local. The impacts of these restructuring processes have been severe for many rural areas, leading to population declines and a cascading effect of dwindling services. For other communities, however, the removal of these structural forces has allowed a blossoming of innovation and place-based identity, leading to highly variegated conditions across our rural examples.

Positive dimensions of place emergence represent the pull factors that are also driving rural change. Communities and regions are organizing themselves, constructing their own visions of development, and establishing innovative networks and responses to new economic opportunities. This form of place-based development, as we will see in the following chapters, is highly dependent on rural capacity (often aided by new forms and types of relationships with government and industry). Nevertheless, the localization and diversification of the rural economy, which are by-products of the place-based approach, present exciting possible futures and lessons for rural areas that are mired in the shock and decline of restructuring.

The Next Rural Economy

Second, while an economic imperative to rural development remains, there is now greater consideration of culture, environment, and community issues and implications. These additional issues are now well-recognized and sought-after assets in the new economy. The chapters in this volume provide valuable lessons and stories of rural development that draw from these and other place-based assets. Importantly, the view that emerges of the next rural economy remains grounded in many of the traditional assets of rural places—the resource sector, natural amenities, and small-town lifestyle—but involves thinking about and mobilizing these assets in different ways. This is important because it does not alienate the existing rural economy and its people in the process of transition. Other critical themes that emerge in the volume include the importance of connectivity, rural innovation, lifestyle, and quality of life—traditional rural strengths that now take on increased importance.

Connectivity

Rural and small-town places have thrived or withered depending on the availability of connected infrastructure. The re-equipping of rural and small-town places to be more competitive in the global economy means attention to "old economy" infrastructure, including roads, rail, airports, and other connecting infrastructure. In addition, places must be equipped to connect with the new economy through the communications tools of that economy, mainly advanced information and communications technologies. The ability to move information is a critical component of the knowledge economy, and if places are to mobilize local assets, they will need to be active in that economy. The "next labour force" demands electronic connectivity to the global community at the same time as it values the quality of life that still defines rural and small-town places. Finally, connectivity is identified in a number of chapters as being crucial to networking across communities with similar interests in order to establish a regional identity or scale-up successful community interventions.

Innovation

In a fast-paced global economy, places need to be flexible and responsive to new opportunities. Establishing place-based flexibility involves attention to, and support of, innovation. Innovation refers to strategic processes of area networking and investment that can stimulate inter-sector and inter-firm advancement. Such innovation grows from the density of local/regional connections and is further supported by a recursive commitment to learning and ongoing human-capacity development. Depending upon the assets and aspirations of individual places, several of the chapters identify ways to support innovation through the creative identification of opportunities and the implementation of supportive public policy and investments.

Quality of Life and Lifestyle

Quality of life and rural lifestyle have historically been important for holding businesses and residents in small-town places. Increasingly, however, the global economy also demonstrates that these assets are valuable economic commodities. Looking forward to the "next labour force," many of the chapters in this book make it clear that quality of life and lifestyle assets will be key to attracting and holding creative people and the economic activities they generate. Lifestyle is also a critical force in retaining residents and influencing their willingness to participate in transition processes. Quality of life and lifestyle assets in rural and small-town places are critical ingredients for attracting and retaining mobile capital and attracting the next generations of workers.

Urban–Rural Ties

Many of the contributors highlight the importance of an old notion: that rural and urban places are intimately bound together in a single economic structure. Each has a different, but connected, role to play within integrated regional economies. The debate in many places over the last 20 years has become divorced from this recognition of connectedness, and the research stories that follow inform us that we must renovate this relationship. The importance of connectivity between rural and small-town places and metropolitan cores is important in practice, in policy, and in directing our investments. A reinforcing point on the need to renovate our understanding of rural and urban ties comes from those examples of rural places that are being "drowned by an urban tide." Development pressures that are not well integrated into thoughtful rural and urban planning processes can generate terrific pressure on local property and housing markets, and may lead to negative outcomes for rural and small-town places that otherwise may have benefited from such an influx of development interest.

Not a Case of Either / Or Solutions

One of the prominent messages inculcated through the following chapters is that rural and small-town places must approach the latest economic development "fads" or trends with caution. Researchers raise concerns about the "next big idea" and "flavour of the month" solutions that have so often come to characterize rural development actions and investments. The need for a careful and balanced multi-faceted approach that is built upon local, place-based assets and aspirations means that we should consider opportunities that emerge based on how well they fit with those assets and aspirations. Attention to purposeful development and a common vision can assist with the coordination of policy support, local initiatives, and investment decisions. In the end, leaping from disjointed opportunity to disjointed opportunity will be a poor solution for the effective renewal of rural economies and a poor use of our limited community-development supports. Such reactive policies and projects also contribute little toward building more resilient, vibrant, and proactive rural and small-town places that are able to meet the challenges of the global economy over the long term.

Governance

Third, new governance regimes and creative policy prescriptions are central to the place-based economy. Governance implies a re-drawing of the lines of accountability and control, away from centralized state power, to be dispersed among a greater diversity of local and extra-local actors and institutions. The following chapters highlight new forms of governance, ranging from formal structures of regional government ministries and development offices to informal regional networks. Common to these governance reflections is a need to consider new roles for senior governments (often noted as a gap in research of localist approaches to development) and the challenges that governance mechanisms place on local institutions.

Role for Senior Government

Most of the case studies highlighted in the following chapters illustrate a general neo-liberal-inspired policy withdrawal by senior government from rural and small-town development issues. However, also evident are stories of the key role that senior governments continue to play in supporting place-based development. Senior governments retain key policy levers that may enable particular local ideas to succeed, key fiscal powers to support needed investments in social and physical infrastructure, and a critical body of capacity and expertise that can assist locally generated development processes. Rather than simply critiquing government offloading of responsibility, these chapters highlight the need for a return to careful intervention by senior governments through partnerships with regions and communities that are now increasingly comfortable with identifying and collectively mobilizing toward their own imagined futures.

Challenge of Local Capacity

The burdens of restructuring and the challenges associated with assuming greater levels of development responsibility put considerable pressure on rural local governments and agencies. Given their comparatively smaller institutional size, rural organizations often require assistance with building and maintaining capacity or with accessing specialized skills. Many of the chapters reinforce the need for continued attention to "continuous capacity renewal." Place-based development demands that rural capacity-building programs exist as legitimate efforts to enable renewed forms of localized governance. In the absence of substantive capacity, rural development programs serve only to mask neglect. They also ultimately inhibit rural places from effectively and productively transitioning to the next rural economy, representing a waste of the original investment.

Rural Investment

Finally, a place-based economy requires active investment to construct and maintain place competitiveness. The dynamic nature of an economy driven by competitive advantage requires renewal and a reversal of recent rural development patterns that have largely ignored the importance of re-investment. In the 21st century, we must stop viewing rural areas as a "resource bank" from which to withdraw funds to support development in metropolitan cores. The future of both rural and urban areas depends upon a willingness to re-invest a larger portion of funds from the resource bank back into rural areas. The rural infrastructure platforms that have fuelled growth in all resource sectors are crumbling. The chapters in this volume speak to the opportunities that exist for rebuilding rural infrastructure using a place-based orientation, thereby enabling a foundation for development that benefits both rural and urban areas. Guiding concepts to ensure the efficacy of rural re-investment include the multi-functionality and coordination of public investments.

Multi-functionality

Multi-functionality refers to the potential flexibility of infrastructure investments to serve a variety of potential uses and users. In resource industry terms, this is the economic equivalent of moving away from monoculture forests or fields. Attention to multi-functionality can reduce vulnerability and enhance options for local economic diversification—even if those opportunities are not readily apparent at the time of construction. Multi-functionality also requires that we employ different legal, administrative, and even cultural processes in the design of these investments in order to accommodate different users and value systems. The pressure for rural landscapes to meet multi-functional needs/demands is widespread, and a failure to accommodate these needs/demands through a more constructive and inclusive approach will result in increasing levels of conflict.

Coordinated Public Sector Investments

While the need for rural re-investment is clear, many of the chapter authors indicate that there are limited funds available across all the national contexts for rural and small-town renewal. The core message is that if we are to invest our limited funds, we need to spend them wisely. This message is particularly prescient given recent attention to government stimulus initiatives that may free up investment dollars for rural infrastructure projects. We must ensure that we generate the greatest benefit for the largest number of communities for each dollar invested. The need for coordinated investments must also be built around a new understanding of competitiveness that recognizes the importance of community transportation, communication, energy efficiency, quality of life, and related infrastructure. This includes the strategic value of building social infrastructure as well as physical infrastructure—an investment that reinforces local capacity and motivation to make communities sustainable. Here again, the place-based approach presents a framework for effectively integrating and contextualizing much-needed rural investment.

Chapter Guide

It is our hope that *The Next Rural Economies* provides a variety of contributions to the rural development discourse. First, the range of OECD nations represented in the volume provides an important lens through which to view and contrast both the similarities and differences emerging in rural development and policy. The book underscores the extent to which different nations are confronting common challenges associated with the structural forces of globalization, while at the same time highlighting and comparing the context-specific nature of local and regional responses to rural change. Second, the book provides a comprehensive look at the emergence of place-based development. Place-based development is often the focus of a single contribution in edited volumes of rural issues. By asking the contributors to this volume to prioritize place as *the* core theme of their rural research, the book offers a comprehensive and varied contribution to understanding the role of place in rural development and how it may be effectively mobilized to construct more competitive and resilient rural economies.

The Next Rural Economies is divided into five parts. Below we provide an introduction to each part as well as a brief summary of each chapter. We feel that the thematic consistency of the volume makes each contribution appealing to a wide variety of interests and audiences, allowing readers to see how different places confront common challenges of development. Nevertheless, the following abstracts may help readers find specific issues or community contexts that offer particular relevance to their areas of study, work, or community.

Part One

In the first part, "Demographics, Migration, and Immigration," five chapters raise and discuss issues concerning population change. In- and out-migration, together with in-situ demographic changes, flow from and link to the changing economies of rural and small-town places.

The chapter by Argent, Walmsley, and Sorensen follows the story of two rural communities in Australia that serve as examples for understanding the broader restructuring that has taken place in Australia under the guise of neo-liberalization. The main themes of the chapter cover the persistence of traditional industries in rural areas and their continued importance as contributors within the overall economy. While these industries remain economically important, they also continue to bind local places to forces of instability linked with industrial and political restructuring. The authors illustrate the burden of responsibility that is placed on local actors (i.e., government officials, mayor, and councillors) when dealing with issues of economic transition. Diversification efforts are being grounded in a reframing of traditional comparative advantages toward more place-based opportunities for valued-added production and agriculture. The chapter illustrates the persistence or continued importance of traditional factors of economic advantage, but reframed from the perspective of place-based development.

The chapter by Harrington examines changing settlement patterns across the Great Plains region of the United States. These small settlement places are set within a larger, rather more ubiquitous, space. Harrington reviews changing relations between agricultural intensification and the application of irrigation. While supporting economic diversification in the short term, the intensive reliance on declining water sources creates long-term vulnerability. Despite knowledge of this vulnerability, there has been a lack of diversification from agricultural investments across most Plains communities, often due to a lack of local leadership. Harrington's chapter makes an important contribution to the challenge of identifying place-based assets across broadly similar resource-development regions.

Furuseth investigates the impact of Latino immigration into a rural and small-town region of the southern United States and the extent to which it creates differentiated restructuring impacts on urban and rural settlements. Latino immigration into rural areas is creating new opportunities and a new community-development paradigm for the rural south. The author follows the development of immigrant businesses in rural areas that begin as unstructured, low-capital investments, but which over time build local capacity by creating important business and training opportunities. The study also shows that as the immigrant businesses diversify and become more complex over time, they integrate with non-immigrant communities, leading to overall rural revitalization. Furuseth shows how attention to immigration reform and immigrant settlement by both local and senior governments may affect economic opportunities for rural revitalization linked to these different business communities.

The chapter by Walford explores the connections between rural and urban places through an examination of migration flows over time. Following a long period of population decline, the Welsh study areas in Walford's research experience significant in-migration after the 1960s. The author explores the source and destination ends of the migration chain and asserts the importance of local amenity features, economic development investments, and lifestyle choices as driving different migration streams. The net result is an uneven spatial process of population change that highlights place-based development across this rural Welsh region. The study illustrates the important role of place-based investments and assets in supporting demographic change and creating new rural economies.

Gayler studies the tensions and contradictions that exist between urban and rural planning in southern Ontario, Canada. Specifically, the author focuses on the challenges associated with urban growth and containment, and the conservation of the rural resource base. His core theme traces the importance of top-down senior-government planning and authority in directing place-based development. Senior governments are seen to have the necessary power and authority to protect and nurture such place-based development. Local and regional governance institutions, which have had quality land-use plans, do not necessarily have the authority or the jurisdiction to implement them effectively. Gayler discusses how the protection of the agricultural resource base in the region creates an inherent tension between the greater public good of regional land-use planning and the private interests of the farmers, who view selling out to urban expansion as an opportunity to escape the price-cost squeeze and an overall decline in farm competitiveness.

Part Two

The second part of the book comprises four chapters that examine "emerging economies." In each case, place-based attributes pay key roles in supporting new activities, but it is the creative action of residents, decision makers, and entrepreneurs that mobilize the opportunities.

Cawley examines the changing scale of tourism in the rural and small-town places of County Galway, Western Ireland. Galway has a long history of tourism activity but is currently seeking to grow the local benefits derived from tourism via an integrated rural tourism model. The core of this approach is to protect and nurture essential social and environmental characteristics in the area, rather than allowing additional economic activity to threaten or destroy them. The author identifies the significant supplementary economic role that small-scale tourism activities can generate in rural and small-town places. Such supplements include both income and employment opportunities. However, growth in tourism activity is creating management challenges that may ultimately degrade the place-based competitive advantages of Western Ireland. Participants in Cawley's study called for a more supportive and coordinated policy approach so as to mitigate negative externalities from tourism growth.

Che examines a fruit-growing region in northwestern Michigan. She describes how the unique coincidence of environmental and settlement features have created a viable and valuable fruit belt. Recent changes associated with international markets and the global economy have exerted various forms of cost-price and market pressures on mid-sized fruit growers. To maintain viable communities and local economies, these fruit farms have turned to farm tourism as a significant additional opportunity for raising income and maintaining the viability of farm households. The conversion of agricultural land to urban and residential uses places a particular urgency on the need to find solutions for farm viability in this northern area of the United States. The chapter highlights how grassroots innovation, coupled with place branding and regional agricultural cooperation among producers, still needs supportive public policy in order to maintain a viable response to more generalized new rural economy pressures. By building upon place-based experiences and assets, northwest Michigan fruit farmers have been able to diversify local interests both within the agricultural sector and across new sectors such as tourism and "agritainment."

Ramsey looks at rural restructuring in the new economy, providing case examples in Germany and Canada. He illustrates how restructuring forces are affecting areas of both countries in similar ways, particularly concerning efforts to diversify in settings with limited land availability. There are a variety of thematic dimensions to the chapter, including the influence of policy at different scales (local, regional, county, provincial, federal, and international) and the way in which local conflicts arise as a result of broader restructuring forces. Ultimately, these local conflicts are about differing views and approaches to redefining place within the context of changing local production.

Bruce's chapter examines the application of a cluster development strategy to foster the creative economy in a rural and small-town context. He uses the animation sector, an emergent sector in Miramichi, New Brunswick, as his case study and looks at the overall impact of restructuring taking place in the region and the extent to which the Miramichi town and region have been attempting to revitalize themselves through a variety of development strategies. The chapter examines how the setting of place provides opportunities to attract members of the creative class and develop a creative industry that may merge into some form of a cluster through supportive frameworks of education and associated economic development. The chapter also highlights many of the challenges associated with attracting and maintaining creative industries and creative class employees in a rural setting.

Part Three

The third part of the book contains three chapters that draw out specific issues related to "rural policy and governance." A key finding in all three contributions is that the "recipe" for rural and small-town development success involves both strong local actors and supportive senior-government investments and policies.

The chapter by Bryant draws upon the challenges identified in a broad survey of rural and small-town settings ranging from the peri-urban fringe to peripheral places. Bryant links the heterogeneous experiences of these places to the themes of place-based development in a new rural economy. The central argument in the chapter is that assessing changes requires attention to the roles and impacts of governance and government structures. Bryant asks, "What are the most appropriate and effective forms of governance for transforming rural communities?" The key message is that while the ability to manage change is within the grasp of local and regional actors, senior governments continue to play an important role in facilitating processes. Drawing upon the specific case of agriculture in the peri-urban fringe, the chapter explores these governance issues in concert with the roles of researchers in nurturing and supporting local processes and action. The chapter finishes with a guide to co-creating conditions for supporting place-based rural and small-town transition into the new rural economy.

The purpose of Storey's chapter is to challenge the presumed idealism of the "local turn" in rural planning and development. While recognizing the inherent values of a local approach, in terms of community empowerment and contextual specificity, the chapter raises a series of questions as to the overall authenticity of local development, using cases of "town branding" from rural England. Here, place-based development is seen to promote a homogenized presentation of rural heritage rather than an authentic representation of rural distinctiveness. Other barriers to attaining the local ideal include the professionalization of rural development as an industry, which further removes it from place ownership. The chapter stresses that many of these strategies may prove to be authentic or successful; however, the lack of a regulatory and facilitative framework leaves local development as vulnerable to manipulation as it is to achieving real empowerment.

Drawing upon the example of rural Wales, Woods argues that both space and place continue to be central to the futures of transforming rural and small-town communities and that distance still requires investments in infrastructure by senior governments to help offset the costs of space. Rural researchers and developers must consider the multi dimensional roles of both space and place as they combine into unique and shifting assemblages of spatial relations. By understanding space and place in this way, policy makers and practitioners will be able to grapple with the complexities of heterogeneous rural and small-town encounters with the pressures of global economic change. The attention to place making requires attention to partnerships. Such partnerships, as illustrated in the Welsh rural examples, extend across public, private, and community sectors. The uneven implications of new rural economies need to be at the centre of our responses to cope with the uneven capacities and amenity attributes of individual rural localities.

Part Four

The three chapters that make up the fourth part of the book each directly address the issue of rural–urban relationships. In this "rural–urban exchange," the opportunities and challenges of spatial relationships are explored through their impacts on place-based rural and small-town development.

Aragau and Charvet examine a rural and small-town region around the peri-urban fringe of Paris, France, that has been affected by the development of a new expressway connecting urban Paris and coastal Brittany. They examine how changes in the accessibility of the region have had several interacting implications for local communities, and they adopt a systemic approach for examining "life basins." Their results indicate that while urban influences continue, there has been a more important shift in local trading areas and networking, which has resulted in more vibrant and resilient services and commercial foundations across the rural and small-town places of this peri-urban region.

The chapter by Loudiyi adopts a spatial perspective of the Volcans rural–urban fringe region in France and describes the consequences of economic restructuring as two rural areas focus on internationally known place-based assets. The concept of rural "place marketing" is a theme connecting the two cases. A key theme in the chapter concerns the importance of local identity and how a regional agglomeration copes with and constructs a new sense of identity. The chapter shows how local resources are shaped and appropriated by local actors to define a new local identity and provide for local, economic, and social opportunities.

From the perspective of a rural–urban fringe area in southern Japan, the chapter by Ouchi explores a suite of strategies being employed by a set of small towns. While urban development pressures may be ubiquitous, each of these small towns is pursuing specific development directions rooted in place-based assets and fitting with place-based aspirations.

Part Five

The final part of the book includes three chapters that explore place-based development issues in the context of "renewal in resource peripheries." All three chapters focus on Canadian settings, and each describes how economies built on comparative advantages are being modified as competitive advantages become paramount, shifting from space-based development to place-based development.

Vodden uses stories of rural restructuring in Newfoundland and Labrador to elaborate on the tensions between top-down control and development versus bottom-up organization and initiative. The top-down/bottom-up nexus takes on a particularly dramatic style in Newfoundland and Labrador, given the history of strong personalities in positions of authority. The chapter explores two contradictions. First, the tension between "hero" dependency and strong local initiative is evident in Newfoundlanders' struggle between acquiescing to senior leadership while also being committed to their communities and local action. Second, Vodden outlines the tension between the pattern of resettlement of Newfoundland outports and the overall centralization of the population over time versus a strong attachment to place, even if that sense of place persists only in the form of a recreational amenity.

Markey isolates the rising phenomenon of the use of fly-in/fly-out (FIFO) workcamps for resource extraction as a particularly dramatic example of rapid rural restructuring. At first glance, FIFO appears to be the pinnacle of "place-less" development—completely flexible, isolated, and temporary. However, on closer review, it is clear these operations have significant direct and indirect impacts at local, regional, national, and even international levels in terms of economic contribution or opportunity costs, social and cultural impacts, and environmental implications. A new regionalist perspective provides both theoretical and practical tools for assessing impacts and for reconciling the place-less dimensions of FIFO with the place-based realities of rural and small-town economies in northern British Columbia.

The chapter by Halseth explores the case of northern British Columbia and the transformation of its forest-dependent economy. Examples from rural and small-town communities highlight the value of mobilizing place-based assets that fit with global economic opportunities and local aspirations respecting the future of the community. Critical to mobilizing place-based initiatives is the need for senior governments' strategic involvement through infrastructure investments and supportive public policy.

Reimer's chapter closes the book and provides a conceptual synthesis for the entire volume, using a framework consisting of the stressors, assets, governance, and outcomes of rural development. Reimer shows how rural areas responding to stressors and planning for the future must accommodate place-based perspectives. Particular challenges facing place-based development are the generality of policy and the policy process, as well as the difficulty of effectively and efficiently incorporating contextual specificity. Reimer draws from a variety of themes, suggesting mechanisms and points of inspiration that will allow a place-based perspective to assert itself, both in terms of local and regional development processes and at a broader level of implementing place-based policy.

Conclusion

Place has emerged as a fundamental ingredient for rural and small-town development planning. We must pay deliberate attention to equipping places to be flexible and responsive in pursuing their economic futures. Where territory matters more than sector, and competitive advantage more than comparative advantage, purposeful actions are needed—whether these are supporting public policy or local actions. Recurrent throughout the chapters, however, is a warning that our actions must be grounded in the assets of place and the aspirations of local residents. Assets refer to those potential characteristics that may support one or a number of economic futures. Aspirations are the visions that residents have for their place in the future.

The collective message voiced in these chapters is that place-based development offers a trajectory of hope for rural areas that have long been under the siege of restructuring. Importantly, this message is not offered naïvely, with a lack of awareness of the challenges associated with place-based rural futures. The stories told in the following chapters highlight the benefits of place development, including local ownership fostered by participatory engagement, efficiencies achieved through collaboration, and innovations in the rural economic enterprise revealed by truly understanding the competitive appeal of place. Equally, however, the authors warn of the pitfalls associated with false leadership, inauthentic place branding, and overburdened local capacity. It is the job of rural researchers, community leaders, and government officials to "co-construct" the re-mapping of rural futures that finds an appropriate balance between the contextual specificity of place and the structural generalities of policies and programs that will help to foster the next rural economies.

References

Apedaile, L.P. (2004) The new rural economy. In: Halseth, G., and Halseth, R. (eds.) *Building for Success: Exploration of Rural Community and Rural Development*. Rural Development Institute, Brandon University, Brandon, MB, 111–136.

Bradbury, J. (1989) The social and economic imperatives of restructuring: A geographic perspective. In: Kobayashi, A., and Mackenzie, S. (eds.) *Remaking Human Geography*. Unwin Hyman, London, 21-39.

Bradford, N. (2004) Place matters and multi-level governance: Perspectives on a new urban policy paradigm. *Policy Options* 25(2), 39–45.

———. (2005) *Place-based Public Policy: Towards a New Urban and Community Agenda for Canada* (Research Report F-51). Canadian Policy Research Networks Inc., Ottawa.

Cairncross, F. (1997) *The Death of Distance*. Harvard Business School Press, Boston.

Cloke, P. (1977) An index of rurality for England and Wales. *Regional Studies* 11, 31–46.

du Plessis, V., Beshiri, R., Bollman, R., and Clemenson, H. (2002) *Definitions of Rural*. Minister of Industry, Statistics Canada, Ottawa.

Fluharty, C. (2006) Written statement for the record. Presented to the US House of Representatives, House Committee on Agriculture. Subcommittee on Conservation, Credit, Rural Development and Research, www.rupri.org/Forms/testimony.pdf (accessed 10 June 2008).

Halseth, G., Manson, D., Markey, S., Lax, L., and Buttar, O. (2007) The connected north: Findings from the Northern BC Economic Vision and Strategy Project. *Journal of Rural and Community Development* 2(1), 1–27.

Harvey, D. (1990) *The Condition of Postmodernity: An Enquiry into the Origins of Cultural Change*. Blackwell, Oxford.

Hoggart, K., and Buller, H. (1987) *Rural Development: A Geographical Perspective*. Croom Helm, London.

Lovering, J. (1991) The restructuring debate. In: Peet, R., and Thrift, N. (eds.) *New Models in Geography*. Unwin Hyman, London, 198–223.

Markey, S., Halseth, G., and Manson, D. (2006) The struggle to compete: From comparative to competitive advantage in northern British Columbia. *International Planning Studies* 11(1), 19–39.

———. (2008) Challenging the inevitability of rural decline: Advancing the policy of place in northern British Columbia. *Journal of Rural Studies* 24(4), 409–421.

Massey, D. (1984) Geography matters! In: Massey, D., Allen, J., and Anderson, J. (eds.) *Geography Matters! A Reader*. Cambridge University Press and Open University, Cambridge, 1–11.

O'Brien, R. (1992) *Global Financial Integration: The End of Geography*. Council of Foreign Relations, New York.

Organization for Economic Co-operation and Development. (1994) *Creating Rural Indicators for Shaping Territorial Policies*. OECD, Paris.

———. (2006) *The New Rural Paradigm: Policies and Governance*. OECD Publishing, Paris.

Partridge, M., and Rickman, D. (2008) Place-based policy and rural poverty: Insights from the urban spatial mismatch literature. *Cambridge Journal of Regions, Economy and Society* 1(1), 131–156.

Statistics Canada. (1999) *1996 Census Dictionary* (Cat. No. 92-351). Statistics Canada, Ottawa.

Stinchcombe, A. (1968) *Constructing Social Theories*. Harcourt, Brace and World, New York.

Wellman, B. (1999) *Networks in the Global Village*. Westview Press, Boulder, CO.

Chapter 2

Something Old, Something New, Something Borrowed, Something...? Rediscovering the Comparative Advantage of the "New" Pastoral Economies of Northern New South Wales, Australia

Neil Argent, Jim Walmsley, and Tony Sorensen

What developmental options lie open for traditional, remote, productivist-oriented rural economies of "settler societies" such as Canada, New Zealand, and Australia? In this chapter we address this question by examining the recent economic, demographic, and social restructuring of Guyra and Inverell, two relatively remote, agriculturally dependent communities in the northern tablelands of New South Wales, Australia. We also aim to document the multi-scalar processes that are driving economic change within both places, including the increasingly vital role of local agency and advocacy.

The chapter is divided into four sections. First, we discuss the major structural constraints facing the rural economies of former colonial countries—such as Australia and Canada—in their quest for long-term social and economic viability. Second, we set out the historical and locational context for Guyra and Inverell as towns and broader rural communities, and we discuss the major economic and demographic trends affecting both places since the 1970s. A key focus here is the recent development of new enterprises and the substantial role that these are playing in the social, economic, and demographic rejuvenation of both communities. Third, given the continuing centrality of the small-farm sector to the fortunes of both communities, we consider the economic and social linkages between local farmers and "their" towns, and how these are changing over time. Finally, we explore the role of local agency (in the guise of key local government representatives) in shaping the renaissance of Guyra and Inverell.

Rural Development in an Era of Multi-functionality?

Despite its inherent flaws, the concept of productivism/post-productivism has brought into sharp relief some of the major structural shifts that have occurred and are continuing to occur in rural economies of the developed world. In the former colonial nations of Canada, New Zealand, and Australia, the rural sector effectively underpinned national economic growth and development during the 19th and well into the 20th centuries via the export of farm and other extractive industry commodities to the imperial core (Powell, 1975; Williams, 1975; Bolton, 1978). Hence the famous aphorism that neatly captured the macro-economic contributions of the farm sector to Australia during the 1950s and 1960s: "Australia rides on the sheep's back." Since this halcyon period, though, Australian rural communities and economies have increasingly experienced the enervating effects of the long-run cost/price squeeze, itself a product of deeper sectoral trends and tendencies, such as the relatively low income elasticity of demand for most agricultural goods. This malaise is evident in a discourse of decline that has pervaded much Australian rural geographical and sociological scholarship since the 1980s.

There is a large degree of commonality in the experiences of peripheral rural economies in these former colonial countries, and a similar level of near unanimity on the generally narrow range of remedies to rural economic decline. "Post-productivism" stresses the potential efflorescence of a range of alternative niche-farm and non-farm industries and enterprises in agricultural heartlands, triggered by a complex combination of pluriactivity and counterurbanization, with largely ex-urban migrants bringing their own interpretation of rural life to their new locale (Cloke and Thrift, 1990; Phillips, 1993; Cloke *et al.*, 1995; Boyle and Halfacree, 1998), and landholders seeking to capitalize on the sudden influx of people and tastes. While some have seen in this trend the gradual gentrification of the "working countryside," others have discerned new developmental opportunities for rural communities. As Reed and Gill (1997, p. 2019) observe, "the conceptualization of the social and economic processes associated with postproductivism can assist in an understanding of how tourism, recreational, and amenity (TRA) values are incorporated into the institutional framework that regulates land use in rural areas."

A related strand of thought conceives these dynamics as part of a shift to the creation of multi-functional rural landscapes (Wilson, 2001; Argent, 2002; Holmes, 2006) moulded by three driving forces: (1) agricultural overcapacity; (2) the emergence of "market-driven amenity uses"; and (3) "changing societal values" (Holmes, 2006, p. 143). "Changing societal values" refers to society's growing concerns over the sustainable management of natural resources, together with an associated expansion of consumer interest in "clean," safe, and humane food and fibre production. "Agricultural overcapacity" relates to the fact that roughly 80% of Australian farm profit at full equity is attributable to approximately 1% of Australian farmers (Barr, 2000, 2005). The rise to prominence of alternative, amenity-oriented, rural land uses overlaps substantially with the previous point. In strategically located regions, rural land is being progressively valued not for its productive capacities but for its perceived aesthetic, capital gain, and status features. Hence, rugged coastal ranges are sought after for homesites overlooking the ocean and coastal valleys; small towns and old dairy farms are desired for their "country" ambience and accessibility to large regional centres. In other words, rural settlement and land use are driven increasingly by consumption values and not solely by production ones.

In these contexts, rural communities face a number of potential threats and opportunities. Continued reliance upon extensive broadacre industries that offer few local "value-adding" opportunities will almost certainly lead to continuing deterioration of the local economy as lower population densities and diminishing local trade combine to produce a classic vicious cycle of decline (Sorensen, 1990). Where better-positioned communities are able to successfully market their "TRA values" to non-local consumers, a "geographical transfer of value" may occur if towns lack both the infrastructure (e.g., quality accommodation) and the operators needed to retain the fleeting tourist dollar within the local economy (Holmes, 2002; Walmsley, 2003). There is also the danger that a high-TRA-value locality or region will eventually be "loved to death" by the sustained rapid in-migration of aspirational middle classes in search of their own version of the rural idyll (Bunce, 1994; Woods, 2007). On the upside, the restructuring of rural communities and economies associated with Holmes' (2006) three driving forces opens up fresh opportunities to innovate and experiment with new, higher-value industries and enterprises, possibly redefining the traditional comparative advantage of regions.

A Tale of Two Rural Communities

In the balance of this chapter, we explore the subtly changing character of two highly agriculturally-dependent economies in northern New South Wales, Australia. The historical development of both Guyra and Inverell in many respects follows that of the archetypal inland rural town and its farming hinterlands: the emergence and subsequent development of both townships hinged on the fortunes of the surrounding farm sector, but as the profitability of agriculture began its general if periodically interrupted wane from the 1970s, so Guyra and Inverell also suffered. Both are located in the northern New England Tablelands, an agriculturally rich region in New South Wales lying approximately equidistant between Sydney (about six hours' drive south of the region's centroid) and Brisbane (about five hours' drive north) (Fig. 2.1).

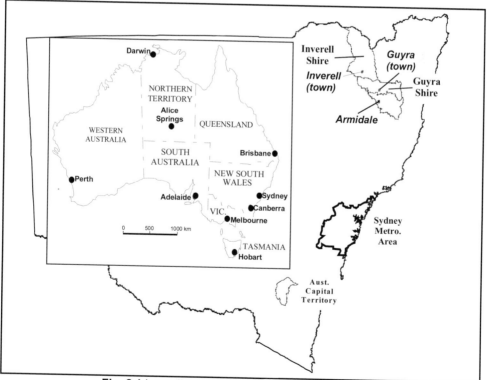

Fig. 2.1 Inverell and Guyra shires and town locations.

According to the dominion capitalism thesis (Ehrensaft and Armstrong, 1978; Armstrong and Bradbury, 1983; Schwartz, 1989), the historical development of settlement and industry in rural hinterlands such as the New England Tablelands must be understood in the broader context of the Australian nation's incorporation within the British Empire's orbit from the late 18th century. The open, savannah-type grasslands of the tablelands were seen as ideal for wheat, meat, and fine wool production (Lea *et al*., 1977) after the local indigenous peoples—notably the Anaiwan and Kamilaroi Aboriginal tribes—had been subjugated, dispersed, or exterminated. Drawn into the imperial trade networks by the gravitational pull of England's demand for minerals, wool, wheat, and meat, squatters in the northern New England Tablelands saw their raw farm produce—chiefly wool, cereal grain, and meat—drained from the region via the dendritic transportation routes that centred on major port cities.

Table 2.1, which displays the major agricultural industries within Guyra and Inverell shires, shows that there has been surprisingly little apparent structural change in the regional farm sector, with remarkable stability in overall farm numbers and average farm size. The difference between "Estimated Value of Agricultural Operations" thresholds from one census date to the next may conceal some minor trends in farm-size change, but in many other parts of rural Australia, farm numbers and the mean size of holdings have moved in opposite directions. Nonetheless, Table 2.1 disguises some significant shifts within the major farm industries since the early 1990s. Most noticeably, sheep numbers and the size of the wool clip have dropped substantially in the wake of the near total collapse of the national wool industry following the 1991 deregulation of wool marketing. Despite the New England Tablelands' comparative advantage in fine wool production, the Merino flock has experienced a major decline, with local producers moving into beef cattle and/or fat lamb production, the two major viable alternatives available to farmers in this grass-fed production system.

Table 2.1 Selected agricultural indicators, Guyra and Inverell shires, 1976–1977 and 2005–2006.

Indicator	Guyra		Inverell	
	1976–1977	2005–2006	1976–1977	2005–2006
Number of farms	439	421	750	671
Average farm size (ha)	844.72	787.21	940.28	902.92
Area of cereal crops (ha)			39,450	27,300
Sheep and lambs (head)	821,048	533,379	512,730	
Wool shorn (kg)	2,758,000			
Beef cattle (head)	122,427	108,000	132,736	132,000

Source: Australian Bureau of Statistics, 1978, 2008.
Note: The "Estimated Value of Agricultural Operations" (EVAO) thresholds for farm survey data to be included in final published statistics vary between the two years reported here.[1]

A recent survey of Guyra and Inverell farmers conducted by the authors shows that less than one-quarter of farm respondents are now predominantly woolgrowers. The majority of respondents (59.3%) regarded themselves as predominantly cattle graziers, with cropping and fat lambs making up the remainder. Further, nearly three-quarters (73%) had adjusted their operations to at least some extent since 2000. Two-thirds had increased their farm size, with the average size of all farms exceeding 1,500 ha—well above the mean obtained through the Australian Bureau of Statistics agricultural census data from 2005–2006 (see

Table 2.1). Two-thirds of respondents also indicated that they ran other enterprises besides the farm. Most of these involved activities that made use of existing farm plant and machinery or the owners' talents, including machinery contracting.

In many respects, Guyra's and Inverell's historical pattern of economic development conforms to the "staples trap" thesis (Innis, 1995; Hayter and Barnes, 1990, 1997). The export of relatively untransformed agricultural commodities has been the region's dominant and propulsive sector (measured by employment, output volumes, and value) for much of its history, allowing local farmers to enjoy buoyant economic conditions for most of the 20th century. Nonetheless, staples commodities markets tend to operate close to textbook "perfect competition" conditions, with markets clearing readily. This renders staples sellers "price takers" rather than "price makers" (Barnes, 1996). Further, due to this "export mentality" (Barnes, 1996, p. 49), there have been few attempts to diversify the regional economy, save for some basic downstream processing of local pastoral commodities (e.g., abattoirs). This apparent inability to develop alternative major industries is also in part attributable to the quite strongly regulated nature of farm commodity marketing throughout much of the 20th century, with producers forced to sell their output to the umpteen boards that formed a protective filter between the small producer and end markets (both domestic and international) (see Pritchard, 2000).

Nevertheless, some structural shifts within the local labour market have occurred. Guyra's and Inverell's changing relative economic dependence on agriculture is plainly evident in Table 2.2, which shows trends in employment by industry spanning a quarter century for the two shires. In Guyra, the farm sector never employed less than one-third of the shire's total workforce from 1981 to 2006, despite the overall 25% decline in the size of the agricultural workforce. The only sector to rival farming's employment dominance has been manufacturing, which employed nearly one-quarter of Guyra workers during the early 1990s. The vast majority of these people were employed by the local abattoir, which employed as many as 400 people in 1990 (Stayner, 2003, p. 45). However, with the closure of the meatworks in May 1996, manufacturing employment dropped by almost 70% between the 1991 and 1996 censuses, causing a dramatic downturn within the local economy. It is this event, perhaps above all others, that best defines Guyra's recent developmental renaissance.

In the immediate aftermath of the abattoir's closure, local government and community organizations introduced a range of events, campaigns, and strategies to stem out-migration and attract business and population to the town. However, the enterprise that helped shore up Guyra's economy and workforce—if only for several years—came to the district almost irrespective of these efforts. Ruddweigh was a family manufacturing firm based in Sydney whose main output was precision livestock scales and weighing systems. The Ruddweigh proprietors were drawn to Guyra via a family connection, the cheap land, the town's location on a major highway midway between two major cities (Sydney and Brisbane), and the area's strong pastoral economy. They established a "high-tech" manufacturing plant for electronic livestock scales in the main street during the late 1990s. At its peak, the business employed approximately 30 people, providing a substantial boost to the town. Local, domestic, and international demand for Ruddweigh products bloomed, and the company established a strategic alliance with Waratah, a manufacturer of fencing wire (including electric fencing equipment). Unfortunately for Guyra, the Ruddweigh plant closed its doors in 2004 after the parent company moved the scale assembly business to a cheaper production site in New Zealand. Yet again, the Guyra community's hopes for a sustainable, employment-generating industry had been dashed by the restructuring strategies of a multinational corporation.

Table 2.2 Employment by industry, Inverell and Guyra shires, 1981–2006.

Category	1981		2006		% change in numbers employed, 1981–2006	
	Inverell	Guyra	Inverell	Guyra	Inverell	Guyra
Agriculture, etc.	24.83	48.01	15.89	34.16	-34.01	-25.33
Mining	1.32	1.27	0.64	0.54	-50.00	-55.00
Manufacturing	9.49	3.55	10.38	7.72	12.82	128.57
Construction	6.40	3.17	7.33	4.65	18.21	54.00
Wholesale and retail trade	20.75	14.25	21.43	15.15	6.53	11.56
Transportation	2.87	3.99	2.95	2.35	6.06	-38.10
Electricity, gas, water	3.22	1.52	0.91	0.78	-70.81	-45.83
Finance, property and business services	7.02	3.80	6.69	6.88	-1.73	90.00
Public administration, defence	2.95	4.50	4.58	4.04	60.00	-5.63
Communications	2.31	2.03	0.84	0.60	-62.41	-68.75
Community services	13.47	10.45	20.35	16.42	55.87	64.85
Recreation, personal services	5.37	3.48	8.02	6.70	54.05	101.82

Source: Australian Bureau of Statistics, 1989, 2007.
Note: The first four columns show the percent of total employment. The last two columns relate to change in numbers in each industry (1981-2006), not the shifting share of employment.

In terms of local and regional demographic trends, Guyra Shire's population has declined by over 17% from 1971 to 2006, while that of Inverell Shire dropped by 10%. The main towns have fared better, with Guyra experiencing a net decline of only 1.7% over the same period. Inverell town's rate of population loss was closer to 6%. Both shires did experience modest growth in the most recent intercensal period (2001–2006), as did Guyra township. Of course, this brief summary overlooks some more complex dynamics—and their causes—and these are discussed further below.

Table 2.3 shows that the total populations of both towns' social catchments have also declined between 1981 and 2001. Guyra's rate of population loss has been greater than Inverell's, reflecting the impact of the abattoir closure in 1996. Nevertheless, the rural population of Guyra—which accounted for over 40% of the entire social catchment population in both 1981 and 2001—decreased more rapidly than the town population, indicating that restructuring in the local farm sector has also had its impact. Inverell, on the other hand, has experienced relative stability over the 20-year study period, though, as already observed, this trend conceals considerable change.

Perhaps surprisingly, the density of rural (i.e., excluding the towns) occupied dwellings has actually increased, particularly in Inverell. This can, in part, be attributed to the in-migration of new residents into the area and the growth of rural residential allotments near the town. An interesting example of new settlement development on rural land is the case of the Bruderhof community, which established itself on a 40 ha portion of an iconic farming property 25 km east of Inverell township during 1999. On this property, the community built 15 residential dwellings, a light manufacturing factory (for state-of-the-art playground equipment), and a worship centre (Gutteridge Haskins and Davey Pty Ltd., 2000), with firm plans to expand its population to 400 persons over the decade to 2009.

As already noted, both Guyra and Inverell's economic dependence on agriculture is substantial. Employment in agriculture and other primary extractive industries accounted for over 40% of all jobs in the Guyra social catchment in 1981, and this had only declined to about 37% by 2001. Inverell's reliance on farm-based employment is much less— approximately 17% in 1981 and under 15% by 2001. Regardless of the varying importance of farming to both communities' economies and workforces, it is clear from Table 2.3 that the Guyra and Inverell agricultural labour forces are in relative decline. The broader economic implication of this trend can be seen in the changing industrial diversity index (IDI) figures in Table 2.3, which reveal that Guyra's economy has become more balanced over time, indicating that non-farm industries have been absorbing more of the local workforce. While Inverell's IDI has decreased, indicating greater concentration of employment, its score is nevertheless quite healthy for both census years.

Table 2.3 Selected indicators for the Guyra and Inverell social catchment areas, 1981–2001.

	1981		2001	
	Guyra	Inverell	Guyra	Inverell
Total population	3,243	14,851	2,954	14,447
Rural population	1,03	3,642	1,229	3,663
Rural population density*	20.20	22.45	21.50	27.75
Percentage of workforce in agriculture	42.98	16.91	36.69	13.59
Industrial diversity index	38.35	57.98	40.44	47.06

Source: Australian Bureau of Statistics, 1989, 2003.
Note: Density is measured as number of occupied dwellings/100 sq. km

Social and Economic Interlinkages between Farm and Broader Community

To complement this broad statistical snapshot of Guyra and Inverell, we collected primary data in connection with the Australian Research Council "rural heartlands" research project. The sample in each case was a randomly selected group of farming properties (19 in Guyra and 40 in Inverell). Owners took part in a lengthy face-to-face interview, answering questions on general farm practices and enterprise mix, employment trends, and community interaction, as well as household information.

In relation to perceptions of local interaction in Guyra, the pattern that emerges is one of slow change. In most cases, respondents reported the same level of engagement as existed a decade earlier (Table 2.4). However, where change is apparent in Guyra, it tends to have been positive. This is particularly the case with shopping; the majority of respondents estimate that they are doing more locally, no doubt reflecting increased service provision as the local economy has grown. There is also a fairly widespread feeling that involvement in local organizations is either the same or has increased, suggesting an increased degree of vibrancy. Opinion is more divided in relation to the local concentration of general socializing, banking, health care delivery, and sport, where approximately one in four respondents report a decrease in involvement.

Table 2.4 Level of interaction with the local area in the 10 years since 1997 (%).

	Guyra	Inverell	Guyra	Inverell	Guyra	Inverell	Guyra	Inverell	Guyra	Inverell	Guyra	Inverell
	Shopping		Socializing		Banking		Health care		Sport		Local orgs.	
More	58	5	32	18	17	0	24	5	18	14	31	39
Same	42	80	42	53	61	74	52	77	58	24	56	32
Less	0	15	26	29	22	26	24	18	24	62	13	39

Despite some evidence of disengagement, the picture in Guyra is much more positive than the one for Inverell. In Inverell's case, there is little sign of change in local shopping or in health care delivery, perhaps because, being a somewhat larger centre, facilities were already relatively adequate. Elsewhere the picture is more negative, particularly in the case of sport, where a large majority of respondents reported lower levels of involvement. This is important because of sport's significance in contributing to the development of social capital in rural communities (Tonts, 2005). Perhaps understandably, given its more complex economy, banking in Inverell is tending to drift away from the immediate area, helped no doubt by the widespread availability and use of Internet banking. No respondents in Inverell reported an increase in local banking. It would be wrong, however, to paint a bleak picture of interaction in Inverell (and in Guyra). For all cases outlined in Table 2.4, except for sport in Inverell, respondents reported the same or more local interaction. This suggests that the communities are resilient in spite of the challenges they face.

In order to gain further insight into the embeddedness of rural communities within their "home" area and the reasons for any changes in local affiliation, we asked respondents to rate the quality of certain aspects of the local area now and ten years ago, using an ordinal scale that went from 1 ("very poor") to 7 ("excellent") (see Table 2.5). Increased shopping in Guyra was clearly linked to a perception that there had been a major improvement in shopping facilities. Curiously, the perception was that Inverell's shopping facilities had also improved, although this had not led to increased local activity. In Guyra's case, improvements to the main street may have reduced the leakage to nearby towns. The striking feature in Table 2.5 is the perception that job opportunities have increased very significantly in Guyra. This is not surprising given the changes and policy initiatives outlined elsewhere in this chapter. A marked improvement in job opportunities was also evident in Inverell.

Interestingly, improvements were also seen in the quality of the physical environment. This was perhaps strange at a time of drought, but it might reflect greater environmental consciousness in the population generally. In contrast, little change was evident in relation to community spirit and social belonging. Other positive changes that became apparent were an improvement in educational facilities in Guyra (but little change in Inverell) and an improvement in leisure-time facilities in Inverell (but not in Guyra). On the downside, the success of the local economy seemed to be associated in respondents' eyes with a deterioration in housing provision. This was reflected in very tight housing markets for both ownership and rental. The other area of perceived deterioration was health care delivery. However, this perception did not seem to translate into increased use of primary health care services in neighbouring towns, possibly because of the relatively long distances involved at a time of illness. Interestingly, Inverell seemed to be characterized by a perception that crime was becoming more common, although there are no published crime statistics at the local level to corroborate this.

Table 2.5 Changing perceptions of the quality of life in the local area now compared to ten years ago.

	Guyra	Inverell	Guyra	Inverell	Guyra	Inverell	Guyra	Inverell	Guyra	Inverell	Guyra	Inverell
	Shopping		Socializing		Banking		Health care		Sport		Local orgs.	
More	58	5	32	18	17	0	24	5	18	14	31	39
Same	42	80	42	53	61	74	52	77	58	24	56	32
Less	0	15	26	29	22	26	24	18	24	62	13	39

Note: Figures relate to the movement of scores on a seven-point scale that ran from 1 ("very poor") to 7 ("excellent").

In addition to describing their level of local interaction, respondents were asked, in an open-ended question, to describe the "the best things about your local area...what it has got going for it." They were also asked to describe "the most significant problems that your local area faces." In each case, respondents were invited to give up to three responses. Interestingly, positive responses outweighed negative responses. Moreover, there were differences in the outlook of respondents in Guyra and Inverell. In Guyra, the ratio between "best things" and "significant problems" was 1.6:1. In Inverell, it was somewhat lower but still positive at 1.3:1.

A sense of community and lifestyle figured prominently among the "best" things listed by more than one in five respondents in both Guyra and Inverell. Interestingly, lifestyle was rated particularly highly by Inverell respondents. This augurs well for the future given the rising importance of amenity- and lifestyle-led migration (Bell, 1996; Argent *et al.*, 2007). Also prominent in the lists for both Guyra and Inverell was an appreciation of the productivity of the land, reflecting the obvious business interests of the farmers.

The listing of "problems" in both Guyra and Inverell was less extensive than the listing of positive features. The most significant concerns in both areas were with infrastructure and health care services. Levels of concern were higher in Inverell than in Guyra, perhaps reflecting Guyra's relative proximity (about 40 km) to Armidale, the regional centre (population approximately 22,000). Ranking below infrastructure and health were more diffuse concerns about the nature of government (Guyra) and overall anxiety about the state of the economy (Inverell). The problem of crime was not prominent in Inverell despite the perception that this is a bigger problem now than it was a decade ago.

Regional Development Strategy at the Local Level

In many countries, Australia included, governments and communities attempt to play active roles in shaping the economic and social transformation of their communities. Australian approaches to the task have metamorphosed substantially over the last 30 years, with Guyra and Inverell in the vanguard of such changes. Critical to an appreciation of the subtly varied approaches to "place development" adopted by both shires is the understanding that, during the last three decades, Australia has switched from being a highly regulated and protected economy to becoming one of the world's most open market-oriented economies (Walmsley and Sorensen, 1993; Sorensen, 2002). This structural shift has reshaped both city and country alike.

For example, the value of government support for the farm sector has shrunk from an initial 8% of the value of production, low by world standards, to about half that amount. This coincided with the abolition of most controls on the volume and destination of production, the activities of commodity marketing boards, import controls, and other price support schemes. The agricultural mainstay of Guyra and Inverell—livestock production— is among the most deregulated and export oriented of Australia's primary industries. Thus, regional farm incomes are heavily dependent on a combination of contemporary technology, producer efficiency—including scale economies—global commodity prices, and the value of a freely floating Australian dollar, which is now more highly valued on a trade-weighted basis than it has been at any time in the last 25 years.

Pressures on the farm sector to become more efficient and self-reliant are reflected in both public administration and community governance. Australia's global integration has been accompanied by a redistribution of powers between the three tiers of government: Commonwealth, state, and local (Sorensen *et al.*, 2007). The Commonwealth has steadily acquired more control from the states over many sectors, including corporations law, industrial relations, taxation and fiscal strategy, social security, public infrastructure, health and education, and environmental regulation. Simultaneously, the states have devolved further elements of social policy, environmental management, and local development to ill-prepared local governments, which account for only approximately 5% of public revenue and outlays. The Commonwealth and the states keep their fingers in the development pie, if only because it is a hot political issue. Earlier state-level attempts to promote top-down local economic development foundered on inadequate funding, the targeting of industry sectors over which governments had only weak control, and the diversity of rural problems and opportunity. Regional development is a state responsibility under Section 51 of the constitution, but that responsibilitiy now largely resides with local government and associated community groups.

Low population densities, extensive territories, and weak budgetary capacity appear to have imposed great responsibility on local leaders to drive economic development forward. More often than not, as is the case in Guyra and Inverell, the leader is the local mayor (Sorensen and Epps, 1996), who assumes the role due to his or her official capacity as a community leader. In some cases the leadership ranks are swelled by activist general managers, regional development professionals in the larger councils, or the CEOs of large businesses or infrastructure agencies. Their task is formidable and multi dimensional. It can include the following duties:

- Identifying and promoting new growth industries, often in partnership with private investors;
- Paving the way for private investment through the delivery of necessary physical infrastructure, which itself has to be funded and constructed;
- Working with local business leaders to expand their markets and improve local networking to source inputs locally rather than from further away; this can occur through intermediary organizations such as Chambers of Commerce and industry bodies;
- Improving the local skills base by working with educational providers including the Technical and Further Education (TAFE) system;
- Exercising a degree of psychological manipulation that promotes effort, self-belief, future orientation, and community cooperation;
- Wringing support and investment from other public agencies;
- Teaching the general skills of place promotion;
- Even, in some localities, raising or organizing capital.

On a precautionary note, the elements of this agenda work slowly and cumulatively over long time periods. It is difficult to attribute local change to the work of particular leaders against a background of technological improvement, changing global demand and supply, the tide of corporate decisions, fickle currency movements, environmental regulation, and ever-shifting national macro-economic settings. That said, the quality of local leadership is potentially critical to local economic and social well-being (Sorensen and Epps, 1996).

Both Guyra and Inverell have benefitted in recent years from the efforts of their respective mayors, Robyn Jackson and Barry Johnston, who illustrate the diversity of opportunity and approach. Robyn Jackson's ambition for her community was to grow its population from 2,500 to 10,000 in a decade on the back of several major projects, both current and anticipated. Given the previous demographic data, this goal might appear fanciful, but as of late 2006, Guyra council had approved $75 million worth of development projects in the previous year, compared with a long-term norm of $1 to $2 million. Those projects, which collectively herald the possible incipient rise of a new rural economy, include expansion of a recently developed tomato farm, a new feed-pellet business, redevelopment of part of the former abattoir into an industrial park, the growth of a local mohair rabbit business based on imported French animals, and a wind farm. The tomato farm is the most important of these, with its eightfold expansion from 5 ha to 40 ha now well underway. The current operation employs 70 people. Each additional 5 ha will create employment for another 50 to 60 workers, indicating a potentially massive population expansion. As already noted, there is a widespread perception that the local housing market has greatly tightened, and this feeling is supported somewhat by the fact that there is currently no surplus rental accommodation in town.

Most of the developments reported here result from private initiative, and council's role has been more reactive in the sense of trying to facilitate development by providing infrastructure, fast-tracking planning decisions, and promoting Guyra in various media. Good leadership is important for these tasks and involves using persuasive argument to smooth feathers ruffled by economic and social change. Guyra participates in a networked council arrangement with nearby Armidale, and Guyra's council has tried to keep development prospects confidential to prevent their leakage to a larger centre.

Mayor Johnston runs a much larger and more diversified economy than Guyra's, but his council has no economic development officer, relying instead on his personal leadership, aided by such senior officers as the general manager. In Johnston's view, the reason local attempts at integrated regional development have failed is, at least in part, because the organizations created have little power and most councils are competing with each other for development. He is wary of the state's local industry development board, having previously been a member and witnessing its lack of outcomes. That said, he is pleased with the level of support received from the NSW Department of State and Regional Development (DSARD), which he sees as more important than input from the Commonwealth's Department of Transport and Regional Services through its local Area Consultative Committee. DSARD played a crucial brokerage role in the Bruderhof community's decision to locate near Inverell (GHD, 2000).

Both mayors recognize the need for self-help in local development, and have developed personal styles to help realize economic and social improvement tailored to their council's resources and environment. It is a fluid task, driven by the mayors' experience, personalities, and connections, and by the rapidly changing Australian economy in which they are embedded. In both areas, economic expansion depends largely on private investment, and council's role is mainly enabling, providing timely infrastructure and quality of life to attract and retain businesses, and creating a forward-thinking environment receptive and adaptable to change. The mayors, too, are ambassadors for their communities, raising place profiles in the public eye. Both mayors stress the crucial role of leadership in all these tasks.

Conclusion

By most objective measures, or at least those set out within this chapter, communities like Guyra and Inverell have the dead weight of their economic history and geography against them. As traditional providers of basic agricultural staples to global markets, they have seen the opportunities for industrial diversification and, thus, the development of more robust, sustainable local economies and diverse workforces and communities restricted to some downstream processing of local commodities. These sectors have proved to be notoriously volatile and susceptible to corporate takeover and capital flight, leaving the local community bearing the full costs, over the short and long term, of unemployment, underemployment, population loss, and economic downturn.

In addition, both Guyra and Inverell are locationally disadvantaged, remote from the major capital cities, and "off the beaten track" of major tourist markets and migration corridors. Like most rural Australian communities, they perceive that the public services (e.g., primary health care, education, policing) they once took for granted as part of their citizenship rights are declining in quality and quantity. Despite these problems and constraints, the evidence presented in this chapter demonstrates that local farmers and key local leaders have attempted to deal with the developmental deficiencies of their regions in a highly adaptive fashion, and one that speaks of their strong attachment to place and the people that live in it. There have been few attempts to "reinvent" either place as a high-amenity theme park in order to attract footloose, affluent, ex-urban migrants (though some place marketing along these lines has been attempted). Equally, there has been no rush to develop new "sunrise" industries or to chase "smokestack" industries that could relocate from the cities. Intriguingly, the most successful enterprises—the businesses that are now providing more jobs and attracting in-migrants to Guyra and Inverell—are those that have simply reinterpreted the comparative advantages of both places and developed highly cost-effective production and distribution strategies accordingly. The recent economic successes of both can be attributed not so much to a radical redefining of the local economic base through the discovery and exploitation of tourism, recreational, and amenity values, but to making the most of the inherited comparative advantage of both places. In this sense, the forging of the "next rural economies" in Guyra and Inverell is simultaneously a passé *and* novel occurrence. It is through this deep sense of place—as a unique biophysical environment; as a node and hinterland within a broader (Thünenian) space economy; and as a location in which the people who make up communities struggle together, not always in harmony, to defend their access to a decent life—that the next economies of inland rural Australia are being forged.

Note

[1]The EVAO for 1976–1977 was $1,500 (nominal); for 2005–2006 it was $5,000 (nominal).

Acknowledgements

The research reported on in this chapter is the product of two Australian Research Council-funded grants: "Regional Governance in Rural NSW: Emerging Issues and Future Options" (DP05584000) and "Australia's Rural Heartlands: Declining Economic Fortune or Dynamic Regional Adjustment?" (DP0771418). We are grateful to the respondents involved in both projects. Since interviews were conducted in 2007 as part of the field work for DP05584000, Robyn Jackson has stood down as mayor, perhaps a reflection of the stresses and time-intensive nature of local leadership. Finally, we thank the participants at the "Space to Place" conference held at the University of Northern British Columbia in May 2008 and this book's referees for comments on an earlier draft of this chapter. The usual disclaimer applies.

References

Argent, N. (2002) From pillar to post? In search of the post-productivist countryside in Australia. *Australian Geographer* 33, 97–114.

Argent, N., Smailes, P., and Griffin, T. (2007) The amenity complex: Towards a framework for analysing and predicting the emergence of a multifunctional countryside in Australia. *Geographical Research* 45, 217–232.

Armstrong, W., and Bradbury, J. (1983) Industrialisation and class structure in Australia, Canada and Argentina: 1870 to 1980. In: Wheelwright, E., and Buckley, K. (eds.) *Essays in the Political Economy of Australian Capitalism*, Vol. 5. Australia and New Zealand Book, Sydney, 43–74.

Australian Bureau of Statistics. (1978) *Handbook of Local Statistics 1978, New South Wales* (Cat. No. 1304-1). Author, Canberra.

_____. (1989) *1981 Census on Supermap*. Author, Canberra.

_____. (2003) *2001 Census on CData*. Author, Canberra.

_____. (2007) *2006 Basic Community Profile Series* (Cat. No. 2001.0), www.censusdata.abs.gov.au (accessed 20 April 2008).

_____.(2008) *Agricultural Commodities: Small Area Data, Australia, 2005/2006*, www.abs.gov.au/AUSSTATS/abs@.nsf/ProductsbyCatalogue/9B391A9A73B84B3CCA2573D7 00178528?OpenDocument (accessed 30 April 2008).

Barnes, T. (1996) External shocks: Regional implications of an open staple economy. In: Britton, J. (ed.) *Canada and the Global Economy: The Geography of Structural and Technological Change.* McGill-Queen's University Press, Montreal, QC, and Kingston, ON, 48–68.

Barr, N. (2000) *Structural Change in Australian Agriculture: Implications for Natural Resource Management, Theme 6, Project 3.4.* Natural Resources and Environment Victoria, Melbourne.

_____. (2005) *The Changing Social Landscape of Rural Victoria.* Victorian Department of Primary Industries, Melbourne.

Bell, M. (1996) *Understanding Internal Migration.* Bureau of Immigration, Canberra.

Bolton, G. (1978) How we got to here. In: van Dugteren, T. (ed.) *Rural Australia: The Other Nation.* Hodder and Stoughton, Sydney, 1–20.

Boyle, P., and Halfacree, K. (1998) *Migration into Rural Areas: Theories and Issues.* Wiley, Chichester, UK.

Bunce, M. (1994) *The Countryside Ideal: Anglo-American Images of Landscape.* Routledge, London.

Cloke, P., and Thrift, N. (1990) Class and change in rural Britain. In: Marsden, T., Lowe, P., and Whatmore, S. (eds.) *Rural Restructuring.* David Fulton, London, 165–197.

Cloke, P., Phillips, M., and Thrift, N. (1995) The new middle classes and the social constructs of rural living. In: Butler, T., and Savage, M. (eds.) *Social Change and the Middle Classes.* UCL Press, London, 220–238.

Ehrensaft, P., and Armstrong, W. (1978) Dominion capitalism: A first statement. *Australian and New Zealand Journal of Sociology* 14, 352–363.

GHD Pty Ltd. (2000) *Justification Report for Amendment to Inverell Local Environmental Plan 1988: Development of an Integrated Community.* Author, Coffs Harbour, Australia.

Hayter, R., and Barnes, T. (1990) Innis' staple theory, exports and recession: British Columbia, 1981–86. *Economic Geography* 66, 156–173.

_____. (1997) Troubles in the rainforest: British Columbia's forest economy in transition. In: Barnes, T., and Hayter, R. (eds.) *Troubles in the Rainforest: British Columbia's Forest Economy in Transition* (Canadian Western Geographical Series, vol. 33). Western Geographical Press, Victoria, BC, 1–14.

Holmes, J. (2002) Diversity and change in Australia's rangelands: A post-productivist transition with a difference? *Transactions of the Institute of British Geographers* 27, 362–384.

_____. (2006) Impulses towards a multifunctional transition in rural Australia: Gaps in the research agenda. *Journal of Rural Studies* 22, 142–160.

Innis, H. (1995) *Staples, Markets and Cultural Change: Selected Essays.* Ed. D. Drache. McGill-Queen's University Press, Montreal, QC, and Kingston, ON.

Lea, D., Pigram, J., and Greenwood, J., eds. (1977) *An Atlas of New England.* Vol. 2, *The Commentaries.* Department of Geography, University of New England, Armidale, Australia.

Phillips, M. (1993) Rural gentrification and the process of class colonisation. *Journal of Rural Studies* 9, 123–140.

Powell, J. (1975) Conservation and resource management 1788–1860. In: Powell, J., and Williams, M. (eds.) *Australian Space, Australian Time: Geographical Perspectives.* Oxford University Press, Melbourne, 18–60.

Pritchard, B. (2000) Negotiating the two-edged sword of agricultural trade liberalisation: Trade policy and its protectionist discontents. In: Pritchard, B., and McManus, P., (eds.) *Land of Discontent: The Dynamics of Change in Rural and Regional Australia.* UNSW Press, Sydney, 90–104.

Reed, M., and Gill, A. (1997) Tourism, recreational, and amenity values in land allocation: An analysis of institutional arrangements in the postproductivist era. *Environment and Planning A* 29, 2019–2040.

Schwartz, H. (1989) *In the Dominions of Debt: Historical Perspectives on Dependent Development.* Cornell University Press, Ithaca, NY.

Sorensen, A. (1990) Virtuous cycles of growth and vicious cycles of decline: Regional economic change in northern NSW. In: Walmsley, D.J. (ed.) *Change and Adjustment in Northern NSW.* Department of Geography and Planning, University of New England, Armidale, Australia, 41–59.

_____. (2002) Regional economic governance: States, markets and DIY. In: Bell, S. (ed.) *Economic Governance and Institutional Dynamics.* Oxford University Press, Melbourne, 262–285.

Sorensen, A., and Epps, R. (1996) Leadership and local development: Dimensions of leadership in four central Queensland towns. *Journal of Rural Studies* 12, 113–125.

Sorensen, A., Marshall, N., and Dollery, B. (2007) Changing governance of Australian regional development: Systems and effectiveness. *Space and Polity* 11, 297–315.

Stayner, R. (2003) Guyra, New South Wales. In: Cocklin, C., and Alston, M. (eds.) *Community Sustainability in Rural Australia: A Question of Capital?* Centre for Rural Social Research, Wagga Wagga, Australia, 38–64.

Tonts, M. (2005) Competitive sport and social capital in rural Australia. *Journal of Rural Studies* 21, 53–65.

Walmsley, D. (2003) Rural tourism: A case of lifestyle-led opportunities. *Australian Geographer* 34, 61–72.

Walmsley, D., and Sorensen, A. (1993) *Contemporary Australia: Explorations in Economy, Society and Environment.* Longman Cheshire, Melbourne.

Williams, M. (1975) More and smaller is better: Australian rural settlement 1788-1914. In: Powell, J., and Williams, M. (eds.) *Australian Space, Australian Time: Geographical Perspectives.* Oxford University Press, Melbourne, 61–103.

Wilson, G. (2001) From productivism to post-productivism...and back again? Exploring the (un)changed natural and mental landscapes of European agriculture. *Transactions of the Institute of British Geographers* 26, 77–102.

Woods, M. (2007) Engaging the global countryside: Globalization, hybridity and the reconstitution of rural place. *Progress in Human Geography* 31, 485–507.

Chapter 3

The US Great Plains, Change, and Place Development

Lisa M.B. Harrington

> Our citizens being so prone to rambling, and extending themselves on the frontiers, will, through necessity, be constrained to limit their extent on the west to the borders of the Missouri and the Mississippi, while they leave the prairies, incapable of cultivation, to the...Aborigines of the country.
> —Zebulon Pike, *Exploratory Travels through the Western Territories of North America*

Zebulon Pike considered the prairies and Great Plains region of the United States unsuitable for agriculture and a desirable natural barrier that would prevent the spreading of the nation's Anglo-Americans too sparsely across the continent (Pike, 1811). His assessment proved incorrect, with settlement coming to the region in spite of the sometimes difficult environment, and in spite of Stephen Long's label of "The Great American Desert" broadly plastered over early maps (Long and James, 1823). Although there was a strong pull drawing settlers across the region to Oregon and California in the 1840s and 1850s, homestead claims only really began in the Plains states in early 1863,[1] shortly after passage of the Homestead Act of 1862. With the coming of the railways and promotional activity to settle the region, increasing numbers of settlers were attracted from other parts of the country, and from overseas.

Over the past century, residents of the Great Plains have made significant changes in agriculture and resource use. However, the region continues to be open and generally sparsely settled (Webb, 1931), and the basis of its economy has been agriculture ever since the arrival of American and European settlers. Although the region has continued to be agricultural in nature and dependent on natural resource use, neither agriculture nor communities remain static. Economy and agricultural production respond to stresses and opportunities, including changes in climate, resource availability, economic conditions, and government policy. This chapter presents the changing conditions of a subregion and a specific place embedded within the larger region (space) of the Great Plains. From a general overview of the Great Plains, through a discussion of a portion of its High Plains subregion, and ending with a specific Kansas community, the focus is on general economic and environmental conditions. While some places within the larger space of the North American Great Plains/prairie region may find the wherewithal to succeed in the longer term—by capitalizing on local features and local entrepreneurial strength—these are likely to be exceptional in a large and relatively sparsely populated region.

The Great Plains Region

Environment and Population

John Wesley Powell's report on the "arid lands" of the United States (1879), though focused on more western states, included western portions of the Great Plains. He noted that agriculture would be dependent on irrigation and that this would require "the use of the large streams" (p. 11). Large streams are a rarity across the Great Plains, and where streams cross state boundaries there is a high level of state-to-state competition for water resources (see Harrington and Harrington, 2005). The characteristic flow regime of many streams has been changed from perennial to ephemeral as a result of withdrawals of alluvial groundwater for irrigation (Sophocleus and Wilson, 2000; Worster, 2004). The region is known for extremes in weather and a high level of interannual variability in precipitation (Kincer, 1923; Skaggs, 1978; Rosenberg, 1986).

Government policies, including homestead legislation, railroad grants, agricultural subsidies, and environmental programs, have played important roles in the settlement and use of the land of the Great Plains. Growth occurred during a period of boosterism, relatively small farms (given the Plains reality), and relatively high rainfall. However, much of the 20th century, continuing into the 21st, has been a period of adjustment to changes in the reality of technologically-based farming, expanding farm sizes, and diminished labour needs (Easterling *et al.*, 1993; Fitzgerald, 2003; Hart, 2003; Wishart, 2006).

In general, the region has fewer than ten people per square mile (Fig. 3.1), and many parts of the Great Plains achieved their population highs in the late 1800s to early 1900s. For example, the population of McHenry County, North Dakota, peaked at 17,627 people in 1910; there were 5,987 residents in 2000, and the county was estimated to have lost another 9.3% between 2000 and 2006 (US Census Bureau, 1995b, 2008b). Grant County, Nebraska, reached 1,486 for the 1920 census and recorded 747 in the 2000 census; the 2006 estimate was down to 660 (US Census Bureau, 1995a, 2008b). Some authors have found these population declines "disturbing" (Rathge and Highman, 1998), and the trend has led others to question the longterm viability of the Great Plains as a working landscape (Popper and Popper, 1987),[2] although others have seen it as simply an adjustment to reduced labour and household size requirements as farm and ranch sizes have increased (Hudson, 1996). As noted by Mather (1972), the most-travelled routes across the Plains states run east to west; the region lacks strong north–south connections. For most US residents, the Great Plains is seen as an area to fly over or drive across...as quickly as possible.

Following the environmental and social disaster of the Dust Bowl in the 1930s, when drought and winds following on the heels of excessive land clearing caused extensive erosion and loss of income in a large part of the Great Plains, the federal government established the Soil Conservation Service (now the Natural Resources Conservation Service) and instituted an acquisition program for highly erodible land. In response to another major drought in the 1950s, Congress created the Soil Bank, a temporary retirement program for farmland. At one point, about 14.1 million acres were set aside in the Great Plains (Laycock, 1988), but the program was ended due to costs (Bedenbaugh, 1988). With the 1985 Farm Bill (Food Security Act of 1985), Congress created another environmentally (and production) oriented means to temporarily retire land, the Conservation Reserve Program (CRP). The program provides payments to farmers who enroll eligible cropland with highly erodible soils. The CRP's key goals originally were soil conservation and reduced overproduction in the agricultural sector. Since 1985, protection of wildlife habitat also has been recognized as an important benefit and purpose of such resource protection, and there has been growing interest in the program's carbon sequestration potential. Some farmers have enrolled in the CRP in order to obtain more reliable income. There are concerns, however, that with upcoming contract expirations, much of the land currently enrolled will be converted back to crop production, largely due to high commodity prices. With good crops and high prices, the average net farm income in Kansas in 2007 was $115,035, as compared with $46,593 in 2006, according to the Kansas Farm Management Association (*Topeka Capital-Journal*, 2008). Incomes were highest for irrigated crop operations, with an average of $280,585; ranches did less well, with cattle ranching operations averaging a net income of $23,633.

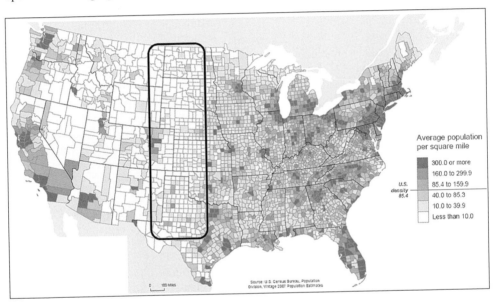

Fig. 3.1 Population density, July 2007 (US Census Bureau, 2007).
The box indicates the general area of the US Great Plains.

Livestock and Crops

Large cattle operations, first free range and then ranch-based, were introduced after bison were cleared from the Great Plains through excessive sport and market hunting and the desire to remove the traditional livelihood of native peoples. Even in 1923, Kincer noted that the "drier portions of the region, considered from a climatic standpoint, are pre-eminently grazing areas, and must so remain until moisture is artificially supplied by irrigation" (p. 80). Ranching activities, and dryland (unirrigated) agriculture based generally on winter wheat, continue to be the key agricultural activities where supplemental water is unavailable. Since about World War II, concentrated livestock raising in feedlots or feedyards has been established in a number of areas of the Great Plains, beginning in southwestern Kansas and northeastern Colorado. A vertically integrated agricultural economy serving national and international markets typifies parts of the region, although other areas have been described as a "buffalo commons." Where there is sufficient space, water for animals and for growing feed, and connections to rail and highway transportation, beef cattle feedlots have reached capacities in excess of 100,000 head. High-capacity packing plants are often found nearby.

Since the 1990s, some parts of the Plains states have seen growth in other types of concentrated animal feeding operations (CAFOs), with the appearance of large hog operations, especially after the establishment of a packing plant in the panhandle of Oklahoma (Hart and Mayda, 1997), and movement of dairy operations into southwestern Kansas, joining the beef CAFOs long established there. Milk cow numbers have increased, especially in eastern New Mexico and southwestern Kansas, but also in parts of the Texas and Oklahoma panhandles and southern Nebraska. These operations do not have the capacity of the beef CAFOs, but they add to the mix of agricultural activities and have been seen by some as opportunities for economic diversification. Large dairy operations are affected by both push and pull factors, with competition for land pushing the activity out of parts of California, for example. Stringent environmental controls provide a push from some parts of the country, and places with more accommodating controls contribute a pull in response. The Great Plains region also offers plenty of space and reduced likelihood of conflicts with neighbouring landowners.

Shifts in scale of production have been widely noted for the last half century, but other changes are also notable. In the High Plains, many adjustments have been made based on the availability of water and can be seen in geographic shifts responding to drought, changing groundwater access, and government programs that may be used to augment income (such as the Conservation Reserve Program). Drought has been a periodic hazard for agricultural producers in the region (e.g., Rosenberg, 1986). There is considerable spatial variability in water resources, and areas that have had access to groundwater resources like the Ogallala–High Plains aquifer system are now seeing reduced water availability due to several decades of withdrawals greatly exceeding recharge rates, and due to high energy prices.[3] Crops and land cover have shifted in response to changes in water availability and enrollment in agricultural programs; CRP enrollment has offered some farmers an opportunity to stabilize income and has created situations where agricultural land use has changed as a result of federal policy and program availability. Researchers and policymakers must recognize and understand these changes and their implications for the vulnerability, resilience, and adaptive capacity of agricultural enterprises and rural communities in the face of environmental variability, including the potential effects of global climate change.

Evolution of the "Buffalo Commons"

In 1987, Deborah and Frank Popper suggested that population decline in the Great Plains would lead to the creation of a vast re-naturalized area they referred to as the Buffalo Commons. They saw a bleak future for virtually all Plains communities:

> It is hard to predict the future course of the Plains ordeal. The most likely possibility is a continuation of the gradual impoverishment and depopulation that in many places go back to the 1920s. A few of the more urban areas may pull out of their decline, especially if an energy boom returns. And a few cities—Lubbock and Cheyenne, for example—may hold steady as self-contained service providers. But the small towns in the surrounding countryside will empty, wither, and die. The rural Plains will be virtually deserted. (p. 16)

This led to strong negative reactions from Great Plains residents (to put it mildly), who disparaged the Poppers for their lack of understanding of the region and its people. Indeed, the Poppers' initial interpretation that land depopulation created unused land was wrong in some ways: although few people occupy large parts of the region, lack of occupancy does not mean lack of use. On the other hand, although the federal reacquisition and management of the area that the Poppers originally envisioned has not occurred, parts of the region have indeed reverted to buffalo (*Bison bison*) grazing.

By 1999, the Poppers noted that there were changes consistent with a Buffalo Commons "metaphor" for change in parts of the Great Plains. These included adoption of bison as livestock by ranchers, growth in membership in the National Bison Association, creation of the North American Bison Cooperative (for meat processing), and creation of the InterTribal Bison Cooperative to promote bison raising and the place of bison in Native American culture. Over the last 20 years, bison—and other native wildlife—have received growing attention as a tourism resource (Popper and Popper, 2006; Kurlantzik, 2008). This holds promise as a contributing economic activity for portions of the Great Plains, though it should be remembered that tourism can be highly sensitive to broader economic conditions. Beyond tourism benefits, the appeal of bison meat as a healthy alternative to beef and the desirability of an animal that is well adapted to regional environmental conditions also constitute reasons for shifts and hope for a reliable income source. According to a National Bison Association press release in 2007, bison meat sales saw double-digit increases in each of the previous three years, and expectations are for continued increases in production and sales. The release cited several reasons for expansion:

> People have discovered that bison is a great tasting, healthy meat that is sustainably produced by North American ranchers...At the same time, our marketers have done a great job in developing a national distribution system that is bringing bison to foodservice and retail outlets across the country. And, smaller rancher-marketers have continued to develop a strong customer base among people looking for locally-raised food.

Energy

Energy has played an important role in the economic and social development of the Great Plains. In the early days of settlement, energy development was beside the point: most power was provided by horses, mules, and oxen (sustained by locally grown feed) to work the fields and provide transportation, and by wind to pump water. However, as the nation industrialized and discovered the wonders of fossil fuels, first the petroleum of Texas was tapped, and then oil field development spread to states like Oklahoma and Kansas. Natural gas fields were developed later on. In many cases, derelict well pumps may be seen where the remaining oil is no longer of sufficient quantity to withdraw. In other areas, such as the Hugoton Field region running from the Texas panhandle into southwestern Kansas, natural gas resources have been depleted to the point where options like infilling (increasing well density) or forcing remaining gas toward the surface by adding other fluids are being employed.

Wind power has long been used at the farm scale for bringing water up from below, but only since the latter 1990s and early 2000s have large windfarms feeding into the national grid been developed in the Great Plains. Kansas has three wind energy projects of 100 MW capacity or more, all brought online since 2000, and another is planned for 2008 (American Wind Energy Association, 2008). Other Plains states have a variety of small to large wind facilities, with most dating after 1998. These can be meaningful in their energy provision to communities and in their economic benefits to farmers, who can receive about US$2,000 per year for each wind tower.

A number of ethanol production plants have been built throughout the Great Plains. The same is true for much of the country, with corn serving as the feedstock of choice at the present time. The United States had record corn production in 2007, and 2008 saw the second highest corn acreage planted since 1946, with 87.3 million acres (down 7% from 2007) (National Agricultural Statistics Service, 2008). Feed grain prices are expected to remain high, which will continue to trouble livestock producers. Rising corn prices, driven by the ethanol boom from an average of US$2.00 per bushel in January 2006 to US$4.28 in January 2008 (Beaubien, 2008), also have had a negative effect on other crop production and on subsectors of agriculture.

Rising fuel prices—for gasoline and, especially, diesel—have created further problems for farmers and ranchers. Most farm equipment and trucks run on these fuels, so higher prices increase the cost of bringing in agricultural supplies and shipping out agricultural goods, as well as increasing farm household costs. Agrochemical costs also rise with petrochemical costs. In addition, pumping groundwater requires energy use (very often fossil-fuel based), and more energy is required to lift water from increasing depths as groundwater resources are depleted.

The Southwestern Kansas High Plains

The southwestern corner of Kansas is in the High Plains portion of the Great Plains region and has many of the more general regional characteristics described above. Because of its Dust Bowl location, repeated droughts, and changes made possible by use of the Ogallala–High Plains aquifer system, this area has long received particular attention from historians, sociologists, geographers, and others.

The Kansas High Plains and contiguous Oklahoma and Texas panhandle areas were in the core of the 1930s Dust Bowl region. The (highly variable) precipitation generally averages under 20 inches of rainfall annually. Additional major droughts occurred in the 1890s and the 1950s, with less extreme periods of drought at other times. In spite of the relatively difficult environment, this region has been thriving in recent years, unlike many other parts of the Great Plains. As noted by Powell (1879),

> There are two considerations that make irrigation attractive to the agriculturist. Crops thus cultivated are not subject to the vicissitudes of rainfall; the farmer fears no droughts; his labors are seldom interrupted and his crops rarely injured by storms. This immunity from drought and storm renders agricultural operations much more certain than in regions of greater humidity. (p. 11)

Early settlers and inhabitants up to the 1950s had to rely on the relatively rare surface water and on the storage and diversion structures that were built in conjunction with the major streams (Sherow, 1990), but eventually means were developed to tap into a vast underground water system (Kromm and White, 1992). Starting in the 1950s, but particularly from the 1960s through the 1980s, the use of water from the Ogallala–High Plains aquifers underwent tremendous expansion, and groundwater came to support a large area of irrigated agriculture (Fig. 3.2). This decreased the impact of drought on farming:

there has been a reduced relationship between cropland harvested and drought with the expansion of irrigation. The southwestern corner of the state is dominated by agricultural land use, with 93% in rangeland or crop production (Harrington *et al.*, forthcoming). A cattle culture and an agriculture support base have, in turn, supported expansion of beef cattle feeding operations, large packing plants, and associated support activities—from irrigation equipment supply sales to manufacturing of boxes for the shipment of beef. Reliance on agriculture, particularly groundwater-supported agriculture, is high.

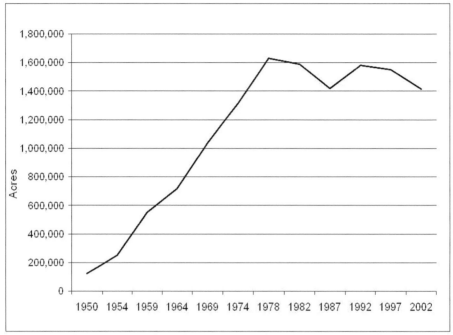

Fig. 3.2 Increase in irrigated land area, southwestern Kansas (19-county area). US Census of Agriculture, various years; the irregular intervals are due to irregular census dates in earlier years.[4]

In western Kansas, many adjustments are driven by the availability of water, with agricultural shifts in response to drought, changing groundwater access, and government programs that may be used to augment income. For the western third of the state, where there is very little surface water, there has been great variability in access to water resources, particularly the Ogallala–High Plains aquifer system. Although irrigation has helped mitigate agricultural sensitivity to climate variability (Bloomquist, *et al.*, 2002, following on Bell, 1942), it may actually increase vulnerability in the long term (Dregne, 1980). As the groundwater resource upon which the region has become reliant is depleted, agriculture will be forced to change again in response to this stress (Harrington, 2005). In some parts of western Kansas, the loss of access to sufficient groundwater means irrigation is no longer economically viable. Previously irrigated fields have reverted to dryland agricultural use (Kettle *et al.*, 2007). For the 14 southwesternmost counties in the state, Leatherman *et al.* (2004) estimated that, should cropping shift to dryland (non-irrigated) only, there would be a total income loss of $89 million (in 2003 dollars), with 2,178 jobs lost. This is in spite of increased production values for the dryland crops of sorghum, hay and pasture, and sunflowers. It should be noted, however, that much of the area is not now irrigated: range makes up 64.5% of all agricultural land for the 19-county region (60.4% of the total land area), and only 42% of cropland is irrigated (Harrington *et al.*, forthcoming).

Two wind farms, Spearville Wind Energy Facility (100.5 MW capacity) and Gray County Wind Farm (112.2 MW), are now located in southwestern Kansas. There are also ethanol production plants in western Kansas, and a large coal-fired power plant in the region. Although the power plant sits atop the Hugoton natural gas field, it relies on coal imported from Wyoming (Harrington and Kaktins, 1998).[5] Energy-related activities are important, but not key, to the economics of the area. With continued attention to renewable energy, the importance of these activities may increase; commercial wind power generation contributes to farm income and is thus linked to the already dominant agriculture of the region.

White (1994) noted that a few communities in western Kansas, particularly Garden City, Liberal, and Dodge City, were "gainers" in terms of population; these are the key trade centers in the area and have good access to groundwater resources. Gains have largely been linked to the immigration of Hispanics to work in packing plants, and an influx of Southeast Asian refugees in the 1970s/early 1980s (Broadway, 1994). Much of the rest of western Kansas has seen (and is seeing) population loss, with younger residents leaving and many of the older residents aging in place. Even Garden City, the largest community in southwestern Kansas, has experienced recent declines, from an estimated 1 July population of 28,547 in 2000 to 26,629 in 2007 (US Census Bureau, 2008a). Much of this loss can be attributed to the closing of a large beef packing plant following a fire in 2003.

The area's current dependence on natural resources and agricultural production contributes to its potential economic vulnerability (Harrington, 2005). Irrigation use of the Ogallala–High Plains aquifer system is not sustainable; its management has been based on the concept of "managed depletion," with the idea of extending the useful life of the resource, but not making it sustainable long into the future. Moves to prolong the use of the aquifer have been based on increasingly efficient irrigation technologies and crop changes. Residents of the region retain a sense of adaptability and resiliency to changing conditions. However, although farmers in southwestern Kansas and other parts of the Great Plains have been able to adapt to a highly variable climate system and overcome drought and other climatic hazards (Harrington *et al.*, forthcoming), uncertainties associated with climate change are on the horizon.

Disaster as Opportunity: Greensburg, Kansas

Just one county to the east of the southwestern Kansas High Plains area described above, a small town has become a focal point for place development. Greensburg, the county seat of Kiowa County, is a typical Great Plains community. The Greensburg population is mostly white (97% white; less than 2% Hispanic) and declining (from 1,574 in 2000 to an estimated 1,452 in 2004). Estimates show a loss in county population, as well: from 3,255 in 2000 to 2,953 in 2007 (US Bureau of the Census, 2007).

In May 2007, Greensburg was hit by an EF-5 tornado (the most intense—and destructive—category). The tornado killed 11 people and destroyed virtually the entire town. The irony is that the disaster, while a tragedy, also brought the community tremendous attention—including multiple news stories and a 13-episode series on Discovery Communications' Planet Green television network—and donations ranging in size from US$5 (through the One Million $5 Donations campaign) to much larger gifts and other support. The almost complete demolition of Greensburg also created an opportunity for "green" redevelopment. In the wake of the disaster, Governor Kathleen Sebelius declared, "We have the opportunity of having the greenest town in rural America" (Rothschild, 2007). Greensburg plans to build all city structures to the US Green Building Council Leadership in Energy and Environmental Design (LEED) Platinum standards (City of Greensburg, 2007). A nonprofit organization, Greensburg GreenTown, has been "established to provide the residents of Greensburg, Kansas with the resources, information and support they need to rebuild Greensburg as a model green community" (Greensburg GreenTown, 2008). A variety of businesses and organizations, from the GM dealership to the Baptist Church, are planning "green" buildings at some level. The city's long-term recovery plan highlights "sustainable (green) development," focusing on building programs and energy alternatives. It appears that some residents who might otherwise have moved away have been energized to remain in Greensburg. President George W. Bush attended the May 2008 high school graduation in recognition of the disaster and recovery process.

Thousands of similar small communities have not received such attention (and do not have a "clean slate" on which to build more sustainable conditions), but could benefit greatly from assistance with transitioning to economic, social, and environmental sustainability. In the Greensburg case, it will be years before we know if this type of place-based development works in the long term. In the meantime, other communities of a variety of sizes throughout the region lack the resources to address development needs and are unlikely to be focal areas for economic growth; many of these communities will likely experience continued population decline.

Space, Sector, Place, and Economic Development

In 2003, Governor Sebelius convened a Rural Life Task Force to address issues affecting rural parts of Kansas (Governor's Rural Life Task Force, 2003). The task force report identified a number of concerns regarding social and economic sustainability in Kansas. Environmental connections were not addressed as part of the committee's concerns, although these can be critical to local well-being. Although the task force was formed in recognition of the need to address issues in rural areas, no further action appears to have been taken. In a way, Greensburg may have become the "poster child," and certainly the focal point, for rural development in Kansas.

With the exception of anomalous situations like that of Greensburg, and the few destination locales in the Plains (e.g., the scenic Black Hills/Rapid City area), it does not appear that "place" is apt to replace "sector" as the focus of economic strength in many parts of the Great Plains. Places are found within the vast space of the Plains and prairies, but are weakly differentiated and have characteristics that attract a small proportion of the general populace. There continue to be adjustments—largely reductions—in social services, school consolidations, and other changes associated with local decline. Key individuals can be important to development activities, but local leadership can be lacking in small communities, and progress can stop with the loss of a primary leader.

As illustrated elsewhere in this volume (e.g., Argent, Halseth, Markey, Vodden), development of rural places, specifically those not occupying urban fringe or near-fringe locales, is still highly contingent on natural resource use and connections to external markets. Both the space of the Great Plains and most of the places within the region remain closely linked to the agricultural sector. Demand for food will continue, and global as well as national markets create a reason for continued agricultural activity across the region. Although place matters, national policy development for the rural United States, including the Great Plains, is likely to continue to focus on general applications of policy to agricultural concerns, with other economic, social, and environmental concerns of secondary interest. With the exception of renewable energy development, there is little short-term opportunity for economic diversification or sector-independent development of place. In some parts of the Great Plains, multi-functionality of agricultural areas has been a possibility—generally in the form of farming, conservation, and recreation (Laingen, forthcoming)—but the entire region cannot rely on such possibilities for much economic or social betterment.

In addition to the social and economic stresses now being felt in the Great Plains, environmental stresses always loom; both may limit rural development. In addition to what Great Plains inhabitants have experienced as drought over the last century, there is evidence that prior droughts were more severe and of longer duration (Woodhouse and Overpeck, 1998; Sauchyn *et al.*, 2003). Climate change uncertainties contribute to what we *don't* know about the stresses that may affect Great Plains regional well-being in the future; a temperature increase is likely, as is a decrease in precipitation throughout the Plains (Intergovernmental Panel on Climate Change, 2007). Potential changes to seasonality of precipitation, greater severity and frequency of storms, potential evapotranspiration and crop stress, and variability within the larger climate pattern are possibilities.

In addressing the construction of rural place in a global economy, we need to consider the key questions for specific rural places. Beyond the economy, the key sustainability goals in rural areas and small towns need to be explored. We need to discover how local priorities are determined and how varying goals related to sense of place, economy, environment, and social connections are to be balanced against each other. How are environmental goods and services (natural capital) balanced against other interests (social, financial, human, and built capital)? How are the societal benefits and costs of rural services balanced? Local rural places often provide goods and environmental services or benefits for populations beyond their own inhabitants, but the equitability of costs and benefits may be questioned. All these themes will be vital in the global economy and the pursuit of a sustainability transition (National Research Council, Board on Sustainable Development, 1999).

Acknowledgement

I would like to acknowledge constructive comments from John A. Harrington, Jr. in the development of this chapter.

Notes

[1]In this chapter, the term "Great Plains states" encompasses North Dakota, South Dakota, Nebraska, Kansas, and Oklahoma. The eastern portions of these states are not properly included in the Great Plains, but much of their identities are tied to the Plains. General statements about the Great Plains would apply to the eastern Rocky Mountain States (Montana, Wyoming, Colorado, and New Mexico) as well.
[2]See US Census Bureau (2007); the map showing population change between April 2000 and July 2007, for example, indicates population decline on a large proportion of the Great Plains. This follows the long-term trends in the region.
[3]As depth to groundwater increases, the energy requirement to pump it to the surface increases. Overall costs to acquire water are then exacerbated by rising energy prices, in combination with greater energy needs.
[4]The counties included are: Clark, Finney, Ford, Grant, Gray, Greeley, Hamilton, Haskell, Hodgeman, Kearny,

Lane, Meade, Morton, Ness, Scott, Seward, Stanton, Stevens, and Wichita.
[5] In 2008, a proposal to greatly expand coal-fired energy production in western Kansas became a focus of contention between supporters of coal expansion and environmental interests. Although state legislators attempted to override the Kansas Secretary of Health and the Environment, who denied a permit based on air quality and carbon dioxide (climate change) concerns (Tollefson, 2007), the Governor's veto held.

References

American Wind Energy Association. (2008) U.S. wind energy projects, www.awea.org/projects/ (accessed 7 May, 2008).

Beaubien, J. (2008) Ethanol demand, prices boost farm communities. National Public Radio, 4 March, www.npr.org/templates/story/story.php?storyId=87782087 (accessed 12 November 2008).

Bedenbaugh, E. (1988) History of cropland set aside programs in the Great Plains. In: Mitchell, J. (ed.) *Impacts of the Conservation Reserve Program in the Great Plains* (GTR RM-158). Rocky Mountain Forest and Range Experiment Station, USDA Forest Service, Fort Collins, CO, 14–17.

Bell, E. (1942) *Culture of a Contemporary Community: Sublette, Kansas* (Rural Life Studies: 2). US Bureau of Agricultural Economics, US Department of Agriculture, Washington, DC.

Bloomquist, L., Williams, D., and Bridger, J. (2002) Sublette, Kansas: Persistence and change in Haskell County. In: Luloff, A., and Krannich, R. (eds.) *Persistence and Change in Rural Communities*. CABI Publishing, Wallingford, UK, 23–43.

Broadway, M. (1994) Beef stew: Cattle, immigrants and established residents in a Kansas beefpacking town. In: Lamphere, L., Stepick, A., and Grenier, G. (eds.) *Newcomers in the Workplace: Immigrants and the Restructuring of the U.S. Economy*. Temple University Press, Philadelphia, 25–42.

City of Greensburg. (2007) Official website of Greensburg, Kansas, www.greensburgks.org/ (accessed May 2008).

Dregne, H. (1980) Task group on technology. In: Rosenberg, N. (ed.) *Drought in the Great Plains: Research on Impacts and Strategies*. Water Resources Publications, Littleton, CO, 19–42.

Easterling, W., Crosson, P., Rosenberg, N., McKenney, M., Katz, L., and Lemon, K. (1993) Agricultural impacts of and responses to climate change in the Missouri–Iowa–Nebraska–Kansas (MINK) region. *Climatic Change* 24, 23–61.

Fitzgerald, D. (2003) *Every Farm a Factory: The Industrial Ideal in American Agriculture*. Yale University Press, New Haven, CT.

Governor's Rural Life Task Force. (2003) *Rural Kansas: Past, Present, Future*, www.oznet.ksu.edu/library/misc2/RLTFReport.pdf (accessed 7 September 2007).

Greensburg GreenTown. (2008) Greensburg GreenTown website, www.greensburggreentown.org/ (accessed 7 May 2008).

Harrington, L. (2005) Vulnerability and sustainability concerns for the U.S. high plains. In: Essex, S., Gilg, A., Yarwood, R., Smithers, J., and Wilson, R. (eds.) *Rural Change and Sustainability: Agriculture, the Environment and Communities*. CABI Publishing, Wallingford, UK, 169–184.

Harrington, L., and Harrington, J., Jr. (2005) When winning is losing: Arkansas River interstate water management issues. *Papers of the Applied Geography Conferences* 28, 46–51.

Harrington, L., and Kaktins, S. (1998) Policy and local utility greenhouse gas emissions, or: Why a coal-fired power plant in a natural gas production area? Paper presented at the 21st annual Applied Geography Conference, Louisville, KY. (Abstract is included in *Papers and Proceedings of the Applied Geography Conferences* 21, 469).

Harrington, L., Lu, M., and Harrington, J., Jr. (forthcoming) Southwestern Kansas: Agricultural vulnerabilities in the High Plains–Ogallala region. In: Yarnal, B., and O'Brien, J. (eds.) *Sustainable Communities on a Sustainable Planet*. Cambridge University Press, Cambridge.

Hart, J. (2003) *The Changing Scale of American Agriculture*. University of Virginia Press, Charlottesville.

Hart, J., and Mayda, C. (1997) Pork palaces on the panhandle. *Geographical Review* 87(3), 396–400.

Hudson, J. (1996) *The Geographer's Great Plains* (Kansas State University Occasional Publications in Geography). Department of Geography, Kansas State University, Manhattan.

Intergovernmental Panel on Climate Change. (2007) *Climate Change 2007* (Fourth Assessment Report, Working Group 1). Cambridge University Press, Cambridge.

Kettle, N., Harrington, L., and Harrington, J., Jr. (2007) Groundwater depletion and agricultural land use change in the High Plains: A case study from Wichita County, Kansas. *Professional Geographer* 59(2), 221–235.

Kincer, J. (1923) The climate of the Great Plains as a factor in their utilization. *Annals of the Association of American Geographers* 13, 67–80.

Kromm, D., and White, S., eds. (1992) *Groundwater Exploitation in the High Plains*. University Press of Kansas, Lawrence.

Kurlantzik, J. (2008) Journeys: The Great Plains. Back to nature and ready for guests in the Great Plains. *New York Times*, 8 June, travel.nytimes.com/2008/06/08/travel/08journeys.html (accessed 10 June 2008).

Laingen, C. (forthcoming) The past, present, and uncertain future of South Dakota pheasant hunting. *Focus* 51(3).

Laycock, W. (1988) History of grassland plowing and grass planting on the Great Plains. In: Mitchell, J. (ed.) *Impacts of the Conservation Reserve Program in the Great Plains* (GTR RM-158). Rocky Mountain Forest and Range Experiment Station, USDA Forest Service, Fort Collins, CO, 1–6.

Leatherman, J.C., Cader, H.A., and Bloomquist, L.E. (2004) When the well runs dry: The value of irrigation to the western Kansas economy. *Kansas Policy Review* 26(1), 7–20.

Long, S., and James, E. (1823) *Account of an Expedition from Pittsburgh to the Rocky Mountains, Performed in the Years 1819 and 1820*. Maps and Plates. H.C. Carey and I. Lea, Chesnut Street, Philadelphia.

Mather, E. (1972) The American Great Plains. *Annals of the Association of American Geographers* 62(2), 237–257.

National Agricultural Statistics Service. (2008) USDA report assesses corn and soybean acreage. News release, 30 June.

National Bison Association. (2007) Bison industry poised for strong growth in 2008. News release, 27 December, www.bisoncentral.com/bison-news.php (accessed 16 June 2008).

National Research Council, Board on Sustainable Development. (1999) *Our Common Journey: A Transition toward Sustainability*. National Academy Press, Washington, DC.

Pike, Z.M. (1811) *Exploratory Travels through the Western Territories of North America*. Reprint, W.H. Lawrence and Company, Denver, 1889.

Popper, D.E., and Popper, F.J. (1987) The Great Plains: From dust to dust. *Planning* 53(2), 12–18.

_____. (1999) Buffalo Commons: Metaphor as method. *Geographical Review* 89(4): 491–510.

_____. (2006) The onset of the Buffalo Commons. *Journal of the West* 45(2), 29–34.

Powell, J. (1879) *Report on the Lands of the Arid Region of the United States, with a More Detailed Account of the Lands of Utah*. Government Printing Office, Washington, DC.

Rathge, R., and Highman, P. (1998) Population change in the Great Plains: A history of prolonged decline. *Rural Development Perspectives* 13(1), 19–26.

Rosenberg, N. (1986) Adaptations to adversity: Agriculture, climate, and the Great Plains of North America. *Great Plains Quarterly* 6, 202–217.

Rothschild, S. (2007) Officials hope to build "green" Greensburg. *Lawrence Journal-World*, 12 May, www2.ljworld.com/news/2007/may/12/officials_hope_build_green_greensburg/ (accessed 16 September 2008).

Sauchyn, D., Stroich, J., and Beriault, A. (2003) A paleoclimatic context for the drought of 1999–2001 in the northern Great Plains of North America. *Geographical Journal* 169(2), 158–167.

Sherow, J. (1990) *Watering the Valley: Development along the High Plains Arkansas River, 1870–1950*. University Press of Kansas, Lawrence.

Skaggs, R. (1978) Climate change and persistence in western Kansas. *Annals of the Association of American Geographers* 68(1), 73–80.

Sophocleus, M., and Wilson, B. (2000) Surface water in Kansas and its interaction with groundwater. In: *An Atlas of the Kansas High Plains Aquifer*. Kansas Geological Survey, Lawrence, www.kgs.ku.edu/HighPlains/atlas/atswqn.htm (accessed 12 November 2008).

Tollefson, J. (2007) Air permit blocks Kansas coal plants. *Nature* 449, 953.

Topeka Capitol-Journal. (2008) Report: State farm income doubled in '07. *CJ Online* (AP story), 10 May, cjonline.com/stories/051008/bus_277594205.shtml (accessed 12 November 2008).

US Census Bureau. (1995a) Nebraska population of counties by decennial census: 1900 to 1990, www.census.gov/population/cencounts/ne190090.txt (accessed 10 June 2008).

_____. (1995b) North Dakota population of counties by decennial census: 1900 to 1990, www.census.gov/population/cencounts/nd190090.txt (accessed 10 June 2008).

_____. (2007) Population estimates, www.census.gov/popest/ (accessed 10 June 2008).

_____. (2008a) Population estimates: Cities and towns, www.census.gov/popest/cities/ (accessed 20 September 2008).

_____. (2008b) State and county QuickFacts: Nebraska; North Dakota, http//quickfacts.census.gov/qfd/states (accessed 10 June 2008).

Webb, W. (1931) *The Great Plains*. Reprint, University of Nebraska Press, Lincoln, 1981.

White, S. (1994) Ogallala oases: Water use, population redistribution, and policy implications in the High Plains of western Kansas, 1980-1990. *Annals of the Association of American Geographers* 84(1), 29–45.

Wishart, D. (2006) Natural areas, regions, and two centuries of environmental change on the Great Plains. *Great Plains Quarterly* 26(3), 147–165.

Woodhouse, C.A., and Overpeck, J.T. (1998) 2000 years of drought vulnerability in the central United States. *Bulletin of the American Meteorological Society* 79(12), 2693–2714.

Worster, D. (2004) The waters of Kansas, past and present. *Kansas Policy Review* 26(1), 2–6.

Chapter 4

A New Rural North Carolina: Latino Place-Making and Community Engagement

Owen J. Furuseth

As the American South ended the last century and moved into a new millennium, dramatic social and economic shifts were underway. Some observers argue that the most important of these regional changes was demographic: specifically, the emergence of the American South as the second-largest home for Hispanics/Latinos in the United States.[1] The speed and scale of Latino immigration caused historian Raymond   Mohl to suggest that the end of the 20th century marked a segue from the "New South" to the "Nuevo South" (Mohl, 2005).

While the pace of Latino immigration has changed the face of southern cities, the size and complexity of metropolitan centres have enabled them to absorb the immigrant stream with relatively modest impacts. Indeed, large and moderate-sized southern cities have been among the fastest-growing and economically most robust urban areas in the United States during this period. Metros like Atlanta, Charlotte, Raleigh-Durham, Tampa, Nashville, Orlando, and northern Virginia have relied on immigrant labour to meet the demand for construction trades, services, and other low-wage jobs that undergird local economies.

The immigration experience in large parts of the rural South has been equally dramatic. But economic differences and socio-political contexts have created different sets of outcomes and challenges. The most fundamental difference between the rural and urban South is economic status. Trade liberalization and the national economic downturn of the 1990s greatly impacted broad sections of the rural South. For example, between 1990 and 2006, manufacturing employment in North Carolina fell by 31% (Quinterno, 2008). In rural North Carolina, where low-wage, low-skill manufacturing has been more important than agriculture, these job losses have been devastating. Indeed, only 49% of the workers in rural areas who were laid off in 2002 had found a job one year later, and those lucky workers were earning 27% less (Quinterno, 2008).

In rural communities facing economic and out-migration challenges, the influx of new Latino residents may offer the potential for a new community development paradigm for the rural South. In this chapter I explore the impacts of Latino settlement in rural North Carolina, examining changes in local immigrant settlement geography and place-making, with a focus on the reception and community development impacts of the newcomers. In this context, this chapter is focused on three interrelated issues. First, what are the impacts of Latino entrepreneurship and economic activity on rural North Carolina? Second, within the receiving communities, what are the spatial dimensions of the Latino economic activities? And finally, from a policy perspective, what are the challenges to fostering and building stronger Latino economic success and engagement in rural communities?

Latino Newcomers in North Carolina

Historically, North Carolina had the second-largest agricultural migrant labour force on the East Coast (Bailey, 2005). Latino participation in North Carolina's agricultural economy has been important since the 1970s. Initially, Latinos represented a modest proportion of the temporary agricultural workforce that moved through the orchards and the vegetable and tobacco fields, augmenting local labour, primarily African-Americans, in the spring and fall planting and harvesting periods. Eastern North Carolina, the core of North Carolina's tobacco and small farm economy, and the western region, noted for tree fruits and Christmas tree farms were the primary destinations of these sojourners. By and large, most of this labour force was native or naturalized Mexicans, who regularly crossed the border to harvest crops and perform stoop labour in conjunction with US agricultural needs and then withdrew back to their home villages.

In the 1980s and 1990s, Latino immigration to North Carolina was dramatically transformed. First and foremost, the size of the immigrant stream grew to unprecedented levels. In a state where rural communities were regularly losing black and white residents, Latino newcomers were replacing the growing out-migration stream. Second, former agricultural sojourners returned to North Carolina looking for permanent jobs and brought their families with them. North Carolina had gained status among the native and international Latinos as a desirable place to live and a preferred immigration destination.

Why Rural North Carolina, and Why This Time?

The emergence of North Carolina as a principal destination for Mexican and other Central American immigrants has replicated a model reported by earlier analysts. In seminal ethnographic research, collaborators Rúben Hernández-León and Victor Zúñiga (2000) provided detailed and insightful analyses of the Latino settlement and place-making activities in Dalton, a small city in northwestern Georgia that is home to a cluster of carpet-making factories, which began to attract Latino immigration nearly 40 years ago. The lessons and findings from Dalton have spurred a small but increasingly active group of scholars examining Latino immigration to rural and small-town communities in the South, Midwest, and Rocky Mountain regions. Research centred on North Carolina includes Cravey's (1997) story of Latino poultry-processing workers in Asheboro, North Carolina; Fink's (2003) ethnographic study of Mayan industrial labour in western North Carolina; Torres *et al.*'s (2006) work on Greene County, North Carolina; and Emery *et al.*'s (2006) analysis of woodland resource conflicts in Yancey County, North Carolina.

In every case, Latino immigrants were attracted to communities with expanding economies that required low-skill labour which native or nearby labour pools did not have the capacity or willingness to provide. These empirical findings are supported by the macro-scale statistical analyses carried out by Kandel and Cromartie (2004). Their research reported a correlation between rural counties with high rates of Hispanic population increases and counties with a significant proportion of workers concentrated in three employment clusters: agricultural processing (poultry, beef, and pork); furniture and textile manufacturing; and high-amenity resort areas.

A second, widely reported finding about the new destinations is antecedent settlement. That is to say, in most instances these communities had earlier immigration experiences, as well as an in-situ Latino social network. The research showed that immigrants were often returning to rural communities where they had worked previously or to communities where relatives or friends currently resided. The popular term "settling out" is used to describe a process in which formerly transitory immigrant labourers return to earlier work communities and establish permanent residence. This activity often includes bringing family members to the new residence or making plans to resettle family members as economic circumstances allow. The critical difference between settling out and traditional sojourning is the nature of employment. Returnees, unlike sojourners, are drawn by offers or opportunities for permanent, year-round employment and higher earnings. It is widely reported that employers eager to recruit Latino labour will pay bonuses to current employees to find and deliver new workers.

In new destinations where there is no existing ethnic population or settlement history, employers often engage in elaborate and expensive strategies to recruit Latino labour. This has included offering attractive financial or quality-of-life inducements to workers so they will relocate to a new community. Zúñiga and Hernández-León (2005) report, for example, that the initial movement of Latino workers to Dalton, Georgia, was spurred by employment recruiters in the El Paso, Texas, area, who were hired by carpet manufacturers in the 1970s. Similarly, IBP, Inc., the United States' largest beef packer and second-biggest pork-processing firm in the 1990s, faced with high labour turnover and a growing shortage of workers, greatly expanded its existing Latino labour force by sending recruiters to Texas and New Mexico border cities and advertising on Spanish-language radio stations that broadcast into the labour markets of northern Mexico (Stull and Broadway, 2008).

At a national level, the short-term labour certification programs enacted by the federal government, the H2-A (temporary agricultural work permits) and H2-B (temporary non-agricultural work permits), offer another mechanism for attracting Latino immigrants to new rural destinations. Both programs have emerged as critical mechanisms for supplying labour to the American agricultural and rural resort industries. Legal residence in the United States under these temporary worker programs is restricted to one year, so Latino labour is recruited, deployed, used, and then returned to Mexico. Thus, these programs provide a constant supply of reliable, plentiful, and low-wage workers who are always in place or ready in a queue. Not unexpectedly, rural destinations using H-2 contract labour have experienced dramatic increases in Latino populations.

North Carolina's focused empirical research has reported on both the settling-out process and the new destination models. Cravey's (1997) research in the Piedmont region; Torres *et al.*'s (2006) coastal plain study; Fink's (2003) Appalachian foothills work; and Emery *et al.*'s (2006) Appalachian mountain project provide broad geographical coverage in all parts of rural North Carolina. In all of the case studies, elements of these divergent processes are at work. Clearly, no simple or single settlement process describes the growth of new Latino rural place-making.

Research Framework

Study Communities: Latino High-Growth Rural Counties

To examine the place-making and entrepreneurial impacts of Latino settlers, I set out to identify counties experiencing sustained Latino immigration. Following Blewett *et al.* (2004) and Casey *et al.* (2004), the criteria for selection required that the county have (1) a Latino population of at least 1,000 residents in 2000; (2) at least 5% of the population identified as Latino; and (3) a Latino population growing at least 50% from 1990 to 2000. Eight of North Carolina's 60 rural counties fit the criteria (Table 4.1). As Fig. 4.1 shows, the eight counties were located across the state, from the Appalachian foothills and Piedmont regions to the coastal plain. From a settlement perspective, they varied from urban shadow counties (Harnett, Lee, and Lincoln) to deep rural (Duplin, Montgomery, Surry) jurisdictions. All of the study counties shared common economic and social roots. In the middle and late 20th century, they were slow-growing jurisdictions that attracted few new residents and contributed to North Carolina's tradition of out-migration. Local economies were centred around small farm agriculture, augmented by rural manufacturing jobs. Social and political cultures in every case were conservative and framed by a white–black racial dichotomy.

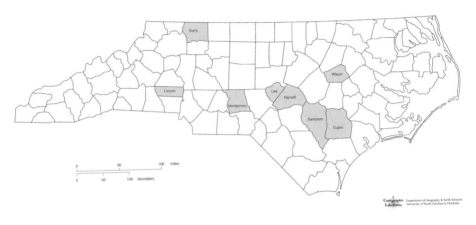

Fig. 4.1 Latino high-growth rural counties in North Carolina.

Table 4.1 Latino high-growth rural counties in North Carolina.

County	Number of Hispanic residents, 2000	Percentage of Hispanic residents, 2000	Percentage of Hispanic population increase, 1990–2000	Number of Hispanic residents, 2006	Percentage of Hispanic population increase, 2000–2006
Duplin	7,426	15.1%	631.6%	10,540	41.9%
Harnett	5,336	5.9%	360.4%	8,524	59.7%
Lee	5,715	11.7%	614.4%	8,422	47.4%
Lincoln	3,656	5.7%	541.4%	6,075	66.2%
Montgomery	2,797	10.4%	403.1%	4,112	47.0%
Sampson	6,477	10.8%	790.9%	9,805	51.4%
Surry	4,620	6.5%	667.4%	6,382	38.1%
Wilson	4,457	6.0%	730.0%	6,469	45.1%

Source: US Census Bureau, 2007.

Table 4.2 Selected Latino characteristics of study communities, 2000.

County Characteristics	Duplin	Harnett	Lee	Lincoln	Montgomery	Sampson	Surry	Wilson
Foreign-born (Proportion of total Hispanic population)	5,161 (70.5%)	2,744 (53.0%)	3,947 (69.7%)	2,556 (72.7%)	1,831 (67.1%)	3,844 (60.2%)	3,101 (70.8%)	2,914 (70.7%)
Entered the United States between 1990 and 2000	4,264	2,518	3,054	2,324	1,617	3,138	2,367	2,607
From Mexico	3,346	2,377	3,102	1,086	1,788	3,197	2,967	2,729
From Central America (excluding Mexico)	1,646	270	884	1,351	34	663	126	160
Not a US Citizen (Percentage not citizens)	4,889 (88.6%)	3,022 (72.3%)	3,806 (81.4%)	2,487 (80.8%)	1,840 (85.5%)	3,486 (81.5%)	3,119 (83.1%)	2,905 (79.9%)
Median household income (Proportion of countywide median household income)	$25,298 (84.6%)	$31,468 (89.6%)	$35,690 (91.6%)	$29,255 (70.6%)	$30,509 (92.7%)	$27,080 (85.2%)	$24,583 (74.4%)	$26,359 (79.6%)
Poverty status (Income below poverty level)	34.7%	26.0%	24.9%	26.2%	32.3%	31.9%	32.8%	40.2%
Educational attainment (Less than high school graduate)	73.4%	58.8%	68.1%	42.1%	84.5%	67.7%	80.4%	82.6%
Proportion of linguistically isolated households[2]	40.7%	22.3%	44.6%	27.9%	38.3%	36.4%	34.5%	27.5%
Proportion of households living in overcrowded residences	39.90%	27.20%	41.60%	32.10%	48.30%	40.40%	42.50%	50.30%

Source: US Census Bureau, 2007.

A review of Table 4.2 provides a contemporary demographic and economic snapshot of the Latino population in the study communities. Most of this population is new to North Carolina and the United States. It is generally made up of working-class Mexicans or Central Americans. In this regard, most lack a high school-level education. These newcomers are filling low-wage jobs in the agriculture, food-processing, manufacturing, and service sectors. High levels of poverty, overcrowding, and linguistic isolation are evidenced in all the communities. The hard-edged economic and social profile for immigrants in the study communities is not unique to rural North Carolina. Rather, these conditions are widely reported by analysts examining Latino immigration in other rural communities throughout the United States. One local impact of this settlement process is that Latino newcomers emerge as the most disadvantaged group in their new rural settings.

Data and Methods

In order to answer the research questions, I used a quantitative data-screening process and community profiles (US Census Bureau, 2007) as secondary data sources, complementing a larger, more extensive, qualitative research design. I carried out community interviews and windshield surveys in 12 small cities and towns in the study counties (Fig. 4.2), selecting the interview sites using county-level population data from the 2000 census, followed by recommendations from Latino-oriented service providers. The critical criterion for choosing each place was a significant Latino population in the community and surrounding area. The length of residence by Latinos and the economic status of the place were not selection factors. However, both variables were important in the subsequent analyses.

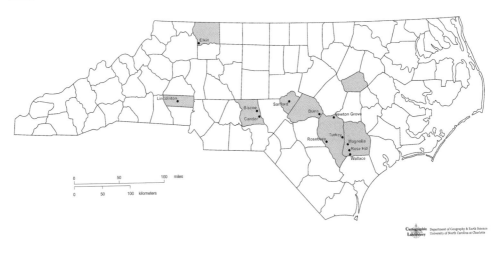

Fig. 4.2 Community interview sites.

Following selection of the interview cities and towns, I made contact with local Latinos and native business interests. These initial interviews and conversations were accompanied by calls to faith community leaders for recommendations regarding Latino entrepreneurs and community leaders. From the two sets of contacts, I arranged and carried out unstructured interviews with 33 Latino community leaders. In all of the interviews, English was the primary language. Follow-up conversations with a native Spanish speaker were used to augment and clarify interview findings. With only one exception, all the community interviews were cordial and completed with no hesitancy or problems. In the exceptional case, wariness around undocumented status and the risks of talking to an unfamiliar Anglo ended the conversation with little information provided.

Research into Latino Entrepreneurship and Business Practices

The role of immigrants as place-makers and active entrepreneurs in urban America has been extensively documented and analysed by social scientists and business scholars (Portes and Bach, 1985; Kaplan and Li, 2006; Robles and Cordero-Guzmán, 2007). Research focused on urban ethnic business development and the impact of ethnic populations on community revitalization and restructuring is widely reported. In recent years, the popular media has translated and extended this scholarship in stories highlighting immigrant settlers' activities in declining suburban areas and the economic revitalization that these newcomers have produced (Katz and Puentes, 2006; Miroff, 2006; Vitullo-Martin 2007).

Given the recency of large-scale Latino settlement in rural America, similar empirical research has been limited. At the present time, community-based research carried out at the University of Northern Iowa (UNI) on immigrant entrepreneurial activities in the Midwest is the most important resource (Grey *et al.* 2004; Grey and Woodrick, 2005; Iowa Center for Immigrant Leadership and Integration, 2006; Oberle, 2007). The UNI research reveals, through broad themes, the activities and processes at work among new immigrant settlers in other rural areas. One of the Iowa researchers' primary findings is that the urban ethnic business model and rural immigrant business development share a parallel structure and occupational characteristics. In both situations, entrepreneurial activities during the start-up phase are small and focused on providing goods and services to co-ethnic customers. These businesses lack strategic plans and are undercapitalized and deeply embedded within ethnic social networks.

Despite challenges to their economic viability, pioneering immigrant businesses provide widespread economic and social benefits to their ethnic community. Admittedly, financial returns to the business owner are modest, but employment and training spillover benefits to co-ethnic employees foster and incubate new entrepreneurship and business development. At the same time, the small immigrant retail and service businesses serve as informal community centres and networking spaces for newcomer communities. Situated in larger, majority cities or towns, the ethnic store or business offers a comfortable, familiar place where newcomers sense belonging and social inclusion.

UNI researchers report that immigrant businesspeople, taking advantage of the ongoing population and economic decline, are concentrating their activities in downtown shopping districts, where high vacancies, low rents, and economic development interests steered business location. An important difference between urban and rural environments is the service radius or hinterland for rural immigration business operations. In the urban or suburban setting, travel times are barriers to immigrant business growth and sustainability; but in rural areas, immigrants are accustomed to travelling longer distances between home and work or home and shopping, so that, generally, travel distance does not preclude patronage of ethnic businesses and services.

Research Findings

Latino Business Activity in Rural North Carolina

The evolving pattern of Latino entrepreneurship in rural North Carolina cities and towns was remarkably similar in all of the study communities. In general, conventional business geography models and real estate literature were not good predictors for Latino business location and growth. Rather, individual entrepreneurs' behaviour was opportunistic and instinctive, and not guided by formal business plans. All of the Latino businesspeople interviewed in the study selected their business locations based on space availability, rent costs, relationship with the landlord, or recommendations from other Latino entrepreneurs. Conventional concepts of market area analysis and strategic planning were never mentioned in the interviews. For example, one Latino entrepreneur in Duplin County commented that he knew Latino customers would find their way to his downtown location because he was respected in the community, so people would want to patronize his store.

The spatial implication of this business location model translated into a somewhat unpredictable business landscape. The most ubiquitous business was the "tienda," a Latino version of the corner store, but with a much broader range of goods and services. It is a combination grocery store, lunch counter, money-wiring service, and social centre. Tiendas were widely dispersed across the study communities. Their locations ranged from downtown commercial business districts to rural crossroads. Virtually any type of vacant business space could be transformed into a tienda.

The tienda was the basic starting point for Latino business development, and all the interviewees mentioned it as a critical entry point, personally and for their communities. With minimal financial requirements, no sophisticated business skills, and community demand to buy ethnic products, novice entrepreneurs could open a tienda. Using family and friends as labour, owners were able to keep their existing jobs while running their businesses. Although economic returns from the stores were usually low, tiendas offered valuable business experience and training for the operators. Moreover, they incubated spinoff businesses and helped train new Latino entrepreneurs. A common story in many interviews was of the Latino business owner with a modest background, working-class social status, and no formal business training or experience, who used the tienda experience to start new enterprises or invest in businesses or services started by family members or close friends.

The most common spinoff business was a restaurant. Like the tienda, the Latino restaurant required modest business training and financing. It was also a business activity in which family, especially women and children, could play an important role. On another level, the restaurant served as an additional site for social integration and networking with the Latino community. However, community support and patronage were critical for this kind of business, given the higher operating costs and expenses associated with meeting government regulations. The locational requirements for a restaurant business were more stringent than those for a tienda, and requirements for equipment and room size offered less flexibility. Former restaurant spaces, both traditional and fast-food buildings, were popular options for new Latino dining establishments. In general, as restaurants increased in size and evolved to serve non-Latino clients, their location moved toward conventional business location models. The shift from Latino-centric restaurants to Latino-themed restaurants for general clients was one of the most important economic development trends identified in this research. This shift marked a significant move from a more informal business model, referred to in the business literature as a "lifestyle business," to mainstream commerce. When this happened, capitalization and business plans were more common, employment impacts were significantly larger, and the business had far greater economic impact for the community. In small communities adjusting to the arrival of Latino newcomers, the establishment and operation of a "Mexican" (Latino) restaurant was a major step toward initiating and building multiculturalism.

Following the establishment of tienda and restaurant businesses, the development of other Latino businesses increased in response to the need for a wider array and complexity of goods and services. The population size of the Latino community in the town or city and surrounding places and counties was a key determinant. In addition to sheer numbers, business growth was also affected by the demographic character of the community. That is to say, as Latino settlement grew and matured, with more female settlers and traditional family structures, there was a transition to stronger and more diverse markets for ethnic products and services.

A widely reported business practice in all the study communities was the incubator model, which included a strong spatial proximity overtone. Simply stated, successful small businesses spurred the establishment of new related and associated businesses, with a location near the original store or office a preferred site for the new operations. Many of the people interviewed recounted a "tienda first" case study. In this model, a Latino entrepreneur opened a tienda, with staffing and funding provided by the family. The store started out as a general merchandise and service provider, offering a wide range of retailing and services. As the businesses become more successful, staffing was increased, and the business began to narrow the mix of products and services. Originally, the tienda would offer hot food service and western clothing. But with business growth and market maturity, the store owner moved the food and clothing sales to new sites. In choosing locations for the new enterprises, the tienda owner was attracted to adjacent or nearby sites. Thus, staff and management functions could be shared, and cross-shopping by customers was facilitated. In the process, a small Latino business cluster developed in a downtown area or a strip shopping centre.

There was another, transformative, version of the "tienda first" model, less frequently reported, but also occurring, in which the tienda grew into a "mercado" (supermarket). In this process, the tienda outgrew its space and customer demand for goods and services, and the business owner moved to a significantly larger store site. In the study communities, former grocery or furniture stores provided the low-cost rental space for the shift. In the new location, specialized foods and services were added to the business. For example, in one instance, fresh native fruits and vegetables, a butcher processing Latino meats and cuts, a larger array of canned and processed foods, and western clothing and jewelry sections were incorporated into the floor plan. Taking advantage of the larger scale of retailing, a back-room portion of the mercado operated as a wholesaling business, where bulk items and products imported from Mexico or Central America were broken down and reprocessed in small quantities for Latino businesses around the state and in South Carolina. The floor space and parking requirements for a mercado meant they were less suitable for downtown sites. Those issues, combined with rental costs, pushed these businesses into abandoned strip centres located on highway bypasses or on the edge of towns.

Along with increases in the size and scope of business activity, the economic impact and community development effects of these business expansions are significant to rural North Carolina. Latino business development translates into employment growth, enhanced real estate and property values. Indeed, increased Latino retail and service patronage translates into cross-shopping with non-Latino businesses. While the interviewees were reluctant to discuss specific financial details of their enterprises, all acknowledged a significant increase in employment that accompanied business expansion and restructuring. Consider, for example, that a traditional tienda would employ family members, as well as non-family members part-time. In contrast, a restaurant has 10 to 30 employees, and mercados hire 25 to 35 employees. (These general employment data were offered by the interviewed entrepreneurs.) At the current time, all the businesses employ Latinos exclusively, although professional services were provided by non-Latinos. All the interviewees said they were willing to hire non-Latinos in the future.

A related social impact of the Latino entrepreneurial model is the workplace opportunities provided to women. Within the machismo (male domination) of Latino culture, women have few chances to work outside the home. In rural North Carolina, employment prospects for low-skill female labour are restricted further by transportation limitations and the absence of job opportunities. Latino businesses offer women employment that is not otherwise available. Small-scale retail and service providers depend on women to serve clients and manage daily operations. Restaurants and clothing stores rely heavily on traditional female skills and talents. In the course of this research, it was not unusual to visit a tienda in one of the study communities and find two or three women operating the store while tending to their small children. The casual environment of the small enterprise offers flexible and accommodating terms for a working Latino mother that would not be available in a regular US business.

Clearly, at this time, the scope of Latino business activity in rural North Carolina is largely focused on meeting the immediate needs of the Latino population. Higher-order business activities, such as wholesaling, manufacturing, and sophisticated service provision, are largely missing. Only limited, small-scale wholesaling and manufacturing of Latino foods and beverages is underway. A lack of financing and formal business training were cited by respondents as explanations for the absence. Moreover, the growth of these business sectors is likely to remain modest, given the educational and economic characteristics of the rural Latino population. The weak capacity means larger US or international Latino businesses would need to move into the area, a prospect that is inconceivable at this time. Thus, continued "grassroots" entrepreneurship is the best path to further Latino business growth.

One indication that rural North Carolina has gained status as a Latino settlement frontier in the eyes of the national Latino business community is an international bus service. Specifically, two bus lines based in Houston, Texas—Adame and Tornado—offer regularly scheduled service from the study counties to cities across Mexico, with connecting service to Central America. These companies have rudimentary bus stations located in conjunction with tiendas and/or restaurants. Ironically, the level of public transportation these Latino-oriented businesses provide to the southwestern United States and international locations far exceeds public transportation options offered by nationally oriented carriers in rural North Carolina.

Latino Entrepreneurship and Place-Making

Across the study communities, Latino entrepreneurship and economic development have reshaped the business landscape. In rural small towns, central business districts hollowed out by the closing or relocation of small businesses and national chains to shopping centres on the highway bypass have been revitalized by Latino business enterprises occupying the vacant shop fronts. In some town centres, the Latino businesses are clustered; in other places, the store or business locations appear random. In rundown or empty blocks, the Latino store or shop often stands out, appearing almost frenetic. Colourful and busy exteriors, with prominent signage, display a strong visual signal to potential customers. In virtually every instance, downtown commercial districts have been strengthened and enhanced by the new business activity. Nonetheless, one challenge raised by natives is the description of Latino storefronts as untidy or as something that "doesn't fit." Clearly, the normal street façades of Latino businesses reveal a cultural gap when compared to Anglo façades. Where one person may see vibrancy and attractiveness, another may interpret the storefront as messy and even threatening. With that caveat, the overwhelming reaction to the business newcomers was positive. New Latino tenants mean more traffic and more opportunities for all businesses.

Along the bypass highways, Latino businesses have primarily moved into derelict or high-vacancy strip centres. The massing of Latino stores associated with downtown districts is translated here into clumps within a single strip centre, dispersed along the roadway. The vibrant visual impressions created by the Latino businesses, however, mimic the downtown. Along the bypass, bright colours and Spanish language signage seem more commonplace in a landscape dominated by flashy billboards, fast-food architecture, and monotonous strip shopping centres. In general, the bypass business environment is more robust, so contiguous, low-cost commercial space is less available and clustering patterns are diminished.

Conclusions: Latino Entrepreneurship and the Next Rural Economy for North Carolina

At a time when the traditional economic base of agriculture and low-skill manufacturing sectors is declining, and the conventional economic development models for revitalizing rural North Carolina are challenged, a rapidly growing Latino immigrant population has emerged. These newcomers present incipient evidence that they offer a new way to grow and revitalize the economic and social fabric of declining rural places. As this chapter has emphasized, Latino entrepreneurs have begun to actively build grassroots-level business clusters in towns and small cities. Operating like urban ethnic groups, the rural Latino entrepreneurs are initially serving the retail and service needs of their fellow immigrants. But over a short period they have already begun to incubate new businesses, helped revitalize declining commercial districts, and increasingly reoriented their business start-ups to attract non-Latino customers. The overall outlook for Latino business interests' sustained impact on rural economies is optimistic. But growing political challenges and structural issues need to be resolved.

In the immediate future, the single most significant impediment to enhancing Latinos' economic contribution is immigration reform. Immigration in the United States is a national or federal government issue. The last significant reform of US immigration policy, the Immigration Reform and Control Act (IRCA) of 1986, is over 20 years old. The lack of updated federal policy, exacerbated by a record number of undocumented immigrants from Latin America, has spurred fierce debates over the status and future of undocumented residents. One trend emerging from the federal stalemate is localized immigration policies, including local or state-level policy actions to either exclude and/or punish undocumented immigrants or protect the newcomers from federal anti-terrorist programs.

In North Carolina, the state legislature has enacted anti-immigrant legislation, most notably a 2006 state law that excludes undocumented adults from applying for driver's licences. Recently, across North Carolina, there has been a movement toward extreme anti-immigrant actions at all levels of government. The political leadership championing these initiatives is often linked to the racialized politics of the late 20th century. Such politicians harp on the economic and social costs of newcomers, especially the illegal (undocumented) immigrants. Fortunately, a countervailing group of progressive community leaders, both business and political, have countered the xenophobic conservative rhetoric. At this juncture, both sides are competing for control of the political policy process at the state level and in individual counties.

Ironically, the nativist political interests are advocating public policies that ignore growing economic development research that encourages population diversity and the infusion of newcomers in stagnant and struggling communities. The "Creative Class" paradigm, closely linked to Richard Florida and other new economic development scholars, offers powerful empirical evidence of the propulsive stimuli that "outsiders" or nonconventional newcomers bring to places (Florida, 2002, 2005). Within this context, international immigrants are agents for new economic initiatives and growth that spread across a community. The research findings in this chapter align with this "new economy" model. Although they are poor and lack formal business acumen, Latino entrepreneurs are making significant economic improvements in their rural home communities.

The current turmoil will only be solved with the enactment of fair and reasonable federal immigration reforms. In the absence of action from Washington, localized immigration policies have a chilling effect on the plans of immigrants, both legal and undocumented, for the future of Latinos in North Carolina. Indeed, it was aggressive, state-level, anti-immigrant action in California in the 1990s that contributed to the Southeast emerging as an immigration destination. Ironically, the federal government will play a critical role in discouraging rural development in North Carolina under the aegis of the Department of Homeland Security, rather than the Department of Agriculture.

At the state level, the North Carolina Department of Commerce, the agency charged with providing business services and community development programs, should play a stronger role in fostering and supporting rural economic development strategies that engage Latino entrepreneurs. The department currently gives a limited amount of funding to the non-profit agency Good Work, which provides business skill development and technical assistance to Latinos and other new or potential entrepreneurs. Programming is delivered in Spanish. Good Work has a successful program and broad partnerships with community groups, educational institutions, and governments across the state. However, the major focus of the Department of Commerce is not small-scale businesses nor Latino entrepreneurship.

Admittedly, in the current politically charged environment surrounding immigration, new state-level funding initiatives or programs to assist Latino business development are likely unattainable. However, state-level support is crucial to this effort. In particular, policies and planning similar to what was proposed by the UNI researchers, including the establishment of investment programs and the provision of training opportunities in Spanish, are critical initiatives.

At the county and local government levels, the need to reach out and build linkages between Latino entrepreneurs and the local business community and public economic development interests is critical. Cultural differences and fears about "outsiders" and "not belonging" have kept newcomers and natives apart. On an individual basis, Latino entrepreneurs have made connections and, in some cases, have even established business relationships with natives. But the larger associations are missing. For example, no Latino businesses were members of local Chambers of Commerce in the study communities.

The established business community's resistance or inability to build partnerships with newcomers handicaps community development. Programs connecting businessperson to businessperson should be priority actions for local community leaders. Where language and cultural barriers are challenges, investment in facilitators is warranted. The faith community and community colleges are well positioned to assume leadership in these bridging programs. Ultimately, local business interests need to recognize that a multicultural business setting is an asset that can benefit the entire community.

Rural North Carolina is at a crossroads. The future presents challenges, but opportunities exist to build and sustain a vibrant commercial and community infrastructure. The Latino newcomers are an asset that needs to be incorporated into the community development framework in order to achieve complete success.

Acknowledgement

This research would not be possible without the support and cooperation of Latino community members. Their openness to strangers and their willingness to talk about their lives and hopes for the future are encouraging harbingers for our state.

Notes

[1] The US Census Bureau uses "Hispanic" as the identifier for persons of Latin American ancestry. The term "Latino" is a preferred descriptor among members of this community. Consequently, the terms are used interchangeably in this chapter and refer to persons of both genders.
[2] A "linguistically isolated household" is one in which no member 14 years old and over (1) speaks only English or (2) speaks a non-English language and speaks English "very well." In other words, all members 14 years old and over have at least some difficulty with English.

References

Bailey, R. (2005) New immigration communities in the North Carolina Piedmont triad: Integration issues and challenges. In: Gozdziak, E., and Martin, S. (eds.) *Beyond the Gateway: Immigrants in a Changing America*. Lexington Books, Lanham, MD, 57–86.

Blewett, L., Casey, M., and Call, K. (2004) Improving access to primary care for a growing Latino population: The role of safety net providers in the rural Midwest. *Journal of Rural Health* 20(3), 237–245.

Casey, M., Blewett, L., and Call, K. (2004) Providing health care to Latino immigrants: Community-based efforts in the rural Midwest. *American Journal of Public Health* 94(10), 1709–1711.

Cravey, A. (1997) Latino labor and poultry production in rural North Carolina. *Southeastern Geographer* 37(2), 295–300.

Emery, M., Ginger, C., and Chamberlain, J. (2006). Migrants, markets, and the transformation of natural resources management: Galax harvesting in western North Carolina. In: Smith, H., and Furuseth, O. (eds.) *Latinos in the New South: Transformations of Place*. Ashgate, London, 69–87.

Fink, L. (2003) *The Maya of Morganton: Work and Community in the Nuevo New South*. University of North Carolina Press, Chapel Hill.

Florida, R. (2002) *The Rise of the Creative Class: And How It's Transforming Work, Leisure, Community, and Everyday Life*. Basic Books, New York.

_____. (2005) *Cities and the Creative Class*. Routledge, Oxford.

Grey, M., and Woodrick, A. (2005) Latinos have revitalized our community: Mexican migration and Anlgo responses in Marshalltown, Iowa. In: Zúñiga, V., and Hernández-León, R. (eds.) *New Destinations of Mexican Immigration in the United States: Community Formation, Local Responses and Inter-Group Relations*. Russell Sage Foundation, New York, 133–154.

Grey, M., Rodriguez, N., and Conrad, A. (2004) *Immigrant and Refugee Small Business Development in Iowa: A Research Report with Recommendations*. New Iowans Program, University of Northern Iowa, Cedar Falls, IA.

Hernández-León, R., and Zúñiga, V. (2000) Making carpet by the mile: The emergence of a Mexican immigrant community in an industrial region of the U.S. historic South. *Social Science Quarterly* 81(1), 49–66.

Iowa Center for Immigrant Leadership and Integration. (2006) *A Rural Service Provider's Guide to Immigrant Entrepreneurship*. Regional Business Center/Small Business Development Center, University of Northern Iowa, Cedar Falls, IA.

Kandel, W., and Cromartie, J. (2004) *New Patterns of Hispanic Settlement in Rural America* (Rural Development Research Report Number 99). Economic Research Service, US Department of Agriculture, Washington, DC.

Kaplan, D., and Li, W. (2006) *Landscapes of the Ethnic Economy*. Rowman and Littlefield, Lanham, MD.

Katz, B., and Puentes, R. (2006) Extreme Makeover: Nassau. *New York Times,* 29 January, www.nytimes.com/2006/01/29/opinion/nyregionopinions/29LIkatz.html?_r=1&oref=slogin (accessed 29 January 2006).

Miroff, N. (2006) Bringing Nueva Vida to Aging Strip Malls. *Washington Post*, 18 December, www.washingtonpost.com/wpdyn/content/article/2006/12/18/AR2006121801448.html (accessed 19 December 2006).

Mohl, R. (2005) Mexican immigration/migration to Alabama. In: Odem, M. and Lacy, E. (eds.) *Mexican Immigration to the U.S. Southeast: Impact and Challenges*. Instituto de Mexico, Atlanta, 85–107.

Oberle, A. (2007) Immigration rhetoric versus economic redevelopment: The role of Latino businesses in revitalizing Iowa towns. Presentation at Association of American Geographers Annual Meeting, San Francisco, CA.

Portes, A., and Bach, R. (1985) *Latin Journey: Cuban and Mexican Immigrants in the United States*. University of California Press, Berkeley.

Quinterno, J. (2008) What about N.C. workers? *Charlotte Observer,* 6 April, 22A.

Robles, B., and Cordero-Guzmán, B. (2007) Latino self-employment and entrepreneurship in the United States: An overview of the literature and data sources. *Annals of the American Academy of Political and Social Science* 613, 18–31.

Stull, D., and Broadway, M. (2008) Meatpacking and Mexicans on the high plains: From minority to majority in Garden City, Kansas. In: Jones, R. (ed.) *Immigrants outside Megalopolis: Ethnic Transformation in the Heartland*. Lexington Books, Lanham, MD, 115–133.

Torres, R., Popke, J., and Hapke, H. (2006) The South's silent bargain: Rural restructuring, Latino labor, and the ambiguities of migrant experience. In: Smith, H., and Furuseth, O. (eds.) *Latinos in the New South: Transformations of Place*. Ashgate, London, 37–67.

US Census Bureau. (2007) *American FactFinder,* factfinder.census.gov (accessed 11 May 2008).

Vitullo-Martin, J. (2007) Save our cities. *Wall Street Journal,* 30 March, www.manhattan-institute.org/html/_wsj-save_our_cities.htm (accessed 30 March 2007).

Zúñiga, V., and Hernández-León, R. (2005) Mexican immigration to the South: Community and cultural change in Dalton, Georgia. In: Odem, M., and Lacey, E. (eds.) *Mexican Immigration to the U.S. Southeast: Impact and Challenges*. Instituto de México, Atlanta, 109–126.

Chapter 5

Connecting Rural and Urban Places: Enduring Migration between Small Areas in England and Wales

Nigel Walford

Rural and urban places are inextricably connected with each other, and such links have persisted and manifested themselves in respect of demographic, economic, social, and environmental factors since human populations first adopted settled rather than nomadic forms of civilization. Throughout much of human history, the general direction of population movement has been from rural to urban areas and has been closely associated with the overall processes of urbanization and industrialization. However, the main focus in this chapter is on the demographic connections pertaining in more recent times and on a relatively constrained portion of geographic space. Although the factors influencing people's experience and participation in such migratory movements are many and varied, the notion remains of "factors" pulling and pushing people in possibly contradictory directions between countryside and town or city. This provides a broad theoretical framework for conceptualizing the nature of the myriad individual decisions and migratory flows that result in people relocating from one place of residence to another.

The closing decades of the 20th century witnessed a slowing down and ultimately a reversal of the long-established and predominant direction of movement from countryside to town. Evidence for this change first emerged in the United States (Beale, 1975; Morrison and Wheeler, 1976), but Fielding (1982) soon identified similar trends in western Europe, Keddie and Joseph (1991) in Canada, and Paris (1994) in respect of Australia. Variously interpreted as a reaction to the increasingly claustrophobic and impersonal lifestyle of urban living, as a search for a more idyllic and meaningful lifestyle in a safe and secure environment, or perhaps less commonly but even more idealistically as a return to nature, the outcome has been heralded as "rural repopulation," "population turnaround," and "rural population renaissance." Whereas many of the former rural-to-urban migrants during the long period of rural depopulation seemed willing to forsake their cultural heritage and assume values associated with the modernizing melting pot of urban living, recent reverse migrants generally seem to have cherished, and sought to retain, certain economic and social aspects of their urban lifestyles and to have brought these with them into the setting of their new rural residence.

"Counterurbanization" emerged as a conceptual framework for understanding these changes of attitude among migrants, which reflected an underlying rejection of urbanism as the dominant mode of living, and of urbanization as the principal process of socio-economic development. However, this terminology is not without its critics, who argue that members of an elite socio-economic group capable of migrating to countryside and rural areas have cherry-picked favoured elements of an urban lifestyle and transposed these into a different environmental context. Following this line of argument, such migrants may be viewed as not so much rejecting urban living but as differentially choosing the elements they wish to retain and those they seek to discard.

Structural and behavioural accounts of counterurbanization exist, stressing, on the one hand, the population dynamics of post-industrialist societies (Renkow and Hoover, 2000), and on the other, the expression of people's collective search for an "imagined geography of rural life" (Cloke *et al.*, 1998, p. 139). Although now widely recognized in different geographical contexts, counterurbanization has emerged selectively, privileging those social and economic groups able to buy into the process. Incomers to rural areas are socially and geographically differentiated from those unwilling or unable to participate in the process, with Boyle (1995) showing that members of the mobile middles classes from southern England were overrepresented among migrants to the Highlands and Islands of Scotland. Two particular age groups dominate the migration flows: the family and homemaker generation, and those at later pre- or post-retirement stages of their life course.

A minority of individual migrations running counter to the general direction of urbanization have accompanied the dominant inter-regional flows during both the historical out-migration from, and contemporary in-migration to, rural areas. Undoubtedly an uneven distribution of demographic change underpins the overall impression of population growth across rural areas of the United Kingdom and other countries. Neighbouring settlements and communities have experienced contradictory population trends reflecting their individualistic character and relative attractiveness as destinations (Spencer, 1995, 1997; Walford, 2001), and moves from metropolitan and urban areas toward the countryside may be punctuated by intermediate stops in a migration cascade (Champion and Atkins, 1996). Furthermore, over the last ten years, UK government policy to address the shortage of housing by setting a 60% target for house completions on previously developed or "brownfield" land, the majority of which is located in urban, formerly industrial areas, has to some extent distorted the overall impression of where population growth is occurring. However, this has not halted migration to rural areas among those with sufficient resources to achieve this lifestyle objective.

This chapter focuses on one specific rural area in Britain, which experienced successive decades of depopulation falling from a peak in 1871. Such was the severity of population decline and resultant demographic and socio-economic dysfunction in this area of Mid-Wales that the national government in the early 1960s called for a Royal Commission, which led to publication of the Beacham Report (Beacham Committee, 1964). Although the area experienced further depopulation up to 1971 (Halfacree and Boyle, 1992), ironically, just as this commission was carrying out its deliberations, a groundswell of change was beginning that would subsequently reverse the long-established trend of depopulation and result in the area becoming a major focus of population growth during the 1970s and 1980s, which abated only slightly through the 1990s. In this chapter I explore the unevenness and persistence of inward migration to Mid-Wales from England and other parts of Wales during these decades and, by examining the geodemographic character of migrants' origins, investigate how incomers are reshaping the character of rural places. I thereby demonstrate the central role that demographic change plays in bringing about the development of rural places and how the development of a new rural economy of the area depended upon establishing and fostering both internal and external linkages. The population and economic turnarounds in this region offer insights into how rural economies in other countries may be reinvigorated as we move into the 21st century. In the remainder of this chapter I address the themes of this volume by providing a general background to demographic and economic restructuring in the area of Mid-Wales studied by the Beacham Commission (Beacham Mid-Wales hereafter), highlighting localities that have been relatively more or less attractive as destinations for external in-migrants, before considering the current population trajectories in the area.

Mid-Wales Population Change

The area that came under the Beacham Commission's attention is a largely mountainous region of Mid-Wales, dissected by valleys carved out during the last major glacial period. The population is scattered in villages and hamlets with a small number of moderate-sized towns, including the university town of Aberystwyth on the coast of Cardigan Bay. The region's economy was traditionally based on primary industries—for example, slate quarrying at Blaenau Ffestiniog in the northwest, and widespread forestry and agriculture, particularly cattle and sheep rearing. The region was already becoming economically marginalized by the 1960s, and the changing structure of British agriculture over the closing decades of the 20th century meant that agriculturalists in the area were farming on the edge of economic viability. Those remaining have become increasingly dependent on financial support for their production and for maintaining public goods, such as countryside and traditional landscape features. As Mid-Wales is a scenically attractive area, the development of tourism, together with small-scale manufacturing and service industries, represents the main direction for recovering the region's economic viability.

It was a period of protracted population decline that led to the establishment of the Beacham Commission and to publication of its report, entitled *Depopulation in Mid-Wales* (Beacham Committee, 1964). The area covered by the enquiry encompassed all or part of five counties containing 43 "old" (pre-1974) local authorities (LAs) (Fig. 5.1). The analysis presented in this chapter employs the Beacham area as a constant geographical reference area, even though subsequent reorganization of local government has significantly redrawn its administrative geography for the periods 1974–1996 and 1996 onwards. In each section of Fig. 5.1, those parts of the LAs extending beyond the Beacham Mid-Wales area are shown with lighter shading. Similarly, the lighter shading in the fourth section shows that three of the statistical wards (see below) associated with the 2001 Census, used in the present analysis, extended beyond the Beacham area in the northeast and southeast.

The Beacham Report and others of the time highlighted issues of rural depopulation not only in this part of the world but also in many regions of Britain and other developed countries. Mid-Wales was by no means alone in experiencing this phenomenon; nevertheless, the long period of population decline from a peak in 1871 (Williams, 1985) had by the 1960s produced an unbalanced demographic structure in which older age groups were dominant. Younger people had departed in search of employment in the urban and suburban centres that were growing as part of post-World War II reconstruction and industrial restructuring. Deaths exceeded births in some parts of Mid-Wales in the 1960s as a result of the exodus of people of childrearing age, and the rate of in-migration was insufficient to ameliorate this demographic deficit.

It is, therefore, perhaps even more remarkable that less than 15 years after the Beacham Commission reported, the same area was experiencing unprecedented population growth

(Champion *et al.*, 1987; Day, 1989), exceeding most other rural regions of the United Kingdom and contrasting with depopulation in many urban centres in Britain (Fielding, 1982). Post-1960s population growth in Mid-Wales took place within Balsom's (1985) "*Y Fro Gymraeg* (Welsh speaking and Welsh identifying heartland) to the west and in British Wales (lack of Welsh speaking and Welsh identifying) to the east" (Walford, 2004, p. 313). Growth continued during the 1980s and 1990s, although, not surprisingly, at a lower rate than in the 1970s given the low level reached previously and the suddenness of the upturn. According to Champion (1994), the general area of Mid-Wales represented one of the final destinations in a counterurbanization cascade (Champion and Atkins, 1996), as people moved to rural areas from urban and suburban centres via intermediate stopping-off points rather than in a single movement.

Table 5.1 records the different experiences of population growth and decline within the three types of old LAs in the Beacham Mid-Wales area for the periods 1961–1971, 1971–1981, and 1981–1991, noting that the proportion of the total Mid-Wales population in each type of LA remained virtually constant over the period. County boroughs grew during the 1960s, while the smaller urban districts and sparsely populated rural districts (RDs) declined. During the following decade the situation was completely reversed, and growth rather than decline occurred overall. During the 1980s, population decline became even more pronounced in the old county boroughs and emerged as a feature of the former urban districts, whereas the level of growth in the rural districts more than doubled. Several explanations have been advanced to account for this remarkable population turnaround. The impact of rural development policies, with funding provided to build manufacturing and service industry infrastructure, encouraged a number of companies to establish branches and even head offices in the region (the Laura Ashley base and factory in Carno was a case in point, although this has now closed). These provided employment opportunities, not only retaining younger people in the area who might otherwise be contemplating out-migration, but also attracting highly skilled, higher-income workers from elsewhere. Some people have moved to the area because they see it giving them the opportunity to change their employment status by becoming self-employed in various kinds of craft, tourism, leisure, and similar types of enterprises. Retirement migrants' moves to the area in search of an attractive and peaceful environment are often founded on previous visits to the area for holidays and on the recommendation of friends who have already moved. Recent migrants regard Mid-Wales as a safer and cleaner environment in which to raise children away from the temptations and pressures of urban centres, even if such children may ultimately become disaffected with areas that claustrophobically smother their teenage aspirations for more excitement than Mid-Wales can offer (Valentine, 1997).

In the early years of the 21st century, the old LAs referenced in Table 5.1 are clearly problematic as a basis for investigating population change. They become increasingly anachronistic the further the analysis moves on from when they were current (up to 1974). They also constitute rather large spatial units in which to detect the subtle nuances of population increase and decrease, which have been shown to vary considerably over relatively short distances (Spencer, 1995, 1997; Walford, 2001). We therefore turn to the question of identifying small spatial units that can form the basis for more detailed analysis. The results presented in this chapter are based on units known rather formally as 2001 Standard Table Wards (see lower right section of Fig. 5.1). The principal reason for this choice is that the origin–destination migration flows for each of the last three population censuses are available for these areas (Economic and Social Research Council Census Programme, 2008).

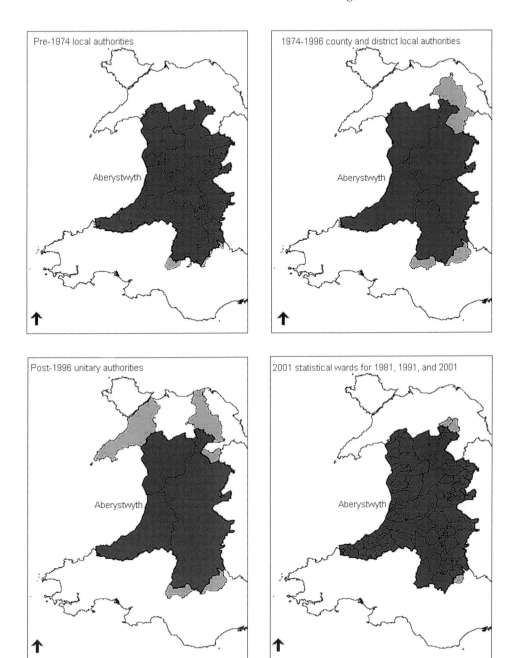

Fig. 5.1 Changing local authority boundaries, and the consistent statistical wards, in relation to Beacham Mid-Wales study area (Office for National Statistics, population censuses). Note: The light shading shows where local authorities at least partially covered by the Beacham Report's (1964) Mid-Wales area (dark shading) extended beyond this study area.

Table 5.1 Summary of population change in Mid-Wales, 1961–1981.

	1961	% change 1961–1971	1971	% change 1971–1981	1981	% change 1981–1991	1991
County boroughs	32,772	11.6	36,624	−0.3	36,531	−4.5	34,877
Urban districts	36,029	−1.2	35,585	16.9	41,606	−23.1	32,011
Rural districts	109,745	−4.7	104,550	6.9	111,780	15.1	128,608
	178,546	**−1.0**	**176,759**	**7.4**	**189,917**	**2.9**	**195,496**

Source: Office for National Statistics, population censuses.

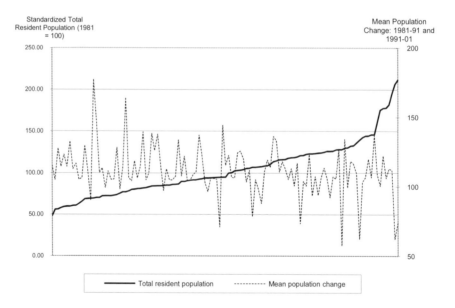

Fig. 5.2 Resident population change in Mid-Wales wards, 1981–1991 and 1991–2001 (Office for National Statistics, population censuses).

The majority of wards in Mid-Wales experienced population growth during the last two intercensal periods (1981–1991 and 1991–2001). However, population decline occurred in a minority of wards (16%), and there appears to be some evidence of a relationship between change and overall total population size. Most of the wards that experienced substantial reductions in their population (more than 10%) were above the overall standardized total population for the period (Fig. 5.2). The population figures have been standardized with a base of 100 to avoid problems associated with quantifying changes for areas with small and large totals. The overall impression is that wards along the entire spectrum of population size were as likely to gain population as they were to lose it, and that wards throughout Mid-Wales experienced significant levels of growth. Focusing on the extreme cases, 60% of the wards where the population increased by at least 15% in each of the last two intercensal periods had lower gains in the second. The accelerated growth in Aberystwyth East, Faenor, and Llanafanfawr is almost certainly connected with an expansion in tertiary education and the inclusion of students at their term-time address in the adjacent university town of Aberystwyth in 2001. Conversely, three of the five wards whose population decreased by 15% in each period experienced a greater fall in the second one.

Migration Flows into and within Mid-Wales Wards

Population change in Mid-Wales, as elsewhere, results from natural increase associated with the interaction between birth and death rates, and from inter- and intra-regional migration. General population aging and lower fertility, which have become important features of developed societies in recent decades, contributed to population growth in Mid-Wales. Analysis of migration in Britain is typically based on the one-year migration figures in the period before each census. The Special Migration Statistics (SMS) from the last three British censuses include selected characteristics of migrants and interaction matrices of flows between origins and destinations. Although differences in the format and confidentiality measures applied to these counts mean that analysis of the data can be problematic, this series of SMS datasets does allow migration trends to be explored. The present analysis has focused on the wards within the Mid-Wales area as the destination of migrants from equivalent units in England and the rest of Wales, and as the origins and destinations of flows within this region. In 2001 there were 123 statistical wards in Mid-Wales, and the SMS for 1981 and 1991 have been re-aggregated to this configuration. The source area (England and the rest of Wales) contained 8,678 wards, although less than 30% of these wards contributed in-migrants to Mid-Wales.

Wards in England and the rest of Wales that were included in the process of in-migration to the region can be divided into two groups. A core group of 420 (the "core wards"), comprising some 5% of the total (8,678), contributed migrants to inward migration flow to wards in Mid-Wales at each census; these ranged from 18% to 23% of the total wards contributing to the inflow on each occasion—2,187 wards in 1981, 2,358 in 1991, and 1,794 in 2001 (Fig. 5.3a). The second group, "one-off" wards, supplied in-migrants to the region at the time of only one of these censuses. The proportion of one-off wards in 2001 was notably lower than in either of the previous censuses, which, taken with the core wards constituting a larger percentage of participating wards, suggests that migratory connections have strengthened. The core wards contributed some 36% of in-migrants to Mid-Wales in each migration period, and the one-off group a reduced percentage in 2000–2001 (Fig. 5.3b). Not surprisingly, the rest of Wales and the neighbouring West Midlands region in England dominated as the source areas for migrants from core wards to Mid-Wales; 40% and 34% respectively were located in these regions, accounting consistently for some 18% and 13% of the inflow. England's South East region, including London, ranked third, with 15% of core wards, but typically only 3% of the flow (Fig. 5.3c).

Migration of people between the wards within Mid-Wales to some extent reinforces the geographical distribution of the destinations of migrants from outside the region. Figure 5.4 plots the Mid-Wales wards in ascending order of their average in-migrants from wards in England and the rest of Wales across the last three censuses. It shows a relatively smooth curve, with 55% gaining between 50 and 110 in-migrants. In addition the dashed line shows the ratio of inter- to intra-regional migrants averaged over the same one-year pre-census periods. Although the ratio fluctuates considerably along the range, with some wards receiving a higher number of internal as opposed to external migrants, the general upward trend is reasonably similar. The level of connectivity of wards within the Mid-Wales area with each other and with wards in England and the rest of Wales indicates the strength of migratory linkage.

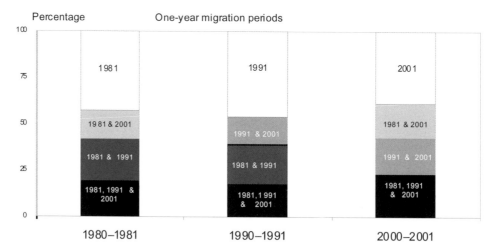

Fig. 5.3a Wards involved in in-migration (Office for National Statistics, population censuses).

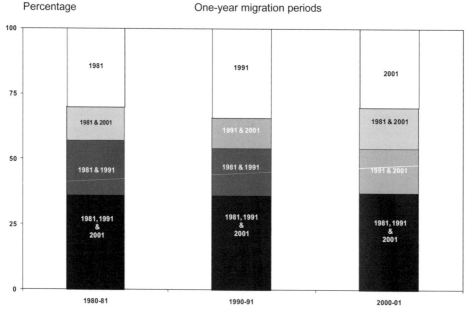

Fig. 5.3b Contribution to in-migration flow (Office for National Statistics, population censuses).

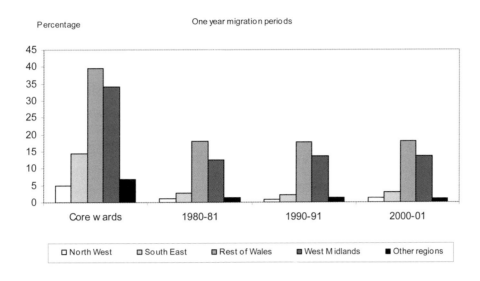

Fig. 5.3c Regional contribution to in-migration flow (Office for National Statistics, population censuses).

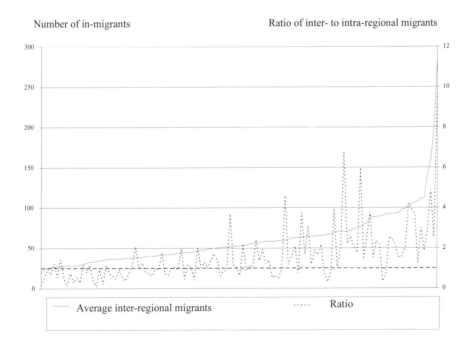

Fig. 5.4 Inter- and intra-regional migrants to Mid-Wales wards (Office for National Statistics, population censuses).

Figure 5.5 explores variations in connectivity averaged over the three one-year pre-census migration periods in three ways. In general, wards with a high number of in-migration links within the region were mainly concentrated in a central swath stretching from the border with England across to Aberystwyth, most notably occurring in and around this regionally important town. Mid-Wales wards with strong links to the external sources of migrants were more widely dispersed, although wards to the north and south of the region were mainly in the lowest quartile, signifying fewer migratory linkages. The lower part of Figure 5.5 suggests that wards with a relatively high level of out-migration connectivity to wards in England and the rest of Wales are spatially concentrated across the central zone.

Wards in the region are, therefore, differentiated in terms of their attractiveness to incoming migrants, and this has produced variations in the changing demographic and socio-economic characteristics of the areas over the study period. The Beacham Report expressed concern about the future of the whole area in respect of employment opportunities and demographic composition, but this chapter has confirmed the findings of other researchers (Champion *et al.*, 1987; Halfacree and Boyle, 1992), who concluded that the demographic and economic fortunes of the area overall have markedly improved. However, it is important to examine the differences between wards that were relatively more or less attractive to migrants, especially to those migrants originating outside the region. Table 5.2 shows a selection of indicators for the top and bottom five wards, ranked according to the ratio of inter- to intra-regional migrants averaged across the one-year pre-census periods. Higher ratios indicate that the ward received more migrants from outside the Mid-Wales area; thus Presteigne, the highest-ranked ward, received nearly 10 times more migrants from outside than inside the region. Apart from Presteigne, the wards in this group were categorized as "Sparse—Village, Hamlet and Isolated Dwellings" in the government's recent categorization (National Statistics, 2005). Presteigne was "Sparse—Town and Fringe." In contrast, the least popular wards for inter-regional migrants were found in some of the larger settlements (such as Aberystwyth and Welshpool), categorized as "Sparse—Urban >10k," except for Welshpool Gungrog, which was "Sparse—Town and Fringe." This seems to indicate that in-migrants from outside Mid-Wales sought out more sparsely settled, countryside areas. The indicators in Table 5.2 suggest that the two groups of wards experienced different changes in their demographic and socio-economic characteristics over the period 1981–2001. Wards most favoured by external in-migrants saw a reduction in the percentage of children, an increase in the percentage of elderly people (65 years and over), and a negligible reduction in unemployment. The least popular wards for inter-regional migrants showed a substantial increase in the percentage of children and older people, and a modest, but significantly different, rise in unemployment. Inter-regional migrants, therefore, seem to be attracted by the prospect of living in small settlements in the countryside, whereas their intra-regional counterparts favour small provincial towns.

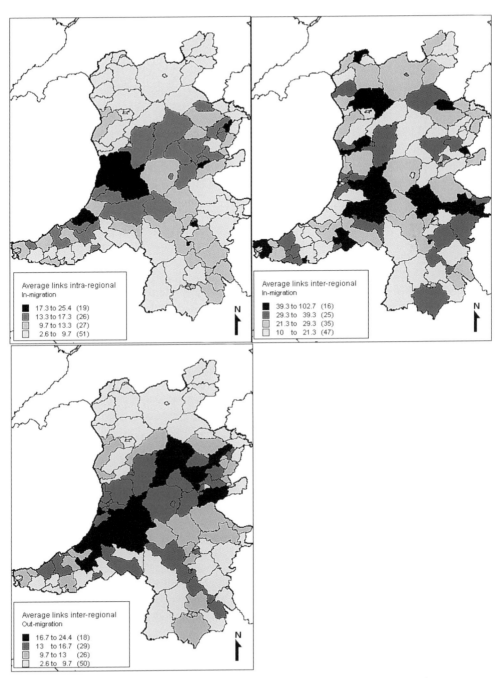

Fig. 5.5 Average pre-census intra- and inter-regional in-migration connections of one-year migrants within Mid-Wales, 1981, 1991, and 2001 (excluding within-ward moves) (Office for National Statistics, population censuses).

Table 5.2 Demographic and socio-economic changes in most and least favoured destination wards in Mid-Wales, averaged over three pre-census one-year migration periods.

	Ratio	Children % change	Older people % change	Unemployment % change
Top five wards for inter-regional in-migrants				
Presteigne	9.7	-2.5	7.2	-2.5
Llanrhaeadr-ym-Mochnant	6.8	-5.3	7.4	-5.3
Old Radnor	6.0	-1.3	4.0	-1.3
Llangybi	4.9	-2.5	4.0	-2.4
Llandrillo	4.6	2.5	2.2	2.5
Average		-2.5	6.7	-0.5
Bottom five wards for inter-regional in-migrants				
Welshpool Gungrog	0.3	-3.8	3.3	0.7
Llanbadarn Fawr—Padarn	0.2	4.4	11.1	-4.4
Aberystwyth Bronglais	0.2	3.3	16.9	-0.6
Aberystwyth Gogledd/North	0.1	2.6	12.8	-2.2
Aberystwyth Canol/Central	0.1	3.3	18.8	3.1
Average		3.0	12.5	0.9

Source: Office for National Statistics, population censuses.
Note: Using a Student's t-test, there is a significant difference at the 0.05 level between the two groups of wards in respect of the mean (average) for each of the indicators. The figures in the ratio column refer to the ratio of inter- to intra-regional migrants averaged across the one-year pre-census periods, with a migrant defined as a person with a different residential address on census night in comparison with 12 months previously.

Geodemographic Connectivity Associated with Migration

The previous analysis has shown that there are a significant number of wards in England and the rest of Wales persistently contributing to in-migration to Mid-Wales. Some wards in the region are preferentially selected by migrants and have greater connectivity. As discussed earlier, it is often argued that migrants to Mid-Wales and other countryside locations are motivated by a search for a safer and cleaner environment and a more communitarian lifestyle. But are people moving to areas demographically and socio-economically similar to the area from which they are departing? In other words, are people in England and the rest of Wales migrating from sparsely settled, countryside areas to the same type of locality in Mid-Wales? Complementing previous research exploring people's reasons for engaging in the migration process (Stockdale, 2006), this section examines whether certain types of areas are more likely to act as sources of migrants irrespective of their geographical location.

Geodemographic classification or "area profiling" seeks to characterize the multi dimensional demographic and socio-economic character of small areas (Harris *et al.*, 2005). Such classifications have been produced under the auspices of the government's statistics office in Britain since the late 1970s (Webber and Craig, 1978) and by companies in the commercial sector since the early 1980s. These area classifications are typically generated from a multivariate analysis of census statistics often accompanied, in the case of commercially produced profiles, by lifestyle data obtained from survey and administrative sources. Although they may be criticized for trying to encapsulate the complex variability of living conditions in deceptively simple descriptions along the lines of "Older affluent professionals" (CACI, 2008), they can, provided their limitations are recognized, offer a means of typifying localities consistently across countries or regions.

The 2001 geodemographic classification of areas produced by the Office for National Statistics has been used as a basis for "typing" the demographic and socio-economic character of the wards that contributed migrants to Mid-Wales. It is a hierarchical classification with three levels; for reasons of simplicity, only the general "Supergroup" categories have been used in the present analysis.[1] Table 5.3 indicates the nine categories that relate to the whole of the United Kingdom and shows that the percentage of migrants into Mid-Wales in the pre-census years 1980–1981, 1990–1991, and 2000–2001 were very consistent within each of the groups, varying in most cases by less than 1%. The final column is a so-called penetration index that indicates whether the Supergroups contributed more (>100) or less (<100) than might be expected to the in-migrant flow. Overall wards in England and the rest of Wales categorized as "Coastal and countryside," "Student communities," and to a lesser extent "Built-up areas" contributed more than would be expected. In contrast, "Multicultural metropolitan," "Prospering metropolitan," and "Suburbs and small towns" provided fewer migrants. Repeating this analysis with respect to the core group of 420 wards that contributed migrants at each of the last three censuses (lower part of Table 5.3) further reinforces the importance of the first set of area types and the unimportance of the latter set. Thus, although some migrants moved between similar types of areas (e.g., "Coastal and countryside"), others originated from quite different types of areas—in one case possibly indicating the return of graduates from a student area to their parental home, and in the other people seeking to leave a built-up environment.

Table 5.3 Characteristics of migrant source areas.

Type of source area	Percentage of total in-migrants to Mid-Wales			
All wards	1981	1991	2001	Index (2001)
Industrial hinterlands	19.3	17.0	17.8	85.8
Traditional manufacturing	6.2	6.4	7.1	75.1
Built-up areas	2.4	1.9	2.3	115.7
Prospering metropolitan	3.0	2.5	2.0	56.7
Student communities	6.0	7.6	7.0	132.2
Multicultural metropolitan	3.6	4.4	3.2	42.1
Suburbs and small towns	21.8	19.5	22.2	76.1
Coastal and countryside	29.5	31.3	30.0	177.3
Accessible countryside	8.3	9.3	8.6	154.3
Core wards				
Industrial hinterlands	6.9	5.6	7.1	92.9
Traditional manufacturing	2.3	2.4	2.5	71.1
Built-up areas	0.7	0.8	0.7	91.6
Prospering metropolitan	0.4	0.2	0.3	25.8
Student communities	3.1	3.7	3.8	191.9
Multicultural metropolitan	0.8	1.0	0.9	31.3
Suburbs and small towns	4.1	3.2	4.0	37.2
Coastal and countryside	16.0	16.6	15.6	247.9
Accessible countryside	1.5	2.0	2.2	108.9

Source: Office for National Statistics, population censuses.

Conclusions

In this chapter, I have sought to demonstrate that the future of rural places is very much interconnected with the future of urban places. Rural Mid-Wales experienced depopulation over many decades until the 1970s. Since then it has enjoyed a turnaround in its population and in its economic fortunes. This has been achieved by policies aimed at reinvigorating the local economy, by seeking to retain young people as they move from education into employment, and by establishing viable economic connections between local and global organizations. The predominant and visible character of the area was defined by the intimate association between an economy based on agriculture, forestry, and extractive industries and their manifestation on the land surface in a largely mountainous region with a sparse and diminishing population. The new economic basis of the area has been founded on restructuring carried out by the occupiers and owners of this landscape: notably by farmers reinventing themselves as part of the leisure and tourism sector, and by employers attracted by the opportunities and the incentives to settle or relocate within an area with an improving, although arguably still restricted, infrastructure.

However, of at least equal importance in the case of Mid-Wales has been its attractiveness and proximity as a destination for migrants seeking an alternative lifestyle. Understanding the motivations of people migrating between rural and urban areas constitutes one of the important elements in anticipating the future economies of rural (and urban) places. The results presented in this chapter indicate that some small areas (wards) in England and the rest of Wales have persistently acted as sources of migrants to Mid-Wales over the course of the last three censuses. The analysis has been based on population and one-year-migrant counts derived from the Census Special Migration Statistics for 1981, 1991, and 2001 with respect to the Beacham Report's Mid-Wales area, where a long period of population decline has been reversed since the 1960s. Some sparsely settled wards in Mid-Wales are clearly more attractive to migrants from outside the region than to their counterparts seeking to move within the region. Inevitably, when dealing with aggregate data, analysis will mask local variations with the larger areas. Thus we should be prepared to expect that the next rural economies will include uneven development, with certain places favoured over others that are eschewed. Policy makers should seek to ameliorate these differences by ensuring a sustainable local infrastructure connecting places in a mutually supportive network.

The analysis of the geodemographic types of areas contributing to the migration flow also helps to indicate how the character of rural areas might change in the future. Although past research has shown that many migrants are searching for a different lifestyle when they move to the countryside, and it would therefore be unwise to conclude that they will inevitably take the socio-economic and cultural characteristics of their source areas with them, or indeed that they are typical of these areas, it seems equally unlikely that they would abandon these characteristics entirely. Variability in the extent of population growth and patterns of in-migration to Mid-Wales indicates that migrants favour certain localities over others, which makes counterurbanization a spatially uneven process within a relatively small area. Inconsistencies in data sources, particularly in respect of boundary and definitional changes, inevitably mean that small absolute or percentage differences should be treated with a certain amount of caution. However, the replication of inter- and intra-regional flows and the high levels of connectivity associated with some wards over the three censuses examined here indicate a certain degree of consistency, and the central message arising from the core results is reasonably reliable.

Acknowledgements

The research reported in this chapter uses data derived from a project titled *Creating a Consistent Census-Based Statistical Geography, 1971–2001*, which received financial support from the Economic and Social Research Council (ESRC) (RES-000-22-0668). The work is based on data provided with the support of ESRC and Joint Information Systems Committee and uses boundary material that is copyright of the Crown and the ED-LINE Consortium. The work is based on 2001 Census Output Area Boundaries, Crown copyright 2003. Crown copyright material is reproduced with the permission of the Controller of HMSO. The work is based on an Ordnance Survey/EDINA supplied service, copyright Crown Copyright/database right 20(01). This work is based on data provided through EDINA UKBORDERS with the support of ESRC and JISC and uses boundary material that is copyright of the Crown.

Note

[1] The Office for National Statistics carried out a hierarchical area classification using a K-means clustering technique. The Supergroup comprises nine broad area types and sits above Group and Subgroup in the threefold hierarchy.

References

Balsom, D. (1985) The three Wales model. In: Osmond, J. (ed.) *The National Question Again.* Gomer, Llandysul, UK, 1–17.

Beacham Committee. (1964) *Depopulation in Mid-Wales.* HMSO, London.

Beale, C. (1975) *The Revival of Population Growth in Non-Metropolitan America* (Economic Research Service Report No. 605). US Department of Agriculture, Washington, DC.

Boyle, P. (1995) Modelling population movement into the Scottish Highlands and Islands from the remainder of Britain, 1990–1991. *Scottish Geographical Magazine* 111(1), 5–12.

CACI. (2008) New ACORN classification map, www.caci.co.uk/acorn/acornmap.asp (accessed 9 June 2008).

Champion, A. (1994) Population change and migration in Britain since 1981: Evidence for continuing deconcentration. *Environment and Planning A* 26(10), 1501–1520.

Champion, A., and Atkins, D. (1996) *The Counterurbanisation Cascade: An Analysis of the 1991 Census Special Migration Statistics for Great Britain* (Seminar Paper 66). Department of Geography, Newcastle University, Newcastle upon Tyne, UK.

Champion, A., Green, A., Owen, D., Ellin, D., and Coombes, M. (1987) *Changing Places: Britain's Demographic, Economic and Social Complexion.* Arnold, London.

Cloke, P., Goodwin, M., and Milbourne, P. (1998) Inside looking out: Outside looking in. Different experiences of cultural competence in rural lifestyles. In: Boyle, P., and Halfacree, K. (eds.) *Migration into Rural Areas.* Wiley, Chichester, UK, 134–150.

Day, G. (1989) A million on the move? Population change and rural Wales. *Contemporary Wales* 3, 137–159.

Economic and Social Research Council Census Programme. (2008) Interaction data, census.ac.uk/guides/Interaction.aspx (accessed 9 June 2008).

Fielding, A. (1982) Counterurbanisation in Western Europe. *Progress in Planning* 17(1), 1–52.

Halfacree, K., and Boyle, P. (1992) *Population Migration, within, into and out of Wales in the Late Twentieth Century: A General Overview of Literature* (Migration Unit Research Paper No. 1). Department of Geography, University of Wales, Swansea, UK.

Harris, R., Sleight, P., and Webber, R. (2005) *Geodemographics, GIS and Neighbourhood Targeting.* Wiley, Chichester, UK.

Keddie, P., and Joseph, A. (1991) The turnaround of the turnaround: Rural population change in Canada, 1976 to 1986. *Canadian Geographer* 35(4), 367–379.

Morrison, P., and Wheeler, J. (1976) Rural renaissance in America. *Population Bulletin* 31(3), 1–27.

National Statistics. (2005) Rutland the most rural area in England and Wales, www.statistics.gov.uk/pdfdir/rural0305.pdf (accessed 9 June 2008).

Paris, C. (1994) New patterns of urban and regional development in Australia: Demographic restructuring and economic-change. *International Journal of Urban and Regional Research* 18(4), 555–572.

Renkow, M., and Hoover, D. (2000) Commuting, migration, and rural-urban population dynamics. *Journal of Regional Science* 40(2), 261–287.

Spencer, D. (1995) Counterurbanisation: The local dimension. *Geoforum* 26(2), 153–173.

_____. (1997) Counterurbanisation and rural depopulation revisited: Landowners, planners and the rural development process. *Journal of Rural Studies* 13(1), 75–92.

Stockdale, A. (2006) Migration: Pre-requisite for rural economic regeneration? *Journal of Rural Studies* 22(3), 354–366.

Valentine, G. (1997) A safe place to grow up? Parenting, perceptions of children's safety and the rural idyll. *Journal of Rural Studies* 13(2), 137–148.

Walford, N. (2001) Reconstructing the small area geography of Mid-Wales for an analysis of population change 1961–95. *International Journal of Population Geography* 7(5), 311–338.

_____. (2004) Searching for a residential resting place: Population in-migration and circulation in Mid-Wales. *Population Space and Place* 10(4), 311–329.

Webber, R.J., and Craig, J. (1978) *Socio-Economic Classifications of Local Authority Areas* (Studies in Medical and Population Subjects 35). Office of Population, Censuses and Surveys, London.

Williams, G. (1985) Recent social changes in Mid-Wales. *Cambria* 122, 117–138.

Chapter 6

Ontario's Greenbelt and Places to Grow Legislation: Impacts on the Future of the Countryside and the Rural Economy

Hugh J. Gayler

Ontario's 2005 Greenbelt Act and Greenbelt Plan for the Greater Golden Horseshoe (GGH) area around Toronto marked the beginning of a new era for urban and rural planning (Government of Ontario, 2005a). Traditional, low-density, car-oriented suburban development was being challenged as economically, socially, and environmentally unsustainable; and the new Greenbelt Plan aimed to conserve the rural resource base and redirect the ways in which urban areas within the Greenbelt could grow in the future. Accompanying legislation—the Places to Grow Act—would meanwhile provide the planning framework for the wider regional economic development of southern Ontario and indicate where urban growth and infrastructure development would take place (Government of Ontario, 2006).

This chapter will briefly examine the background to the restrictive policies of urban containment and rural development presented in the Greenbelt Plan; and now that they are in place, it will critique a number of contentious issues associated with urban and rural development in the future. First, this new exercise in top-down planning is a placed-based policy, which is likely to create local and regional resentments because the central or provincial level of government will use scarce agricultural and rural resources in an optimal fashion, and in so doing will undoubtedly favour development in some areas over others. Second, the Ontario government, in adopting principles of Smart Growth in its Provincial Policy Statement, is not only challenging traditional development, but is effecting a change in the balance between new and better greenfield developments and the intensification of existing urban areas (Government of Ontario, 2005b). Third, the Greenbelt Act and the Places to Grow Act have set in motion a series of trajectories for dealing with problems relating to land-use policies and rural economies in southern Ontario.

These issues will be exemplified with respect to the Niagara Region at the western end of the GGH (Figs. 6.1 and 6.2). This place has long been distinguished from other parts of the GGH by various environmental and economic problems, especially extensive urban and rural sprawl; the Greenbelt and Places to Grow legislation, inter alia, is viewed as key to a space–place transition to a better economic future (Gayler, 2004, 2005).

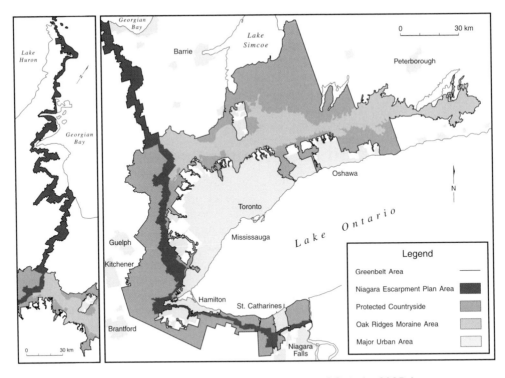

Fig. 6.1 Greenbelt Plan area (Government of Ontario, 2005a).

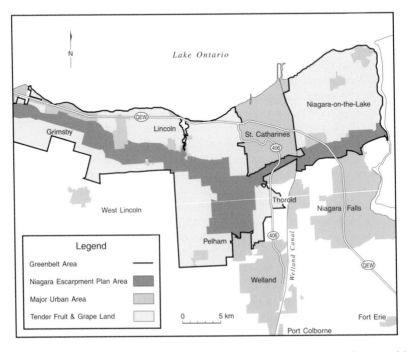

Fig. 6.2 Niagara Peninsula tender fruit and grape area (Government of Ontario, 2005a).

Background to the Problem

The GGH, with a population of nearly 7.5 million, is one of North America's fastest growing areas and is expected to increase by a further 3.7 million over the next 25 years (Greenbelt Task Force, 2004). Various studies suggest that the traditional pattern of land-hungry development is becoming harder to sustain in terms of services, transportation, community development, and quality of life issues; and there is a need to redesign new urban areas and intensify existing urban areas in order to reverse these trends (Blais, 1995; IBI Group, 2002). Moreover, years of lax or non-existent land-use planning and compliant landowners and local politicians have allowed an invidious urban sprawl to take place in the countryside within easy commuting distance of urban areas. Such sprawl adds to infrastructure costs and takes away from the public's expectations of the amenity value of the countryside (Porter *et al.*, 2002; Gurin, 2003; Fischler and Wolfe, 2006).

Low-density urban sprawl, especially, conflicts with the protection of southern Ontario's rural resource base (Reid, 2001; Caldwell and Weir, 2002; Planscape, 2003; Paraskevas, 2005). Much of Canada's Grade 1 agricultural lands lie in the path of urbanization in this area. In particular, 40% of the unique tender-fruit and grape lands in the northern part of the Niagara Region have already been lost since World War II, and much of the rest is under constant threat (Hofman, 2001; Hofman *et al.*, 2005).

This low-density urban sprawl has been carried out for over half a century in a supportive political and planning culture (Gayler, 2004). The major instrument of planning, the Ontario Planning Act, was set up to promote low-density urban sprawl at the local and regional level. Since the 1970s, provincial policy statements have been aimed at protecting valuable agricultural land, but local and regional official plans had only to "have regard to" the Provincial Policy Statement, rather than adopt the more strict "be consistent with."

It was not as if measures to protect valuable agricultural land were not already part of local and regional plans (Gayler, 2004). The Region Niagara Policy Plan of 1981, which finally had to be completed by the quasi-judicial Ontario Municipal Board (OMB), put in place some of Ontario's most restrictive policies relating to where urban development could take place. These policies also were aimed at protecting Niagara's unique tender-fruit and grape lands and redirecting development to poorer lands in the southern part of the region once urban-area boundaries were reached in northern municipalities. In practice, however, these restrictions were of dubious value. Exceptions to the rule through official plan amendments almost seemed to become the rule, and thus it was perhaps fortuitous that Niagara had very slow growth, which protected its fruit lands from extinction. Conservation groups in Niagara were among the most vigorous proponents of better top-down planning from the Ontario government, and the promised Greenbelt legislation in 2003 from the newly elected Liberal administration was regarded as manna from heaven.

Traditionally, urban sprawl was seen at the very least as a subsidy for farmers whether or not there was a pressing economic need. However, despite strong support from farmers for continuing such policies, professional, political, and industry opinion had long focused on securing a better future for the agricultural sector. Closing off the opportunities for urban expansion through the Greenbelt Act raised the ire of farmers, but it brought to the fore the need to win over farmers through better public- and private-sector promotion of measures that would secure their economic future.

Top-Down Planning and Local and Regional Conflicts

The 2005 Greenbelt Act and Places to Grow Act, and their subsequent plans, were seen as positive ways forward in an area under pressure from unsustainable urban growth. A strong Provincial Policy Statement, and the requirement for local and regional official plans to "be consistent with" it, seemingly put in place a very restrictive set of development policies over the vast 1.8 million-acre tract of the Greenbelt. The legislation passed with comparative ease. Opposition from the previous government largely related to process rather than policy, and the development and home-building industries were more concerned about where, rather than if, they could build. Ironically, the most strident, almost threatening, opposition came from farmers, especially those in the Niagara Region. They mistakenly believed that they could still do what they wanted with their land, and that any urban land use would secure a better economic future for them than farming.

In general, local and regional governments were supportive of the legislation; indeed, their planning departments were verging on the ecstatic! Finally, the Ontario government was doing what they had been unable to do up to now at a local level. However, support came because of different interpretations of what the legislation meant for future development. Research by the Neptis Foundation indicated that the Greenbelt allowed for more than enough developable land to satisfy future needs, even at existing densities (Neptis Foundation, 2005) and given that densities would increase, the Greenbelt could have been more extensive. When the Places to Grow areas beyond the Greenbelt are factored in, a considerable surplus of potential land for development is likely, fuelling competition between local municipalities (Bergsma, 2000; Reid, 2000; Gayler, 2004).

At the local level, Greenbelt municipalities differed about where developable greenfield sites will run out in the short term. Grimsby, in west Niagara (Fig. 6.2), sought ways to extend urban-area boundaries before 2005, amending its draft official plan and extending the status quo since then. St. Catharines, on the other hand, has consistently supported the 1981 Region Niagara Policy Plan, and planned for greenfield sites running out by promoting intensification and brownfield development, and encouraging greenfield development in neighbouring municipalities.

St. Catharines' position as Niagara's largest city and de facto regional centre has garnered support from the Ontario government as one of the 25 growth centres in its Places to Grow Plan (Fig. 6.3). Official plans will reflect these centres being the focus for public infrastructure investments as well as private-sector investment in employment and residential and non-residential developments.

For a region that has long promoted (at least on paper!) the redirection of urban development away from its unique agricultural lands, Niagara initially received the plan not to have any designated urban growth centres in the area beyond the Greenbelt as a slap in the face. Part of the reasoning no doubt involved recognition of Niagara's slow growth since 1966, its poorer accessibility relative to other areas of the GGH, and the need to focus on Greater Toronto, where people and jobs have migrated. Niagara had already identified two future growth areas as part of its redirection policy: the area between Niagara Falls and Fort Erie and the Welland Canal Corridor between Thorold and Port Colborne (Fig. 6.4). The former was designated a Gateway Economic Zone in the Places to Grow Plan, recognizing its proximity to major international border crossings and its unique economic importance to both the region and Ontario (Fig. 6.3). After lobbying by regional and local governments in Niagara, Welland was eventually recognized as a Gateway Economic

Centre, although it remains unclear what is meant by this and how dreams of development in south Niagara will come to fruition.

Local and regional municipalities argue that actual growth is inhibited by the failure to complete a 1950s provincial road-planning scheme: Highway 406 between St. Catharines and Port Colborne (it currently terminates in north Welland) and the long-awaited development of a Niagara–GTA highway from Fort Erie to Hamilton, which would relieve future congestion on the Queen Elizabeth Way (QEW) (Fig. 6.4). However, this failure is perhaps a reflection of slow growth and an existing highway infrastructure that has been improved (Government of Ontario, 1976, 2001).

While the future Niagara–GTA highway aims to spur economic growth in south Niagara, regional and local politicians view it, with what some would regard as twisted logic, as part of their Smart Growth policies: building this highway would relieve future pressures on the QEW and Niagara's unique agricultural lands between Grimsby and Niagara-on-the-Lake. Smart Growth supporters, meanwhile, would regard the Greenbelt Act and the freezing of these agricultural lands as sufficient protection, recognizing that Smart Growth envisages the de-emphasizing of the car–truck culture in favour of bus and rail transportation.

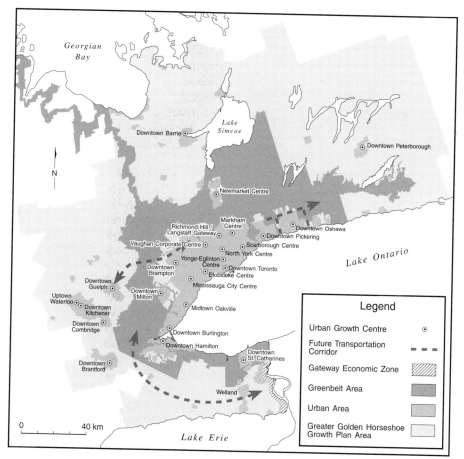

Fig. 6.3 Greater Golden Horseshoe growth area plan (Government of Ontario, 2006).

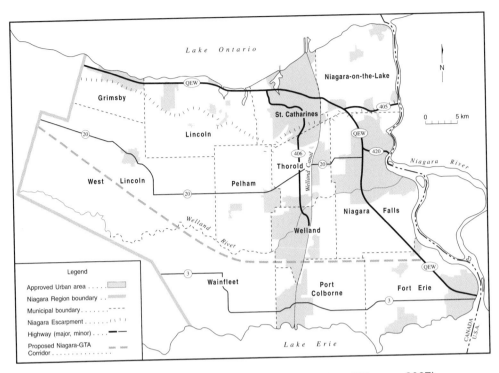

Fig. 6.4 Niagara urban areas (Regional Municipality of Niagara, 2007).

The Way Forward and Changing Urban Design

It is recognized that greenfield development will still form a substantial part of future urban growth. What is difficult to calculate is how much greenfield land will be needed in light of change that points, quite categorically, in the other direction. While the status quo of suburbia remains a reality or a dream for the majority of the population, professional and political leaders are acting otherwise. The Ontario government is setting minimum density figures for all new development and is encouraging such development on underutilized land in existing built-up areas.

The Places to Grow legislation recognizes that the interminable sprawl of the GGH is not sustainable, but there are no clear guidelines as to the proportion of development that will take place in the seven urban growth centres beyond the Greenbelt versus the 18 that lie within it. The Neptis Foundation's research already suggests that there is enough land within the Greenbelt; and rising property prices and public investments in new infrastructure will intensify development still further (Neptis Foundation, 2005). Meanwhile, there is the danger that population growth beyond the Greenbelt, unless accompanied by employment growth, will exacerbate daily commuter car trips into the Greater Toronto area and needlessly encourage expensive public transportation investments.

In Niagara, the redirection of development beyond the Greenbelt remains uncertain. While St. Catharines is about to exhaust its last greenfield sites, it has embraced Smart

Growth principles in its policy and land-use planning, encouraging greenfield development elsewhere and the intensification of development on brownfield and greyfield areas within the city (Regional Municipality of Niagara, 2000a, 2000b; Marshall Macklin Monaghan, 2007). Since clean-up costs are not prohibitive, Niagara's Smart Growth facilitator already sees the realization of much commercial and residential development in such areas in the near future (M. Brickell, Niagara Economic Development Corporation, 2007, personal communication).

Intensifying development and improving urban design in existing areas rather than expanding into the countryside fits perfectly with the Places to Grow legislation and the Provincial Policy Statement. St. Catharines is seeing a steady stream of applications to convert existing developed lots into multiple-townhouse freehold or condominium plans. Much of this intensification relates to deteriorating pre-war commercial and residential areas, but increasingly post-war suburbs are being favoured. Such intensification is often characterized by shoehorning a row of five-to-ten townhouses into the large garden of an existing 1950s house, or by severing a large corner lot for an additional house. While there is strict adherence to good site planning guidelines, most of these developments draw the ire of surrounding residents—the so-called NIMBY factor—on any number of grounds, such as visual impact and loss of a view, increased traffic hazards, perceived loss of property values, and the possibility of a deleterious impact on service provision. Most of these fears are imagined, but even if they were real, the overriding consideration is the wider public good.

As the baby-boom generation continues to age, environmental and economic restrictions are placed on car travel, and public policy increasingly favours one type of development over another, cities are refashioning themselves in a pre-1939 mode. Niagara's land-use policies, and especially its redirection strategy, may need reappraisal in light of changes in intensification.

The Changing Rural Economy

Both redirection to greenfield sites and intensification of existing urban areas afford an opportunity to save Niagara's most valuable agricultural lands in perpetuity. The Greenbelt Act not only froze urban-area boundaries, but it severely restricted the activities that could take place in the countryside beyond. Land not already developed was now limited to agricultural uses or various natural states such as woodlots and wetlands. Moreover, the size of farm unit permitted through subdivision had to be of sufficient size to allow for the continued viability of agricultural uses.

Saving the land for agriculture through top-down planning legislation was seen by the agricultural community as the "final straw breaking the camel's back" (Lafleche, 2002). Five hundred farmers, their families, and their supporters essentially hijacked the Greenbelt Task Force's public hearings in Niagara in November 2004, and noisily demanded that the Ontario government not interfere with traditional property rights by, in particular, selling all or part of their land for some urban-related, and more lucrative, activity. Emotions ran high and many farmers used scare tactics to stir up opposition, such as the government was expropriating their land, preventing them from selling it, or telling them what they had to grow. Farmers argued, without any evidence to support their claim, that land prices would fall and they should be compensated for the loss.

Given the quality of the land, the importance of agriculture to the local economy, the weaknesses of existing local and regional planning, and the need to remove speculation, it was inevitable that the legislation would pass. Farmers regularly note that they are the best stewards of the land, and the Greenbelt Plan could be seen as four-square behind their initiatives. However, farmers have consistently argued that it is first necessary to save the farmer so that the land can be farmed; although of this chicken-and-egg argument one has to ask, what happens if the land to be farmed is no longer there? Thus, it is incumbent on government and the industry to consider both land use and agricultural viability as they examine the changing rural economy. The volatile St. Catharines' public hearings were all about the countless frustrations and uncertainties of farming, and about perceiving the legislation to be no more than a means of preserving the land in perpetuity for the benefit of urbanites who want to enjoy the countryside, rather than as a way to help farmers to make a decent living. The frustrations expressed at the hearings, exemplify an agricultural economy that for many in Niagara has been faltering for some time (Planscape, 2003). Tender-fruit and grape farmers, in particular, have maintained that they face a cost-price squeeze that has been worse than in any other agricultural sector. This has led to a decline in the number of farmers and an increase in the size of farms. Meanwhile, the economies of scale from larger operations have been accompanied by needed innovations as older farmers retire and younger farmers take over. Global competition has meant that the market for Niagara's fresh fruit has declined as transportation has improved and supermarket chains bring in products from the United States and Mexico—the price is cheaper, the season is longer, and the switching back and forth between local and non-local produce makes little economic sense. Selling more local produce in farmers' markets and at the farm gate has helped the situation, and a concerted effort by the Ontario government to promote local produce has finally contributed to an increase in its availability in supermarkets during the growing season.

A high proportion of Niagara's tender-fruit crops used to be sent for local processing in value-added canned fruit, jams, and preserves. However, the last of these processing plants in North America east of the Rockies closed in July 2008 (Blizzard, 2008). Some 120 manufacturing jobs were lost, but also some 150 farmers no longer had a market for peaches and pears. The pears can be sold as fresh fruit, but the peaches are a clingstone variety that is unsuitable for the fresh-fruit market. Various agencies became engaged in a blame game (Downs, 2008). The factory owners, part of an American conglomerate, had little interest in selling out to farmers or other potential competitors; farmers, who were hoping for public subsidies to contribute to either their capital fundraising or to keeping the factory in business, blamed the Ontario government for not working hard enough to realize either of these ventures; and the Ontario government maintained that it tried to save the industry but regrettably did not succeed. But the government stood rightly accused of offering no tax subsidy when other areas of manufacturing attracted multi-millions of dollars. The local press had a field day, particularly at blossom time, emotionally reporting on farmers tearing out fruit trees, but this publicity did not extend much beyond the local community. The plant's closure was perceived as the inevitable end of a once mighty industry in Niagara, and US as other foreign producers took over.

The grape-growing sector has fared better, as the Canadian wine industry re-invented itself after the 1970s. Wine had originally been made from the local *Vitis lambrusca* grape, but it was largely shunned by the cognoscenti in favour of imported wines. This attitude changed, however, after the 1960s when the European *Vitis vinifera* and French hybrid grapes were grown locally. The older and larger wineries converted to using only the

European grape, as did the new small estate-winery businesses that began to develop after 1975. Meanwhile, in 1989, a federal-provincial Grape Acreage Reduction Program subsidized growers to tear out approximately 40% of the old grapes and replace them with the new. However, growers who continued in the grape-juice business with the old varieties did not fare as well. The last juice-processing plant in Niagara closed in 2007, eliciting the same shock, emotional reaction, and blame game that would occur with the closure of the last fruit-processing plant in 2008. The grapes could not go the wine industry, although some did go to juice processors in the United States. In this case, the Ontario government has subsidized growers to tear out the grapes, but shared federal-provincial funding for replanting with wine-making grapes is uncertain.

Converting to wine-making grapes has never resulted in a guaranteed market with local wineries. The need for short-term contracts and issues of price and grape quality have always made for testy relationships with Niagara wineries. Furthermore, local growers continue to lose out to a wine industry in which two major players, producing over 80% of Canadian wine, are permitted to import up to 70% of their wine product, blend it with local grapes, and still call it Canadian wine, using the somewhat deceptive phrase, "Cellared in Canada." Canada remains the only important wine-producing country in the world where the majority of the wine consumed is not from local grapes. In part, this reflects poor marketing, high prices, the continuing snob appeal of European wines, and the amazingly high quality and competitive pricing of wines from other New World countries.

Finally, the faltering agricultural economy has manifested itself in the global–local consequences of the state of the Canadian economy. Since the United States is Canada's largest trading partner, the strength of the Canadian economy is invariably measured by comparing Canadian and US currencies. For much of the last 30 years, the Canadian dollar has been well below its American counterpart, which in turn favours the former's export industries and makes imports more expensive. During times when the Canadian dollar reaches par, exports become more costly while imports are encouraged. Such currency fluctuations have an impact on Niagara's agricultural sector in which US producers offer greater competition. However, since imports are correspondingly cheaper, it may be possible for farmers to match higher costs in one area with lower costs in another.

The expectation and eventual establishment of a Greenbelt in Niagara were the catalysts necessary to get the agricultural sector moving forward on innovations that would reduce uncertainties, raise incomes, and lead to a more secure future. These actions grew out of a panel discussion attended by the author at the annual Smarter Niagara Summit meeting in November 2002. The panel discussion between proponents and opponents of an agricultural land preserve was tense enough, but the question-and-answer session, with approximately 250 people in attendance (most of whom were farmers), degenerated into an ugly, name-calling affair between saving-the-farmer and saving-the-land camps. In order to diffuse the situation, the then Chair of Niagara's Regional Council agreed to form an Agricultural Task Force on the long-term viability of agriculture.

After over a year of discussions, the Task Force's final report seemed to be a win–win solution that finally brought the two sides together to work toward—as the report's subtitle suggested—*A Vision from One Voice* (Regional Municipality of Niagara, 2004). One side agreed to permanently freezing the boundaries of valuable agricultural land in the Greenbelt area in return for new and continued support from all four levels of government, agricultural organizations, and the general public, which would promote a variety of programs, policies, and financial incentives to help farmers.

Sadly, the introduction of the Greenbelt legislation in 2004 derailed this spirit of cooperation. While the Greenbelt Task Force listened to farmers, the ensuing legislation focused only on land use, not on agricultural viability (Greenbelt Task Force, 2004). However, the Agricultural Task Force in Niagara continued its work anyway, receiving a $100,000 Ontario-government grant to implement an agricultural viability plan for the area and completing an Agricultural Action Plan (Planscape, 2006).

A key part to innovation was the recommendation to re-establish the Vineland Research Station in Lincoln. This federal–provincial institution had a 100-year history of providing scientific and educational help to the agricultural community, but much of its work had run afoul of cutbacks in public expenditures. Following effective lobbying, the Ontario government set up the Vineland Research and Innovation Centre in 2007 with a $25-million grant that was matched by the federal government. The Centre has quickly moved forward on a number of fronts that will enhance viability in the industry and inspire confidence in the agricultural community (Ziraldo, 2008).

Part of the Centre's immediate success has been to partner with agriculturally related programs in universities and colleges, to form science and stakeholder advisory committees, and to engage with the agricultural community and the public through a local food initiative. The resulting Buy Local Niagara campaign has focused on the increasingly popular carbon-footprint-reducing 100-mile limit for food in homes and restaurants. Asking the question, "why not Niagara grown?" strikes an even more favourable chord with Niagara farmers since their products are local to nearly seven million people. A local food initiative partnership has been established in order to apply quality standards and to get the food into local supermarkets and grocery stores.

Another important initiative is to grow the near-defunct, value-added processing capability, in effect saying to farmers, "Why not freeze or can your own clingstone peaches now that you are able to market them in one of the supermarket chains?". Many more farmers than ever before are engaging in farm-gate sales. As producers, they never thought they would become retailers, but for the thousands of tourists passing through Niagara, fresh fruit, processed fruit, and various rural crafts, have become part of the agri-tourism experience (Gayler, 2003).

Innovation and value-added activities on the farm have become quite diverse. Many farms are two-career households with spouses having jobs off the farm. A secondary business is permitted for whatever reason as long as zoning and site-plan regulations are not circumvented. Bed-and-breakfast establishments and farm vacations are further sources of extra income, but inns and hotels outside urban-area boundaries are not permitted on the grounds that their accompanying restaurants, bars, and meeting facilities for non-residents are seen more as urban sprawl (Regional Municipality of Niagara, 2007).

The New Countryside

The grape-and-wine industry has made an enormous impact visually on the countryside in Niagara's Greenbelt (Gayler, forthcoming). It has added to the traditional, Niagara Falls-bound tourist industry, because in summer thousands of motorists follow the Wine Route (Fig. 6.5) that connects most of Niagara's wineries (Wine Council of Ontario, 2008). The grape-and-wine industry has resulted in a myriad spin-off activities that can be regarded as part of the agri-tourism experience (Gayler, 2003). Entrepreneurs have invested millions of dollars in turning around a hundred-year-old, down-market industry. Previously the wine industry consisted of only factories in urban areas; they have since closed and the more than 90 wineries today are smaller, more aesthetically pleasing, and are situated amid their own vineyards. The buildings themselves make for appealing destinations, invoking architectural and cultural associations with, for example, a Loire Valley chateau, a Georgian-style farmhouse, an eco-friendly building that could easily be mistaken for an airport terminal, or a Victorian mansion.

This Greenbelt area has been transformed from a countryside of production to one of consumption. Indeed, winery owners have often gone out of their way to hide the production part of their operations so as not to dispel consumer notions of a rural idyll. Media hype and consumer attention are focused on the scenic drive past the vineyards to a winery's various hospitality functions. The actual production of the wine would be seen only on a winery tour.

The growing of this countryside of consumption has not been without its detractors. Rural roads now have far more traffic, and urbanites living there often object to wineries that are little more than well-designed factories with all the attendant noises and smells of machinery and vehicles. Residents ask why such factories cannot go back to an urban industrial park. Many of these people have already endured the development of large commercial greenhouses in this area and have expressed similar sentiments: since the valuable soils underneath the greenhouses are not used, such enterprises should be situated in an urban area. However, both greenhouses and wineries are designated agricultural activities, and are as much a spatially integrated part of the rural economy as tender-fruit and grape growing.

Among the detractors continues to be grape growers who nurse various grievances against some of the wineries. In 2004, a number of the larger and more successful growers built an impressive winery in Niagara-on-the-Lake to produce and market their own wine. Unfortunately, production wildly exceeded consumption, perhaps because the quality was mediocre or the market was suddenly saturated, and the debt load was such that the winery was forced into receivership in 2008.

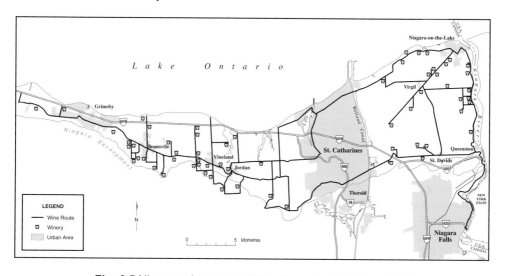

Fig. 6.5 Niagara wine routes (Wine Council of Ontario, 2008).

Behind this idyllic façade lies a wine industry that is still growing and maturing within a contested countryside in which two actors—grape growers and estate wineries—are joined by a number of others, often with competing agendas (Gayler, forthcoming). These other players include the larger, more global wineries; trade associations and grower organizations; the various ministries of the federal and provincial governments; the Liquor Control Board of Ontario, the largest public wholesaler and retailer of wine and spirits in the world; and last, but not least, the consumer who is variously schooled in the appreciation of local wines.

Conclusions

The 2005 Greenbelt Act and Places to Grow Act are revolutionizing the way we now think and plan for urban and rural development in the Greater Golden Horseshoe area of southern Ontario—one of the four fastest-growing regions on the continent. Specifically, we have seen how the intervention of the state (the Province of Ontario) and provincial plans and policy statements have lead to top-down directives about how placed-based development will unfold. It will be largely contained in already designated urban areas, in particular, in the 25 more intensified urban centres. Rural resources, especially valuable agricultural lands and significant environmental features, are to be protected in perpetuity.

Where urban and rural development takes place, and the relative weights given to greenfield versus brownfield/greyfield development, raises various placed-based tensions at the local level. With reference to Niagara's unique agricultural lands, the status quo is no longer an option. Greenfield sites are running out in the Greenbelt municipalities; however, uncertainty remains concerning where development will then take place. St. Catharines has been selected as an urban-growth centre; but the redevelopment of existing sites in this city through intensification could consume much of the population increase, thereby taking away from efforts to redirect development to the south. Moreover, the lack of transportation infrastructure will make redirection difficult, while the surplus of developable lands will likely favour the more accessible (i.e., more northerly) municipalities. The prospects for Niagara, the slowest-growing part of the Greater Golden Horseshoe, are not necessarily good, and especially in those areas that could accommodate more development.

The Greenbelt and Places to Grow plans are just that—land-use plans—but they also greatly affect future rural economies. In Niagara, farmers remain very opposed to this introduction of top-down planning; the safety valve of selling out to urban interests is no longer there, yet the legislation offers no direct ways to grow the rural economy as compensation. However, there is no doubt that accompanying measures and incentives by government, public agencies, grower organizations, the private sector, and the farmers themselves are improving the viability of agriculture and the well-being of the rural community. While many Niagara farmers always hope that a change of government may one day turn back the clock to the "good old days," the acceptance of these place-based policies and the elimination of their politicization are increasingly viewed as the way forward for more sustainable urban and rural development. Indeed, a recent study undertaken by the Canadian Institute for Environmental Law and Policy (Carter-Whitney, 2008) publicized Ontario's Greenbelt as "a model for the world" (Mittelstaedt, 2008, A9). The toughness of its top-down protective policies will ensure a land base for the successful farmer, while it is recognized that other economic measures are necessary to guarantee that success in the first place.

Acknowledgements

The author is indebted to a large number of professional people who have assisted in this research by freely offering information and opinions, including fellow members of the Niagara Region's Smarter Niagara Steering Committee, local and regional planners, farmers, winery owners, and winemakers.

References

Bergsma, M. (2000) Council urges ban on farmland development. *St. Catharines Standard*, 27 July, A3, A6.

Blais, P. (1995) The economics of urban form. In: Greater Toronto Area Task Force (ed.) *Greater Toronto*. Greater Toronto Area Task Force, Toronto, Appendix E.

Blizzard, C. (2008) Bitter harvest for Niagara's fruit farms. *St. Catharines Standard*, 3 May, A14.

Caldwell, W., and Weir, C. (2002) *A Review of Severance Activity in Ontario's Agricultural Land during the 1990s*. School of Rural Planning and Development, University of Guelph, Guelph, ON.

Carter-Whitney, M. (2008) *Ontario's Greenbelt in an International Context: Comparing Ontario's Greenbelt to Its Counterparts in Europe and North America*. Friends of the Greenbelt Foundation, Toronto.

Downs, P. (2008) How the deal went sour. *St. Catharines Standard*, 26 April, A1, A7.

Fischler, R., and Wolfe, J. (2006) Contemporary planning. In: Bunting, T., and Filion, P. (eds.) *Canadian Cities in Transition*. Oxford University Press, Toronto, 338–352.

Gayler, H. (2003) Agritourism developments in the rural–urban fringe: The challenges to land-use and policy planning in the Niagara region, Ontario. In: Beesley, K., Millward, H., Ilbery, B., and Harrington, L. (eds.) *The New Countryside: Geographic Perspectives on Rural Change*. Brandon and Saint Mary's Universities, Brandon, MB, and Halifax, NS, 179–196.

_____. (2004) The Niagara fruit belt: Planning conflicts in the preservation of a national resource. In: Lapping, M., and Furuseth, O. (eds.) *Big Places Big Plans*. Ashgate, Aldershot, UK, 55–82.

_____. (2005) Stemming the urban tide: Policy and attitudinal changes for saving the Canadian countryside. In: Essex, S., Gilg, A., Yarwood, R., Smithers, J., and Wilson, R. (eds.) *Rural Change and Sustainability: Agriculture, the Environment and Communities*. CABI Publishing, Wallingford, UK, 151–168.

_____. (forthcoming) Niagara's emerging wine culture. In: Grant, B., and Nicks, J. (eds.) *Covering Niagara*. Wilfrid Laurier University Press, Waterloo, ON.

Government of Ontario. (1976) Ministry of Transportation and Communications. *Niagara–Lake Erie transportation study*. Author, Toronto.

_____. (2001) Ministry of Transportation. *Niagara Peninsula transportation needs assessment study*. Author, Toronto.

_____. (2005a) Ministry of Municipal Affairs and Housing. *Greenbelt Plan*. Author, Toronto.

_____. (2005b) Ministry of Municipal Affairs and Housing. *Provincial Policy Statement*. Author, Toronto.

_____. (2006) Ministry of Public Infrastructure Renewal. *Places to Grow: Growth Plan for the Greater Golden Horseshoe*. Author, Toronto.

Greenbelt Task Force. (2004) *Toward a Golden Horseshoe Greenbelt*. Prepared for the Minister of Municipal Affairs and Housing. Toronto.

Gurin, D. (2003) *Understanding Sprawl*. David Suzuki Foundation, Vancouver.

Hofmann, N. (2001) Urban consumption of agricultural land. *Rural and Small Town Canada Analysis Bulletin* (Agriculture Division of Statistics Canada) 3(2).

Hofmann, N., Filoso, G., and Schofield, M. (2005) The loss of dependable agricultural land in Canada. *Rural and Small Town Canada Analysis Bulletin* (Agriculture Division of Statistics Canada) 6(1).

IBI Group. (2002) *Toronto-Related Region Futures Study: Implications of Business-as-Usual Development*. Neptis Foundation, Toronto.

Lafleche, G. (2002) Fruit farmers don't like land preserve concept. *St. Catharines Standard*, 28 June, A1–A2.

Marshall Macklin Monaghan. (2007) *Reclaiming Ground in the Neighbourhoods of Oakdale-Moffatt: The Action Plan*. Author, Toronto.

Mittelstaedt, M. (2008) Ontario's greenbelt a model for the world. *Globe and Mail*, 10 April, A9.

Neptis Foundation. (2005) *Neptis Commentary on the Draft Greenbelt Plan*. Author, Toronto.

Paraskevas, J. (2005) Urban sprawl forcing farmers to cultivate poorer soils: Statistics Canada survey details how much of the best farmland has been lost. *Vancouver Sun*, 1 February, A4.

Planscape. (2003) *Regional Agricultural Economic Impact Study*. Prepared for the Regional Municipality of Niagara.

_____. (2006) *Agricultural Action Plan—Growing the Industry: Farm Economic Viability for the Long-Term*. Prepared for the Regional Municipality of Niagara.

Porter, D., Dunphy, R., and Salvesin, D. (2002) *Making Smart Growth Work*. Urban Land Institute, Washington, DC.

Reid, K. (2000) Farm land protection motion criticized. *St. Catharines Standard*, 10 August, A6.

_____. (2001) A place to grow: Niagara's wine industry is eager to expand but finding suitable land is a major challenge. *St. Catharines Standard*, 12 July, A1–A2.

Regional Municipality of Niagara. (2000a.) *Smart Growth for Niagara: A New Approach for Development* (DPD 118-2000). Author, Thorold, ON.

_____. (2000b.) *Niagara—A Special Place Today...and Tomorrow?* (Publication 95-1). Author, Thorold, ON.

_____. (2004) *Securing a Legacy for Niagara's Agricultural Land: A Vision from One Voice*. Report of the Agricultural Task Force. (CAO 13-2004). Author, Thorold, ON.

_____. (2007) *Regional Niagara Policy Plan: Office Consolidation*. Author, Thorold, ON.

Wine Council of Ontario. (2008) *Official Guide to the Wineries of Ontario*. Author, St. Catharines.

Ziraldo, D. (2008) Next stop—Niagara's future and Buy Local: A "Niagara Brand." Presentation to the Smarter Niagara Summit meeting, Welland, ON.

Chapter 7

Adding Value Locally through Integrated Rural Tourism: Lessons from Ireland

Mary Cawley

Tourism is attributed a new economic role in many rural areas affected by local and global restructuring, reflecting renewed emphasis on local places as part of the "new rural economies" (Halseth, 2008). This chapter explores a method of promoting rural tourism more effectively by applying a model of integrated rural tourism (IRT), within a context of "strategic fit," (Porter, 1996), as a way of adding value locally. The model is applied in the context of a rural area in western Ireland, where tourism is long established and some aspects of integration might be expected to be present. The objectives are to assess the role of IRT in promoting "good practice" in adding value within a strategic framework.

Rural tourism has received increased attention in recent decades as an alternative source of income in remote rural areas that have become effectively marginalized from mainstream agriculture (Organization for Economic Co-operation and Development, 1995). Producers have been encouraged by national and international governments and agencies to change their operations from being actively involved in cultivation to adopting a role as conservators of the countryside, and to seek supplementary sources of income through the adaptation of land, labour, and capital to new uses, such as tourism (Wilson, 2001; Walford, 2003; van der Ploeg, 2006). The logic for promoting rural tourism arises, in part, from growing interests in and demands for contact with older ways of life, traditions, and outdoor recreational opportunities by so-called postmodern tourists as alternatives to mass, weakly differentiated, sun-based tourism (Butler *et al.*, 1998; Hall *et al.*, 2003). Incorporating tourism into the rural economy is not, however, achieved without problems arising from structural weaknesses in the sector and from the quite complex bureaucratic structures that are often involved (Hall *et al.*, 2005). To address these problems, Bramwell and Lane (2000) advocate an integrated approach that links tourism with other economic sectors and adopts a governance structure based on partnership and networking. Oliver and Jenkins (2003) propose a more holistic model of IRT, which incorporates environment and society as well as economy. The research reported here draws on the latter's work.

This chapter discusses one approach to attaining greater integration in rural tourism—"adding value" through "strategic fit"—as proposed by Porter (1996) in the context of the firm. While adding value is traditionally associated with economic value, this approach is used to incorporate broader issues relating to the quality of the environment and the support of social and cultural norms, which form part of the distinctive features of rural tourism (Clark and Chabrel, 2007). This chapter begins with a brief introduction to rural tourism in Ireland, and then introduces a model of IRT. The model is discussed with reference to strategic fit and then applied in order to assess the value added by tourism since the early

1990s in a small town and its environs in western Ireland. Broader implications are also identified.

Irish Rural Tourism: Context

The rural landscape features strongly in Irish tourism promotion, and the cultural heritage and welcoming attitude of the population are recognized as being among the main attractions of Ireland for tourists (Millward Brown, 2007). Since the late 1980s, both the state and the European Union (EU) have supported the expansion of rural tourism infrastructure (Deegan and Dineen, 2000). Total capital investment in tourism between 1989 and 1999 amounted to €4.3 billion, 65% of which came from the private sector (Government of Ireland, 2003). Tourism also became a significant contributor to employment gains nationally during this time (Deegan and Moloney, 2005). From the late 1980s onward, tourism received new emphasis in rural development policy, as alternatives were sought to declining employment and income in agriculture and fisheries following reform of the EU's Common Agricultural Policy and Common Fisheries Policy. Irish tourism was prioritized in rural development investment that was channeled through the EU's LEADER program during the 1990s. This program linked activities for the development of the rural economy, and outdoor recreational opportunities received enhanced emphasis (O'Leary and Deegan, 2003).

Notwithstanding the role associated with rural resources in Irish tourism, a rural tourism policy as such does not exist. The relative concentration of accommodation and associated leisure facilities in the larger towns also means that much of the revenue accrues to those centres rather than to more remote locations that attract fewer tourists and where tourism tends to be more markedly seasonal (Deegan and Moloney, 2005). In the Ireland West tourism region of counties Galway, Mayo, and Roscommon, direct and indirect tourism-related employment grew by 30% between 1998 and 2003, accounting for 9,397 full-time equivalents or 5.4% of total employment by 2003 (Deegan and Moloney, 2005). In 2003, tourism accounted for 7.6% of the Gross Value Added in the region (by comparison with 3% in the Dublin capital region). Receipts equalled €1.9 billion, and tourists numbered 2.395 million (plus almost 19 million day visitors). Overseas tourists account for approximately 65% of regional tourism revenue, 76% of which accrues to County Galway. The county contains the main population and accommodation centre of Galway City which in 2006 had a population of 72,414 (Central Statistics Office, 2007). Recent research suggests that synergies exist between urban and rural locations, but the available data do not permit tourist numbers and income to be disaggregated in that way (Deegan and Moloney, 2005). Visitors to the main heritage tourist attraction in the Clifden study area numbered 193,415 in 2006, many of whom would have been Irish day visitors (Fáilte Ireland, 2008). This number is sizeable, particularly in relation to a resident population of 1,495 in the town of Clifden and some 9,000 in the wider electoral district.

Integrated Rural Tourism

Bramwell and Lane (2000) advocate a need for greater integration between rural tourism and other sectors of the economy, and between different resource uses and different stakeholders. Based on extensive research, Oliver and Jenkins (2003) identify the main features that are likely to promote integration as being: sustainable use of resources;

empowerment of local people; complementarity with other economic sectors; prioritization of the local in terms of ownership and resource use; scales of development that are appropriate to the social and geographical context; networking between stakeholders; and embeddedness in local systems.

Definitions of sustainability often draw on the concepts of resource conservation and intergenerational transfer, as articulated in the Brundtland Commission's report of 1987 (World Commission on Environment and Development, 1987). The meaning of sustainability and its operationalization are, however, subject to negotiation between different stakeholders in particular contexts (Sharpley, 2000; Hardy *et al.*, 2002). Attention in the past has often focused on economic and environmental sustainability, but increased recognition is now given to the social and cultural sustainability of local communities (Saarinen, 2006). Promoting sustainability in tourism in lagging rural regions involves supporting the local economy and society in ways that protect, rather than threaten, the essential characteristics of the local culture and the inherent quality of the natural environment (Pigram, 1994, 2000; Aronsson, 2000; Northcote and Macbeth, 2006). State policy is also directing increased attention to empowering local people by encouraging their active involvement in decision making related to rural development, facilitating enterprising behaviour, and reducing unnecessary dependency on the state (Sofield, 2003; Blackstock, 2005).

Oliver and Jenkins (2003) suggest that three features of resource use for tourism are particularly instrumental in promoting integration: complementarity with other types of use; local ownership and appropriate exploitation of the resource base; and a scale of activity that is sympathetic to the local geographical context. By being complementary to existing structures, tourism should contribute more effectively to counteracting economic decline and should harmonize more successfully with environmental and cultural resource uses (Bachleitner and Zins, 1999; Briassoulis, 2002; Hall *et al.*, 2005; Garrod *et al.*, 2006). Local ownership and local collective influence or "agency" in using resources— "endogeneity"—are conducive to promoting "complementarity," and should serve to maximize on the retention of economic benefits within an area (Jenkins, 2000). By contrast, external ownership and external decision making serve to disempower local people (Hohl and Tisdell, 1995). Comparative advantage may be derived from small- and niche-scale activity, characterized by the personalized service offered and particularities of place, which stand in marked contrast to the standardized services provided by large-scale businesses in mass tourism destinations (Butler and Hall, 1998). The potential impact of small businesses and their clients on the natural and cultural resource base is likely to be less than that of their larger-scale counterparts (Long and Lane, 2000; Getz and Carlsen, 2005). In aggregate, small- and medium-sized businesses may make important employment contributions where few alternatives are available (Wanhill, 2000; Andriotis, 2002).

Several authors point to a need for collaboration among small-scale producers and between small-scale producers and other businesses, as a method for overcoming the costs associated with promotion and marketing (Carey *et al.*, 1997; Fyall and Garrod, 2005). The concept of "networking" encompasses the collaboration required to promote business development and marketing. Networking may be closely embedded in local social and economic systems or appropriately disembedded through links to external agencies and markets. The former includes local horizontal actions to create local businesses and products (Kalantaridis and Bifka, 2006), and the latter relates to actions to attract funding and tourists (Fyall and Garrod, 2005). Since the early 1990s, local partnerships, as promoted in the EU's LEADER program, have been known to be conducive to networking at the local level (Vernon *et al.*, 2005). The dimensions of integrated rural tourism and the concept of networking outlined above share features with a strategic approach to adding value in the firm, as discussed by Porter (1996).

Value-Added and Strategic Positioning

A firm is profitable if the value created for buyers (as reflected in the prices paid for products) exceeds the collective costs of performing all of its required activities (Porter, 1990). Value may be added at various points along a chain from production to sale to after-sales service. A firm's value chain is a set of interlinked activities. Change in one activity may have either positive or negative effects on another or result in trade-offs. Gaining competitive advantage means that a firm's value chain is managed as a system rather than as an assemblage of separate parts, and effective management can become a source of competitive advantage over rivals (Porter, 1998).

Porter (1996) expanded on the idea of managing the value chain as a system by introducing the concept of "strategic positioning." In this context, competitive advantage comes from the ways in which activities fit and reinforce each other. The concept of trade-offs is central to this strategic approach, and one activity's costs may be offset by the way in which other activities are performed (as discussed below, this interpretation of trade-off is not appropriate within an IRT model). Porter identifies three types of fit. First-order fit relates to consistency between each activity (function) and the overall strategy. For example, a low-cost strategy should be pursued consistently in all aspects of the firm's activities. Second-order fit relates to reinforcing activities, such as marketing a high-value product to only a (necessarily) limited number of high-value markets. Third-order fit promotes optimization of effort through, for example, coordination and information exchange across activities to eliminate redundancy and minimize wasted effort. Porter suggests that strategic fit among many activities is fundamental to competitive advantage and its sustainability because it is more difficult for a competitor to imitate an interlocked array of activities than to imitate a particular activity. The concept of strategic fit provides a context in which to operationalize an integrated approach to rural tourism development (Cawley and Gillmor, 2008).

A Model of IRT within a "Strategic Fit" Approach

"Value" may be defined as meaning something that creates benefits for firms, visitors, or any part of an area's tourism sector, and it can be added or destroyed at several points between production and consumption. The tourism "value system" is a network of multiple linkages among stakeholders who can influence each other and the multi dimensional environments within which they operate. Such influence can occur in different ways at various points during production, exchange, and consumption. Constant trade-offs in decision making are required if value is to be added rather than destroyed, but these trade-offs must facilitate the maintenance of multi dimensional sustainability rather than economic sustainability alone (Butler, 1999; Sharpley, 2000; Ryan, 2002).

In first-order fit, the trade-off is between activities that either promote or threaten multi dimensional sustainability (Fig. 7.1). Thus, the pertinent tourism stakeholders (e.g., producers, host communities, and support agencies) identify their local competitive advantage—the inherent place-based features of their local physical, social, and cultural environments—and seek to capitalize on that advantage to establish a market niche (Bramwell and Sharman, 1999). The tour operators whom they work with and the tourists whom they target should be sympathetic to the same principles (Carey *et al.*, 1997). The empowerment of local people should form part of a sustainable strategy. Activities that may reduce sustainability and empowerment should be avoided in making trade-offs. Second-order fit relates to promoting the basic sustainability strategy effectively through appropriate resource uses. Rural tourism resource use should be "complementary" to other sectors and activities, involve local resources and local ownership ("endogeneity"), and be pursued at an "appropriate scale." Third-order fit relates to optimizing the effort undertaken. Effective "networking," local "embeddedness," and extra-local "disembeddedness" are recommended as being instrumental in achieving the overall strategy of sustainability and serve as mechanisms to enhance the effectiveness of activities at stages one and two.

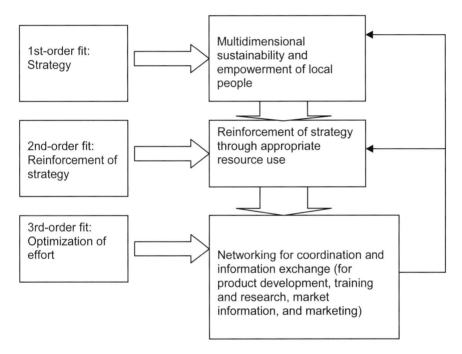

Fig. 7.1 Porter's orders of fit and effective integrated rural tourism promotion.

The Model in Operation

The model of IRT within a context of "strategic fit" was applied in the small town of Clifden (population 1,495 in 2006) and its environs in western Ireland, where seasonal tourism plays an important role in the local economy (Fig. 7.2). The research involved face-to-face interviews with six groups of stakeholders: tourists (T), tour operators (TO), owners/managers of businesses (OM), providers and controllers of environmental, financial, technical, and advisory resources for tourism (RC), institutions involved in tourism planning and management (I), and host community (HC) members (90 persons in total). Research was conducted in 2003 and Table 7.1 shows the types and numbers of stakeholders. All of the stakeholders were selected in purposive ways, following extensive background research, so as to best represent key features of integrated tourism. The business owners/managers, tourists, and host community members were selected to represent the range of types present in these stakeholder groups. The resource controllers, tour operators, and institutional representatives included the main organizations of these types pertinent to the local area and wider region. The interviews solicited views on the seven dimensions of integration and change in tourism impacts since 1992. Selected quotations from the interviews are used later in this chapter to highlight some of the key issues and are attributed by role and interviewee number. The business owners/managers, host community members, and tourists are specific to Clifden; the other interviewees, who had broader geographical remits, are numbered sequentially by group type.

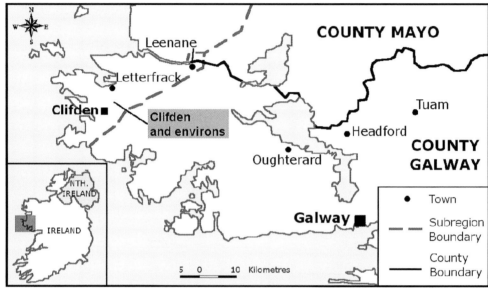

Fig. 7.2 Western Ireland study region.
© *Ordnance Survey Ireland/Government of Ireland. Copyright permit No. MP000709.*

Table 7.1 Stakeholders interviewed.

Stakeholder group	Breakdown of interviewees
Business owners/managers	15 owners/managers of: 1 adventure centre, 5 bed and breakfasts, 1 ferry company, 2 fishing/cruising companies, 1 golf club, 1 guided walking tour company, 2 heritage centres, 1 hostel, 1 hotel
Controllers of resources for tourism	11 local, regional, and national organizations and agencies involved in the provision of physical and environmental resources, finance, training, and advice for rural tourism and tourism entrepreneurs
Tourists	29 tourists interviewed in the town of Clifden and at Letterfrack National Park
Tours operators	6 local, regional, national, and international information providers and tour organizers for tourists
Institutions	17 local, regional, and national institutions involved in policy and planning for tourism and rural tourism
Host community members	12 long-term residents of Clifden and its environs, ranging in age and occupational backgrounds (8 males, 4 females)

First-Order Fit

All of the businesses, except one, operated throughout the year, but most reported a high concentration of trade in June, July, and August. Full-time employment was modest in a majority of cases. Only one hotel and a large interpretative centre employed full-time equivalents (FTEs) of more than 50 persons, comprising full-time, part-time, and seasonal employees (Table 7.2). The contribution of the smaller businesses to local employment was supplementary rather than being a sole source of income, and this was reflected in the relatively modest annual turnover reported. However, virtually all businesses reported increases in both turnover and profits since 1992. All entrepreneurs also reported contributing to a local multiplier effect through purchase of inputs and providing employment. Negative economic impacts, reported by many host community members and tourists, related in the main to inflated food prices in shops and restaurants, arising from opportunistic responses to increased tourist demand.

Table 7.2 Total employment (FTEs) and annual business turnover.

Number of FTEs	Number of businesses
<3	7
4–10	3
11–20	3
50–75	2
Annual turnover in euros	
<20,000	4
50,000–<100,000	3
101,000–<250,000	1
250,000–<500,000	1
500,000–<1,000,000	3
1,000,000–<5,000,000	2

Note: A part-time employee = 0.50 of a full-time employee; a seasonal employee = 0.25 of a full-time employee, except in one case where employment was of eight months' duration and a weighting of 0.75 was applied.

The natural scenic environment was perceived by all stakeholders to be the principal attraction for tourists, and was confirmed by the latter. A female tourist from the United States expressed more widely held expectations, "Beautiful scenery, good food, and hospitality" (Clifden, T #08). A number of tour operators referred to recent housing and infrastructure development as detracting from the green image of the area. Several of the resource controllers had specific remits and statutory powers relating to protecting landscape or water quality, which they highlighted as being essential elements in regional tourism. They identified threats to the quality of the environment arising from poor awareness and poor compliance with regulations among the public, such as seeking permission to build houses in areas of scenic landscape, allowing fertilizer runoff from land into waterways, damaging dune systems through the extraction of sand for construction purposes, and littering. A representative of the Marine Institute, with responsibilities for water-based tourism and leisure, suggested that "good environmental management practices need to be put in place" (RC #17). Business owners/managers and host community members recommended that the county council should implement existing legislation more stringently to control littering along roadsides.

There was universal criticism of a complex of some 100 self-catering cottages that were developed on the eastern fringe of Clifden in the early 1990s as a result of a tax incentive scheme that attracted external investment. A female representative of a local tourism promotional institution referred to these houses as "legoland," and said, "They give the wrong image" (I #9). Second-home development, however, more generally was blamed, in part, for the increased cost of housing locally, although this was a national phenomenon during the 1990s and the early 2000s. All local residents and other respondents, such as tourists, identified traffic congestion on the approach roads and in Clifden as being problematic in the high season of July and August. One local community member who was not involved in tourism said that Clifden "becomes like a city centre in summer" (Clifden, HC #16). Increased prices were identified by the overseas tour operators as posing a threat to the longer-term attraction of the area for tourists.

Socially, tourism was cited as being a valued local source of supplementary or seasonal employment. In the early 2000s, demand for labour exceeded supply, and foreign workers were attracted to work in both lower-skill occupations, such as catering and bar work, and in specialized occupations, such as instructors in recreational activity centres. Some negative social outcomes were identified. For example, a clergyman, attributed (correctly or incorrectly) alcohol abuse by teenagers to the over-involvement of parents in tourism businesses. He stated, "Parents don't have time for (their) children" (Clifden, HC #20). Other negative effects were associated with "stag" and "hen" parties, which were often accompanied by anti-social behaviour, especially on an offshore island where the ferry owner reported, "We have no 'garda' (policeman) and the pub does not close" (Clifden, OM #23). More positively, enhanced local service infrastructure, such as improved bus services to Galway City, was identified as an outcome of tourism growth. A local bank manager listed some of these services as, "an accountant, extra doctors, money raised for an X-ray machine in the local hospital, a dentist" (Clifden, HC #19).

Cultural benefits included the revitalization of traditional sports events and music and dance performances for tourists. A businessman said, "Irish nights in the Town Hall keep alive music and dance" (Clifden, HC #13), although a local school teacher expressed some reservations about a loss of authenticity in the type of music played by stating, "(The) music is all starting to sound the same" (Clifden, HC #17). Contact with tourists was cited by virtually all local residents as being a culturally enriching experience.

Evidence relating to empowerment, the second aspect of first-order fit, related to two dimensions in particular: the opportunities afforded for female entrepreneurship and the sense of "pride of place" attained from having tourists visit. A local female community member commented, "If people travelled this far, it shows us that there is something of value here" (Clifden, HC #21). Most of the smaller accommodation and recreational businesses were owned and operated by a husband-and-wife team, and the wife was usually responsible for the day-to-day operation of the business. The largest interpretative centre in the region was developed by a religious community of nuns who were actively involved in its operation. A need to engage farmers more fully in planning for tourism was identified by a number of host community members as a means to gain greater access to private land for walking and hiking. Most land in Ireland is privately owned, and many landowners are reluctant to afford access because of potential liability for injuries sustained by visitors.

From the views expressed, it appeared that since 1992, tourism had added value to the region economically, environmentally, and socio-culturally. However, value was also lost or was in danger of being lost arising from the negative impacts of tourism and an absence of a more holistic approach to promoting sustainability. Similarly, empowerment of some sectors of the resident population was countered by disempowerment of others.

Second-Order Fit

Second-order fit relates to the extent to which the methods of resource use serve to promote the underlying objectives of multidimensional sustainability. Complementarity was evident, particularly among the farm owners who established tourism businesses to provide an additional source of income, as in one case to help cover the expense of children's education. Some providers owned more than one tourism business that complemented another, for example, a hostel and a walking-tour business. A fisherman provided deep-sea angling experiences for tourists because, his wife said, "John loved fishing and wanted to do something that would let him fish" (Clifden, OM #25).

The landscape and scenery are key features in attracting tourists to the Clifden area and are also the contexts in which a range of recreational activities are pursued (e.g., walking, angling, golfing, horse riding, and sailing). Two large and several smaller interpretative centres focus on local culture and heritage. Local business ownership and control is the norm with the exception of a luxury hotel, which is owned by a group of shareholders, most of whom reside outside the region, and the much-criticized self-catering accommodation complex in which many of the cottages are externally owned. In the latter case, much of the profit from the enterprise was said to leak from the local economy.

A majority of the enterprises were small in scale, and even the larger businesses, with the exception of the self-catering development, were appropriate to their geographical setting. The types of business expansion reported pointed to a concern with retaining personal control over an enterprise and a reluctance to overexpand. Developments on farms, for example, involved providing ensuite bathroom facilities and recreational activities rather than any large-scale expansion. Referring to the importance of protecting the niche character of small-scale businesses, a Paris-based tour operator advised, "Retain small hotels which provide a quality personal service and welcome" (TO #9). Frequent references to traffic congestion on roads approaching Clifden, and in the town itself in July and August, pointed to excessive numbers of vehicles at this time of year. Overcrowding in shops and in pubs was also reported. More generally, however, the business owners/managers suggested that additional numbers of tourists could be accommodated if they could be spread over a longer season.

The structure of tourism in Clifden and the ways in which it has been pursued since the early 1990s have been conducive to adding value locally. The attraction of the town for local people and for visitors is, however, diminished during the high tourist season arising from traffic congestion and overcrowding in pubs and restaurants. These features threaten the retention of value and methods of control require attention.

Third-Order Fit

Third-order fit involves the presence of networks that are both embedded locally and effectively disembedded so as to maximize the benefits of tourism. Most business owners/managers were members of two tourism-related organizations: the Regional Tourism Authority, Ireland West Tourism (IWT), and a local tourism organization, Connemara Tourism. A representative of a local promotional group expressed reservations about the effectiveness of IWT in supporting small-scale providers by stating, "Rural tourism members are not happy...IWT promotes the big hotels" (I #9). Such dissatisfaction seemed to stem partly from the difficulty experienced by numerous individual small-scale providers in attempting to liaise with IWT, which is becoming increasingly dependent on larger businesses for financial support of its promotion and marketing activities. Several businesses were members of a specialist representative organization that gave access to national and international markets. Formal networking took place horizontally for promotion and marketing, and vertically to reach external markets and source funding, advice, and training. Less formal networking was also the norm between accommodation providers referring excess clientele. In the words of one bed-and-breakfast owner about another local business, "I get overflow from her business and I send her mine" (Clifden, OM #21).

Although the networks were closely embedded locally, many businesses also engaged in extra-local, vertical disembedded networking to reach their clientele, using the Internet for example, or by attending overseas trade fairs. While networking was said to be a feature of the area, not all businesses were involved, and the owner of a large interpretative centre said, "It is difficult to get people to cooperate to do anything" (Clifden, OM #28). More generally, a representative of a local tourism promotional group said that tourism policy was too fragmented and that "everything should be under one government group" (I #9). It appeared that some of the larger businesses pursued independent marketing strategies and did not need to engage in extensive local networking. A provider of training for the tourism sector suggested that farmers "could be better integrated with tourism" (RC #16).

The strength of local networking, especially informal networking between businesses, was instrumental in adding value since 1992, when the number of tourists visiting the Clifden area increased. It appeared, however, that networking between large and smaller local businesses and with farmers was not fully developed and required attention.

Conclusion

Tourism is assigned a role of some importance in rural development in many countries as a method of compensating for decline in traditional sectors, utilizing land, capital, and human resources, retaining population and social structures, and reducing dependence on state support. Rural tourism is, however, recognized as being characterized by structural weaknesses. In particular, excessive fragmentation has been associated with the dominant small-scale business structure and with promotional activities. A need for greater integration between providers and between providers and promotional agencies has been identified, but few studies provide methods for attaining these aims. This chapter discussed a model of IRT devised by Oliver and Jenkins (2003) within a framework of "strategic fit" as a method of adding value in a holistic way. The model was applied in the context of a small-town location in western Ireland, where tourism infrastructure and numbers have expanded significantly since the early 1990s. The model permitted the extent to which value had been added or taken away to be assessed in a qualitative way, based on the views expressed by key stakeholders.

There was broad support for multidimensional sustainability as a strategic objective, although economic objectives rather than holistic concerns probably underpinned tourism development in the study area initially. Many stakeholders were critically aware of local tourism in their assessments, valuing its economic contributions but conscious of a need to control some of tourism's environmental, social, and cultural impacts. Equally, there was awareness of a need to protect the quality of the physical environment as a resource for tourism and to more stringently implement regulatory provisions toward that end. Tourism was empowering in providing entrepreneurial opportunities (for women who had limited other employment opportunities available locally) and provided a sense of "pride of place" more generally. Disempowerment was, however, reported among landowners arising from increasing pressure to permit access to their land for walking.

In general, the scale of tourist infrastructure and activities was appropriate to the location. Local ownership dominated, and several enterprises reflected complementarity between tourism and agriculture or fishing. Weaknesses were, however, evident, notably a development of self-catering holiday cottages, which was visually intrusive and was said to have added limited value locally. A need for better complementarity between farming and tourism was identified as being necessary in order to permit greater value to be gained from hiking as a tourist activity. Extensive networking took place both horizontally and vertically, particularly with reference to the promotion of the area and its products to external tourists. Frustration was expressed, however, about the absence of a rural tourism policy, which had the effect of marginalizing small-scale providers from regional and national promotional efforts. While embedded networking took place locally associated with the referral of clients, a series of different networks existed and greater coordination was recommended in order to capitalize on adding value.

The results suggest that the basic model of IRT, as operationalized with reference to strategic fit, is conducive to promoting multidimensional sustainability in tourism and adding value locally by capitalizing on the comparative advantages of local places. As such, the IRT model provides one possible framework within which tourism might be pursued as part of the "new rural economies."

Acknowledgement

The empirical research for this chapter was conducted as part of an EU-funded five-country research project known as Supporting and Promoting Integrated Tourism in Europe's Lagging Rural Regions (SPRITE) CT 2000-01211. Colleague Professor Desmond Gillmor at Trinity College, Dublin, and researcher Róisín Kelly are acknowledged gratefully.

References

Andriotis, K. (2002) Scale of hospitality firms and local economic development: Evidence from Crete. *Tourism Management* 23(4), 333–341.

Aronsson, L. (2000) *The Development of Sustainable Tourism*. Continuum, London.

Bachleitner, R., and Zins, A. (1999) Cultural tourism in rural communities: The residents' perspective. *Journal of Business Research* 44(3), 199–209.

Blackstock, K. (2005) A critical look at community based tourism. *Community Development Journal* 40(1), 39–49.

Bramwell, B., and Lane, B. (2000) Collaboration and partnerships in tourism planning. In: Bramwell, B., and Lane, B. (eds.) *Tourism Collaboration and Partnerships: Politics, Practice and Sustainability*. Channel View, Clevedon, UK, 1–19.

Bramwell, B., and Sharman, A. (1999) Collaboration in local tourism policymaking. *Annals of Tourism Research* 26(2), 392–415.

Briassoulis, H. (2002) Sustainable tourism and the question of the commons. *Annals of Tourism Research* 29(4), 1065–1085.

Butler, R. (1999) Sustainable tourism: A state-of-the-art review. *Tourism Geographies* 1(1), 7–25.

Butler, R., and Hall, C. (1998) Image and reimaging of rural areas. In: Butler, R., Hall, C., and Jenkins, J. (eds.) *Tourism and Recreation in Rural Areas*. Wiley, Chichester, UK, 115-122.

Butler, R., Hall, C., and Jenkins, J., eds. (1998) *Tourism and Recreation in Rural Areas*. Wiley, Chichester, UK.

Carey, S., Gountas, Y., and Gilbert, D. (1997) Tour operators and destination sustainability. *Tourism Management* 18(7), 425–431.

Cawley, M., and Gillmor, D. (2008) Integrated rural tourism: Concepts and practice. *Annals of Tourism Research* 35(2), 316–337.

Central Statistics Office (2007) *Census 2006, Volume 1–Population Classified by Area*. Government Publications, Dublin.

Clark, G., and Chabrel, M. (2007) Measuring integrated rural tourism. *Tourism Geographies* 9(4), 371–386.

Deegan, J., and Dineen, D. (2000) Market services and tourism. In: O'Hagan, J. (ed.) *The Economy of Ireland: Policy and Performance of a European Region*, 8th ed. Gill and Macmillan, Dublin, 286–307.

Deegan, J., and Moloney, R. (2005) *Understanding the Economic Contribution of Tourism to Economic Development: The Case of Ireland West*. Ireland West Tourism, Galway.

Fáilte Ireland. (2006) *Regions–West 2005*. Author, Dublin.

_____. (2008) Top 20 fee-charging attractions, www.failteireland.ie/getdoc/80d0f1fd-91e2-4006-bb8e-d2113bcce66a/top-20-fee-charging-attractions-2006.aspx (accessed 12 June 2008).

Fyall, A., and Garrod, B. (2005) *Tourism Marketing: A Collaborative Approach*. Channel View, Clevedon, UK.

Garrod, B., Wornell, R., and Youell, R. (2006) Re-conceptualizing rural resources as countryside capital: The case of rural tourism. *Journal of Rural Studies* 22(1), 117–128.

Getz, D., and Carlsen, J. (2005) Family business in tourism: State of the art. *Annals of Tourism Research* 32(1), 237–258.

Government of Ireland. (2003) Department of Arts, Sport and Tourism (DAST). *New Horizons for Irish Tourism*. DAST, Dublin.

Hall, D., Kirkpatrick, M., and Mitchell, M., eds. (2005) *Rural Tourism and Sustainable Business*. Channel View, Clevedon, UK.

Hall, D., Roberts, L., and Mitchell, M., eds. (2003) *New Directions in Rural Tourism*. Ashgate, Aldershot, UK.

Halseth, G. (2008) Understanding and transforming a staples economy: The case of place-based development in northern BC, Canada. Paper presented at Space to Place: The Next Rural Economies Workshop, Prince George, BC.

Hardy, A., Beeton, S., and Pearson, L. (2002) Sustainable tourism: An overview of the concept and its position in relation to conceptualizations of tourism. *Journal of Sustainable Tourism* 10(6), 475–496.

Hohl, A., and Tisdell, C. (1995) Peripheral tourism: Development and management. *Annals of Tourism Research* 22(3), 517–534.

Jenkins, T. (2000) Putting postmodernity into practice: Endogenous development and the role of traditional cultures in the rural development of marginal regions. *Ecological Economics* 34(3), 301–314.

Kalantaridis, C., and Bifka, Z. (2006) Local embeddedness and rural entrepreneurship: Case-study evidence from Cumbria, England. *Environment and Planning A* 38(8), 1561–1579.

Long, P., and Lane, B. (2000) Rural tourism development. In: Gartner, W., and Lime, D. (eds.) *Trends in Outdoor Recreation, Leisure, and Tourism*. CABI Publishing, Wallingford, UK, 299–308.

Millward Brown. (2007) *Visitor Attitudes Survey 2006*. Prepared for Fáilte Ireland, Dublin.

Northcote, J., and Macbeth, J. (2006) Conceptualizing yield: Sustainable tourism management. *Annals of Tourism Research* 33(1), 199–220.

O'Leary, S., and Deegan, J. (2003) People, pace, place: Qualitative and quantitative images of Ireland as a tourism destination in France. *Journal of Vacation Marketing* 9(3), 213–226.

Oliver, T., and Jenkins, T. (2003) Sustaining rural landscapes: The role of integrated tourism. *Landscape Research* 28(3), 293–307.

Organization for Economic Co-operation and Development. (1995) *Niche Markets as a Rural Development Strategy*. Author, Paris.

Pigram, J. (1994) Alternative tourism: Tourism and sustainable resource management. In: Smith, V., and Eadington, W. (eds.) *Tourism Alternatives*. Wiley, Chichester, 76–87.

_____. (2000) Tourism and sustainability: A positive trend. In: Gartner, W., and Lime, D. (eds.) *Trends in Outdoor Recreation, Leisure, and Tourism*. CABI Publishing, Wallingford, UK, 373–382.

Porter, M. (1990) *The Competitive Advantage of Nations*, 1st edn. Macmillan, London.

_____. (1996) What is strategy? *Harvard Business Review* 74(6), 61–78.

_____. (1998) *The Competitive Advantage of Nations*, 2nd edn. Macmillan, London.

Ryan, C. (2002) Equity, management, power sharing and sustainability: Issues of the "new tourism." *Tourism Management* 23(1), 17–26.

Saarinen, J. (2006) Traditions of sustainability in tourism studies. *Annals of Tourism Research* 33(4), 1121–1140.

Sharpley, R. (2000) Tourism and sustainable development: Exploring the theoretical divide. *Journal of Sustainable Tourism* 8(1), 1–19.

Sofield, T. (2003) *Empowerment for Sustainable Tourism Development*. Pergamon, London.

van der Ploeg, J. (2006) Agricultural production in crisis. In: Cloke, P., Marsden, T., and Mooney, P. (eds.) *Handbook of Rural Studies*. Sage, London, 258–277.

Vernon, J., Essex, S., Pinder, D., and Curry, K. (2005) Collaborative policymaking: Local sustainable projects. *Annals of Tourism Research* 32(2), 325–345.

Walford, N. (2003) Productivism is allegedly dead, long live productivism: Evidence of continued productivist attitudes and decision-making in South-East England. *Journal of Rural Studies* 19(4), 491–502.

Wanhill, S. (2000) Small and medium tourism enterprises. *Annals of Tourism Research* 27(1), 132–147.

Wilson, G. (2001) From productivism to post-productivism…and back again? Exploring the (un)changed natural and mental landscapes of European agriculture. *Transactions of the Institute of British Geographers, New Series* 26(1), 77–102.

World Commission on Environment and Development (1987) *Our Common Future*. Oxford University Press, Oxford.

Chapter 8

Value-added Agricultural Products and Entertainment in Michigan's Fruit Belt

Deborah Che

The global restructuring of agriculture has particularly affected relatively small, higher-cost domestic producers in advanced industrialized countries. Specialized agricultural regions such as Michigan's Fruit Belt are not immune from this restructuring. While the quality of fruit produced in this region has long been recognized by wholesale buyers, efforts to target retail customers through place-based, value-added agricultural products and entertainment ("agritainment" or "agritourism") can help save small to medium-sized producers and this valuable agricultural land influenced by Lake Michigan. In this chapter I will detail place-based strategies, including production and branding of regional, niche, and heritage foods and regional wines; development of agritourism destinations; and linking sites via tourist trails or routes. I will also discuss recent private- and public-sector developments for fostering such place-based strategies, which may help sustain one of the most important fruit belts in the United States.

Rural Restructuring and the Impact on Michigan's Fruit Belt

Commodity producers in advanced industrialized countries have felt the impact of physical and human limits to production, cost-price squeezes, global competition, and the increased mobility of capital and labour. However, the resource management regimes, systems of governance, and rural development policies implemented in response to the global restructuring of agriculture are different on opposite sides of the Atlantic. In the United Kingdom, the post-World War II, Fordist, agro-industrial dynamic emphasized industrialized domestic food production through the government's top-down technological transfer, subsidies, and preferential policies toward agriculture (Cloke and Goodwin, 1992). Faced with the global restructuring of agriculture and with the environmental and amenity demands for the countryside, the U.K. state increasingly shifted to a system of localized rural service provision to encourage bottom-up entrepreneurship based on regional resources and consumption (e.g., recreation and residential development) (Lowe *et al.*, 1993; Marsden *et al.*, 1993; Goodwin, 1998; Marsden, 2000).

While the agricultural countryside and government policies in the United Kingdom may be considered post-productivist, their North American equivalents are largely productivist and Fordist in nature. Mass, industrial agricultural production, made possible with inputs of machinery, fertilizers, pesticides, hybrid seeds, uniformly bred livestock, and automated feed systems, continues in North America (Troughton, 2005). Cattle production in the United States and Canada, in which large-scale feedlots concentrate thousands of animals and finish them on feed to yield standardized slaughter animals destined for a carcass disassembly line, exemplifies the dominant Fordist model (MacLachlan, 2005). The US government has heavily supported this agro-industrial production process through research funding and government production subsidies/price-support payments targeted at a select group of large producers of major commodity crops (i.e., corn, soybeans, wheat, cotton, sugar, rice) (Troughton, 2005). In the United States, these large producers receive much of the agricultural funding.

This neo-Fordist, intensive agriculture favours large producers of subsidized crops. Mid-sized farms that are unable to achieve economies of scale and/or that produce fruits and vegetables ineligible for US price supports are declining rapidly. According to US Department of Agriculture (USDA) figures, the number of farms with annual sales of more than \$500,000 has increased 23% from 1997 to 2002, while the number of mid-sized farms with sales of \$50,000 to \$500,000 has declined by nearly 65,000, or 14%, in the same period (Barber, 2005). Small farms (5 to 10 acres[1]) have persisted, given their niche production, direct selling, and alternative off-farm income sources (Hamm, 2003). However, mid-sized farms that are too large to sell all their diversified produce through farm and farmers' markets and/or that try to specialize in one commodity and keep up with more efficient large farms (500+ acres) are being squeezed out.

The dilemma facing mid-sized fruit and vegetable farms is of particular concern in Michigan, which depends on specialty crops and where farms average 215 acres (Moses, 1999). While Michigan produces 124 agricultural commodities—more than any state except California—50% of the state's crops do not qualify for federal farm support (Hoogterp, 2002). Michigan ranks first in the world for tart cherry production, sixth in the world for sweet cherries, and fourth in the United States for peaches (*Michigan History*, 2006). In addition to being unable to match the lower-cost production of large farms farther west, Michigan farms also cannot match the output of low-cost producers overseas. With its similar growing seasons and crops, high acreage and output, cheap labour, and low production cost, China has proved to be a major competitor to the United States in many agricultural sectors, and Michigan's small-scale apple producers have felt its impact. In 2000, China exported 161,954 t of concentrated apple juice, valued at \$200 million, to North America and Europe. This figure increased to 227,936 t, or about 35% of the world's total, in 2001 (Zhang *et al.*, 2004). As the Chinese export apple juice concentrate to US wholesalers, states such as Washington and Oregon face increasing pressure to move lower-grade fruit into other markets, thus undercutting Michigan "table fruit" in US Midwest markets (Veeck *et al.*, 2006). US apple producers may soon face additional competition as China, the world's largest apple producer, undergoes a transition from yield to efficiency and quality by restructuring cultivars, concentrating apple plantings to the best-adapted areas, and extending intensive and organic growing practices. Chinese fresh apple exports will thus increase to Asian markets that US producers now supply and may also enter the US market in the future.

At the same time Michigan farmers face competition from low-cost global suppliers of agricultural commodities, demand for farmland for urban residential and commercial uses is increasing. On average, Michigan's land development occurs eight times faster than its population growth. From 1970 to 2000, the number of households in Michigan grew by 43%, while its population grew only 12%. Between 1982 and 1997, farmland acreage in Michigan shrank by almost 1.5 million acres or 13.3%, largely consumed by an increasingly suburban and exurban population (Michigan Land Use Leadership Council, 2003). Farms converted for suburban tracts are lost forever for agricultural production.

Agricultural restructuring is of particular concern in western Michigan's Fruit Belt, one of the most important fruit-growing regions in the United States (Fig. 8.1). The "lake effect"—created by the prevailing westerly winds; the warming effect of Lake Michigan; the low variation between day and night temperatures; the low incidence of frost, stagnant humidity, or fog; and the late spring—produces ideal conditions for specialty fruit production as far as 32.2 km inland, protecting fruit trees and vines from frost in winter and cooling them in summer (Wineman International, 1999). The lake's influence extends the January isotherms of −9.4°C and −6.67°C over 643.7 km northward (Whitbeck, 1920), while deep snows associated with downwind lake-effect sites keep the soil from freezing most years, thus preventing root damage. In summer, temperatures over 29.4°C are rare, and the mild summer days with uniform rains favour fruit production along Michigan's west coast. The area's fruit has long been shipped to Chicago via the Benton Harbor Fruit Market, which is still the world's largest cash-to-grower fruit market (Armstrong, 2006). Western Michigan remains a centre of fruit production and is an agritourism destination for those seeking local foods (Che, 2006). In 2003, Michigan's Fruit Belt produced 81.6 million kg of cherries and 6.6 million kg of peaches (*Michigan History*, 2006). Fifteen hundred acres in the state are devoted to wine grapes. Primarily European vinifera are grown within 40.2 km of Lake Michigan.

Fig. 8.1 Approximate extent of Michigan's Fruit Belt (*Michigan History*, 2006).

While the Fruit Belt's "soils, climate, moisture, and topography" are "unique and irreplaceable" according to Peter Ter Louw, director of the Southwest Michigan Land Conservancy (Ast, 2006, p. 30), cash-strapped growers facing global competition, rising costs, and static or declining returns have sold farmland for residential development as a way to get out of debt and/or retire (Table 8.1). From 1994 to 2004, the amount of land devoted to fruit farming in southwestern Michigan's Berrien, Cass, and Van Buren counties declined from 51,800 to 44,415 acres. The population of Berrien County's Royalton Township, south of the city of St. Joseph, increased 24% from 1990 to 2000, compared to an increase of less than 1% for Berrien County as a whole. The next 20 years will be critical for this fruit-growing region. Since 1969, the number of farms in the area has declined by 60%. Although many of the remaining farms are mid-sized by US standards, scale economies do exist for some specialized fruit farming. A number of family farmers who sell at the Benton Harbor wholesale market are just big enough to stay in business. However, once production falls below a certain volume, the loss of scale economies and market share that make growing profitable may increase pressure on farmers to sell land (Ast, 2006). Place-based strategies, such as focusing on value-added agricultural products and agritourism, can help address concerns with farm income and farmland loss in Michigan's Fruit Belt.

Table 8.1 Agricultural production in Michigan's Fruit Belt counties.

	1987	1992	1997	2002	% Change 1987-2002
Farms	12,081	10,925	10,423	11,721	−3.0%
Land in farms (acres)	1,884,147	1,825,271	1,772,981	1,793,373	−4.8%
Average size of farms (acres)	167	177	174	151	−9.6%
Orchards	2,674	2,410	1,945	1,627	−39.2%
Land in orchards (acres)	143,055	144,492	125,977	105,444	−26.3%

Source: US Department of Agriculture, National Agricultural Statistics Service, 1992, 1999, 2004.
Note: Fruit Belt counties include Charlevoix, Antrim, Grand Traverse, Leelanau, Benzie, Manistee, Mason, Oceana, Newaygo, Muskegon, Ottawa, Kent, Allegan, Van Buren, Kalamazoo, and Berrien.

Place-Based Strategies: Value-Added Agricultural Products and Agritourism in Michigan's Fruit Belt

Researchers in the geography and food marketing departments of Western Michigan University (WMU) conducted research on place-based agritourism development and marketing strategies that could enhance and diversify farm incomes. This research was part of a project funded by the USDA and administered by the Michigan Department of Agriculture (MDA) that also involved convening focus groups of agritourism operators representing the Fruit Belt's diversity of agricultural products, producer locations, customer bases, marketing techniques, and residential and commercial pressures facing farmers. A southwestern Michigan group included tree fruit and vegetable producers. Half of their customers were second-home/cottage owners as well as day visitors from South Bend, Indiana, and Chicago, Illinois. The northern Traverse City-area focus group contained mainly producers of tree fruit (i.e., cherries, other stone fruit, apples), who served second-home owners and longer-distance tourists from Chicago and the Detroit metro area. In a separate, follow-up project, researchers interviewed individuals in charge of marketing activities at Southwest Michigan Wine Trail wineries (i.e., marketing directors and members of the marketing departments, winery owners). The focus groups, interviews, and secondary documentary/archival material highlight how Fruit Belt agricultural businesses' production and marketing of regional, niche, and heritage foods and regional wines; development of agritourism destinations; and linking sites via tourist trails or routes have helped them deal with agricultural restructuring.

Producing and Marketing Regional, Niche, and Heritage Foods and Regional Wines

Michigan's aptly named Fruit Belt is famous for its ripe, ready-to-eat produce. Benton Harbor's famed wholesale market supplies local growers' roadside stands and fruit and vegetable markets throughout northern Ohio and southern Michigan. Such businesses attract vacationers to Lake Michigan (Maynard, 2007). The appeal of the juicy, ripe fruit also appeals to famed restaurateurs in Chicago. Rick Bayless, an award-winning chef-restaurateur, author of the cookbook *Mexican Everyday*, and television personality, uses fruit from Berrien County because it "is locally grown, picked when it is ripe and delivered immediately." Since most varieties of fruit available in grocery stores are picked when they are immature and shipped long distances, Bayless feels many people today "just aren't familiar with the flavor of ripe fruit" (Phillips, 2006, p. 22). They are thus in for a treat at Bayless's restaurants, Frontera Grill and Topolobampo. During the fruit harvest season, Bayless buys hundreds of pounds of fruit a week from Klug Farms for use in summer menus and for use throughout the year in desserts, ices, and sorbets or as a garnish (Phillips, 2006).

Fruit Belt produce literally harks back to a past agricultural heritage. Tree-Mendus Fruit in southwest Michigan is well known for its 200 heritage apple varieties. It supplies one variety, Calville Blanc d'Hiver, a French dessert apple, to French restaurants in Chicago. Tree-Mendus's website claims that its heritage food offerings allow consumers to "sample the simple pleasures of a wholesome past, bursting with incomparable uniqueness and flavor" (Tree-Mendus Fruit, 2008).

In addition to providing distinctive produce for Chicago restaurants, Fruit Belt producers fill an important role by supplying items to develop a regional Fruit Belt food culture. Northwest Michigan is increasingly a culinary tourism destination, described by the *New York Times* as "Michigan's flavorful vacationland," which offers local sweet and tart cherries; value-added foods such as preserves, ice creams, cheese, jams, wine and cider products, and spirits; and innovative regional cuisine (Apple, 2003). One regional winery operator, who produces 32 kinds of wines, buys different fruits from his grower, focusing on "what will make the best product in the world" (Focus group participant).

Local produce is a building block of innovative regional cuisine in the Fruit Belt. Ted Cizma, executive chef of Grand Traverse Resort's fine-dining restaurant Aerie, has long focused on regionalism and seasonality in his cooking. At Aerie, he highlights Michigan foods (e.g., specialty baby vegetables from nearby Werp Farms) and wines to give diners a local experience. The wine list includes at least one red and one white wine from every northern Michigan winery as well as wines from the southwest part of the state. According to Cizma, "Aerie does regionally inspired American food...It's Midwestern sensibility, stylish and aesthetically pleasing. It's not fusion cuisine, not New York; this is northern Michigan" (Silfven, 2007a).

In the southwestern part of the Fruit Belt, more could be done to connect local restaurants and wineries. As one southwestern winery owner said, "I always see on their menus, it says 'fresh Michigan-grown produce,' but the Michigan wines are in the back of the list" (Interview 7). To further develop southwest Michigan's regional cuisine, wineries should focus on this vertical linkage because pairing wine and regional food can boost wine sales and help establish a region's culinary reputation (Telfer, 2000; Hall *et al.*, 2004).

While producing regional foods and cuisine is an important first step, branding and marketing Michigan, the Fruit Belt, and the various viticultural regions can also raise awareness of them as culinary tourism destinations. Given substitutability, which presents one vacation spot as no different than many others, place branding has been used to signify quality, provide identity, and differentiate products from competitors (Morgan *et al.*, 2002). Unique regional foods can help provide a brand identity for their places of origin and convey a sense of place. Recognizing this, states and provinces have used their distinctive foods in destination branding. For instance, Louisiana has used its Cajun cuisine, along with its scenery, architecture, history, culture, and music, to emphasize the unique experience the state offers tourists (Slater, 2002). Likewise, Canadian geographical regions (i.e., Newfoundland, the Maritimes, Quebec, Ontario, the Prairie Provinces, British Columbia, and the North) have highlighted the diversity of Canadian culinary traditions influenced by immigrants, indigenous peoples, and regional products as a way to promote specific regions, and the nation as a whole, as culinary tourism destinations (Hashimoto and Telfer, 2006).

While Michigan, like Canada, is best known for its outdoors, it can use branding to connect and promote its unique natural bounty and agricultural specialties through its Great Lakes, Great Times tourism logo. In a survey for Travel Michigan, the state tourism office, researchers found that Michigan's natural resources—its scenery; nature attractions; and the lakes, shoreline, and other water-related resources—garnered the most frequent positive responses (Spotts *et al.*, 1998). Agritourism is a natural fit with the state's existing tourism assets and the Great Lakes, Great Times brand, given its ties to the natural resources, agricultural scenery, and "lake effect" that make particular types of food production possible.

To promote Michigan-made (grown or processed) agricultural items, the MDA has developed the Select Michigan branding campaign with banners, posters, and shelf tabs in grocery stores and farm markets, and roadside billboards touting Michigan products with a Great Lakes, Great Taste message (*Detroit News*, 1999). The campaign is also explicitly linked to tourism promotion in combination with another Michigan agricultural product campaign, Take Home a Taste of Michigan, which highlights Michigan's specialty food products by listing retailers in the state's major travel destinations who stock the products and by organizing promotional activities, like tastings during festivals and parades, that attract both tourists and local residents. The tourism–agriculture link is especially appropriate for Fruit Belt resort towns on peninsulas north of Traverse City (Che, 2006).

Geographically-based wine tourism, which is a subset of agritourism, can further the reputation of Michigan agriculture, spur economic development, and preserve farmland. Michigan has four American Viticultural Areas, which are grape-growing regions distinguishable by geographic features and growing conditions such as climate, soil, and elevation (Professional Friends of Wine, 2008): Leelanau Peninsula and Old Mission Peninsula in northwest Lower Michigan; Lake Michigan Shore and Fennville in the southwest. In an interview, an individual from one southwest Michigan winery described working with other wineries to focus on the Lake Michigan Shore growing region. The individual said, "[It] puts us on a map of a global scale. Instead of competing against each other, we market together just to promote our region" (Interview 6). Such viticultural regions can help differentiate and brand places and agricultural products.

Development of Agritourism Destinations

For the average American, who has little or no contact with farms, food production, or animal husbandry, the small, independent farm is becoming a popular leisure destination (Nicksin, 1999). People wish to stay on or visit a farm, learn where food comes from, come in contact with the soil, and see live animals. As a result, agritourism—the act of visiting a working farm or any agricultural, horticultural, or agribusiness operation for the purpose of enjoyment, education, or active involvement in the activities of the farm or operation (Lobo, 2001)—is increasing in popularity, and several demographic trends favour future growth of this sector of the tourism industry. For example, the aging of America is a positive development as seniors, with their disposable income and leisure time, are a key market. Agritourism, which involves hands-on, educational activities for children and adults, also benefits from the growing trend of multigenerational travel (Rosenberg, 2000), and it attracts the increasingly urban and suburban boomer and senior populations who hold nostalgic views of farms. According to Jane Eckert, a sixth-generation farm proprietor outside St. Louis, agritourism appeals to urbanites who want to "reconnect with the land and have an opportunity to experience what, for them, is a lost world" (*Fruit Growers News*, 2004, p. 32). Finally, a shift in US domestic travel patterns from traditional two-week vacations to long-weekend trips also favours agritourist operations.

In order to sustain income and save the farm, some Fruit Belt agricultural operators have turned their farms into agritourism destinations, seeking to meet the increasing demand for experiential tourism, which centres on venues and activities that allow tourists to be active participants in their travel experiences. Experiential tourism relies on natural, cultural, and historical resources and helps people learn about their environment and themselves (Fermata Inc., 2005). A Harbor Springs, Michigan, farm operator noted his experiential tourism offerings: "We have a working farm where people can come out and see animals, chickens, sheep, goats, cows... What gets them out there is actually experiencing farm, but they also come out for the vegetables" (Focus group participant). This northern Michigan farmer uses school group visits to the farm to educate children about food production and to generate word-of-mouth reviews that fuel future adult expenditures. Customers who visit an actual farm gain a better understanding of agriculture from encounters with farm animals, connection with the land, and the experience of picking apples off a tree.

Fruit Belt farms also target the growing number of baby boomers and seniors travelling with children and grandchildren who are looking for safe, intergenerational learning and bonding experiences. Farms can provide the setting to create shared family memories, as an Ellsworth family farm operator noted:

> This whole market is not just a store. This is really an experience. And we're doing things, so that dad or grandpa and the kids—we put the Noah's Ark in last year—they have something to do while the women are shopping... We're expanding a memory lane back here. Old farm equipment the men just absolutely love... We're turning this area right in here...is Old Fashion General Store, we have a display of antiques.

Possibly for something to educate and to give them a fun time when they're here. That's probably the most widely used comment. This is a fun place to come to. (Focus group participant)

Linking Sites via Tourist Trails or Routes

Trails and routes connecting businesses and attractions serving tourists can help create a destination. Of all rural tourism routes, perhaps wine routes have been the best developed. Sign-posted, planned wine routes can yield synergistic effects. Itineraries through a well-defined area (region, province, viticultural area) that link wineries, agritourist farms, restaurants, and other retail sites foster visitors' discovery of the region's wine product and associated activities (Brunori and Rossi, 2000). Collaboration between producers and operators can promote a region's development as a wine tourism destination, which in turn generates additional on-site wine and related merchandise sales (Telfer, 2001).

To further wine tourism development and marketing, Michigan's Fruit Belt now has wine routes focused on its four viticultural areas. Along the Southwest Michigan Wine Trail, wineries have formed strong horizontal relationships, which include joint advertising, promotion, and production. They have also built vertical relationships with tour operators, lodging businesses, and restaurants that promote individual wineries as well as the entire wine region. There is considerable potential for growth through an increased presence in restaurants and in packaging tours with accommodations. Adding specialized wine tours, wine festivals, geographical target markets, and a focus on wine education on-site and at educational institutions throughout the region could expand wine tourism and sales (Wargenau and Che, 2006).

Following the success of the winery trails, the MDA awarded Casco and Ganges townships a $50,000 grant to develop an agricultural tourism trail along the Blue Star and Michigan 89 Highways. This trail would promote farmers' markets, orchards, and agritourism-based businesses as well as art dealers in an effort to increase sales of local handicrafts and produce. If this agricultural tourism trail is successful in increasing sales at local businesses, it may serve as a pilot project for other places across the state (Burkert, 2006).

The Next Rural Economy: Public- and Private-Sector Prescriptions for the Fruit Belt

Local heritage foods and place promotion highlighting local distinctiveness have been incorporated into rural development initiatives, although what constitutes the heritage of a place is subject to debate and alternative narratives (Storey, 2008). Recent private- and public-sector developments fostering place-based strategies—including mixed agricultural and residential development, new state and agritourism promotion schemes, and Agriculture in the Middle initiatives to support mid-sized farms—may help sustain one of the most important fruit belts in the United States.

Mixed Agricultural and Residential Development

While there have been substantial losses of Fruit Belt farmland to residential development, new forms of private-sector housing developments may facilitate continued agricultural production, albeit at a smaller scale. Nationwide there has been a rise in planned communities that are zoned for mixed residential and agricultural or viticultural use. In these alternatives to golf course communities, property owners can operate wine-related businesses from their homes. Such properties are not cheap, according to Lloyd Mahaffey, a developer and vintner in Eagle, Idaho. Because vineyards have a certain cachet, Mahaffey says developers can charge a premium of 20% to 25% on the price of land to be used for them (DeParle, 2007).

Such mini-farm or vineyard developments are planned in the Fruit Belt. A Chicago partnership has joined with a longtime Michigan fruit farmer to propose a new housing complex that includes vineyards and a management team caring for them. Using the Douglas Valley Organic Vineyard Community, a 640-acre historic organic fruit farm in Manistee, the developers plan to create an organic, agricultural-based community that will keep 70% of the land in agriculture. Douglas Valley would have a limited number of five- to ten-acre "estate farms" with a vineyard and a house of prairie or farm-style design. The property currently has 120 acres of apple and cherry trees. Ten acres of wine grapes, or 2,000 vines each of Chardonnay, Riesling, Pinot Grigio, and Pinot Noir, have been planted (Silfven, 2007b). While such vineyard developments would not increase production on larger farms for the wholesale or retail market, they would preserve some farmland and open space.

Tourism and Agritourism Promotion

Other initiatives have centred on tourism promotion to the Fruit Belt as well as to Michigan as a whole. Travel Michigan, the state's tourism agency, has developed the Pure Michigan advertising program, which highlights Michigan's natural resources, recreational activities, and cultural attractions via the Michigan.org website, public relations programs, billboards, and television and radio ads narrated by actor and Michigan native Tim Allen (*Grand Rapids Press*, 2008). Given the decline in Michigan's manufacturing and payroll jobs, the campaign is targeting out-of-state visitors from Chicago, Illinois; Milwaukee, Wisconsin; Cincinnati and Cleveland, Ohio; southern Ontario; and Indiana, all within a relatively short drive of Michigan.

The Pure Michigan campaign began in 2006 with a $15 million, two-year state jobs grant. However, the state legislature has recognized the importance of the $18.8-billion-a-year tourism industry and allocated $10 million for 2008 tourism promotion. According to economist Scott Watkins, a consultant with Anderson Economic Group in East Lansing, for each dollar spent on tourism, two dollars are generated for the state treasury. Consumers used the Pure Michigan website an average of 34,951 times a day in 2007, making it the most popular state tourism website in America, according to Hitwise, an online measurement company. The Travel Industry Association of America has also named Pure Michigan the best state tourism campaign (Youssef, 2008). The campaign can raise awareness and bring more people to the state, to the Fruit Belt, and to agritourism and value-added agriculture operations, as it includes information on wineries, the coast, etc.

To promote agritourism specifically, including destinations in the Fruit Belt, industry members established the Michigan Farm Marketing and Agri-Tourism Association (MI-FMAT). MI-FMAT fosters collaboration among individual farm market and agritourism business owners and operators (Jackson, 2006) and represents their views on regulatory issues, such as zoning and site inspections, at the local, regional, and national levels. The association also creates promotional and educational programs to increase visitation (Long, 2006). By supporting agritourism, MI-FMAT strengthens a form of agriculture that educates consumers and helps communities thrive (Jackson, 2006).

Agriculture of the Middle Initiatives

In response to the problems of mid-sized farms, mentioned at the beginning of this chapter, the national Agriculture of the Middle initiative was started to save these farms and the benefits they produce in the form of land stewardship and community social capital. Supported by the USDA's Rural Development/Cooperative Services program, the initiative, which is in the development phase, has three strategic dimensions: (1) create business networks or "value chains" that link mid-sized farms and ranches with food system partners to meet a growing demand for differentiated, high-quality food products; (2) implement public policy changes, both short-term changes that directly affect middle-market development, and longer-term, systemic changes that "equalize the economic playing field" for such farms and ranches; and (3) provide support for the first two dimensions in the form of research and education at the regional and national levels (Agriculture of the Middle, 2005). As Bryant (2008) noted, central government programs like this one can facilitate local and regional processes that are key to managing change.

In the northern part of the Fruit Belt, in the Traverse City area, such small to mid-sized farms have profited from business networks or "value chains" that help meet a growing demand for differentiated, high-quality food products. As previously noted, the Werp Farm supplies the Grand Traverse Resort's Aerie restaurant, but it also provides specialty baby vegetables to 14 other restaurants in Traverse City, Detroit, and Mackinac Island. Compared to conventional corn growers in the region, who may earn $300 an acre, the Werps' total annual revenue is $150,000, or $15,000 an acre, and is increasing. According to Bill Palladino, a small-business development specialist in the Traverse City region, this entrepreneurial "value-added agriculture is based locally, uses local resources, and takes those resources and extends them to the marketplace here" (Schneider, 2004, p. G7). A regional food guide funded by the Traverse City Area Chamber of Commerce's foundation and the W.K. Kellogg Foundation helps link entrepreneurial farmers with local customers who want farm-fresh foods. In the Fruit Belt and beyond, local and state governments and the business community are doing more to bring the two groups together. Michigan's Select a Taste of Michigan program has promoted asparagus and nine other fresh market crops, which has led to an increase in fresh market prices (Schneider, 2004). While operators of mid-sized Fruit Belt farms face challenges to keep the land in agriculture, place-based strategies can assist them in their struggles.

Acknowledgements

The author thanks the US Department of Agriculture and the Michigan Department of Agriculture for financially supporting this research, and she thanks Anne Gibson for cartographic assistance.

Note

[1] One acre (ac) is equivalent to 0.4046863 hectares (ha).

References

Agriculture of the Middle. (2005) Agriculture of the middle, www.agofthemiddle.org/ (accessed 11 May 2008).

Apple, R.W., Jr. (2003) Up north: Michigan's flavorful vacationland. *New York Times*, 30 July, www.nytimes.com/2003/07/30/dining/30MICH.htm (accessed 31 July 2003).

Armstrong, K. (2006) The secret ingredient: How soil, climate, and hard work helped to produce the world's finest fruit. *Michigan History* 90(3), 6–12.

Ast, W., III. (2006) Fruit belt futures. *Michigan History* 90(3), 28–31.

Barber, D. (2005) Stuck in the middle (editorial). *New York Times*, 23 November, A27.

Brunori, G., and Rossi, A. (2000) Synergy and coherence through collective action: Some insights from wine routes in Tuscany. *Sociologia Ruralis* 40(4), 409–423.

Bryant, C. (2008) Co-constructing rural communities in the 21st century: Challenges for central governments in working effectively with local and regional actors. Paper presented at Space to Place: The Next Rural Economies Workshop, Prince George, BC.

Burkert, B. (2006) Townships receive $50,000 grant to bolster agri-tourism. *South Haven (MI) Tribune*, 5 November, A1, A6.

Che, D. (2006) Select Michigan: Local food production, food safety, culinary heritage, and branding in Michigan agritourism. *Tourism Review International* 9(4), 349–364.

Cloke, P., and Goodwin, M. (1992) Conceptualizing countryside change: From post-Fordism to rural structured coherence. *Transactions of the Institute of British Geographers* 17, 321–336.

DeParle, J. (2007) Where the good life demands grape views. *New York Times*, 13 September, www.nytimes.com/2007/09/13/garden/13vineyards.html (accessed 13 September 2007).

Detroit News. (1999) Farmers pitch Michigan products: State campaign hopes to end red ink and save farms. *Detroit News*, 6 December.

Fermata Inc. (2005) *Experiential Tourism Strategy for the Kansas Flint Hills*. Author, Austin, TX.

Fruit Growers News. (2004) Agritourism helps bring more people to the farm. *Fruit Growers News* 43(2), 32–33.

Goodwin, M. (1998) The governance of rural areas: Some emerging research issues and agendas. *Journal of Rural Studies* 14(1), 5–12.

Grand Rapids Press. (2008) Pure Michigan launches ad campaign. *Grand Rapids (MI) Press*, 6 May, www.mlive.com/travel/index.ssf/2008/05/pure_michigan_summer_advertisi.html (accessed 8 May 2008).

Hall, C., Johnson, G., Cambourne, B., Macionis, N., Mitchell, R., and Sharples, L. (2004) Wine tourism: An introduction. In: Hall, C., Sharples, L., Cambourne, B., and Macionis, N. (eds.) *Wine Tourism around the World: Development, Management and Markets*. Butterworth Heinemann, Oxford, 1–23.

Hamm, M. (2003) How to cultivate entrepreneurial agriculture. Panel presentation at Seeds of Prosperity: Food, Farms, and Michigan's Economic Future conference, Thompsonville, MI.

Hashimoto, A., and Telfer, D. (2006) Selling Canadian culinary tourism: Branding the global and the regional product. *Tourism Geographies* 8(1), 31–55.

Hoogterp, E. (2002) Michigan bounty—long on diversity, short on federal aid; most farm support goes to states producing wheat, corn, soybeans, cotton and rice. *Grand Rapids (MI) Press*, 15 December, E1.

Jackson, P. (2006) New agri-tourism association formed. *Michigan Farm News*, 28 February 2006, http://www.michiganfarmbureau.com/farmnews/transform.php?xml=20060228/agritourism.xml (accessed 8 May 2008).

Lobo, R. (2001) Helpful agricultural tourism (agri-tourism) definitions. Small Farm Program, University of California, Davis, www.sfc.ucdavis.edu/agritourism/definition.html (accessed 25 January 2001).

Long, S. (2006) New farm marketing association kicks off membership drive, ANR Communications, College of Agriculture and Natural Resources, Michigan State University, www.anrcats.msu.edu /press/110106/113006_farmmarketing.htm (accessed 8 May 2008).

Lowe, P., Murdoch, J., Marsden, T., Munton, R., and Flynn, A. (1993) Regulating the new rural spaces: The uneven development of land. *Journal of Rural Studies* 9(3), 205–222.

MacLachlan, I. (2005) Feedlot growth in southern Alberta: A neo-Fordist interpretation. In: Essex, S., Gilg, A., Yarwood, R., Smithers, J., and Wilson, R. (eds.) *Rural Change and Sustainability: Agriculture, the Environment and Communities.* CABI Publishing, Wallingford, UK, 28–47.

Marsden, T. (2000) Food, nature, and the rural economy: Regulating rural uneven development. Paper presented at the 96th annual meeting of the Association of American Geographers, Pittsburgh, PA.

Marsden, T., Murdoch, J., Lowe, P., Munton, R., and Flynn, A. (1993) *Constructing the Countryside.* UCL Press, London.

Maynard, M. (2007) In the fruit belt, selling summer off the truck. *New York Times,* 15 August, www.nytimes.com/2007/08/15/dining/15frui.html?_r=1&oref=slogin (accessed 9 May 2008).

Michigan History. (2006) The top crops. *Michigan History* 90(3): 13.

Michigan Land Use Leadership Council. (2003) *Michigan's Land, Michigan's Future: Final Report of the Michigan Land Use Leadership Council.* Prepared for Governor Jennifer Granholm and the Michigan Legislature.

Morgan, N., Pritchard, A., and Pride, R. (2002) Introduction. In: Morgan, N., Pritchard, A., and Pride, R. (eds.) *Destination Branding: Creating the Unique Destination Proposition.* Butterworth Heinemann, Oxford, 3–10.

Moses, A. (1999) Life on the farm becoming a tough sell; Uncertain weather, low profits make farming a stressful occupation. *Detroit News,* 26 November, C8.

Nicksin, C. (1999) Dude farms. *Country Journal* 26(5), 16–19.

Phillips, K. (2006) Cooking with local flavor. *Michigan History* 90(3), 21–23.

Professional Friends of Wine. (2008) American Viticultural Areas, www.winepros.org/consumerism/ava.htm, (accessed 8 November 2008).

Rosenberg, J. (2000) 50-plus on the move. *Advertising Age* 71(29), S2.

Schneider, K. (2004) Sell in bulk, lose farm. Sell locally, and watch revenues grow (Small Business) (Agriculture). *New York Times,* 21 September, G7.

Silfven, S. (2007a). Grand Traverse Resort a wine and food destination; Mackinaw Trail winery picks up steam. *Detroit News,* 19 July, info.detnews.com/wine/columns/silfven/details.cfm?id=407 (accessed 23 August 2007).

_____. (2007b) Douglas Valley and Tabor Fields turn residential living into a wine experience in Michigan. *Detroit News,* 13 September, info.detnews.com/wine/columns/silfven/details.cfm?id=414 (accessed 13 September 2007).

Slater, J. (2002) Brand Louisiana: "Come as you are. Leave different." In: Morgan, N., Pritchard, A., and Pride, R. (eds.) *Destination Branding:Creating the Unique Destination Proposition.* Butterworth Heinemann, Oxford, 148–162.

Spotts, D., Kim, D., Carr, J., and Holecek, D. (1998) An analysis of Michigan's image as a tourist destination. Paper presented at the 20th annual conference of the Travel and Tourism Research Association, Fort Worth, TX.

Storey, D. (2008) Contemporary approaches to rural development: Lauding the local. Paper presented at Space to Place: The Next Rural Economies Workshop, Prince George, BC.

Telfer, D. (2000) Tastes of Niagara: Building strategic alliances between tourism and agriculture. *International Journal of Hospitality and Tourism Administration* 1(1), 71–88.

_____. (2001) Strategic alliances along the Niagara wine route. *Tourism Management* 22(1), 21–30.

Tree-Mendus Fruit. (2008) Antique apple varieties, www.treemendus-fruit.com/heritage.htm, (accessed 12 May 2008).

Troughton, M. (2005) Fordism rampant: The model and reality, as applied to production, processing, and distribution in the North American food system. In: Essex, S., Gilg, A., Yarwood, R., Smithers, J., and Wilson, R. (eds.) *Rural Change and Sustainability: Agriculture, the Environment and Communities.* CABI Publishing, Wallingford, UK, 13–27.

US Department of Agriculture, National Agricultural Statistics Service. (1992) Census of agriculture, highlights of agriculture: 1992 and 1987—Michigan, http://www.nass.usda.gov/census/census92 /atlas92/datafile/mic003.txt .../mic005.txt, .../mic010.txt, .../mic011.txt, .../mic015.txt, .../mic028. txt, .../mic039.txt, .../mic041.txt, ./mic045.txt, .../mic051.txt, .../mic053.txt, .../mic061.txt, .../ mic062.txt, .../mic064.txt, .../mic070.txt, .../mic080.txt (accessed 15 June 2008).

_____. (1999) *1997 Census of Agriculture: Michigan—State and County Data.* Author, Washington, DC.

_____. (2004) *2002 Census of Agriculture: Michigan—State and County Data.* Author, Washington, DC.

Veeck, G., Che, D., and Veeck, A. (2006) America's changing farmscape: A study of agricultural tourism in Michigan. *Professional Geographer* 58(3), 235–248.

Wargenau, A., and Che, D. (2006) Wine tourism development and marketing strategies in southwest Michigan. *International Journal of Wine Marketing* 18(1), 45–60.

Whitbeck, R. (1920) The influence of Lake Michigan upon its opposite shores, with comments on the declining use of the lake as a waterway. *Annals of the Association of American Geographers* 10, 41–55.

Wineman International. (1999) 1999 Michigan wine industry fact sheet, http://www.thewineman.com /MI_winefacts.com (accessed 3 January 2004).

Youssef, J. (2008) Tourism pitches aim at Michigan neighbors; More near-state visits deemed essential to industry, *Detroit News*, 13 February, www.detnews.com/apps/pbcs.dll/article?AID= /20080213/BIZ/802130359 (accessed 13 February 2008).

Zhang, J., Sun, J., and Liu, Y. (2004) A new era for Chinese apples: China's apple industry is transitioning from an emphasis on yields to quality. *American/Western Fruit Grower* 124(6), 18.

Chapter 9

Rural Restructuring and the New Rural Economy: Examples from Germany and Canada

Doug Ramsey

Economic restructuring is not unique to agriculture, nor is agricultural restructuring unique to one particular region of the world. While one constant across sectors is the increasing scale of operations, certain sectors have witnessed greater levels of restructuring than others. The agricultural restructuring literature has drawn upon various perspectives over the past 15 years, including political economy, restructuring, and structure and agency economy (Cloke et al., 1990; Johnsen, 2004; Woods, 2005; Higgins, 2006). While more recently the discourse has explored the notions of post-productivism (Mather et al., 2006), critics have charged that rural geographers ought to return to more relevant and appropriate models of agricultural restructuring (Evans, forthcoming). Within this call is the implicit recognition of political economy perspectives. Simply stated, specific regions and/or commodities tend to be affected by changes in the commodities and agricultural structures that characterize that region (e.g., grain production on the Canadian prairies, citrus fruits in the southern United States, dairy production in Switzerland). External forces that affect one region, whether they take the form of policies, economic conditions, or weather variability, do not necessarily affect other regions. Responses to restructuring forces have been characterized in a number of ways, including alternative farm enterprises (Ilbery et al., 1998), pluriactivity (Bessant, 2006), adaptation (Smit and Skinner, 2002), and diversification (Bradshaw, 2004; Chaplin et al., 2004). In this chapter I take the view that adaptation is the model for responding to forces of change. Diversification is a response at the farm scale and an outcome at the regional scale.

I will address agricultural sectors and regions that are limited in their ability to expand operations, focusing on two regions that have developed distinct identities which include agricultural production, and where it has proven difficult to ensure the farms' financial stability in response to forces of restructuring. In southern Ontario, Canada, a small region known locally as "the Tobacco-Belt" has been dominated by either burley or flue-cured tobacco production since the end of the 19th century. In the past 25 years, tobacco farmers have faced three distinct reductions in production quotas, which occurred in 1984, 2005, and 2008. By comparison, the Reichenau Island in southern Baden-Württemberg, Germany, has a much longer agricultural history dating back to the Reichenau Monastery founded in 724. Both case studies provide examples of rural localities that were once wealthy agricultural economies that now struggle to expand and diversify, most significantly because of land limitations and saturated commodity markets.

In the first section of the chapter I will provide an overview of the rural communities and economic restructuring in both regions. In the second, I highlight place-based policies and economic development considerations that have influenced the rural economies in both case study regions. I conclude the chapter by focusing on population and policy implications with the aim of identifying possible "next rural economies."

Rural Communities and Economic Restructuring

The Reichenau Island (Baden-Württemberg, Germany) and Tobacco-Belt (Ontario, Canada) are both located at the southern limits of their respective provinces and are close to lakes that provide both tourism opportunities and lake-influenced microclimates that offer greater potential for agricultural production. Both economies have been dominated by agriculture: vegetable and grape production in the Reichenau Island and tobacco in the Tobacco-Belt. Responses to restructuring have been quite different in the two regions, however. Farming in the Reichenau Island has become more specialized, with products being marketed through a centralized vegetable cooperative. Farmer participation in the cooperative is mandatory. Diversification has been the response to restructuring in the Tobacco-Belt, and the central marketing agent of tobacco, a grower-owned marketing board, is currently in danger of being dismantled.

Reichenau Island, Germany

The federal state of Baden-Württemberg is located in southwestern Germany, bordering France, Switzerland, and Austria (Fig. 9.1). The Reichenau Island is the largest of three islands located in Lake Constance (Bodensee), which is bordered by Germany, Austria, and Switzerland. Benedictine monks founded the Reichenau Monastery on the island in 724. In 2000, UNESCO added the island to its list of World Heritage Sites for three reasons related to the monastic history: its religious and cultural role as a Benedictine monastery of the Middle Ages, the presence of three Romanesque churches dating between the 9th and 11th centuries, and its significance as an artistic centre in the 10th and 11th centuries, exemplified by its wall paintings and illuminations.

The Reichenau Island is 4.5 km long by 1.5 km wide or about 430 total ha (Fig. 9.2). Settlement is scattered across the island, and there are also three official villages. The total island population is between 3,000 and 4,000 depending on the season. While it is still referred to as an island, a causeway has joined Reichenau Island to the mainland for more than 50 years. The mainland city of Konstanz is a ten-minute drive from the causeway. Paved bike paths and public transit (bus and train) also connect Konstanz and other villages to the causeway. Beyond agriculture, other economies on the Reichenau Island include services, tourism, a commercial fishery, and recreation. The Reichenau Island also serves as a "bedroom community" for Konstanz.

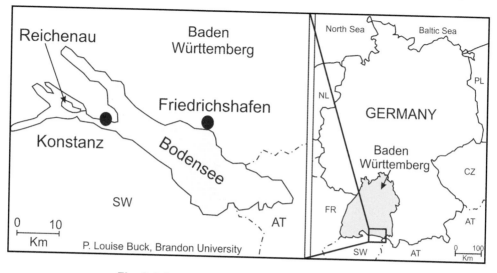

Fig. 9.1 Location of Reichenau Island, Germany.

Fig. 9.2 Bayern Reichenau Island, Germany.

Until 1929, agriculture was characterized by vineyards for the monasteries. However, a cold snap that year destroyed the vines. This was the first phase of restructuring as farmers wanted to diversify in order to reduce their risk and identified crops that allowed for several harvests each year. There is presently one winery on the island, with 17 ha of grape production. The remaining active farmland is used for vegetable production. All farmers must belong to the only cooperative on the island, Gemuse Reichenau, which was established in 1994 in an effort to provide central wholesaling and marketing, thus improving efficiencies and stabilizing, if not increasing, prices. Prior to the formation of Gemuse Reichenau there were six collection points on the island for vegetables alone.

Gemuse Reichenau currently has 289 members, of which 144 are active growers and 145 are retired. In total, the active producers are using 120 ha for open field crops and 40 ha for greenhouse production. The remaining 100 ha of farmland available on the island is idle (e.g., cover crops or pasture). The average farm size is currently 0.65 ha under glass and 1.35 ha in open field. Cauliflower, broccoli, kohlrabi, lettuce, fennel, radishes, celery, courgette (zucchini), and herbs are produced in open fields. Greenhouse production is concentrated on cucumbers, tomatoes, and lettuce. There are also three flower-growing operations on the island that do not belong to the cooperative.

Recent trends include a decline in the number of producers. The reasons are similar to those in other jurisdictions throughout the world and include a lack of interest in farming and a belief there is no future in farming. However, farmers in the Reichenau Island are also confronted by a limited land base that is fragmented into very small holdings. Even if a farmer were able to afford to purchase several units, the fields would be scattered across the island.

The recent trend has been to shift from open field to greenhouse production. There are three main reasons for this: greenhouses offer higher productivity per hectare; they offer a greater degree of seasonal independence because the Reichenau Island's microclimate allows for efficient greenhouse production year-round; and their produce is of a more consistent quality, which is crucial given the competition for markets. The manager of the cooperative feels that open field production will decline further and specialization will continue, with an emphasis on those crops that dominate greenhouse production (i.e., cucumbers, tomatoes, lettuce). A negative consequence of this increased specialization is the general risk associated with limiting the products offered by the cooperative to the open market.

This is not to say that the transition to greenhouse production is without conflict. Individuals and companies involved in tourism and recreation, the other major economic sectors on the Reichenau Island, fear that landscape impacts of further greenhouse production will affect the island's ability to draw visitors. In particular, plastic structures, whether temporary or permanent, tend to be less visually appealing. Already, there are "hot spots" of visual conflict. These include areas of flat topography and areas adjacent to existing greenhouse production, paved roadways, and settlements. Two areas with the least conflict are the shorelines, which are protected by regulations set out by UNESCO and Baden-Württemberg, as well as the knoll in the mid-section of the island, which is the location of the 17 ha of vineyards.

The Tobacco-Belt, Canada

Aboriginal peoples in the area that is now Ontario, Canada, first cultivated tobacco centuries ago. The most notable aboriginal growers were the Petun people, also known as the Tobacco Nation. The first post-colonial cultivation was documented in the 1600s. Commercial production of dark, or burley, tobacco began in about 1800. It was not until World War I that flue-cured cigarette tobacco came into favour (Tait, 1968; Ramsey *et al.*, 2002). Throughout the first half of the 20th century, commercial production expanded, concentrating on the Norfolk Sand Plain region on the north shore of Lake Erie (Fig. 9.3). During this period, a number of grower associations and boards, both regional and provincial, were formed and dissolved. The modern era of flue-cured tobacco began with the creation of the Ontario Flue-Cured Tobacco Growers Marketing Board (OFCTGMB) in 1957. This board is still in existence today. Farmers must purchase quota through the board or from other growers. Until 2008, a grower had to hold quota in order to grow tobacco. Also, prior to 2008, the OFCTGMB allocated the percentage of the quota a quota owner could grow based on consultations with cigarette manufacturers regarding demand and price.

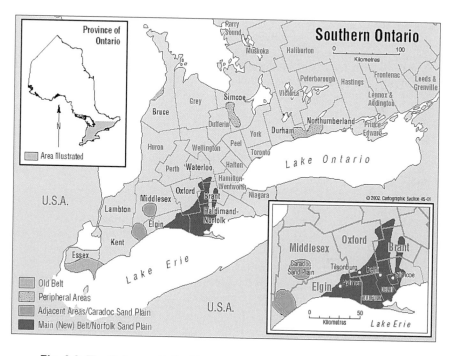

Fig. 9.3 The Tobacco-Belt of Southern Ontario (Ramsey *et al.*, 2002).

Tobacco farming in Canada has undergone distinct phases of restructuring, particularly since 1961, when the number of tobacco farms peaked at 5,600 (Ramsey *et al.*, 2002). By 1991 this number had declined to 1,500, and by 2001 it had dropped to 900. The most recent restructuring has taken place since then. In 2005, 580 growers planted a tobacco crop, followed by 520 in 2006, and 280 in 2007 (OFCTGMB, 2007). A number of factors led to this restructuring, including continued health concerns over tobacco use, health promotion programs, restrictive tobacco-use legislation, increasing levels of cigarette taxes, the closure of all cigarette manufacturing plants in Canada, and trends common to other agricultural sectors (e.g., increasing input costs, market uncertainty). In 2005, the federal and provincial governments and the OFCTGMB initiated a quota-buyout program on behalf of farmers that saw 225 growers permanently exit tobacco farming (Ramsey, forthcoming).

Whereas in the Reichenau Island the trend has been toward specialization, farmers in the Tobacco-Belt have been encouraged and financially supported to diversify into other agricultural commodities. While a number of programs based on commodities have been implemented since the late 1980s, the most recent program (Community Transition

Program or CTP) focused on enterprise development (Ramsey, forthcoming). This $15-million program funded 76 projects throughout the four-county Tobacco-Belt. Within the "Sustainable, Diversified Economy" category, 67 projects were funded in the following subcategories: crop diversification (27), manufacturing (10), food processing (9), business expansion (9), tourism (7), and agritourism (5). The largest project funded was a Toyota Corporation parts plant to be located in Simcoe, Ontario. In total, crop diversification (27%) and manufacturing (23%) accounted for half the total funding. The CTP was a one-time initiative, and there is no replacement program on the horizon (Community Transition Program, 2007).

The following three factors limit diversification into other agricultural sectors:

1. **Restrictions on size of land parcels.** More than half (54%) of all farms in Norfolk County, the core tobacco-production county within the Tobacco-Belt, are between 10 and 130 ha. By comparison, 44% of farms across Ontario fall within this category. (These smaller farms are surrounded by other small farms, so if farmers wish to expand their land base, they must purchase land that is not adjacent to, or often even near, the home farm.)

2. **Soil.** The soil in the Tobacco-Belt is sandy, which, by its nature, is low in organic matter. Thus any commodity to replace tobacco must be profitable using a rotational system that includes a year for rebuilding soil nutrients. Such a system is used for tobacco production.

3. **Markets.** The markets for such commodities as tomatoes, cucumbers, and strawberries have been met, and the transition into niche markets, such as ginseng, has been fraught with problems. Ginseng, a popular crop since the 1980s, takes three to five years to grow, which causes market uncertainty. In fact, the market was flooded and prices fell well below the cost of production throughout the mid-1990s and into the early 2000s (Government of Ontario, 2003).

Place-Based Policy and Economic Development

Policies that have influenced the rural economies of the Reichenau Island and the Tobacco-Belt, including some policies that have forced restructuring and others that have responded to it, have come from many levels: international, national, provincial/state, and local. While the Reichenau Island has benefited from the UNESCO designation, global shifts in agricultural policy, particularly related to state subsidies, have created the urgent need for farms to become more commercially viable. At the same time, international, national, and provincial/state initiatives aimed at reducing tobacco use have had negative impacts on farms growing tobacco. The consequences have been felt particularly hard in the area with the greatest concentration of tobacco farms, the Tobacco-Belt.

Reichenau Island, Germany

There are two conflicting directives for local economic development on the island. First, as already described, is the transition from open field to greenhouse production in agriculture. The second is promotion of the island for tourism and recreation. In addition to the UNESCO designation, a municipal island tourism office (Insel Reichenau im Bodensee), which is open year-round, and an industry association promote the religious institutions, cultural landscapes, monuments, nature, and recreation (Table 9.1 lists the local tourism facilities). The island has a network of paved roads and bike/walking trails as well as some footpaths along the shoreline. The entire shoreline is protected under environmental legislation passed by the State of Baden-Württemberg. For example, the owners of the campground are not allowed to backfill sand for their beach, and they are not allowed to plant palm trees permanently, although the trees can remain in pots for the tourist season (G. Beyer, owner/operator of Insel-Camping-Platz-Sandseele, pers. comm., 23 April 2007).

Table 9.1 Tourist services on Reichenau Island.

Accommodations	Other tourism-related businesses
Hotel – 5	Restaurants – 15
Vacation dwellings – 64	Bakeries – 3
Pension – 2	Flowers/garden centres – 3
Private room – 7	Artisanal crafts – 3
Vacation homes – 2	Photos/souvenirs – 2
Campground – 1	Fish processor (with retail) – 1
	Winery (with retail) – 1
	Vegetables – 1

Source: Insel Reichenau im Bodensee, 2007.

There are concerns within the tourism industry about the changing vistas and cultural landscape on the island as a result of the increased greenhouse production. As yet, there are no regulations restricting or limiting such development, and in an apparent contradiction, the restaurant sector proudly markets the island's products, including wine, fish, and vegetables (G. Beyer, pers. comm., 23 April 2007; J. Bliestle, general manager of Gemuse Reichenau, pers. comm., May 2007). However, given that both the agricultural cooperative and the tourism association are actively, successfully, and aggressively meeting the demands of the new rural economy, conflicts seem certain. A point of connection between the two sectors, however, is that both use island food and wine in product development and marketing.

The Tobacco-Belt, Canada

Before the Community Transition Program of 2005–2006, the Ontario government had implemented three programs with the aim of finding alternative commodities for tobacco farmers to grow. The three programs, which ran between 1989 and 1996, were open to tobacco growers throughout Ontario (Ramsey, 2003). In contrast, while the CTP was also a provincial program, it was regionally specific—targeted solely to the four-county Tobacco-Belt—and was not limited to tobacco farmers. In addition to farmers, municipal governments, local organizations, and corporations were eligible to apply for funding. This expanded focus was in part a reflection of the provincial government's fear of being seen to support tobacco growers, particularly as the Liberal Party governing Ontario at the time had a "tobacco-free" policy. The CTP also acknowledged the need to assist a community negatively affected by the economic downturn caused by declining tobacco farm numbers. This was consistent with the quota-buyout program of 2005, in which the federal government funded the purchase of quota while the provincial government paid for "obsolete" farm equipment and buildings (Ramsey, forthcoming).

Norfolk County accounted for 60% of the area where tobacco was grown in 2006 (OFCTGMB, 2007). In response to the "crisis" in the tobacco farming sector, the County of

Norfolk developed a Tobacco Community Action Plan in 2004, which was laid out in the report *Norfolk at the Crossroads: Directions for a Prosperous Future in Norfolk County* (Norfolk County, 2004). The report states that "diversification has not been easy and many individuals and families have suffered losses" (p. 2). It also indicates that "tobacco is expected to continue as a viable crop, although acreage may fall substantially" (p. 3). The first statement has proven to be correct, while the second, which is discussed in the next section, is more questionable. Having said this, the plan includes five recommendations:

- **Manage the transition**—to administer the Transition Program and to help individuals and families identify and secure alternative sources of income.
- **Maintain a viable agricultural economy in Norfolk**—to sustain existing farm enterprises and develop new value-added opportunities for high-value agricultural products.
- **Build community capacity for growth**—to increase commercial and industrial development, and the infrastructure and educational facilities to enable growth.
- **Support innovation and entrepreneurship**—to enable Norfolk area agri-food industry players to benefit from world-class technologies and expanded markets.
- **Protect and enhance Norfolk's environment**—to sustain the land and water resources for the benefit of all.
- **Protect the safety of Canadians**—to ensure agri-food products consumed in Canada meet domestic standards for traceability and for pesticide and pathogen content.
- **Expand tourism opportunities and development**—to allow Norfolk to reap the rewards from its natural beauty and country charm. (Norfolk County, 2004, p. ii)

Perhaps the greatest negative consequence for the tobacco farming community is the failure to secure a final exit strategy in the form of a final quota-buyout program. The OFCTGMB devised an exit strategy based on three objectives:

1. Proactively address the needs of tobacco growers and their communities as part of Federal and Provincial Government tobacco control strategies.
2. Implement a plan that will provide an orderly, managed and fair exit program for Ontario tobacco farmers over the life of the industry.
3. Provide transition support for those communities that have long been economically dependent on tobacco production and who suffer from its decline. (OFCTGMB, 2008)

In separate efforts, the OFCTGMB and a local organization called Tobacco Farmers in Crisis (TFIC) lobbied for this kind of exit strategy after the completion of the 2005 quota-buyout program. However, the OFCTGMB has been in turmoil since 2007, and in April 2008 the chair was "ousted" in a board vote (Heldson, 2008). The TFIC has been inactive since mid-2007, in part because some members felt that negotiation needed to be replaced by civil action while others did not (M. Bannister, founder/former executive member of Tobacco Farmers in Crisis, pers. comm., October 2007).

Unfortunately for the remaining 1,074 tobacco quota owners (OFCTGMB, 2007), in April 2008 the federal government announced that no quota buyout or exit strategy would be forthcoming (Novak, 2008a). Soon after, a consortium of farmers calling itself the New Tobacco Alliance Committee announced it was starting a lawsuit against the governments of both Canada and Ontario. Tobacco farmers have also launched individual lawsuits against the OFCTGMB. It is impossible to obtain an estimate of the number of farmers who planted a crop in 2008. However, all agree that it is a fraction of the number of quota owners, and the volume planted is a fraction of the quota owned.

Thus, there is conflict within the community. Table 9.2 lists a sample of headlines from the only local daily newspaper that originates in Norfolk County, the *Simcoe Reformer*. They begin with examples of frustration and acts of civil disobedience in response to failed negotiations (December 2007 to January 2008) and proceed to the failure to include financial assistance in the federal budget (February to March 2008), lawsuits launched (April 2008), failure of the member of Parliament (MP) to meet with farmers (April 2008), and the announcement to fight contraband cigarette manufacturing and sales (May 2008). Regular protests have bedeviled Conservative MPs who represent portions of the Tobacco-Belt. Most notably, Diane Finley, the MP for Haldimand-Norfolk, who is also minister of Immigration and Citizenship, has faced protests and rallies. On 24 April 2008, she was scheduled to attend a meeting with tobacco farmers, but cancelled at the last minute. Her office indicated the reason was that she had received death threats unrelated to the tobacco farming issue. However, Finley herself indicated that she met with OFCTGMB officials but that the farmers' "forum was inappropriate to get the message out, to hear from farmers in an appropriate circumstance" (Novak, 2008b).

Table 9.2 Conflict in the countryside as evidenced in the local media.

Headline	Date
Rogue Protest Planned for Tobacco Exchange in Delhi	05/12/07
Tobacco Rally Organizer Talking Tough	06/12/07
Angry Farmers Prepare to Give Tobacco to Six Nations	10/12/07
Nothing to Lose*	10/12/07
Bales of Garbage: Plan B for Tobacco Farmers	18/01/08
Tobacco Farmers Given 'False Hopes' by Conservatives, Dion Says	21/01/08
Tobacco Buyout Hopes Dealt Setback	25/01/08
Farmers Prepare to Trash Tobacco	31/01/08
No Mention of Buyout in Federal Budget	27/02/08
Budget Fallout*	27/02/08
Buy Out Farmers, Province Tells Ottawa	03/04/08
Sucker Punch*	03/04/08
Release the Lawyers*	21/04/08
Inappropriate Behaviour*	30/04/08
Smoke Screen*	08/05/08

Source: *Simcoe Reformer*, archival search with keyword "tobacco" at http://cgi.bowesonline.com/pedro.php?id=305&x=archives_result.
Note: * indicates an editorial title; all others are articles.

The lack of a solution and the dearth of information have fuelled anger in the community, which was increased by a Liberal Party motion from the federal Agricultural Advisory Committee that called on the ruling Conservative Party to "implement the buyout program put forward this spring by the Ontario Flue-Cured Tobacco Growers' Marketing Board" (Pearce, 2008). In May 2008, the federal Minister of Public Safety, Stockwell Day, announced that his department and the Royal Canadian Mounted Police would be increasing efforts to address growing production and sales of contraband cigarettes. This announcement was met with skepticism within the Tobacco-Belt, as noted in a newspaper editorial titled "Smoke Screen" (Schwass, 2008). The RCMP will be targeting illegal production and sales in three Canadian First Nations' communities, including those on the Six Nations reserve located adjacent to the Tobacco-Belt.

Prospects for the Future: Policy, Economics, and Population

It is no secret that rural restructuring is a global phenomenon. With restructuring and change, some communities and regions will succeed and grow, others will fail, still others will simply survive. The notion of sustainable development implies growth, so perhaps the notion of "rural maintenance" is more apt for some rural communities than growth or expansion.

There are both similarities and differences in the two case studies presented in this chapter. Similarities include a relatively stable population, the lack of large tracts of available and affordable land for agricultural expansion, issues of competitiveness in agricultural production, a progression toward tourism markets, and the presence of external forces that have a direct impact on the communities. Differences include the degree of specialization and diversification, and the restructuring of commodity-based marketing organizations. In this final section I provide a brief accounting of these similarities and differences, with a few words on future prospects.

Reichenau Island, Germany

The word Reichenau is derived from the words "Reiche" and "Au," which mean "Rich Island." The island is steeped in history that is now protected by UNESCO and the federal state of Baden-Württemberg. While the population of the island is stable, the number of members of Gemuse Reichenau who are actively growing, is declining. Residential growth continues on the Reichenau Island, which, along with the success of the tourism market, seems to bode well for the Island.

Farming will continue to face issues of commercial viability. While on one hand there is a limited land base, the fact that only 120 of the 220 ha of open fields available for crop production are actively being farmed is cause for concern. The transition to greenhouse production is capital intensive during start-up, but there is less need for capital once the greenhouse is in operation, and the limits to such growth are not known. However, conflicts between the tourism and agricultural sectors seem inevitable—even if the markets are not mutually exclusive. There are worries that UNESCO regulators might decide that the transition to greenhouse production is detracting from the cultural landscapes of the island. Having said this, the hospitality industry of the Reichenau Island, which prides itself on island fish, wine, and vegetables, is also price sensitive. Thus, the clash between commercial viability and historic preservation will likely take place in the not-too-distant future.

The first response to the need for stability and commercial viability in the farming system of the Reichenau Island was the establishment of Gemuse Reichenau. While technically a cooperative, owned and operated by members, participation is mandatory and there is no guaranteed income. If the crop does not sell, payments are not made. However, there is no quota system, so farmers are free to grow whatever they wish, in whatever quantity they choose. Thus, the farmer can decide to specialize in certain commodities, such as tomatoes, cucumbers, and lettuce, which are marketed by the cooperative. This is quite different from the situation in the Ontario Tobacco-Belt, where it could be argued that specialization in one commodity has been partially responsible for the crisis in the farm community.

The Tobacco-Belt, Canada

The population of the Tobacco-Belt has remained relatively stable throughout the various phases of restructuring. Norfolk County, for example, grew by 2.8% between the 2001 and 2006 census years (with a population of 60,487 and 62,563, respectively). This compares to a provincial average of 6.6% growth. Nevertheless, compared to other rural regions of Canada (e.g., Newfoundland, the Prairies, and remote rural Canada), 2.8% would be considered a success story. However, the farm population in Norfolk County declined from 1,651 to 1,525 over the same period. While only a decline of 126, it represents an 8.2% decline that compares to the provincial average of 4.2%. Further, the number masks the true picture. In 2001, 1,100 farms reported a tobacco crop. This number fell to 520 in 2006, a 53% decline. By the next year, this number dropped to 280, a one-year decline of 240 farms or 51%. In 2001, farms reporting tobacco accounted for 1.7% of total farms in Ontario. By 2006, this percentage had declined to 1.0% (Statistics Canada, 2006). Thus while the total population of Norfolk, which represents the core of the consolidated Tobacco-Belt, remains stable, the farm population is anything but.

Added to this is the small farm size in much of southern Ontario. This is in part due to the tradition of tobacco farming, which was capital and labour intensive but required small areas of production. However, it is also a reflection of the Tobacco-Belt's location in the Windsor–Quebec City corridor, with its high demand for land. In fact, part of the non-farm population growth is due to retirees relocating from large urban centres (e.g., Hamilton or London) into the countryside, particularly along the Lake Erie shores. This is similar to what is happening on the Reichenau Island, albeit on a different scale. Also similar is the transition toward tourism, with Norfolk now marketing itself as "Ontario's South Coast" (www.norfolktourism.ca). Similar to the circumstances on the Reichenau Island, Lake Erie fish, wineries, and local produce are marketing points for the tourism sector.

Perhaps more than any other agricultural sector, tobacco farmers face the greatest external pressures, particularly those related to the elimination of tobacco production. While domestic demand for tobacco products in Canada is declining, it still exists. The difference is that the demand will now be met by importing products from other countries. This is a frustration for both the farmer and the farming community. It is also, increasingly, recognized as a loss of tax revenue for provincial and federal levels of government. Domestic production was highly regulated by government, the OFCTGMB, and the cigarette manufacturers, and as it declines, there is equivalent growth in the black market. The prospect for a future tobacco-farming sector in Canada is not good. Thus, while farmers in the Reichenau Island are specializing to meet market demands, farmers in the Tobacco-Belt are diversifying their operations. For decades, the search for alternative crops has continued. While there have been some successes, most replacements have been small-scale niche crops. Other growers have shifted their focus to processing commodities. Continued success, however, seems to depend on others not engaging in the same sector. Ginseng is the prime example: The first growers were profitable, but when others saw the opportunities and switched to ginseng, the market was flooded and prices dropped.

A final difference between the two regions relates to marketing. While Gemuse Reichenau is a successful operation, welcomed by the farming community, the OFCTGMB will likely be dissolved. However, even this is uncertain, as the OFCTGMB's exit strategy was turned down by the federal government, and 2008 was the first year since its inception in 1957 that the board did not establish quota levels for production. As a result, no one knows how many farmers are planting a tobacco crop nor how much they are planting. More importantly, those who are planting a crop have no selling point. While options include selling Ontario-grown tobacco to the new cigarette-manufacturing facility on the Six Nations Reserve or to firms in the United States and Mexico, the mechanisms for selling the product are unclear. The tobacco farming community, including farmers, the OFCTGMB, and TFIC, is still waiting for implementation of the tobacco quota-buyout program announced in the summer 2008. Until this is in place, discussions about future tobacco sales and marketing are up in the air.

Acknowledgements

I would like to thank Gernot Beyer and Johannes Bliestle for participating in the research in the Reichenau Island and for giving me tours and information about tourism and agriculture on the island. I would also like to thank Manfred and Heidi Schöpflin for their hospitality in Konstanz. In Ontario, I would like to thank Anthony Boerkamp, Tracey and Shelley Boerkamp, Clark Hoskins, and Mark Bannister for their support, information, and time.

References

Bessant, K. (2006) A farm household conception of pluriactivity in Canadian agriculture: Motivation, diversification and livelihood. *Canadian Review of Sociology and Anthropology* 43(1), 51–72.

Bradshaw, B. (2004) Plus c'est la meme chose? Questioning crop diversification as a response to agricultural deregulation in Saskatchewan, Canada. *Journal of Rural Studies* 20, 35–48.

Chaplin, H., Davidova, S., and Gorton, M. (2004) Agricultural adjustment and the diversification of farm households and corporate farms in Central Europe. *Journal of Rural Studies*, 20, 61–77.

Cloke, P., Le Heron, R., and Roche, M. (1990) Towards a geography of the political economy perspective of rural change: The example of New Zealand. *Geografiska Annaler B* 72, 13–25.

Community Transition Program. (2007) *Process Evaluation*. Prepared by Harry Cummings and Associates Inc. Site accessed at: http://www.communitytransition.com/pdf/ctp_processaudit.pdf

Evans, N. (forthcoming) Adjustment strategies revisited: Agricultural change in the Welsh Marches. In: Winchell, D., Koster, R., Ramsey, D., and Robinson G. (eds.) *Rural Change, Connections and Scale: Agriculture and Environment*. Eastern Washington University Press, Spokane.

Government of Ontario. (2003) Ministry of Agriculture, Food and Rural Affairs. Marketing and export of ginseng, www.omafra.gov.on.ca/english/crops/facts/ginmkexp.htm (accessed 11 August 2008).

Heldson, J. (2008) Board chair ousted. *Simcoe Reformer*, 15 April, http://www.simcoereformer.ca/News/index.html (accessed 9 May).

Higgins, V. (2006) Re-figuring the problem of farmer agency in agri-food studies: A translation approach. *Agriculture and Human Values* 23(1), 51–62.

Ilbery, B., Shaw, A., and Bowler, I. (1998) Farm-based tourism as an alternative farm enterprise: A case study from the Northern Pennines, England. *Regional Studies* 32(4), 355–364.

Insel Reichenau im Bodensee. (2007) *Gäste-Journal 2007*. Author, Reichenau, Baden-Württemberg, Germany.

Johnsen, S. (2004) The redefinition of family farming: Agricultural restructuring and farm adjustment in Waihemo, New Zealand. *Journal of Rural Studies* 20, 419–432.

Mather, A., Hill, G., and Nijnik, M. (2006) Post-productivism and rural land use: Cul de sac or challenge for theorization. *Journal of Rural Studies* 22, 441–455.

Norfolk County. (2004) *Norfolk at the Crossroads: A Tobacco Community Action Plan.* Prepared by the Team Advising on the Crisis in Tobacco.

Novak, K. (2008a.) Budget fallout (Viewpoint). *Simcoe Reformer*, 27 February, http://www.simcoe reformer.ca/Editorial/379696.html (accessed 27 February).

_____. (2008b.) Inappropriate behaviour (Viewpoint). *Simcoe Reformer*, 30 April, http:www.simcoe reformer.ca (accessed 1 May).

OFCTGMB. (2007) *Ontario Flue-cured Tobacco Growers' Marketing Board—Annual Report.* Author, Tillsonburg, ON.

_____. (2008) *Ontario Flue-cured Tobacco Growers' Marketing Board—Annual Report.* Author, Tillsonburg, ON.

Pearce, D. (2008) Buy out farmers, province tells Ottawa. *Simcoe Reformer*. 3 April, www.simcoereformer.ca/News/389700.html (accessed 3 April).

Ramsey, D. (2003) Responding to restructuring forces: Diversification in the Tobacco-belt, Southern Ontario. In: Beesley, K., Millward, H., Ilbery, B., and Harrington, L. (eds.) *The New Countryside: A Geography of Rural Change.* Brandon University and St. Mary's University, Brandon, MB, and Halifax, NS, 90–104.

_____. (forthcoming) Agricultural restructuring and adaptation in the Ontario Tobacco-Belt. In: Winchell, D., Koster, R., Ramsey, D., and Robinson G. (eds.) *Rural Change, Connections and Scale: Agriculture and Environment.* Eastern Washington University Press, Spokane.

Ramsey, D., Stewart, C., Troughton, M., and Smit, B. (2002) Agricultural restructuring of Ontario tobacco production. *Great Lakes Geographer* 9(2), 71–92.

Schwass, K. (2008) Smoke screen (Viewpoint). *Simcoe Reformer*, 8 May, www.simcoereformer.ca/Editorial/399098.html (accessed 9 May).

Smit, B., and Skinner, M. (2002) Adaptation options in agriculture to climate change: A typology. *Mitigation, Adaptation Strategies and Global Change* 7, 85–114.

Statistics Canada. (2006) Census of agriculture, www.statcan.ca/english/agcensus2006/index.htm (accessed 29 October 2008).

Tait, L. (1968) *Tobacco in Canada.* Flue-cured Tobacco Growers' Marketing Board, Tillsonburg, ON.

Woods, M. (2005) *Rural Geography.* Sage, London.

Chapter 10

Nurturing the Animation Sector in a Peripheral Economic Region: the Case of Miramichi, New Brunswick

David Bruce

In 2007, Enterprise Miramichi commissioned a study to develop a long-term strategy for the potential growth and development of the animation sector in Miramichi, New Brunswick (Marlin *et al.*, 2007). The purpose of the study was to provide an understanding of the local and global context for the animation sector, with a view to determining the elements that both contribute to and hold back potential business and labour force growth for the sector in Miramichi.

As of 2008, the animation sector in Miramichi consisted of a post-secondary educational institution and two key companies. The New Brunswick Community College (NBCC), Miramichi campus, began offering animation and gaming programs in the late 1990s. The campus is now a Centre of Excellence in Multimedia Learning Technology. In recent years, Fatkat Animation Studios and the Child Safety Research and Innovation Center have emerged in Miramichi as employers of graduates from NBCC programs and of people from all over Canada, the United States, and other countries (Marlin *et al.*, 2007). The animation sector in Miramichi fits with regional, provincial, and Atlantic-wide economic development interests related to growing business success within knowledge-based industries.

This chapter considers the potential for nurturing growth in an emerging animation sector as a key component of the Miramichi regional economy. The sector has its roots in the business start-up of a local entrepreneur. Subsequent plans and investments made by key public sector agencies are now attempting to move this region to a serious place-based player in a rapidly expanding global economic sector.

Community and Economic Restructuring in Rural New Brunswick

The City of Miramichi was created in 1995 from the amalgamation of five individual towns and villages and several rural local service districts. The City is located along the banks of the Miramichi River on the northeast coast of New Brunswick. With a population of 18,129 (2006 census), it is the largest city in the province's northeast (Fig. 10.1). The Miramichi region includes the City of Miramichi, several neighbouring smaller towns and villages, and a vast expanse of sparsely settled territory. The region has a combined population of

48,868 and a long economic history based on natural resources—most communities are forest dependent. More recently, conscious efforts have been directed at diversifying the local and regional economies. In 1998, NBCC Miramichi began to emphasize knowledge industries (such as computer animation) by offering new animation and gaming programs.

Fig. 10.1 Miramichi locator map (Government of New Brunswick, n.d.).

In recent years, Miramichi and the region have suffered economic setbacks, including the closure of the former Canadian Forces Base Chatham in the mid-1990s and the ongoing restructuring of the pulp-and-paper sector. The forest economy and forest-dependent communities have undergone a fundamental transition. Forest industry changes are driven by higher Canadian dollar values, increasing global competition, aging infrastructure, and an unsatisfactory softwood lumber arrangement with the United States. Companies have cut costs, eliminated jobs, and closed mills (Natural Resources Canada, 2006). Between 2003 and 2007, eight mills closed in New Brunswick—three of them permanently (Parkins and White, 2007). Across the province, only 16 of the 85 mills that were operating in 1995 are still running at full capacity (CBC News, 2008). Despite the local setbacks, the industry remains important to the provincial and regional economy (Gordon *et al.*, 2008).

In the Miramichi region, the forest industry employed 2,700 people in 1996 (14.2% of the total labour force). That number has dropped significantly with recent closures of local operations of multinational corporations. The region's largest employer was the UPM-Kymmene pulp-and-paper operation, which closed permanently in 2008, with 600 jobs lost. Weyerhauser's oriented-strand-board mill closed in June 2007, resulting in 140 jobs lost. Other smaller forest-related operations in Miramichi have also closed. The net impacts are significant. The Miramichi region suffered a net loss of more than 1,950 people between 2001 and 2006 (a 3.8% decline), while the City of Miramichi lost 2% of its population. Out-migration was the major contributor to the lower population rates, as only 135 people moved into the region over this period.

Out-migration affected the key age categories of children (0–17 years), youth (18–24 years), and young working-age adults (25–44 years). Most troubling was the net loss of almost 1,000 young people (Table 10.1).

Table 10.1 Age of migrants, Miramichi region, 1999–2004.

	In-migrants	Out-migrants	Net
0–17 years	1,300	1,559	-259
18–24 years	1,177	2,156	-979
25–44 years	2,171	2,846	-675
45–64 years	938	823	115
65+ years	385	373	12
Total	5,971	7,757	-1,786

Source: Adapted from Statistics Canada, 2006.

These changes in Miramichi are consistent with those experienced by many forest-dependent communities and regions, and the consolidation of the forest industry over time and the introduction of labour-saving technology have driven them. Additional pressures affecting the demand of forest products are underpinned by energy costs, inflation, housing starts, and interest rates for mortgages. Looking back on the recent history of the sector, we note that during the Fordist era of the 1950s and 1960s, lumber, plywood, and pulp production increased. However, the 1970s and 1980s was marked by downsizing and closures. The plywood industry suffered problems stemming from a decline in the supply of large logs, competition from new products, and lower-priced particle board products (Barnes and Hayter, 1992). Forestry towns also experienced problems in the 1970s when energy costs fueled inflation. Fluctuations in the demand for lumber and wood products, along with interest rates for home mortgages, contributed to a high turnover among secondary-sector workers in forest towns (Humphreys, 1990; Luloff, 1990).

Most notably, the 1980s were marked by a shift to computer-based production that reduced manufacturing employment and required a flexible labour force (Barnes and Hayter, 1992). The number of jobs created per unit of production declined (Williamson and Annamraju, 1996), and while some mills closed, others modernized, resulting in a large reduction of employment (Barnes and Hayter, 1992). This shift could be described as marking the beginning of a period of decline in many forestry-dependent communities that still continues today.

A Brief, Recent History of Local Development Planning Efforts

As a result of ongoing changes in the forestry sector and their impacts on local communities, many community leaders identified the need to plan for a future with a more diversified economy. Led by the newly formed Enterprise Miramichi (a community economic development agency funded by all three levels of government), a slowly evolving community-based approach to economic development planning has emerged in the region. However, it has not been without its challenges given the region's traditional dependence on forestry and its desire to hold jobs in that sector, as well as maintain a sense of frontier and industrial identity.

A variety of strategic plans have been prepared for Miramichi in recent years on economic development, tourism, community growth, transportation, and downtown revitalization (Daniel K. Glenn Ltd., 1999; SGE Group, 2002; Baker Consulting, 2005; PK Consulting, 2005, 2007a, 2007b; SGE Acres Limited, 2005a, 2005b; City of Miramichi, 2006; ADI Limited, 2007). The most common actions identified in the plans involved economic development (including tourism and entrepreneurship), community infrastructure (such as beautification, revitalization, signage, heritage and cultural infrastructure), social issues (namely retention and attraction of youth, improvement of education attainment levels), and tourism and entertainment issues (such as the need for more museums and theatres).

Key economic strategies/plans in the evolutionary turn toward a knowledge-based economic sector included the following:

- In 2002, the City's *Final Report: Miramichi Economic Development Initiative* (SGE Group, 2002) identified that Miramichi was not on the radar of potential investors and that it was not a "new economy" leader. The report identified a number of challenges for the City, the need to attract foreign investment, and that the most profitable sectors over a five-year period were in traditional forestry and manufacturing areas. In 2005, a plan was prepared to activate a forestry and manufacturing cluster in the Miramichi region (PK Consulting, 2005).

- In 2005, a plan was developed for downtown revitalization (SGE Acres, 2005b) in Miramichi's two former town centres—one in Chatham (the Historic Water Street Business District) and one in Newcastle. The plan provided strategic direction, a process, and partners to improve, diversify, and expand the range of services in each downtown area to support retail attractiveness and expansion of tourism economies. It included physical improvements, marketing, and improved signage.

- A parallel strategy for downtown signage, imaging, and marketing (SGE Acres 2005a) recommended updating the branding of the two downtown areas (specifically the Water Street and Ritchie Wharf areas). The report recommended a historical redesign, a tourism awareness program, the creation of tourism packages, organization of festivals, and a particular focus on the Toronto, Montreal, and New England markets.

- The City of Miramichi's 2006 Strategic Plan recommended commercializing the Miramichi Open River Museum, which is a network of 11 cultural, heritage, and natural attractions stretching along 55 km of the Miramichi River within the City (City of Miramichi, 2006). Commercializing the museum was intended to strengthen the community's social, recreational, heritage, cultural, educational, and quality of life characteristics, as well as increase property values.

- In 2007, transportation strategies in support of economic development were outlined (ADI Limited, 2007). Addressing critical infrastructure issues, the strategies presented focused on connecting the City and region with the wider world as part of a more comprehensive and strategic approach to economic development. For the first time, prominent among the recommendations was the need to develop educational and human resources training and opportunities in research and development.
- Also in 2007, a community growth strategy (PK Consulting, 2007a) identified four economic-sector priorities: forestry and forestry-based manufacturing; tourism; value-added manufacturing (metal fabrication and value-added wood products for export); and knowledge-based industries (animation and upscale customer-contact centres).
- Finally in 2007, a completed strategic plan for the whole Miramichi region (PK Consulting, 2007b) showed that between 2003 and 2006 the animation sector produced close to 70 net new jobs. The plan focused on three key sectors: knowledge-based industries (animation and call centres); value-added manufacturing (metal fabrication and value-added wood); and tourism.

The spate of plans and strategies underscores the region's sense of urgency to find workable place-based solutions to local economic challenges. It also demonstrates how decision makers have grappled with development fads (clusters) and moved from traditional (forestry) to knowledge (animation) economy options. There is no shortage of ideas, but there are significant hurdles to implementation. These include, among others, few resources, weak implementation strategies, dependency on the private sector and federal/provincial government programs, and so on.

Policy Context

A number of larger policy initiatives are in place to support the region as it copes with changes to its economic foundation. The Miramichi Regional Economic Development Fund (MREDF) was established by the province in 2004. The commitment is $25 million and the province's Regional Development Corporation will manage the funds until 2009. MREDF's purpose is to fund economic and social development activities to facilitate the transition from a resource-based economy to the new global economy, including education and training, research and development, economic diversification, and strategic infrastructure.

The Province of New Brunswick released its Self-Sufficiency Action Plan in 2007, which has resulted in the following investments in the Miramichi region:

- Funding for a new community action committee ($160,000, a storefront operation in collaboration with the companies and respective unions in the Miramichi region to provide a variety of services to the workers and families affected by the mill closure).
- Labour force expansion funding for Fatkat Animation Studios ($370,000, 35 new jobs). Fatkat Animation Studios also received four New Brunswick Film Tax Credits for its work on recent productions ($405,842).
- Funding for new seats for NBCC Miramichi students ($151,000, eight new seats for carpentry and 14 new seats for welding training).

- Up to 150 new jobs by partnering with the ATCON Group (an important Miramichi-based manufacturer) to support the creation of a new $21.5-million Centre of Excellence in Steel Fabrication in Miramichi. ATCON also received a $3,250,000 repayable loan, a $3,060,000 forgivable loan, and $1,190,000 under the MREDF; to create highly skilled, sustainable employment for people in the region (Government of New Brunswick, 2007a; 2007b; 2007c).

In addition, the federal government announced a national Community Development Trust Fund in 2008 in response to the deepening crisis of job losses and industry closures, primarily in rural Canada and in the natural resources sector. New Brunswick's share was $30 million, and the provincial government identified several immediate measures for the fund. These measures included:

- Supporting economic adjustment in hard-pressed communities such as Miramichi;
- Funding research and development related to innovative uses of engineered wood, biofuels, and energy efficiency;
- Analysing the New Brunswick forest industry's competitive position in world markets;
- Examining opportunities for supplying natural gas to northern communities in order to lower industry energy costs;
- Accelerating mining opportunities (Government of Canada, 2008).

Animation and Its Place in the Provincial Economy

Animation (including computer, flash, 2-D, 3-D, Claymation, traditional drawing, and other media) is part of a wider set of knowledge- and creative-based economic activities. Animation and related activities are found in information and cultural industries, as well as in arts, entertainment, and recreation industries. Related sectors include motion pictures, post-production, broadcasting, Internet publishing, telecommunications, Internet service providers, film publishing, and amusement arcades. Additional sectors include advertising, marketing, and simulation, and educational gaming, among others. Figure 10.2 presents a conceptual model of the animation cluster.

In 2004, New Brunswick's gaming, simulation, and animation (GSA) industry included 45 companies and educational institutions (mostly in the province's three larger urban centres). The sector employed 1,500 people. At that time, there were few start-up companies; most were at least five years old. Most private and educational organizations were, however, optimistic about growth (Red Hot Learning Inc., 2004). The five most common vertical markets for GSA companies at that time were entertainment, manufacturing, Internet telecommunications, post-secondary academic institutions, and subcontracting from other firms. This broad range of potential markets—local, regional, national, and international—spoke to the potential for growth.

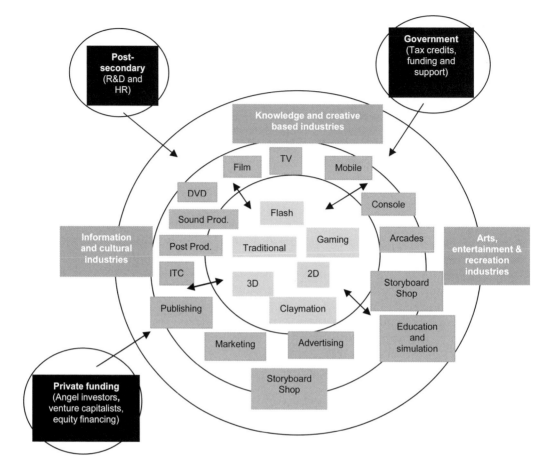

Fig. 10.2 The animation cluster.

The Literature: Cluster Development and Creative Cities

In recent years, clusters have been seen as a means to stimulate local and regional economies. Cortright (2006, p. 3) defines a cluster as a set of "firms and related economic actors and institutions that draw productive advantage from their mutual proximity and connections." More specifically, a knowledge cluster has been defined as "an innovative, interrelated group of firms that gain competitive advantages from side-to-side building and transmitting knowledge between local actors and institutions. A cluster can revolve around a certain industry, or it may involve technologies that cross industry boundaries" (Hubert H. Humphrey Institute of Public Affairs, 2004, p. 14). One element that sets a cluster apart from a simple constellation of like firms and businesses is the ongoing collective sharing of knowledge and technology, through both formal agreements and the natural diffusion of information. Knowledge transfer in this manner can involve "both the formal transfer of innovations between firms and researchers at local institutes of higher learning, for example, via technology licensing, as well as more informal processes by which ideas are exchanged (e.g., in cafes, the hiring of graduates, the departure of experienced employees to launch their own firms)" (FAD Research Inc., 2005, p. 76). For the successful development of an animation cluster in Miramichi, there will need to be considerable growth in the number and type of related firms. This will in turn create the critical mass required to facilitate the sharing of knowledge.

Drawing on the initial work of Porter, Cortright (2006) identifies four main elements or conditions required for cluster success:

- Factor conditions: A skilled labour force, specialized infrastructure, and educational institutions are present.
- Demand conditions: Sophisticated and demanding local customers force continuous innovation. Firms cooperate with their customers to meet their needs, which in turn may lead to greater competitiveness in global markets (given the highly global nature of the animation sector, this condition may be somewhat less important in this context).
- Related and supporting industries: Local suppliers and competitive, related industries are needed to create a broad base of support and can lead innovation and the exchange of information and knowledge about processes and products.
- Firm strategy, structure, and rivalry: Individual businesses upgrade and invest continuously to remain competitive. In cases where local competition or rivalry exist, there will be enhanced motivation to be innovative. Together, firm strategy and rivalry contribute to regional competitiveness.

For an animation sector cluster to emerge in Miramichi, new business starts are needed in a variety of complementary sectors, such as media arts, advertising, computer stores, and so on. It will also require fostering a research and development culture among businesses and the NBCC. Investments in these activities—both in the public and private sectors—are part of the multiplier effect of an emerging cluster. As a cluster grows, and there is a larger constellation of complementary businesses within and around it, the spending by the sector remains more localized and enhances the overall economy.

It is not possible to "force" a cluster into existence. Clusters are organic in nature and have a life of their own that evolves over time. What is required is that interested stakeholders make investments in those elements that may create the conditions for a cluster to evolve and grow. In the case of the animation sector in Miramichi, this means investing in quality of life enhancements, entrepreneurship, skills development, labour force development, and industry supports, which will in turn create an environment conducive to business attraction and endogenous business start-ups.

The Creative City in a Rural Region

Animation is first and foremost an artistic endeavour practised by creative individuals. If Miramichi is to attract and retain creative minds, it is necessary to consider the concept of the creative city as a possible strategy. Who comprises the creative class and what features do they look for in a creative city? Can small cities and rural regions be considered creative, too?

The creative class is attracted to places with diversity, quality of place, high acceptance of differences, outdoor recreation, and street-level entertainment. Artists want cafés, sidewalk musicians, local stores, and small bistros. They crave stimulation, not escape, and want many different things to do. Creative cities are unique and authentic communities that have heritage buildings and celebrated local culture and music (Florida, 2002). Florida's empirical work (Florida and Gates, 2001, 2003) suggests that it is medium-sized cities rather than the largest cities that attract the creative class, especially those medium-sized cities that have a more diverse labour force, which is less dependent on service-sector jobs.

Florida's research (2002) shows that communities are generally successful when they attract creative people. However, if communities want to appeal to the creative class, they must be open to creativity and diversity. They need to spend money on projects that will benefit large numbers of residents, such as developing trail systems instead of attracting a professional sports team. Furthermore, communities need to be open to immigration and must develop a successful "people climate." Many cities do not want to focus on attracting young people because they tend to be transient and do not have a lot of money to spend. The focus is often on young families and retirees. However, members of the creative class are "youthful"—they remain young at heart no matter their age, and they infuse energy into community life. They go to concerts, take in art exhibits, and live active lifestyles (they cycle, they walk, and so on). Additionally, members of the creative class want their children to grow up in a community characterized by tolerance, activity, and diversity. Investments in these elements are a necessity.

Bain (2003) notes that the common features of neighbourhoods to which artists are drawn include the availability of the following: marginal, overlooked spaces; improvizational space; rundown areas; old factories and warehouses; and areas that do not reflect dominant social values. The creative class likes to be in areas that are becoming, evolving, and changing. They also value downtown locations because they associate creativity with the energy and intensity of life in a bustling area. In Miramichi, Fatkat Animation recently purchased the former Royal Canadian Legion building in the downtown of former Newcastle and extensively renovated it for its production studios. Immediately, the "life" of the downtown area changed as animators looked for interesting outlets for their creative minds in the immediate neighbourhood. A further advantage in this particular case was that this relatively "small place" had lower real estate costs and offered easy commutes to work, while still being connected to a global economy.

Many of the features of creative cities are also those of high-technology growth cities. With increased creativity comes an increase in technology development (Florida and Gates, 2003). Technology cities tend to be more racially integrated and are socially, culturally, and ethnically diverse. The creative class usually flocks to smaller urban centres. However, as McGranahan and Wojan (2007) note, rural communities also have features that are attractive to the creative class. The authors argue that the quality of life in a rural place may outweigh the lower incomes people may make there. The rural landscape can foster creativity and the imagination. Therefore, rural areas should attract and retain talented young people, as well as families, in order to maintain their talent base and economies.

Looking Ahead: A Vision for the Animation Sector in Miramichi

The Miramichi region has an emerging animation sector with particular strengths in multimedia web design and e-learning subsectors. The main reason for this strength is the local community college and its multimedia program. The region has also established a foothold in the business of customer-service centres. Building on this foundation will serve to provide an important asset to the region as it transitions to a more diversified economy. As of 2007, the broader sector of information computer technology (including animation) included 22 businesses that employ 923 people (5% of the region's total labour force) (PK Consulting, 2007b).

The vision for the animation sector in Miramichi is "a growing, vibrant and internationally recognized animation and gaming sector within a sustainable and diverse Miramichi economy" (Marlin *et al.*, 2007, p. 3).

There are a number of key strengths for the animation sector in Miramichi. The region is an affordable place to live that is friendly and safe, the pace of life is slower than in a larger centre, and the environment is clean. It is a good area for hiking, fishing, and canoeing, and the natural environment afforded by the Miramichi River, ocean, and forests is a perfect backdrop for an arts-and-culture niche. Fatkat offers salaried, full-time positions with health and other benefits, which is uncommon in the animation sector due to the cyclical nature of the business. High-speed Internet covers 90–95% of the City. NBCC Miramichi is home to New Brunswick's only college-level animation and gaming programs and is a Centre of Excellence in Multimedia Learning Technology that attracts instructors from all over the world. The college produces more than 40 highly skilled and qualified graduates from its animation and gaming programs every year (Marlin *et al.*, 2007).

Weaknesses, Challenges, and Opportunities

Miramichi, however, has several weaknesses. The population of Miramichi, like many communities in Atlantic Canada, is decreasing. Because of poor highway conditions and limited regional bus service, Miramichi is isolated from larger centres such as Moncton and Fredericton (and their airports). There is no local public transportation and taxis can be expensive. The amalgamation of towns, villages, and rural areas more than ten years ago continues to present integration challenges for the City and for community organizations. There are perceived rivalries between the old towns of Chatham and Newcastle, and there is no single, focused downtown core. Perceptions about Miramichi as "an old, meat and potatoes, pulp-mill town" remain entrenched. The belief that residents do not readily accept change or diversity is also deeply rooted. Miramichi continues to be thought of as a retirement city (the average age of residents is 40) and has been marketed that way, particularly since the closure of CFB Chatham. There is a large segment of older residents; younger people often do not want to stay because they feel there is nothing for them to do; and people under 40 are not well represented on the municipal council. There is a lack of doctors, after-hours clinics, and affordably priced apartments in the downtown areas, and, as in many cities, other social problems, such as drug use, also exist (Marlin *et al.*, 2007).

There are also some specific challenges for the animation sector. Studios do not have skilled employees, flexible training options, financing, and effective marketing. There is a lack of female employees (and female-oriented businesses) in Miramichi. In this male-dominated sector, a shortage of female employees is a key retention issue for young male employees; if there are relatively few potential life partners with similar interests and values in the region, young males may choose to leave the region. Miramichi does not have the range and types of stores and dining establishments that animators would frequent, such as speciality restaurants, art and music stores, cafés, comic-book shops, and computer stores. There is a general scarcity of entertainment options such as live contemporary music, live theatre, art galleries, night clubs and other social activities. As previously discussed, Miramichi also lacks many of the businesses that are complementary to the animation sector. Another major weakness, for which little action may be possible, is the absence of a critical mass of post-secondary educational institutions to support a research-and-development culture (which in turn stimulates the sector). There is also a perceived lack of communication between stakeholders in the sector. All players need to be aware of what others are doing or have achieved and how they could work together cooperatively to further promote the sector (Marlin *et al.*, 2007).

Despite the apparent shortcomings of Miramichi for the animation sector, there are many external opportunities. Knowledge sectors, such as animation, are likely to continue to be highly successful. Thus, they offer an effective way to diversify the local economy in a sustainable manner. Since significant growth in the animation sector is expected across Canada, the anticipated influx of new people into Miramichi provides opportunities to open new businesses and offer new services, such as shops and dining establishments, entertainment (e.g., live music, buskers, pubs, and radio stations), sound production houses, 3-D animation studios, and female-oriented businesses to support female workers in the animation sector. Furthermore, since production costs in New Brunswick are generally low, up-and-coming technology centres like China, Korea, India, and Malaysia may seek to partner with local firms on animation development projects. With the availability of high-speed Internet, companies in Miramichi can take advantage of opportunities around the world (Marlin *et al.*, 2007).

External threats, however, do exist, which neither Miramichi nor its animation sector can control. If animation companies open in nearby cities such as Moncton or Fredericton, young and highly mobile employees may decide to leave Miramichi for a city with more night life, an active music scene, more stores, and so on. Fatkat has been unique in offering salaried full-time positions with benefits, but other companies in Canada and the United States are catching on. Furthermore, other provinces such as British Columbia, Ontario, and Quebec now offer impressive tax credits for the animation sector whereas New Brunswick currently does not. This may limit the start-up of additional businesses in Miramichi that would help to establish an animation cluster. Furthermore, low production costs in developing countries like India may take work away from local companies in Miramichi.

To combat these possible threats, an action plan has been developed to help grow and nurture Miramichi as an animation hub (Marlin *et al.*, 2007). Since 2007, the City has focused on the following initiatives:

- Implementation of a new public transit service that connects residents and visitors to important shopping-and-service areas, such as Douglastown, the hospital, Acadian Lines, the VIA train station, churches, recreation venues, and so on;
- Beautification and revitalization of the downtown areas by planting more trees along streets to create an inviting urban forest in addition to public gardens and park benches;
- Restoration and revitalization of historic and rundown buildings;
- Establishment of an Animation Task Force that includes:
  - o Enterprise Miramichi, Atlantic Canada Opportunities Agency, Business New Brunswick, the City, the Chamber of Commerce, the Business Improvement Area, and the newly formed Miramichi Regional Multicultural Association,
  - o staff members from Fatkat, the Child Safety Research and Innovation Center, and from any new similar companies,
  - o and instructors and students from the animation and gaming programs at NBCC.

Another positive development is the recent opening of a new information technology company, Hostopia.com Inc., with a customer-support call centre. Hostopia has created 200 new jobs and is helping to grow the range of complementary firms.

Actions the Miramichi Region Needs to Take

To support a robust animation sector, Miramichi should take action on a variety of fronts. Developing new rental housing that is both affordable and aesthetically pleasing is key to attracting newcomers to downtown areas, and reinstating the Miramichi Welcome Wagon service would help them settle into the community. Establishing new arts and culture festivals would highlight animation as well as cultural diversity. Increasing awareness about cultural diversity within the City would help to promote understanding and tolerance of differences. The creation of an arts-and-culture officer post for the City would also help to increase awareness, encourage acceptance of diversity, and celebrate local history and culture. Improving intercity transportation services would provide better linkages to larger centres, especially to Moncton and Fredericton.

Furthermore, the region needs to attract and/or gain support from the businesses that animators and younger people would frequent, such as comic-book shops, clothing stores, art and music stores, ethnic restaurants, and unique pubs and cafés. Business New Brunswick should actively consider offering animation and gaming tax credits on New Brunswick labour that are competitive with other provinces (Marlin *et al.*, 2007). Such tax credits would mean anywhere from 15% (as in British Columbia) to 37.5% (as in Quebec). NBCC should take the lead on developing a culture of research and development in the region, which may involve finding funding opportunities, supporting faculty and staff in grant writing, providing additional research equipment, and so on. Taking the lead also means that NBCC should reach out to the business community and build an inventory of research capacity and interests that may in turn foster research and development more widely in Miramichi.

Conclusion

For a small community or region to have all the core elements in place to support cluster development and the creative class is quite a challenge. Certainly, many of these elements are present in Miramichi, such as a skilled labour force, an educational institution, and innovation among existing animation and gaming firms. However, there is no "local market;" there is a lack of competition between and cooperation among existing local firms (because there are so few of them); there is little in the way of local suppliers and related businesses; and there is a need for a larger critical mass. Despite earlier efforts to implement economic policies focused on the forestry sector, more general attention is now being paid to investing in quality of life and encouraging tolerance and social and cultural diversity—elements that are currently weak and require concerted, specific actions.

What do the features of a cluster suggest about the prospects for developing one in the Miramichi region that is focused on animation? Concerted action on numerous fronts is required to address challenges and to build on strengths. These action items include, but are not limited to the following:

- Investing in research and development, and engaging in knowledge sharing;

- Finding and supporting vertical and horizontal business linkages and companies;
- Creating a strong sense of tolerance and supporting cultural and ethnic diversity;
- Continuing to support and nurture entrepreneurship;
- Investing in basic infrastructure to support quality of life and business needs.

Nurturing the development of an animation cluster in the Miramichi region holds promise for an effective place-based economic development strategy. The region offers some unique attributes and assets for this sector, and strategic investments in community infrastructure (i.e., investments in place) are underway. New investments in retail, cultural diversity, and business attraction are still needed. Enterprise Miramichi is playing a critical role in facilitating the development of the animation sector as a key component in the region's economy. However, serious efforts by the private sector and all three levels of government to invest in "place" are needed to achieve economic development through spinoff businesses complementary to animation and to enhance the "rootedness" of the sector.

References

ADI Limited. (2007) *Final Report: Transportation Strategies in Support of Economic Development in the Miramichi Region*. Prepared for the City of Miramichi and the Atlantic Institute of Transportation and Logistics.

Bain, A. (2003) Constructing contemporary artistic identities in Toronto neighbourhoods. *Canadian Geographer* 47(3), 303–317.

Baker Consulting (in association with Daniel K. Glenn Ltd.). (2005) *Miramichi Open River Museum Business Plan*. Prepared for the City of Miramichi.

Barnes, T., and Hayter, R. (1992) The little town that could: Flexible accumulation and community change in Chemainus. *Regional Studies* 26, 647–663.

CBC News. (2008) Forestry aid gets mixed reaction in New Brunswick, www.cbc.ca/canada/new-brunswick/story/2008/01/11/forestry-react.html (accessed 31 January 2008).

City of Miramichi. (2006) *Strategic Plan*. Author, Miramichi, NB.

Cortright, J. (2006) *Making sense of clusters: Regional competitiveness and economic development*. Discussion paper prepared for the Brookings Institution Metropolitan Policy Program.

Daniel K. Glenn Ltd. (in association with Ekistics Planning and Design and FGA Consultants Ltd.). (1999) *Miramichi Riverfront Strategic Plan*. Prepared for the City of Miramichi.

FAD Research Inc. (2005) *New Media in PEI: Strategy towards Economic Development and Export*. Prepared for the Innovation and Technology Association of Prince Edward Island.

Florida, R. (2002) The rise of the creative class: Why cities without gays and rock bands are losing the economic development race. *Washington Monthly* 34(5), www.washingtonmonthly.com/features/2001/0205.florida.html (accessed 31 January 2008).

Florida, R., and Gates, G. (2001) Technology and tolerance: The importance of diversity to high-technology growth. Center on Urban and Metropolitan Policy, the Brookings Institution, Washington, DC.

_____ (2003) Technology and tolerance: The importance of diversity to high-technology growth. In: Clark, T., and Boyne, G. (eds.) *Research in Urban Policy*. Vol. 9, *The City as an Entertainment Machine*. JAI Press, Stamford, CT, 199–219.

Gordon, P., Shotbolt, K., and Irving, J. (2008) The future of the forestry industry. *Moncton This Week*, January 16, p. A2.

Government of Canada. (2008) Office of the Prime Minister. PM unveils new community development trust, 10 January, pm.gc.ca/eng/media.asp?category=1&id=1959 (accessed 13 March 2008).

Government of New Brunswick. (n.d.) Department of Transportation. The four lane Trans-Canada Highway in New Brunswick, www.gnb.ca/0113/Fed-prov/progress/map-e.asp (accessed 16 June 2008).

_____. (2007a) Premier announces support for Miramichi region, 14 August, www.gnb.ca/cnb/news/bnb/2007e1027bn.htm (accessed 13 March 2008).

_____. (2007b) New investment and jobs coming to Miramichi, 26 September, www.gnb.ca/cnb/news/bnb/2007e1217bn.htm (accessed 13 March 2008).

_____. (2007c) *Our Action Plan to be Self-Sufficient in New Brunswick*. Province of New Brunswick, Fredericton, NB.

Hubert H. Humphrey Institute of Public Affairs. (2004) *Knowledge Clusters and Entrepreneurship in Regional Economic Development*. University of Minnesota, Minneapolis.

Humphreys, C. (1990) Timber-dependent communities. In: Luloff, A. and Swanson, L. (eds.) *American Rural Communities*. Westview Press, Boulder, CO, 34–60.

Luloff, A. (1990) Small town demographics: Current patterns of community development. In: Luloff, A., and Swanson, L. (eds.) *American Rural Communities*. Westview Press, Boulder, CO, 7–18.

Marlin, A., Zwicker, G., and Bruce, D. (2007) *Animation in the Miramichi: Creating the Future.* Prepared for Enterprise Miramichi.

McGranahan, D., and Wojan, T. (2007) The creative class: A key to rural growth. *Amber Waves* 5(2), 17–21.

Natural Resources Canada. (2006) Industries and communities in transition, canadaforests.nrcan.gc.ca/articletopic/7 (accessed 23 January 2008).

Parkins, J., and White, B. (2007) *Assessment of Forest Dependent Communities: A Scoping Report*. Prepared for the Canadian Council of Forest Ministers Forest Communities Working Group.

PK Consulting. (2005) *Final Report: Activation of a Forest and Manufacturing Cluster in the Miramichi Region*. Prepared for Enterprise Miramichi.

_____. (2007a) *Community Growth Strategy for the Miramichi Region*. Prepared for Enterprise Miramichi.

_____. (2007b) *Strategic Plan for the Miramichi Region*. Prepared for Enterprise Miramichi.

Red Hot Learning Inc. (2004) *New Brunswick Capacity Study: Gaming, Simulation and Animation Industry Report*. Prepared for Enterprise Greater Moncton.

SGE Acres Limited. (2005a) *Downtown Strategy—Signage/Image and Marketing Background Report*. Prepared for the City of Miramichi.

_____. (2005b) *Final Report: City of Miramichi Strategic Plan for Downtown Revitalization*. Prepared for the City of Miramichi.

SGE Group. (2002) *Final Report: Miramichi Economic Development Initiative*. Prepared for the City of Miramichi.

Statistics Canada. (2006) Small Area and Administrative Data Division. *Table A: Migration by Age Group, 1999–2000 to 2003–2004* (91C0025). Author, Ottawa.

Williamson, T., and Annamraju, S. (1996) *Analysis of the Contribution of the Forest Industry to the Economic Base of Rural Communities in Canada* (Working Paper No. 43). Industry, Economics and Programs Branch, Canadian Forest Service, Natural Resources Canada, Ottawa.

Chapter 11

Co-Constructing Rural Communities in the 21st Century: Challenges for Central Governments and the Research Community in Working Effectively with Local and Regional Actors

Christopher Bryant

The Context

Small-town and rural communities across Canada are facing major challenges that neither the research community nor central governments have effectively or systematically addressed. The challenges range from rapid population growth in the context of our major urban and metropolitan regions to continued decline or stagnation in resource peripheries because of changes to their economic base. Even within these two broad regional types, there is considerable heterogeneity of circumstances—demographic growth versus stagnation, economic revival versus economic collapse, conflict versus harmonious transformation.

This heterogeneity is firmly linked to the two major themes of this book—place-based rural development and the "next rural economies." Place-based rural development builds explicitly on the specificities of rural territories. Managing change in rural places also calls for a place-based development of appropriate governance processes and structures, a major concern in this chapter as places and their actors determine the course of rural communities, integrating them into the constantly evolving economies—and societies—of rural places, as well as developing those new economies and societies themselves. In this chapter, I tackle two broad types of rural communities—periurban rural communities and more peripheral rural communities—always stressing, however, the essential heterogeneity of communities in each category.

Taking agricultural communities as the example, it is obvious to anyone with field experience that periurban agricultural communities are very heterogeneous. Many such communities are still experiencing the continued transformations that mirror what has been happening in the broader agricultural economy. Others are experiencing decline, and their agricultural territories are in effect undergoing destabilization and degeneration, partly in response to the pressures of urban development and partly in response to other pressures such as interregional and international competition. Still others, apparently defying all odds, function in environments where there are significant pressures, but where the farmers and their families have been able to adapt, proactively, to the pressures and even seize or create opportunities that allow their farm businesses to flourish. This simple framework recalls the threefold categorization of farming landscapes proposed by Bryant (1984): landscapes of agricultural development, landscapes of agricultural degradation, and landscapes of agricultural adaptation. The landscapes of agricultural degradation clearly pose a set of challenges for the agricultural and broader rural communities in those territories.

Other types of periurban communities are also affected by other stresses and processes. For instance, around most major cities there are rural communities that have experienced demographic growth through upmarket residential development involving people—perhaps early retirees or long-distance commuters—who are seeking amenity landscapes to retire to or in which to bring up their families. An example is the municipality of Val-David, 75 minutes north of Montreal in the Laurentian Mountains (Solidarité Rural du Québec, 2008), where an almost continuous influx of migrants over at least 40 years, largely from nearby Montreal, has transformed the community into a dynamic place with an upscale housing market. A number of problems have been identified in Val-David, including how to integrate families attracted by an expanding regional tourism industry that tends to pay lower incomes, making it difficult for such families to access housing.

Rural areas and communities in more peripheral regions confront issues that can be territorially and regionally specific, and others that are more widespread. Population decline remains endemic in many Canadian rural communities, accompanied by an eroding economic base. The cumulative process of stagnation and decline is still a fact of life for many such communities, although some have been able to adapt and develop a renewed economic base, albeit more often than not at a lower population level. Other communities have experienced an expansion of their population base and a rejuvenation of their economic base.

Throughout the rural-agricultural communities of our periurban areas and in more peripheral rural territories and communities, other challenges are widespread, although these issues also generally possess a territorially specific component. One example is the set of issues surrounding agricultural pollution and its impacts on communities and environments. In this case, the consequences and impacts can be transmitted over wide areas, posing real challenges for mitigation and intervention.

Another example is climate change and variability. While this is now overwhelmingly seen as a global phenomenon, the potential impacts, consequences, and appropriate forms of adaptation are increasingly seen as territorially specific because the nature of many of the impacts and consequences are themselves territorially specific (Bryant *et al.*, 2007, 2008). In addition, the ability of communities to adapt to this phenomenon can also be territorially specific, requiring territorially or place-sensitive intervention and support. The phenomenon of climate change may well turn out to be the single most important process and phenomenon to impinge on rural communities throughout the world in the 21st century.

In both the two broad types of issues—those that are distinctly territorially specific or place-based and those that are more widespread—there are challenges in how to deal with them, what form of intervention (individual, community, or governmental) is the most appropriate, and how to construct those interventions. However, in both cases, the issues can always be associated with territory since impacts always affect territories and the communities that are part of them. I argue below that strategic place-based development planning and implementation is what is required to create and maintain sustainable rural communities and allow them to participate in the development of the next rural economies. Already, some territories and their communities have been able to rise to the occasion, frequently—but not always—with support from other levels of government. In relation to all of these issues, a number of questions must be addressed: What are the roles of legislation and the application of rules and regulations? What is the role of other forms of intervention and involvement in the solution of those problems? What is the role of community and regional actors, including the populations themselves? In short, what are the most appropriate and effective forms of governance for these transforming rural communities? The chapter is very much focused on the communities that are most severely affected by the different processes and stresses mentioned above—and there are other stresses too, such as international competition and technological change.

Drawing on field work undertaken in central Canada in rural territorial development, I argue in this chapter that the key to managing change lies within the grasp of local and regional actors, but that central governments (federal and provincial in Canada) can facilitate these processes. Developing territorially sensitive processes and structures of governance, including strategic planning and its implementation, are central to place-based development. Such place-based construction of governance processes and structures does not, of course, occur in a vacuum, and it is important to recognize the significance of local and regional actors combining with other actors, such as federal and provincial governments and their agencies, as well as non-governmental organizations (NGOs), to co-construct those processes and structures. I argue that the researcher can also play a constructive role in this place-based co-construction process, and I suggest that the most rewarding and productive role is to engage in an action research process.

I will begin the chapter with some comments about managing change in rural communities, suggesting a framework that communities and local and regional actors can use to analyse and manage change, and describing the changing role of central government. Then I will discuss the implications for the role of the researcher in investigating rural community management of change.

Managing Change in Rural Communities and Territories

The "Dynamic of Localities" Framework as a Tool of Practice and Research

A useful way of looking at change is through the model of the dynamic of localities (Fig.11.1) (Bryant *et al.*, 1998; Frej *et al.*, 2003). In this framework, there are seven components, which, it is suggested, represent (a) the components of a locality (community, region, ...) that must be analysed if we are to understand the dynamic of the locality, and (b) the building blocks for the analysis, planning, and management of rural communities and localities. The seven components are: (1) actors (local and non-local), characterized by (2) their different interests and objectives, capacities, resources, and power and influence. These actors undertake actions (3) in the pursuit of their interests and objectives. To facilitate their actions, they can draw upon (or construct or re-construct) their networks (4) of relations to help them mobilize support, resources, and information, among other things. These networks represent both the formal organization of a locality (5a) and the informal social organization of space (5b). The cumulative result of the different actions taken by the many actors present gives rise to patterns in time and space resulting in different localities being characterized by different orientations (6). When these orientations can be observed, they are termed actual orientations (6a); when the conditions appear ripe for a specific orientation that has not yet emerged or been recognized, we can label it a latent orientation

(6b). Both—after reflection and choice by the community and local actors—can be used as strategic orientations, in which actions are pursued to achieve the vision the community has constructed for itself. All of this, of course, takes place in specific contexts, at a variety of scales (7). These contexts possess economic, politico-administrative, cultural, and political dimensions, all of which can potentially change and influence the decision-making processes underway in a locality. These contexts also contain various resources that actors can access through the networks they construct (Bryant, 1999a, 1999b).

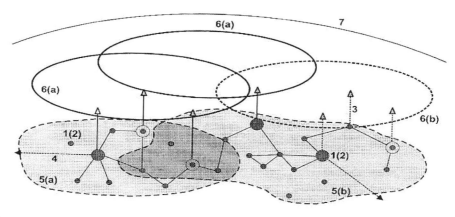

Key
1. Actors; 2. Interests and objectives; 3. Actions; 4. Networks; 5 (a). Formal organization; 5 (b). Informal organization; 6 (a). Observed orientation; 6 (b). Latent orientation; 7. Context.

Fig. 11.1 The dynamic of localities (after Bryant *et al.*, 1998).

The literature discussing dynamic of localities (e.g., Marsden *et al.*, 1993; Bryant, 1995a, 1999b; Frej *et al.*, 2003; Bryant and Mitchell, 2006) has provided useful descriptions and explanations of the different types of strategies actors (including farmers) have adopted in the domain of the adaptation of human activities to external forces (Bryant, 1984, 1995a; Bryant and Johnston, 1992 [2007]).

In the dynamic-of-localities work, the emphasis is on understanding how actors interplay with each other, how they mobilize resources by using and constructing networks in order to achieve their objectives (both personal and collective), how their actions create particular profiles of development for an area, and how this whole dynamic can be influenced by parameters established, and resources located, in the broader political, administrative, socio-cultural, and economic contexts. The work specifically on local actors demonstrates how groups of actors—including collective actors, such as municipalities and their agents, professional associations, and groups of citizens—may combine to resolve issues to their mutual satisfaction. By extension, this more concerted reflection and action can contribute to successful strategic planning and action at the community or territorial level (Bryant, 1995c, 1999b; Bryant and Mitchell, 2006; Claval, 2006).

The Changing Role of Central Government in Relation to Rural Communities and Activities

While it has been common to talk about the retreat of the central government in Western society in the face of globalization, corporate restructuring, and technological change (among other processes), it is perhaps fairer to speak about the redefinition of the role of government in the wake of the multiple transformations that societies and economies have experienced over the last 40 years or so. This redefinition of roles in relation to local, and especially rural, communities has moved at different speeds in different countries (Bryant and Cofsky, 2004), but it has generally involved a move away from central government holding overwhelming importance as a provider of development capital, and a shift toward governmental roles that involve framing community development (through legislation and various programs) and accompanying communities by providing strategic information, counselling, and facilitation to local and regional actors as they pursue their own development planning and action processes.

The challenges are enormous because central governments are not necessarily particularly well suited to these new roles. Given this reality, it becomes even more important to construct productive linkages between the different levels of government—local, regional, provincial, and federal. Even when a central government desires to perform these new roles, it may be more appropriate for the central government to develop partnerships with specific organizations at the local and regional level that may be better placed to discharge such functions. They may, for instance, be better prepared to perform such roles because they have a permanent presence in the area, they may be more credible in the eyes of the other local and regional actors, and they may be more flexible in their ability to deal with other actors.

The Co-Construction of Public and Collective Intervention

Processes of co-construction of communities and their governance processes and structures that involve local, regional, and central state actors, which are beginning to emerge in some Western European countries, appear to hold out considerable hope. However, maintaining equity and respecting the specificities of place pose major challenges for our central governments in terms of the appropriate roles and functions that their own human resource base needs to adopt and of their own adaptive capacity.

Almost any cross-cultural comparison reveals the influence of political culture—e.g., the nature of the relationships between central, regional, and local state and local populations, and the effectiveness of the networks constructed by the different actors (see Bryant and Cofsky, 2004, on the roles and functions of central states in influencing local development processes).

Action Research and Its Potential Role in Managing and Understanding Change

In this section, I will briefly explore the contexts of two different research domains and the potential role of action research. The discussion will then turn to the two types of rural communities and situations introduced at the beginning of this chapter: urban fringe communities with a degrading agricultural structure; and rural communities facing the challenges of climate change and variability.

Action research involves a researcher or team of researchers becoming part of a real-world process. In the context of rural places, the overall aim can be framed in terms of contributing to the resolution of issues and priorities that are particularly important to the communities and populations in those places.

Action research, however, does not involve the researcher in imposing any particular perspectives on the actors (whether they are local, regional, or "external" actors) and communities he or she is working with. The contribution of researchers on the "action" side of the equation of action research is to impart to those actors the researcher's knowledge when the actors ask for it. It puts the researcher in a particularly sensitive position; he or she must always be mindful of the importance of taking a back seat to the discussions, analyses, and diagnostics constructed by the actors.

At the same time, the "research" side of the equation of action research requires the researcher to be diligent and organized in recording the evolving processes—including identifying the actors and how the composition of actors changes and is recognized in the communities, as well as recording the changing pattern of interests of the different actors, their actions, and the development of their networks—and identifying patterns that might contribute to improved conceptual frameworks for understanding and managing place-based development and its integration into, and construction of, the next rural economies.

Action Research: The Case of Urban Fringe Communities with Agricultural Degradation

1. Research on Urban Fringe Agriculture

Much of the early work on urban fringe agriculture had a major focus on the negative impacts of proximity of urban fringe agriculture to the expanding urban area (see a synthesis of this and subsequent work up until the early 1990s in Bryant and Johnston, 1992 [2007]). However, another current of thinking that emerged rapidly after the early 1980s was that all farmers do not react in the same ways to the multiple stressors they are faced with; some are capable of adapting in very positive ways in these environments under pressure (Bryant, 1984).

More recently, researchers have recognized that the capacity of some farmers to adapt to difficult circumstances has been enhanced by the involvement of other actors—and not just actors involved in the implementation of provincial or national programs to protect agricultural land (Bryant and Granjon, 2007). These actors may be interested in revitalizing periurban agriculture that has faced degradation, so that it can play a constructive role in offering other functions to the urban population. The concept of the multi-functionality of agricultural land is all-important here.

Periurban open space, especially agricultural land, can fill a variety of roles and functions around our cities, especially the larger metropolitan agglomerations, but how well it does this depends in part on human decision makers—notably farmers, local and regional actors, and, sometimes, citizen groups. How do some periurban communities with a significant area of agricultural space that has experienced degradation due to a variety of forces come to appropriate those spaces and plan and construct alternative development trajectories for them?

It is suggested that the key is to understand the interplay of the different actors—private and collective (public, associative, professional)—in the construction of these territories, and to understand how this interplay may be used in the effective planning and management of the development of these agricultural spaces. This can lead to the different actors' appropriation of the different functions involved. The local development literature has already, in many contexts, highlighted the role of local actors (e.g., Dale and Pierce, 1999), including their roles in shaping urban fringe agriculture (Bryant and Granjon, 2007; Caldwell *et al.*, 2007).

2. The Concept of Multi-Functionality of Rural and Agricultural Territories

The concept of multi-functionality of rural and agricultural territories has led to a burgeoning literature, especially in Western Europe (e.g., Fleury 2000, 2001a, 2001b, 2004, 2005, 2006). It recognizes the important functions that such spaces can fulfill for the urban and periurban populations (Berger, 2004; Mollard *et al.*, 2007). The concept is also increasingly being used as a tool in the socio-economic development of the most peripheral rural communities and territories.

Multi-functionality of rural agricultural space involves both private and collective functions of the land. The non-agricultural functions of agricultural spaces, especially in the urban fringe, respond essentially to an urban-based type of demand, including open space, recreation, and conservation of natural and cultural heritage resources (Bryant and Charvet, 2003; Granjon and Bryant, 2004; Mollard *et al.*, 2007; Bryant, 2007). Frequently, the private function of agricultural production, which involves providing an income for the farmer and farm family, has conflicted with the development of these more collective functions, although conflicts are not inevitable. Much depends on how the community's development is managed, how the objectives of the community's development are articulated and by whom (for instance, are farmers involved?), and how potential conflicts are anticipated and dealt with. Much, therefore, depends on the dynamic of the local actors, on how they interact with other levels of actors and processes of management and planning, and, generally, on the openness and transparency of the governance processes involved. How this happens, and what can be done to encourage a positive process, remains one of the most important open questions in the field of periurban agriculture.

3. Action Research in the Urban Fringe

Fleury, in particular, has played a significant role in advancing thinking about periurban agriculture and has increasingly become involved in action research (Fleury, 2000, 2004, 2006; Bouraoui *et al.*, 2001; Donadieu and Fleury, 2003; Fleury and Boudjenouia, 2003; Fleury *et al.*, 2004). Action research in relation to periurban agriculture necessarily involves urban planners, but professional organizations and citizen groups take part as well. Examples of action research in the urban fringe exist elsewhere, such as Fleury's participation in action research involving urban planners and the construction of alternative futures for the communities under consideration.

The researcher has two main objectives from the research perspective: (a) to contribute to the construction of the agricultural territories involved by working with the local and regional actors; and (b) to document and analyse the dynamic of the process in order to identify the building blocks of successful processes (from the farmers' and community's perspectives) that allow for sensitive transference and application elsewhere. The researcher's documentation and analysis is also useful in the development of appropriate practices and strategies for working in other types of rural communities experiencing other stresses.

For both objectives, there is a common set of preliminary stages that appear necessary:

a) Identifying actors and profiling the community, its agriculture, and recent history;

b) Approaching the actors and obtaining their consent to the researcher's or research team's accompanying them in the strategic reflection on, planning for, and management of the periurban territories concerned;

c) Recognizing that, although the actors will be principally local and regional, some central government actors may be essential (e.g., in the case of attempts by several actors in the City of Longueuil, Quebec, to construct a viable agricultural zone from a zone where farming had become destructured, Planchenault [2008] indicates that participation of the Ministry of the Environment was necessary);

d) Agreeing to an involvement based on appropriate forms of accompaniment, counselling, participation in planning, and integration of farm populations;

e) Establishing a data-collection process based on identifying the actors, their interests, their actions, the networking that evolves, and the actions posed—i.e., the ingredients of the dynamic-of-localities model (e.g., Bryant, 1995a; Frej *et al.*, 2003)—throughout the whole process.

Action Research: The Adaptation of Rural Communities to Climate Change and Variability

Since the early 1990s, a team of researchers in the climate change and adaptation domain at the Université de Montréal has integrated climate scenario modelling at the regional, and, more latterly, the relatively local level, with interviews and focus groups involving sets of farmers and managers of tourist facilities (e.g., downhill ski facilities and golf courses), as well as other related professionals (Singh *et al.*, forthcoming). From May 2007 to March 2008, in relation to agriculture, the research has shifted to working with a set of decision makers and actors—governmental, professional, and regional and local organizations, including municipalities—to co-construct appropriate planning mechanisms and forms of collective intervention to reinforce their own and farmers' capacity to adapt to changing climate conditions (Bryant *et al.*, 2008).

The research involves a form of action research. Specifically, the researchers have worked with farmers and other experts to refine the planning tools that will help farmers assess the adaptation strategies they have before them more readily. The researchers have also worked with farmers and other regional actors (two regions were the focus of the most recent research project—the Montérégie and the Saguenay Lac Saint Jean regions) to better assess the implications of climate change and variability, and to identify appropriate forms of strategy as well as which actors might be better suited to carry out the roles and activities involved in those strategies (Bryant *et al.*, 2008). The research provides a good example of the territorialization of collective intervention.

Action Research Generally

Action research (e.g., Bryant, 1999b), therefore, involves going beyond simply transferring appropriate information to decision makers. Much of the earlier work on the research themes identified above has been pursued by researchers observing and codifying what has been occurring, with relatively little attention paid to the decision processes involved, and also with little direct transfer of knowledge to the decision makers in those processes.

Action research can lead to a much more profound understanding of the processes of change, conflict, and negotiation (Mollard *et al.*, 2007; Torre *et al.*, 2007) in the territories where it is followed. It requires the researcher to accompany actors and implicate himself or herself in the process (without imposing any particular solutions or values); at the same time, the researcher records and analyses the processes of transformation, reflection, conflict and negotiation, and identification of potential solutions and their implementation.

The function of transfer of knowledge and construction of knowledge is based on the researcher performing the roles of educator, counsellor, and provider of strategic information as he or she accompanies actors in their deliberations and decision making. It does not require the researcher to impose approaches or any sets of ideas, but, rather, to respond to the different actors' needs and requests as the process evolves. It inherently involves the reinforcement of the researcher's, the actors', and their communities' capacities.

Conclusions

It is obvious but bears repeating: rural communities are heterogeneous. Not only do they have varying resource bases, which respond in different ways to external stressors, but they also vary in terms of their capacity to cope and, more importantly, adapt. As part of their capacity to adapt and manage their own affairs, they can draw upon and construct the social capital in their community or territory necessary for successful collective planning and action, and therefore they can put in place appropriate structures and processes of governance. Place-based development necessarily includes and, many would argue, starts from the construction of such territorially- or place-specific processes and structures.

Managing change does not mean planning and taking action in a vacuum (Bryant, 1995a, 1995b); local and regional actors may require, and more generally benefit from, support and resources from central government. Because the conditions in a locality (community, region) are so variable, and the consequences of the impact of different stressors equally variable, it has become increasingly common to speak about the territorialization of public policy and collective intervention. For instance, such an approach has become commonplace in rural France and France's regions. The following conditions appear to be necessary for successful co-construction of intervention related to rural and small-town communities.

On the part of central governments:
- Recognition of the need to territorialize public policy and the different forms of public and collective intervention;
- Recognition of the value of the contributions of local and regional actors to policy construction;
- Recognition of the limits of central government intervention.

On the part of local and regional actors:
- A readiness to implicate actors who are not necessarily in the immediate domain of interest; for example, for an agricultural problem, being ready to include non-farmers with an environmental orientation in the deliberations;
- Adoption of an open and transparent process to include all actors and a readiness to include new actors as they emerge.

For researchers involved in studying the transformation of rural territories, one of the most important preoccupations has become how to influence the construction of the next rural territories, taking into account the tremendous variety of rural territories. This brings us full circle, to suggesting one of the responses to the theme of this chapter, the co-construction of rural territories and the emerging next rural economies in the 21st century or, in short, how to construct appropriate processes and structures of governance for them.

Naturally, researchers involved in this domain must recognize the heterogeneity of rural communities and territories. It has been suggested above that action research holds out considerable promise, both in terms of research and in terms of the rural territories involved. Two broad orientations of action research appear to be essential:

- All such research must be grounded on the actors present, as well as being capable of involving newly emerging actors as they appear.

Clearly, this necessitates acquiring a sound understanding of the actors, their interests and objectives, and the way in which they take action and mobilize the necessary resources through their networks of social relations. This brings us back to the importance of the dynamic-of-localities model, or some similar framework, for organizing and collecting the data on which to ground appropriate structures and processes of governance (see, for example, Bryant, 1995b, 1999a, 1999b; Frej *et al.*, 2003).

- At the same time, the construction of appropriate forms of governance for rural areas demands that the actors present be the ones who develop the appropriate structures and processes of governance, including, of course, how these structures and processes—and the territories themselves—can be co-constructed with all levels of government and segments and sectors of the population. It is in this context that processes of action research are essential to a successful outcome.

Action research also implies the collection of data to document the dynamic of the processes as they are constructed by local and regional actors (and co-constructed with actors from other levels in society, including governments and NGOs). This begins—and continues—with the production of knowledge on the construction of networks, the mobilization of resources, the participation of actors, and the development of approaches that are essentially cooperative (Morin, 1992a, 1992b; Lavoie *et al.*, 1996). At the same time, involvement in action research processes will help researchers construct theoretical frameworks that can be of much broader application (Saint-Arnaud, 1992; Barbier, 1996). Through all this, the researcher engages in the roles of accompanier, counsellor, provider of strategic information, and facilitator for the networks of actors that exist and are created to tackle the transformation of rural territories (in many ways, the researcher's roles are similar to the emerging functions for central governments identified earlier). Action research is not an innovation in itself (Liu, 1997; Greenwood and Levin, 1998; Crézé and Liu, 2006), but it is certainly at the avant-garde of social science research, and nowhere is this more apparent than in the domain of the co-construction of rural territories, where it contributes to the construction of novel and appropriate forms of governance of rural territories undergoing transformation. These forms of governance, which are inevitably based on participation of all pertinent actors and segments of the population, can be seen as essential to mobilizing the creative energies within the communities and building their capacities to identify and create the developmental trajectories and processes that will sustain them into the future. It is these local actors, through the processes and structures of governance that they themselves construct, and with the support of central governments and the research community, who will define what the next rural economy means for their communities and territories.

Acknowledgements

The author would like to thank the SSHRC for a 2008 research grant dealing with the redynamization of periurban agricultural zones. He would also like to acknowledge the financial support provided by Natural Resources Canada, Climate Change Impacts and Adaptation Division, for various research contracts over the last 10 years for research on agricultural adaptation to climate change, and the professional input as well as financial support provided by Ouranos, Montreal.

References

Barbier, R. (1996) *La recherche action*. Éditions Economica, Paris.
Berger, M. (2004) *Les périurbains de Paris*. CNRS Éditions, Espaces et Milieux, Paris.
Bouraoui, M., Donadieu, P., and Fleury, A. (2001) L'agriculture périurbaine, une chance pour l'aménagement du grand Tunis. *Cahiers agricultures* 10, 261–269.
Bryant, C. (1984) The recent evolution of farming landscapes in urban-centred regions. *Landscape Planning* 11, 307–326.
_____. (1995a) The role of local actors in transforming the urban fringe. *Journal of Rural Studies* 11(3), 255–267.
_____. (1995b) *Strategic Management and Planning for Local and Community Economic Development: I. The Organization*. Sustainable Community Analysis Workbook 2. Econotrends Ltd., St. Eugène, ON.
_____. (1995c) *Strategic Management and Planning for Local and Community Economic Development: I. The Community*. Sustainable Community Analysis Workbook 3. Econotrends Ltd., St. Eugène, ON.
_____. (1999a) Community-based strategic planning, mobilisation and action at the edge of the urban field: The case of Haliburton County. In: Bowler, I., Bryant, C., and Firmino, A. (eds.) *Progress in Research on Sustainable Rural Systems* (Série Estudos, No. 2). Centro de Estudos de Geografia e Planeamento Regional, Universidade Nova de Lisboa, Lisbon, 211–222.
_____. (1999b) Community change in context. In: Dale, A., and Pierce, J. (eds.) *Community Perspectives on Sustainable Development*. Vol. 2 of *Sustainable Development Series*. Sustainable Development Research Institute, University of British Columbia, Vancouver, 69–89.
_____. (2007) A place des espaces ruraux périurbains et de l'environnement dans le développement régional. In: Mollard, A., Sauboua, E., and Hirzak, M. (eds.) *Territoires et enjeux du développement régional*. Éditions Quæ, Versailles, 159–171.
Bryant, C., and Charvet, J. (2003) La zone périurbaine: Structure et dynamiques d'une composante stratégique des régions métropolitaines. *Canadian Journal of Regional Science/Revue canadienne des sciences régionales* 26(2/3), 241–250.
Bryant, C., and Cofsky, S. (2004) *Politiques publiques en développement économique local: Comparaison internationale des approches, des programmes et des outils*. Research report for Développement Économique Canada, Montréal.
Bryant, C., and Granjon, D. (2007) Agricultural land protection in Quebec: From provincial framework to local initiatives. In: Caldwell, W., Hilts, S., and Wilton, B. (eds.) *Farmland*

Preservation—Land for Future Generations. Centre for Land and Water Stewardship, University of Guelph, Guelph, 61–86.

Bryant, C., and Johnston, T. (1992 [2007]) *Agriculture in the City's Countryside.* Pinter Press, London, and University of Toronto Press, Toronto, 1992. Translated into Japanese for Association of Agriculture and Forestry Statistics of Japan, Tokyo, 2007.

Bryant, C., and Mitchell, C. (2006) The city's countryside. In: Bunting, T., and Filion, P. (eds.) *The Canadian City in Transition: The Twenty-First Century,* 3rd edn. Oxford University Press, London, 234–248.

Bryant, C., Desroches, S., and Juneau, P. (1998) Community mobilisation and power structures: Potentially contradictory forces for sustainable rural development. In: Bowler, I., Bryant, C., and Huigen, P. (eds.) *Dimensions of Sustainable Rural Systems* (No. 244). Netherlands Geographical Studies, Utrecht and Groningen, 233–244.

Bryant, C., Singh, B., Thomassin, P., and Baker, L. (2007) *Farm-Level Vulnerabilities and Adaptations to Climate Change in Quebec: Lessons from Farmer Risk Management and Adaptations to Climatic Variability.* Research report submitted to Climate Change Impacts and Adaptation Program, Natural Resources Canada, Ottawa.

Bryant, C., Singh, B., and Thomassin, P. (2008) *Evaluation of Agricultural Adaptation Processes and Adaptive Capacity to Climate Change and Variability: The Co-Construction of New Adaptation Planning Tools with Stakeholders and Farming Communities in the Saguenay-Lac-Saint-Jean and Montérégie Regions of Québec.* Research report for project A1332, submitted to Climate Change Impacts and Adaptation Program, Natural Resources Canada, Ottawa.

Caldwell, W., Hilts, S., and Wilton, B., eds. (2007) *Farmland Preservation—Land for Future Generations.* Centre for Land and Water Stewardship, University of Guelph, Guelph.

Claval, P. (2006) *Géographie régionale: De la région au territoire.* Armand Colin, Collection U, Paris.

Crézé, F., and Liu, M. (2006) *La Recherche-action et les transformations sociales.* Éditions L'Harmattan, Paris.

Dale, A., and Pierce, J., eds. (1999) *Community Perspectives on Sustainable Development.* Vol. 2 of *Sustainable Development Series.* Sustainable Development Research Institute, University of British Columbia, Vancouver.

Donadieu, P., and Fleury, A. (2003) La construction contemporaine de la ville-campagne. *Revue de géographie alpine* 91(4), 19–28.

Fleury, A. (2000) Les nouveaux rapports ville campagne dans l'espace périurbain. *Comptes Rendus de l'Academie d'Agriculture de France* 86(3), 199–213.

_____. (2001a) L'agronomie face aux nouveaux enjeux de l'agriculture: Formes et fonctions de l'agriculture périurbaine. *Comptes Rendus de l'Academie d'Agriculture de France* 87(4), 129–138.

_____. (2001b) Vers une nouvelle agriculture? *Cahiers de l'OIPRA* 2, 33–35.

_____. (2004) La multifonctionnalité de l'agriculture périurbaine en Méditerrannée. In: Nasr, J., and Padilla, M. (eds.) *Interfaces: Agricultures et villes à l'Est et au sud de la Méditerranée.* IFPO, Delta, Paris, 96–111.

_____. (2005) L'agriculture dans la planification de l'Ile-de-France. In: Fleury, A. (ed.) Multifonctionnalité de l'agriculture périurbaine, a special issue of *Les cahiers de la multifonctionnalité* 8, 33–46.

_____. (2006) Quelle ingénierie pour l'agriculture de la ville durable? *Natures sciences sociétés* 14(4), 399–406.

Fleury, A., and Boudjenouia, A. (2003) Urban and periurban agriculture in Setif. *Urban Agriculture Magazine* 11, 22–23.

Fleury, A., Laville, J., Darly, S., and Lenaers, V. (2004) Dynamiques de l'agriculture périurbaine: Du local au local. *Cahiers Agricultures* 1, 1–6.

Frej, S., Doyon, M., Granjon, D., and Bryant, C. (2003) La construction sociale des localités par des acteurs locaux: Conceptualisation et bases théoriques des outils de développement socio-économique. *Interventions économiques* 30(1), http://www.teluq.uquebec.ca/interventionsecon omiques (accessed 14 November 2008).

Granjon, D., and Bryant, C. (2004) La dynamique des localités périurbaines: Les défis de la multifonctionnalité et l'atteinte d'un développement communautaire durable. In: Ramsey, D., and Bryant, C. (eds.) *The Structure and Dynamics of Rural Territories: Geographical Perspectives (A Collection of Essays from the Rural Geography Study Group, Canadian Association of Geographers, 2001 and 2002 Annual Meetings)*. Rural Development Institute, University of Brandon, Brandon, 79–88.

Greenwood, D., and Levin, M. (1998) *Introduction to Action Research: Social Research for Social Change*. Sage, London.

Lavoie, L., Marquis. D., and Laurin, P. (1996) *La recherche-action: Théorie et pratique, manuel auto-formation*. Presses de l'Université du Québec, Quebec City.

Liu, M. (1997) *Fondements et pratiques de la recherche-action*. L'Harmattan, Paris.

Marsden, T., Murdoch, J., Lowe, P., Munton, R., and Flynn, A. (1993) *Constructing the Countryside*. Westview Press, Oxford.

Mollard, A., Sauboua, E., and Hirzak, M., eds. (2007) *Territoires et enjeux du développement régional*. Éditions Quæ, Versailles.

Morin, A. (1992a) *Méthodologie et étude de cas*. Vol. 1 of *Recherche-action intégrale et participation coopérative*. Éditions Agence D'arc, Laval, PQ.

_____. (1992b) *Théorie et rédaction du rapport*. Vol. 2 of *Recherche-action intégrale et participation coopérative*. Éditions Agence D'arc, Laval, PQ.

Planchenault, M. (2008) Le projet pilote «Continuum ville-campagne» de Longueuil: De la résilience territoriale à la gouvernance responsable. In: Loudiyi, S., Bryant, C., and Laurens, L. (eds.) *Territoires périurbains et gouvernance: Perspectives de recherche*. Laboratoire Développement durable et dynamique territoriale, Géographie, Université de Montréal, Montréal, 65-74.

Saint-Arnaud, Y. (1992) *Connaître par l'action*. Presses de l'Université de Montréal, Montréal.

Singh, B., Savoie, M., Bryant, C., Granjon, D., and Pécheux, I. (Forthcoming) Impacts et adaptations aux changements climatiques pour les activités de ski et le tourisme dans le sud du Québec. *Tourisme et territoires*.

Solidarité Rural du Québec. (2008) *Études de cas sur la néo-ruralité et les transformations de la communauté rurale*. Author, Nicolet, PQ.

Torre, A., Aznar, O., Bonin, M., Caron, A., Chia, E., Galman, M., Guérin, M., Jeanneau, P., Kirat, T., Lefranc, C., Paoli, J., Salazar, P., and Thinon, P. (2007) Conflits et tensions autour des usages de l'espace dans les territoires ruraux et périurbains. Le cas de la région Rhône-Alpes et de trois autres zones géographiques françaises. In: Mollard, A., Sauboua, E., and Hirzak, M. (eds.) *Territoires et enjeux du développement régional*. Éditions Quæ, Versailles, in the CD-ROM Appendix.

Chapter 12

Partnerships, People, and Place: Lauding the Local in Rural Development

David Storey

Recent trends in rural development in the United Kingdom (UK) and throughout much of the rest of western Europe reflect a return to, or re-emphasizing of, the local manifested in two interlinked ways. First, the rural development discourse stresses the importance of participation by local agents alongside an espousal of the centrality of community involvement, empowerment, and capacity building. On the face of it, this emphasis on involving local communities appears to reflect a rejection, or at least a questioning, of older "top-down" planning trajectories in favour of a more locally attuned "bottom-up" development process. The second component of this "local turn" is the employment of elements of place distinctiveness (whether drawing on local landscapes, heritage, culture, or identity) in the process of rural regeneration through forms of place promotion and branding. These twin emphases on local involvement and local "resources," raise a series of issues that this chapter endeavours to address. The chapter begins with an overview of debates pertaining to community, partnership, and the "local" and then outlines some points of contention associated with the promotion and commodification of place. The recourse to partnership working and the use of place promotion is then exemplified through reference to market-town strategies in England. The final section of the chapter assesses the implications of this "local turn" for rural development.

Participation, Partnership, Community, and Locality

Rural areas in the United Kingdom (as elsewhere) have undergone substantial transformations in recent decades as productivist agricultural systems, based on intensification, concentration, and specialization, contribute to a radical reshaping of the nature of rural localities (Robinson, 2008). Farm amalgamation into larger units, increased mechanization and technological innovation, and huge reductions in the numbers engaged directly in agriculture have led to the decline of the sector as the mainstay of rural places, thereby forcing many rural areas to seek alternative means of boosting flagging economies. This significant economic and social restructuring, although spatially and temporally uneven, has led to a recognition of the increasingly more complex nature of rural places, and this, in turn, has led to the evolution of a series of rural development initiatives aimed at addressing this heterogeneity. As a result, rural development in recent decades has been characterized by an espousal of the importance of integration and participation. Together with sectoral integration, there is also a strong ethos of organizational integration, whereby various interested partners, organizations, and individuals are encouraged to engage with the development process. A traditional "top-down" development paradigm has been replaced in favour of a more "bottom-up" approach ostensibly centred on the active involvement of local people and deploying the rhetoric of empowerment.

The "top-down" paradigm was much criticized because it neglected the views of local residents, resulting in the advocacy of more "bottom-up" approaches centred on considering the concerns of local people and empowering them to actively participate in devising strategies for their own areas. The approach of involving local individuals and agents makes use of local knowledge and skills and may ensure more success given that it enjoys a degree of local support while tapping into people's identification with locality and community (Moseley, 2002). It is therefore argued that this participatory approach is not just more democratic but also more effective. Furthermore, some suggest that a territorial framework may serve as a mechanism that induces a real sense of community, mobilizes local residents, and facilitates positive practical outcomes (Ray, 1998). In addition, there is a perceived need for locally specific responses to those global processes that have tended to increasingly open up localities to a range of external forces (Woods, 2007). Viewed from a wider political-economy perspective, one might argue that the relative lack of success of top-down initiatives and the rise of a neo-liberal agenda centred on "rolling back the state" have encouraged the off-loading of responsibility onto local actors who can, in turn, be blamed when things don't work out. In any event, there has been a shift away from cross-spatial solutions imposed from outside toward more flexible responses that take local circumstances into account.

This strong emphasis on involving community, empowering people, building capacity, and harnessing the talents of local residents has been reinforced within the United Kingdom (and throughout the European Union and beyond) by using partnership arrangements that bring together interested groups and individuals from the statutory and voluntary sectors, including representatives of relevant agencies and local actors. At the EU level, the Cork Declaration gave more substance to a partnership approach (Commission of the European Communities, 1996), while in 2000, the government's White Paper for Rural England emphasized the need for a vibrant countryside in which local communities shape their own future. The White Paper contained a rhetorical commitment to "give rural communities a bigger say in their own affairs (because) local people are best placed to identify their individual challenges and opportunities and to shape their future" (Department of the Environment, Transport and the Regions, 2000). As a further demonstration of this commitment, the Commission for Rural Communities—established to advise government on rural issues—is ostensibly dedicated to "listening to rural communities and their representatives" (Commission for Rural Communities, n.d.). Underpinning this approach is a view that partnerships may be sources of genuine added value, not just mechanisms for collaboration (Moseley, 2003), while community can be a potentially positive resource (Staeheli, 2008).

Partnerships come in many different forms, and they operate at (and across) a variety of spatial scales (Edwards *et al.*, 2000). These organizational arrangements reflect shifting modes of governance, where power and authority are assumed to extend beyond the formal structures of central and local government, embracing the interactions between a diverse range of actors at various levels in the spatial hierarchy, and having varying degrees of influence (Goodwin, 1998; Murdoch and Abram, 1998). These structures may reflect a generic shift away from centralized forms of state regulation to what might be interpreted as more flexible modes of local regulation (Jones and Little, 2000).

In a positive light, such moves to a more participative and partnership-based approach seem to encourage decentralized decision making, recognize the role of local people in the development process, foster indigenous potential, emphasize rural diversity and local difference, and break down divisions between professional and amateur and between local resident and external expert. Leaving aside the technical issues of the operationalization of partnerships and the best way to evaluate the effectiveness of programs (Moseley, 2003), a more critical perspective is desirable in order to consider the political dimensions of rural development because (like any other form of development) it "is not a neutral, non-political process" (Goverde *et al.*, 2004, p. 7). More attention needs to be paid to issues of the nature of community, representation, power, and co-option. One might also argue that the underlying assumption of giving primacy to the local needs to be more critically examined.

"Community" is a term with potent meaning and one often "swathed in soothing feelings" (Staeheli, 2008, p. 7). Despite its appeal, some simplistic interpretations conflate communities of place with communities of interest, where a commonality is assumed between all those living in a geographically defined area. Territorially based partnership approaches to development tend to elevate residential location and the "local," while brushing over various fault lines such as class, gender, or length of residency in the area (Bell, 1994; Murdoch and Marsden, 1994; Liepins, 2000). In emphasizing community and encouraging the construction of partnerships, developmental initiatives endeavour to find common goals whereby potentially divisive issues may be sidelined in favour of harmony, resulting in what some suggest is a standard set of interventions (Mosse, 2001). This may mean that "easier," achievable, and less contentious options may be pursued, while more problematic issues are ignored in order to minimize potential friction.

It is not necessarily the case that partnership arrangements equate to widespread participation. Some voices are more likely to be listened to while others are ignored or remain silent. It may be the "usual suspects" (those with the time and the energy) who are heard regularly, while a "silent majority" sits outside the consultative framework (Moseley, 2003; Lowndes and Sullivan, 2004, Osborne *et al.*, 2004). There are additional risks in that individuals and groups become incorporated into the development structures allowing more powerful partners, whether central government, local authorities, or other statutory bodies, to "capture" the agenda and sideline dissent. In effect, the discourse of participation, community, empowerment, and so forth disguises the various power relations in operation whereby local people are "involved" but are not necessarily in control.

In many instances, it would appear that partnership has assumed a somewhat functional character; that is, it is adopted in order to gain access to funding (Westholm *et al.*, 1999). In this sense, partnerships may come into being and may behave in particular ways for purely pragmatic or instrumental purposes (Edwards *et al.*, 2000). Some partnerships may be more "real" and meaningful than others, while some may be little more than "paper" partnerships, reflecting a pragmatic response to funding requirements. Partnership could thus be viewed as a hoop to be jumped through in order to attain funding and/or legitimacy. The replacement of a "top-down" orthodoxy by another participative one to which all must subscribe is seen by some as merely indicating a new form of tyranny rather than heralding a new and radical approach to development (Cooke and Kothari, 2001).

Although central and local government may appear to champion participative governance, the existence of informal networks means that some power resides in "elite spaces" beyond direct democratic or community control (Woods, 2005). Although these networks may be colonized by traditional factions of rural society, the professionalization of rural development may have created another elite as a result of the activities of individuals employed by government agencies, local authorities, and rural partnerships, or through the actions of representatives of community groups and the plethora of rural development consultants.

Underlying much of the rural development rhetoric appears to be an assumption that partnership and participation are intrinsically good things (Duff *et al.*, 2001) and that the supposed merits of the approach have become acts of faith not to be challenged (Cleaver, 2001). As well as the problematic issue of who constitutes the local community (who is "in" and who is "out"), obvious questions arise as to what the local actually is in terms of its spatial extent, its territory, its boundaries, and its scale. There appears to be an implicit idea that the local can be both unambiguously defined and lauded as unequivocally "better" (Harvey, 1996). An emphasis on the local, while it may have potentially useful outcomes, may also create or magnify competition and divisiveness among rural localities as each tries to outdo the others in drawing attention to their "deserving" status. This can have the effect of diverting energies into funding bids and creating a case for funding rather than into what might be the more productive activity of devising development strategies.

While it may be sensible to query the supposed external "experts," it does not necessarily follow that local solutions are intrinsically better merely by being "local." Arguably, local knowledge, no more than expert knowledge, does not in itself possess an intrinsic value. It is far from certain that a knee-jerk lauding of the local, in so far as one distinct local can be identified, is in any way intrinsically "better" than an externally imposed view; local knowledge is not fixed, it is contingent and is shaped by various interests (Mosse, 2001). Consequently, there may be a danger "of swinging from one untenable position (we know best) to an equally untenable and damaging one (they know best)" (Cleaver 2001, p. 47). The more romanticized justifications for local involvement tend to gloss over the possibility that some local perspectives may reflect insular and conservative values that can translate into exclusionary practices exerted against specific groups (such as gypsies) or individuals within a locality (Harvey, 2000). An emphasis on place-based communities may serve to legitimate forms of social exclusion.

Promoting Rural Places

The second dimension of this "local turn," alongside partnership and community engagement, involves the employment of elements of the "local" by rural places as they endeavour to reimagine themselves in order to deal with broader processes of rural change and restructuring. This emphasis on the local has manifested itself through various place-promotional activities (initiated by statutory bodies and by various types of partnerships). These activities include an increasing reliance on such things as local heritage and place branding, and a broader commodification through which places are packaged, promoted, and "sold" to visitors (Kearns and Philo, 1993; Ward, 1998; Misiura, 2006). One physical manifestation of place promotion in the British landscape is the increasing array of directional signs on roads and footpaths pointing toward sites of local interest.

Aspects of the "local" are increasingly deployed in the service of place promotion in a highly instrumental manner, and recent years have witnessed an increasing emphasis on local landscape, heritage, or culture as vehicles through which areas can be "developed." While this is not a new phenomenon, it is apparent that there are more and more overt attempts to present places as possessing something of historical or cultural merit that distinguishes them from other places. Distinctive local features are utilized in attempts to put the locality on the map (Cloke, 1992; Hopkins, 1998; Mitchell, 1998; Mordue, 1999). Landscapes, local individuals or families, events, traditions, and building styles, along with other less tangible elements linked to local culture and tradition, become resources pressed into the broader service of rural regeneration. Like partnership approaches to development, the instrumentalist use of "the local" raises both technical and wider political issues.

Technical issues emerge over such things as the elements of the past to be selected, the availability of appropriate artifacts, the usability of these elements and artifacts, and the ways in which they might be employed in place promotion. While pragmatic considerations (such as budgetary or related constraints) may mean it makes sense to focus on some elements, a range of deeper, more "political" questions also emerges centring on what is selected, who does the selecting, and what messages are conveyed (or intended for conveyance) through this process (Wright, 1985; Walsh, 1992; Storey, 2004).

While a range of motivations underlies the phenomenon of the local in place promotion, there is undoubtedly a strand of instrumentalism at work here, reflecting a desire to protect and celebrate those things that seem to make places different in what, for some, is an increasingly homogenous world. The representation of local or regional identity in the face of globalizing forces can be harnessed for functional ends in which rural places are presented as a buttress against modernity. Local distinctiveness becomes a resource to be exploited in order to achieve particular outcomes, and this may give rise to a range of tensions in which cultural objectives linked with education and an understanding and exploration of the past rub up against more instrumentalist concerns with economic benefits. Consequently, these tensions may give rise to questions of authenticity, romanticization, sanitization, and simplification (Hewison, 1987; Rojek, 1993; Samuel, 1994; Lowenthal, 1998; Graham *et al.*, 2000).

Many involved in local rural development are happy to use heritage, culture, and local distinctiveness—feeding on sentiment and nostalgia—as tools in their strategy. Local agencies and partnerships are keen to present their locality as different or possessing something of distinctiveness. Of course, these place-promotional efforts may have a mobilizing impact, providing a focal point around which groups and individuals coalesce, thereby engendering a sense of dynamism in the locality, accentuating people's identification with place, and strengthening attempts at community building and partnership working. However, while these sorts of enterprises have the potential to be informative and genuinely educational, they may also be somewhat superficial. Throughout the United Kingdom, local authorities, other statutory bodies, and a variety of agents and partnerships involved in rural development engage in such activities and, as a result, music festivals, interpretative centres, and heritage trails have all received rural development funding from national and EU sources. Place promotion is evident at various spatial scales and through generic attempts at local branding, as well as through, for example, the development and promotion of visitor trails and the sale of "traditional" local produce.

In the English West Midlands, Herefordshire's tourist authority urges people to visit "a county of unspoilt countryside, market towns of distinctive character and a wealth of varied landscapes from an historic City to fascinating villages," where they are encouraged "to venture down the less travelled roads and explore the myriad of villages and hamlets that pepper the landscape" (Visit Herefordshire, n.d.) in order to fully appreciate the essence of the county. Herefordshire's cultural strategy identifies the need to "protect and enhance Herefordshire's distinct environment [and] to promote and preserve the historic and rural landscape" (Herefordshire Partnership, 2004). Meanwhile, in neighbouring Worcestershire, the local authority promotes the county as "the essence of England," where "charming villages" can be found in "a peaceful countryside with a turbulent past" (Worcestershire County Council, 2008). At a more local scale, individual towns and villages are branded, and the word "historic" is becoming ubiquitous on signage, welcoming people to a "historic riverside village" or yet another "historic market town."

Designated walking or driving routes have a long history, and the introduction of themed heritage trails is a growing phenomenon. One example is the Black and White Village Trail—a driving route of some 64 km—that takes in a series of Herefordshire villages featuring old timber-framed buildings, many of which date from the 16th and 17th centuries. Elsewhere, local historic figures are invoked in order to promote sections of public footpaths or loop walks. The Cleric's Trail along Herefordshire's border with Radnorshire, Wales, takes its name from Francis Kilvert, a local 19th century vicar who wrote a multi-volume set of diaries. The trail is a themed walk reflecting aspects of his life and provides a clear example of how a historic individual is used to promote a particular route through a part of the county, which now bears his name—"Kilvert Country" (Literary Heritage West Midlands, 2002). In a similar fashion, the Simon Evans Way—a walking route through part of neighbouring south Shropshire—is named after a local poet and postman.

In recent years, the promotion and branding of local and regional foods and beverages has become a noteworthy phenomenon (Kneafsey and Ilbery, 2001; Kneafsey *et al.*, 2001), and is bound up with the creating and sustaining of alternative food networks (Cox *et al.*, 2008). Local products can also be the peg on which to hang place-promotional strategies, such as gastronomic tourism (Boyne and Hall, 2004). The town of Ludlow in Shropshire has acquired and subsequently utilized its reputation for good quality restaurants and bar food. Elsewhere, promotional devices, such as "the real Cider Country" route through Herefordshire, have been linked to local produce (Herefordshire Cider Route, 2003). In these various ways, elements of the local are presented as distinct and worthy of further exploration, contributing (it is hoped) to the economic and social well-being of rural places.

Market Towns, Partnerships, and Place Promotion

The rural economic and social restructuring referred to earlier in this chapter has had a considerable impact on market towns in the United Kingdom. Their original *raison d'être* (as centres where agricultural produce was bought and sold) is effectively gone, and they are faced with a dilemma over future directions. In 2000, the government's White Paper for Rural England recognized this problem and identified market towns as foci for growth in rural areas and as places that could act as service centres and hubs for their hinterlands. The White Paper suggested that these towns offered potential places to live, work, and spend leisure time, thereby contributing to the maintenance of sustainable rural communities and the diversification and revitalization of rural economies. Subsequently, a Market Towns Initiative (MTI) was launched in England, and in keeping with the partnership and community-involvement ethos, local people in these towns and surrounding areas were to have a say in future plans. In Shropshire, three towns received "official" funding channeled through the regional development organization (Advantage West Midlands). In these cases, partnerships, consisting of people drawn from local businesses and community groups, as well as local councillors, were either created afresh or evolved out of pre-existing arrangements. These partnerships worked in tandem with the district council to undertake a health check of their towns and environs. In this way, regional, county-level, and local scales were drawn together. Interestingly, many other towns in the county and beyond formed similar local partnerships even though they did not actually participate within the MTI scheme.

Cleobury Mortimer in south Shropshire (a small town of about 2,000) was one of the beneficiaries of MTI funding. For some time, an apparent loss of trade to supermarkets in larger towns had fostered concern among local business people about the town's future. In Cleobury, as elsewhere, a local partnership was formed (with a steering group and five sub-groups), which worked in conjunction with South Shropshire District Council and Advantage West Midlands to undertake an initial health check and commission consultants to research the town's problems, prospects, and potential. Assisted by a market towns officer, the partnership devised an action plan for the town and its hinterland of nine parishes, which identified specific projects and initiatives that might be carried out. Material outcomes included the creation of a business resource centre, a purpose-built, multi-functional centre (currently under construction) to contain offices, conference space, community Internet facilities, and a library, among other amenities. Also undertaken were improvements to the appearance of the main business street.

Like other places, a key element in Cleobury's strategy has been to devise an "angle" that makes the town appear different and, perhaps, more interesting than other places (Barrett *et al.*, 2001; 2004). The use of a place-branding approach has formed a significant dimension of this strategy. While road signs on the approach to the town tell visitors they are entering "The gateway to Shropshire," the partnership decided to adopt the title "Cleobury Country" to refer to the town and surrounding parishes. This branding, accompanied by a logo designed by local schoolchildren, is a clear and explicit element in the town's strategy. Jute shopping bags with the Cleobury Country logo are available from shops in the town. Visitor maps and leaflets of Cleobury Country are also available, including a trail map of Cleobury Mortimer—"at the heart of Cleobury Country"—and information on cycling routes in the area. Guides listing places to stay and places to eat and drink in Cleobury Country have also been produced, and a "Closer to Cleobury" directory provides information on local food producers, farm outlets, and village shops.

The local partnership (like many others elsewhere in the country) has now evolved into a limited liability company, Cleobury Country Ltd., and its website proclaims its ambitions to "promote and celebrate the rural heritage of our special landscape, provide fresh experiences and new opportunities for all and develop and strengthen the Cleobury Country identity and lifestyle" (Cleobury Country, 2009). The Cleobury partnership is just one of many local alliances that exist within the interstices of governance in rural areas. It illustrates both the practice of partnership and the range of ways in which places endeavour to distinguish themselves and promote some version of uniqueness.

Implications for Rural Places

A strong implication within contemporary rural development discourses is that the key to success lies within the "community" at the "local" scale, while partnerships have become the new orthodoxy. This approach may have emancipatory potential by engendering community, mobilizing people around specific issues, providing a framework for fostering a more active citizenship, unleashing local capacity, and strengthening social capital in localities (Moseley, 2002; 2003; Woods, 2006). In addition, the other element in the local turn—the devising of various place-promotional projects—offers similar potential. The positive connotations associated with participation, community, and empowerment, and the implicit assumption that local is good, render it difficult to criticize these twin tracks.

Nevertheless, some problems clearly emerge with regard to the operation of partnerships, the mechanics of their formation, and the instrumentalist nature of some of them. Questions still exist about the "representativeness" of those who become involved and about the potential of particular groups to "capture" the development agenda. The objectives pursued may be those of a particular coterie better versed in the intricacies of partnership working and the formulation of funding applications. While knowledge exchange, cooperation, innovations, and positive material outputs may emerge out of this process, an investigation of the appropriateness of current initiatives to address rural problems needs to consider fundamental issues of power and to explore the agendas of different partners, the extent to which all sections of the rural community are included, and other relevant issues. In one sense, there is an opening up of "development" to local people, but a closing down of options through the pressure to conform to certain structures.

The facilitation of place-promotional initiatives has been one by-product of current development programs. Highlighting local distinctiveness and attempting to utilize local branding may offer some positive outcomes for generating community spirit and togetherness, although they may equally create or exacerbate divisions and tensions. In part, the outcomes may depend on whether the project has an organic base emerging out of the locality or whether it is promoted for more narrowly instrumental reasons. Equally, outcomes may depend on whether initiatives are rooted in a genuine attempt to deal with the depth and complexity of the issues or whether they are more superficial and functional. Focusing on some elements of the locality may be seen as an easy option, allowing the identification of clearly discernible outcomes, thereby providing a "spectacle" that visibly demonstrates that development or regeneration is occurring.

While it seems sensible to adopt a pragmatic approach to the use of heritage and local identity, and employing these as development devices, there is a need to ensure that these elements of locality are genuinely organic and deep rather than imposed and superficial, and that the agenda pursued is not just the narrow concern of local vested interests. Developing what might be seen as territorially based culture economies (Ray, 1998; Kneafsey *et al.*, 2001) by using local resources may seem appealing, but this approach is no guarantee of success and may lack deep roots. There are also risks that these sorts of promotional devices encourage competition between places for scarce funding resources, whereas cooperation might ultimately be more beneficial. Additionally, there is a need to avoid the trap of blindly following notions of place branding and the promotion of tourist trails and routes, which run the risk of homogenizing places rather than emphasizing their differences. Cleobury Country is but one of many attempts throughout the country to reimagine rural localities, and it would be naïve to assume that what works in one location is going to work in all. Similarly, Herefordshire is far from being the only county to lay claim to quaint and historic villages.

We also need to be mindful that accompanying the emphasis on local involvement is an increasing professionalization of rural development characterized by growing numbers of rural development officers (such as market town officers) and a burgeoning number of rural development consultants. Taking note of this growing professionalism is not intended to denigrate the genuine efforts of individuals and groups (professional and amateur, statutory or voluntary) who work in rural development or to imply that positive outcomes cannot emerge from their efforts. Nevertheless, it seems that community, empowerment, and a lauding of the local are tropes regularly deployed in discourses that imply radical change, but which might more accurately reflect shifting tactics within a neo-liberal order. Development practitioners and local activists must explore ways to encourage more widespread participation. There is a need to genuinely listen to, and engage with, local residents to deal with conflicts (rather than ignore or sidestep them), while fostering indigenous potential rather than copying blueprints from elsewhere. In trying to follow these (fairly self-evident) pointers, those involved in development must be realistic about what can be achieved. The results of ventures such as the branding and promotion of Cleobury Country may be difficult to assess and may ultimately be judged successes or failures only many years down the line, well beyond the time frames imposed by rural development practitioners or funding parameters. Moreover, in an increasingly integrated global economy, it seems unlikely that solutions will be unambiguously local as the capacity of local agencies to have a radical impact on processes that transcend the locality is questionable. Finally, within the context of this "local turn" there is a tension between the potential advantages of a "genuine" bottom-up approach on the one hand and the need for regulatory and facilitative frameworks on the other. While emphasizing local decision making, a fine line must be drawn between local control and necessary forms of external regulation and facilitation.

References

Barrett, H., Storey, D., and Yarwood, R. (2001) From market place to marketing place: Retail change in small country towns. *Geography* 86(2), 159–163.

Barrett, H., Storey, D., and Palmer, C. (2004) *Cleobury Mortimer and Hinterland: Survey of Environmental Issues*. Report commissioned by Cleobury Mortimer Partnership/South Shropshire District Council, Centre for Rural Research, University of Worcester.

Bell, M. (1994) *Childerley: Nature and Morality in a Country Village*. University of Chicago Press, Chicago.

Boyne, S., and Hall, D. (2004) Place promotion through food and tourism: Rural branding and the role of websites. *Place Branding* 1(1), 80–92.

Cleaver, F. (2001) Institutions, agency and the limitations of participatory approaches to development. In: Cooke, B., and Kothari, U. (eds.) *Participation: The New Tyranny?* Zed Books, London, 36–55.

Cleobury Country. (2009) Welcome to Cleobury Country, www.cleoburycountry.com/cleobury/www /index.cfm?objectid=DFCB2D73-FAB6-2072-E3D30BBB1B461FB8 (accessed 2009).

Cloke, P. (1992) The countryside as commodity. In: Glyptis, S. (ed.) *Leisure and the Environment: Essays in Honour of Professor J.A. Patmore*. Belhaven, London, 53–67.

Commission for Rural Communities. (n.d.) Our purpose, http://www.ruralcommunities.gov.uk/content/ ourpurpose (accessed 2009).

Commission of the European Communities. (1996) *Cork Declaration: A Living Countryside*. Author, Brussels.

Cooke, B., and Kothari, U. (2001) The case for participation as tyranny. In: Cooke, B., and Kothari, U. (eds.) *Participation: The New Tyranny?* Zed Books, London, 1–15.

Cox, R., Kneafsey, M., Venn, L., Holloway, L., Dowler, E., and Tuomainen, H. (2008) Constructing sustainability through reconnection: The case of "alternative" food networks. In: Robinson, G. (ed.) *Sustainable Rural Systems: Sustainable Agriculture and Rural Communities*. Ashgate, Aldershot, UK, 67–81.

Department of the Environment, Transport and the Regions. (2000) *Our Countryside: The Future. A Fair Deal for Rural England*. Author, London.

Duff, J., Bowen, P., and Partington, G. (2001) Consenting to cooption: Uncertainty and consultation in community development. Paper presented at TASA Conference, Sydney, Australia. (Available from www.tasa.org.au/members/docs/2001_6/Duff,%20Bowen%20&%20Partington.pdf)

Edwards, B., Goodwin, M., Pemberton, S., and Woods, M. (2000) *Partnership Working in Rural Regeneration*. Policy Press, Bristol, UK.

Goodwin, M. (1998) The governance of rural areas: Some emerging research issues and agendas. *Journal of Rural Studies* 14(1), 5–12.

Goverde, H., Baylina, M., and de Haan, H. (2004) Introduction: Power and gender in European rural development. In: Goverde, H., de Haan, H., and Baylina, M. (eds.) *Power and Gender in European Rural Development*. Ashgate, Aldershot, UK, 3–9.

Graham, B., Ashworth, G., and Tunbridge, J. (2000) *A Geography of Heritage: Power, Culture and Economy*. Arnold, London.

Harvey, D. (1996) *Justice, Nature and the Geography of Difference*. Blackwell, Oxford.

_____. (2000) *Spaces of Hope*. University of California Press, Berkeley.

Herefordshire Cider Route. (2003) Welcome, www.ciderroute.co.uk/site/index.html (accessed 27 June 2009).

Herefordshire Partnership. (2004) Herefordshire cultural strategy: Making a difference, www.herefordshire.gov.uk/docs/LeisureAndCulture/hereford_cultural_strategy_2004.pdf (accessed 27 June 2009).

Hewison, R. (1987) *The Heritage Industry: Britain in a Climate of Decline*. Methuen, London.

Hopkins, J. (1998) Signs of the post-rural: Marketing myths of a symbolic countryside. *Geografiska Annaler B* 80(2), 65–81.

Jones, O., and Little, J. (2000) Rural challenge(s): Partnership and new rural governance. *Journal of Rural Studies* 16(2), 171–183.

Kearns, G., and Philo, C., eds. (1993) *Selling Places: The City as Cultural Capital, Past and Present*. Pergamon, Oxford.

Kneafsey, M., and Ilbery, B. (2001) Regional images and the promotion of speciality food and drink products: Initial explorations from the "West Country." *Geography* 86(2), 131–140.

Kneafsey, M., Ilbery, B., and Jenkins, T. (2001) Exploring the dimensions of culture economies in rural west Wales. *Sociologia Ruralis* 41(3), 296–310.

Liepins, R. (2000) Exploring rurality through "community": Discourses, practices and spaces shaping Australian and New Zealand rural "communities." *Journal of Rural Studies* 16(3), 325–341.

Literary Heritage West Midlands. (2002) Francis Kilvert, www3.shropshire-cc.gov.uk/kilvert.htm (accessed 27 June 2009).

Lowenthal, D. (1998) *The Heritage Crusade and the Spoils of History*. Cambridge University Press, Cambridge.

Lowndes, V., and Sullivan, H. (2004) Like a horse and carriage or a fish on a bicycle: How well do local partnerships and public participation go together? *Local Government Studies* 30(1), 51–73.

Misiura, S. (2006) *Heritage Marketing*. Butterworth-Heinemann, Oxford.

Mitchell, C. (1998) Entrepreneurialism, commodification and creative destruction: A model of post-modern community development. *Journal of Rural Studies* 14(3), 273–286.

Mordue, T. (1999) Heartbeat country: Conflicting values, coinciding visions. *Environment and Planning A* 31(4), 629–646.

Moseley, M. (2002) *Rural Development: Principles and Practice*. Sage, London.

_____, ed. (2003) *Local Partnerships for Rural Development: The European Experience*. CABI Publishing, Wallingford, UK.

Mosse, D. (2001) "People's knowledge," participation and patronage: Operations and representations in rural development. In: Cooke, B., and Kothari, U. (eds.) *Participation: The New Tyranny?* Zed Books, London, 16–35.

Murdoch, J., and Abram, S. (1998) Defining the limits of community governance. *Journal of Rural Studies* 14(1), 41–50.

Murdoch, J., and Marsden, T. (1994) *Reconstituting Rurality: Class, Community and Power in the Development Process*. UCL Press, London.

Osborne, S., Williamson, A., and Beattie, R. (2004) Community involvement in rural regeneration partnerships: Exploring the rural dimension. *Local Government Studies* 30(2), 156–181.

Ray, C. (1998) Territory, structures and interpretation: Two case studies of the European Union's LEADER I programme. *Journal of Rural Studies* 14(1), 79–87.

Robinson, G., ed. (2008) *Sustainable Rural Systems: Sustainable Agriculture and Rural Communities.* Ashgate, Aldershot, UK.

Rojek, C. (1993) *Ways of Escape: Modern Transformations in Leisure and Travel.* Macmillan, London.

Samuel, R. (1994) *Past and Present in Contemporary Culture.* Vol. 1 of *Theatres of Memory.* Routledge, London.

Staeheli, L. (2008) Citizenship and the problem of community. *Political Geography* 27(1), 5–21.

Storey, D. (2004) A sense of place: Rural development, tourism and place promotion in the Republic of Ireland. In: Holloway, L., and Kneafsey, M. (eds.) *Geographies of Rural Cultures and Societies.* Ashgate, Aldershot, UK, 197–213.

Visit Herefordshire. (n.d.) Herefordshire and the Wye Valley, www.visitherefordshire.co.uk (accessed 27 June 2009).

Walsh, K. (1992) *The Representation of the Past: Museums and Heritage in the Post-Modern World.* Routledge, London.

Ward, S. (1998) *Selling Places: The Marketing and Promotion of Towns and Cities 1850-2000.* E & FN Spon, London.

Westholm, E., Moseley, M., and Stenlås, N., eds. (1999) *Local Partnerships and Rural Development in Europe: A Literature Review of Practice and Theory.* Dalarnas Forskningsråd, Falun, Sweden.

Woods, M. (2005) *Contesting Rurality: Politics in the British Countryside.* Ashgate, Aldershot, UK.

_____. (2006) Rural politics and governance. In: Midgley, J. (ed.) *A New Rural Agenda.* Institute of Public Policy Research, London, 140–168.

_____. (2007) Engaging the global countryside: Globalization, hybridity and the reconstitution of rural place. *Progress in Human Geography* 31(4), 485–507.

Worcestershire County Council. (2008) Explore the countryside, worcestershire.whub.org.uk/home/wccindex/wcc-countryside/wcc-countryside-exploring.htm (accessed 27 June 2009).

Wright, P. (1985) *On living in an old country: The national past in contemporary Britain.* Verso, London.

Chapter 13

The Political Economies of Place in the Emergent Global Countryside: Stories from Rural Wales

Michael Woods

The perceived shift in emphasis in rural development strategy that forms the theme of this collection, from "Space" to "Place," reflects a transformation in the way rural economies are imagined in popular and governmental discourses. The transformation has occurred over the past few decades and is commonly associated with globalization. The assumption embedded in this transformation is that the old space-based economy, which disadvantaged peripheral rural regions, has been emasculated by technological advances and that the key to rural development is no longer overcoming peripherality but rather enabling rural places to compete effectively in a global economy. In this chapter I adopt a critical stance toward this analysis, arguing that space remains important in understanding the uneven development of rural regions, but that relations between space and place are being reconfigured in an emergent global countryside. After establishing the theoretical context for this argument, I proceed to illustrate and examine the issues raised through a case study of rural Wales, in the west of Britain, before drawing some broader conclusions about space, place, and development in the "next rural economy."

Space, Place, and Rurality

Historically, rural regions were defined by their peripherality, discursively constructed as marginal to a national economy and national infrastructure centred on urban industrial regions. From a governmental perspective, the key challenges confronting rural economies were problematized as distance and accessibility, leading to rural development strategies that prioritized infrastructural development and improved transport and communications links with major conurbations. More recently, this discourse has started to give way to a new representation, in which the disadvantage of distance is argued to have been eroded by improved transport connections, technological advances, and the ubiquity of a global information technology (IT) infrastructure that is not tied to urban localities.

Freed from the tyranny of the space-based economy, rural areas, so the argument goes, can compete with urban centres and with each other for investment and jobs and can sell their services in a global marketplace (see Marsden *et al.*, 1993). The key to economic prosperity for rural localities thus no longer rests on eradicating the problems of distance through infrastructural development, but rather now depends on the capacity of a rural locality to sell itself as an attractive place for economic investment. In some cases, the natural environment and amenity potential of rural places can be mobilized to attract footloose businesses and professionals in hi-tech industries and service sectors, or to build an economy based on tourism and recreation. In other cases, rural localities might sell themselves as a site of cheap land and cheap labour (Epp and Whitson, 2001).

It is a seductive argument, not only for the cheerleaders of depressed rural economies—entrepreneurs, rural development agents, and booster ish local politicians—but also for advocates of neo-liberal governance seeking to claw back the state's involvement in rural development. Conventional rationalities of rural development demanded big state solutions: new roads, new railways, new airports, industrial parks, incentives for inward investment, tax breaks, and government loans. The new rationality of place-based development, in contrast, promotes bottom-up, community-led solutions:

> The emphasis on endogenous, rather than exogenous, forms of development means that the source of this market-led recovery lies in the entrepreneurial skills of local people and their ability to find new, and more innovative, ways of enhancing their competitiveness in the global economy. ... Rather than having governments "prop up" declining regions through welfare payments or other forms of subsidies, or even relying upon "footloose" capital to establish itself in local areas and generate new employment opportunities, the driving force of this kind of rural development is the local entrepreneur. (Cheshire, 2006, pp. 43–44)

For some, this rationality is empowering, creating the opportunity for rural people to develop their economies in the way that they want, rather than having development forced upon them by distant government actors (see, for example, Ray, 1997). Yet the rationality of bottom-up rural development also displaces responsibility and risk from the state to rural communities themselves. If economic development fails, it is the community that is to blame (Herbert-Cheshire, 2000, 2003).

Place-based rural development creates winners and losers, just as the old space economy did, but dangles the lure that any rural community can be successfully regenerated so long as it follows the right approach. A new industry has blossomed, circulating an almost evangelical message through consultancies, reports, and toolkits (see, for instance, Kenyon and Black, 2001). In this way, the place-based rural development discourse disciplines rural communities, codifying forms of correct social practice and discriminating between "healthy" and "unhealthy," "responsible" and "non-responsible" communities, as Cheshire again observes (see also Table 13.1):

> Communities that exhibit individualism, cynicism, defeat and negativity are considered by contemporary commentators as "unhealthy", "unsustainable" and "non-responsible" and can hardly expect to initiate their own successful development programmes unless they have first addressed this problem. "Healthy" communities, on the other hand, are said to foster a positive and self-reliant "can do" spirit and attitude. They place emphasis on consensus building and collaboration and encourage broad community participation. (Cheshire, 2006, p. 67)

Notably, the emphasis here is on social capital and community attitudes, rather than structural characteristics, as the key factors in determining the economic prosperity of a locality. Yet structural factors, including distance from major population centres, continue to be critical in shaping the ability of communities to mobilize the forms of social capital associated with successful communities and to convert this capacity into tangible economic gains. There is, however, no simple correlation between distance and economic success. Remote rural communities can exhibit a strong sense of solidarity and thus social capital, but their potential for attracting tourists, or capturing passing trade, for example, may be severely restricted by poor accessibility. In contrast, periurban communities arguably have greater opportunities to tap into nearby markets, but their capacity to do so may be weakened by high levels of commuting and population turnover, which dilute social capital.

Table 13.1 The healthy/unhealthy communities balance sheet, produced by the IDEAS group.

Healthy communities	Unhealthy communities
Optimism, hope, "we are in this together"	Cynicism
"We can do it"	"Nothing works"
Value intangibles of vision, value	Emphasis only on tangibles
Consensus building	Polarization
Collaboration	Confrontation
Focus on the future	Debate the past
Interdependence	Parochialism
Broad community participation	Few do everything
Leadership renewal	Same old faces
Think and act in long term	Short-term thinking
Listening	Attacking
Reconciliation	Holding grudges
Win–win solutions	Win–lose solutions
Politics of substance	Politics of personality
Patience	Frustration
Diversity	Exclusion
Challenge ideas	Challenge people
Problem solvers	Blockers and blamers

Source: Cheshire, 2006.
Note: The IDEAS group is a consultancy group advising on rural community development in Australia.

Space, therefore, cannot be discarded in an analysis of the next rural economies. Rather, we need to rethink our understanding of space and the way in which spatial relations come together to create places. Space should not be conceived in two-dimensional Euclidian terms, with "places" defined as points on a map separated by distance. Instead, we need to recognize space as multidimensional, able to be crumpled and folded to produce proximities that defy conventional geographical logic, but always dynamic and unstable. From this perspective, places are not static and containable points on a two-dimensional map, but shifting assemblages of spatial relations that leak and smudge and seep between dimensions. Understanding space and place in this way is crucial to understanding the significance of globalization for rural places, as it leads to the rejection of the two great fallacies about globalization: that globalization is homogenization; and that globalization has produced the annihilation of space by time.

As Massey (2005) argues, globalization is rather "a making of space(s), an active reconfiguration and meeting-up through practices and relations of a multitude of trajectories" (p. 83). It is in this (re-)making of space that Massey locates the variegated politics of globalization, recognizing that "local places are not simply always the victims of the global; nor are they always politically defensible redoubts *against* the global" (p. 101).

Applied to the rural context, Massey's argument highlights the differentiated geography of the global countryside. In an earlier article (Woods, 2007), I describe the "global countryside" as "an hypothetical space, corresponding to a condition of the global interconnectivity and interdependency of rural localities" (p. 492), which is defined by ten characteristics that represent the end point of current globalization processes (see Table13. 2). Significantly, however, the "global countryside" does not currently exist anywhere in this idealized form. Rather, the characteristics of the global countryside are partially and differentially articulated in different rural places, reflecting both structural factors and the actions of local and global agents:

> The extent to which any particular characteristic is evident in any particular rural locality is determined not only by the degree of penetration of globalization processes, but also by the way in which those globalization processes are mediated through and incorporated within local processes of place-making. (Woods, 2007, p. 494)

Table 13.2 Characteristics of the "global countryside."

1. Primary sector and secondary sector economic activity in the global countryside feed, and are dependent on, elongated yet contingent commodity networks, with consumption distanced from production.
2. The global countryside is the site of increasing corporate concentration and integration, with corporate networks organized on a transnational scale.
3. The global countryside is both the supplier and the employer of migrant labour.
4. The globalization of mobility is also marked by the flow of tourists through the global countryside, attracted to sites of global rural amenity.
5. The global countryside attracts high levels of non-national property investment for both commercial and residential purposes.
6. It is not only social and economic relations that are transformed in the global countryside, but also the discursive construction of nature and its management. Neo-liberal globalization involves the commodification of nature, and locally embedded discourses of nature are also challenged by the dissemination of "global" values of environmental protection and animal welfare.
7. The landscape of the global countryside is inscribed with the marks of globalization, including deforestation, the opening of new oil fields and mines, the development of global tourism resorts and associated infrastructure, as well as—more subtly—the transplantation of plant and animal species, and the proliferation of symbols of global consumer culture.
8. The global countryside is characterized by increasing social polarization.
9. The global countryside is associated with new sites of political authority.
10. The global countryside is always a contested space.

Source: Woods, 2007, pp. 492–494.

The political economies of place in the emergent global countryside, hence, concern the hybrid reconstitution of rural places—and, by extension, of rural economies—through the negotiation, mediation, and contestation of global and local (and national and regional) economic and political processes, networks, and structures by local and non-local actors and agents. Place-based economic development strategies are part of this process, forming an arena in which local actors seek to respond to the challenges and opportunities presented by globalization through actions that involve the re-articulation of key aspects of place.

Developing Rural Wales

Geographical and Historical Context

Located on the west coast of Britain, with a difficult topography defined by the upland ranges of the Brecon Beacons, Cambrian Mountains, and Snowdonia, and with poor internal and external transportation links, rural Wales has conventionally been constructed as peripheral in relation to the economic cores of Wales, Britain, and the European Union. With a population of around 960,000 and a low population density, in British terms, of 56.3 persons per km^2, the region is dominated by small towns, villages, and farmsteads, with no settlements of more than 20,000 people. The northwestern part of the region is additionally culturally distinctive, with the Welsh language widely spoken.

Historically, the region's economy was based on agriculture, mining, and quarrying. The mines (mostly silver, copper, and lead) closed in the early 20th century, prompting significant out-migration, including emigration to North America, Australia, and New Zealand. The decline of the agriculture and slate industries followed over the course of the century. By the 1960s, rural Wales was widely recognized as a region in crisis, with low living standards—at least a quarter of the houses in Mid-Wales were without a piped water supply, and over 3,000 farms did not have mains electricity (Hooson and Jenkins, 1965)—and limited employment opportunities.

The consequence was mass depopulation. The subregion of Mid-Wales (present-day Ceredigion, Powys, and southern Gwynedd) lost a quarter of its population between 1871 and 1961, more than any other region in Britain. With the rate of depopulation accelerating to around 4% a year between 1951 and 1961, a Royal Commission was established to examine the reasons for the region's decline and to propose action (Beacham Committee, 1964). In its report, the Beacham Commission recommended substantial government investment to increase and diversify employment opportunities by developing export-orientated manufacturing. Recognizing that the peripherality and dispersed population of the region presented a challenge to the development of export industries, the report further proposed that the investment should be focused on 12 "growth centres," accompanied by internal migration and settlement rationalization (Williams, 1985).

Postwar Rural Development Policy

In reaching these conclusions, the Beacham Commission reflected the dominant regional political discourse of the time, which associated economic and population decline with problems of accessibility and overdependence on agriculture, and envisaged the solution in government intervention, improved transportation and communication links, growth poles, and the expansion of export industries. For example, one political pamphlet outlined proposals for the development of Mid-Wales that prominently featured the construction of a regional airport, new motorways, and toll roads, providing the infrastructure for a revitalized economy centred on a "new town" of 60,000 people at Aberystwyth. The presentation of ideas such as a coastal toll road provides an illuminating insight to the faith placed in transportation links as the catalyst for regional development:

> Bridges, or alternatively, barrages should be built to carry this road across the Mawddach and Dovey estuaries. As it would be difficult initially to justify this road on industrial grounds, there is much to be said for it to be a toll road in its early years. Clearly it would have immense attractions to holiday-makers, for it would open up the wonderful panoramic views along this coast. If barrages should prove feasible, they would themselves add to the attraction of the area for boating and sailing. They might also provide fresh water reservoirs. (Hooson and Jenkins, 1965, p. 17)

Hooson and Jenkins's radical vision was never put into practice, nor was a similar alternative plan for a new town of 70,000 people in the more accessible Severn valley (Williams, 1985). Some of the principles and ideas expressed in these reports were, however, incorporated into the regional development policy, notably the "growth pole" approach and government investment in industrial units to attract and stimulate export-orientated manufacturing (Williams, 1985). In Mid-Wales, this strategy was led from 1976 onward by the Development Board for Rural Wales (DBRW), with a sibling organization, the Welsh Development Agency (WDA), performing a similar role in other parts of rural Wales.

The strategy was spectacularly successful in achieving the expansion of manufacturing industry in rural Wales. Between 1977 and 1985, over 200 new factories were established in the DBRW area, increasing manufacturing employment by 61%, from 3,921 to 6,330 (J. Edwards, 1985), against the national trend. However, the impact of this investment on the wider economy and society of rural Wales is questionable. The trajectory of population decline was reversed, but the turnaround arguably owed more to the national trend of counterurbanization, including the in-migration of "back-to-the-land" settlers who bought smallholdings and renovated derelict cottages in areas such as the Dyfi Valley and Mynydd Bach of Ceredigion, attracted by their comparative isolation and remoteness (Halfacree, 2007; see also Jones, 1993; and Walford, Chapter 5 this volume).

Moreover, the growth of key towns such as Newtown and Aberystwyth contrasted with continuing pockets of depopulation in more remote areas and a broader undercurrent of continuing deprivation (Cloke *et al.*, 1997). DBRW's strategy increasingly came under fire from local authorities and community groups for being excessively top-down and overcentralized and for creating jobs for in-migrants rather than local residents. In a particularly strident critique focused on Gwynedd, but with relevance for rural Wales as a whole, Lovering (1983) attacked the postwar development strategy for making the region a "temporary place for small-time businessmen and aspiring managers" (p. 53), dependent on economic conditions elsewhere.

In response, the emphasis of the regional development strategy in Wales shifted in the mid-1980s to encourage "bottom-up" regeneration within the existing settlement structure. As Williams (1985) observed, this refocusing "posed an inherent conflict between strategic objectives relating to *regional* as opposed to *rural* development" (p. 119).

The Challenges of Globalization

At the same time as the regional development strategy was being questioned from below by community actors, the social and economic assumptions on which it was based were being eroded from above by the processes of globalization. Rural Wales is not a region in which the impact of globalization is highly visible. Its dominant industries are not hard-wired into global trading and corporate networks, nor has it become a "global playground," attracting large numbers of international tourists and amenity migrants. As experienced in rural Wales, globalization is a more everyday, banal process of change, an almost insidious development, stealthily transforming place bit by bit.

Nevertheless, we can identify three key challenges that globalization presents for the economy of rural Wales. First, the liberalization of global trade in food and other commodities has increased pressure on traditional industries such as agriculture. When farmers from northern Wales mounted a spontaneous blockade of the port at Holyhead in December 1997, stopping trucks arriving on the ferry from Ireland, they were reacting against insidious globalization (Woods, 2005). Their frustration had been stoked by a situation in which British beef could not be exported due to controls imposed during the BSE scare, and currency exchange rates allowed imported beef to undercut domestic meat in price. The strength of sterling contributed to falling farm incomes across the agricultural sector between 1997 and 2001. This was compounded by other facets of globalization, including the impact of a recession in East Asia and the collapse of the Russian economy on the market for sheepskins—an important by-product of Welsh sheep-farming. In 1999–2000, the average farm income in Wales was just £4,500, and Welsh politicians warned that the farming crisis represented a threat to the sustainability of rural Wales as a whole:

> The increasing number of farms being forced out of business will in turn have implications for the whole social structure of rural Wales, the strength of the Welsh language in its traditional heartlands and the environmental sustainability of the countryside. (Chair of the Welsh Assembly Agriculture Committee in a letter to the UK prime minister, March 2000, quoted by Woods, 2005, p. 145)

Second, so-called new economic sectors in rural Wales are also losing out to global competition. Manufacturing, the boom sector of the 1970s and 1980s and one-time saviour of rural Wales, is now in serious decline, unable to compete with southern Europe and Asia in a footloose global economy. The changing fortunes of manufacturing in rural Wales are symbolized by the story of Laura Ashley, a textile company whose floral print clothing and furnishings achieved popularity in Britain during the 1980s. Initially founded in Kent, the fledgling company relocated to the village of Carno in Mid-Wales in 1961 and opened its first shop in the nearby small town of Llanidloes. By 1979, the company's turnover had exceeded £25 million. As it expanded production capacity to meet demand, the firm remained loyal to rural Wales, opening four more factories in the region. Laura Ashley participated in globalization, opening outlets in a number of countries, but this expansion stretched the company financially and left it vulnerable when exposed to cheaper competition from Asia in the 1990s. Laura Ashley itself began to move production to southeast Asia, and in 1998 it was taken over by a Malaysian corporation, MUI Asia Ltd. The last Laura Ashley factory in rural Wales closed in September 1999 (BBC, 1999).

The IT sector has followed a similar pattern. As late as the mid-1990s, government policy for rural Wales echoed the prevailing logic that new technologies had eradicated the inequities of the old space economy and presented new opportunities for peripheral rural regions:

> The information age, in particular, offers a new era of hope and opportunity for many rural areas. Like no other economic revolution, it promises to make geographical location irrelevant and will open up a vast communications network, connecting rural areas with people and businesses across the world. (Welsh Office, 1996, p. 1)

Alongside "telecottages," or small-scale IT businesses, the development agencies actively courted "call centres," which provide customer support for large service-sector corporations. A decade later, however, the same call centres were relocating to India, where labour costs and overheads were lower. Thus, while 850 jobs were created in call centres in rural Wales between 2000 and 2005, 265 call-centre jobs were lost, largely due to the relocation of operations to Asia (Woods et al., 2007).

Third, rural Wales has more recently been exposed to internationalized labour migration, particularly the arrival of migrant workers from Central and Eastern Europe following the expansion of the European Union in 2004. Since May 2004, over 10,000 migrant workers have arrived in rural Wales, especially from Poland. Although this is a small figure compared to the numbers in some rural regions of Britain, the influx has nonetheless had a significant impact on Welsh rural communities with no history of immigration. In most areas, relations between local residents and migrant workers are amicable, but tensions have flared in some smaller communities, especially where the migrant workforce is dominated by young single men. One such location is Llanybydder in Carmarthenshire, a predominantly Welsh-speaking community of 1,400 residents, which is now home to around 200 Polish migrant workers employed at a local abattoir (Woods and Watkin, 2008). Although a comparatively recent phenomenon, the internationalization of labour in rural Wales presents both challenges and opportunities, on the one hand raising questions about the beneficiaries of rural development and the distinctiveness of local culture, yet on the other hand presenting opportunities for trade and tourism through new links with the migrants' home countries.

The combination of these processes has produced a dynamic and uncertain environment for the economy and society of rural Wales at the start of the 21st century. The region has a steadily increasing population, but the overall pattern of growth disguises a locally differentiated geography of population change in which many smaller rural communities are still experiencing depopulation (Hartwell et al., 2007). Residents of rural Wales as a whole are relatively prosperous compared to residents of the urban South Wales Valleys, but there is persistent hidden poverty (Milbourne and Hughes, 2005). Spiralling house prices reflect demand created by in-migration, gentrification, and local prosperity, but they have also generated a crisis of access to affordable housing across the region (Kitchen and Milbourne, 2006). Regional centres such as Aberystwyth and Carmarthen are booming with significant property development, but other small towns have become pockets of deprivation as factories and services close (Woods et al., 2007). The western part of the region qualified, along with South Wales, for funding under Objective 1 of the European Structural Funds in 2000, indicating that its GDP was below 75% of the European Union average.

In developing responses to these challenges, current regional development policy—in contrast to the policy of the postwar period—now prioritizes endogenous development rather than exogenous investment, and it focuses on enhancing accessibility within the region rather than building stronger outward connections (Welsh Assembly Government, 2003). Thus space is still a critical factor for rural development but is now problematized on two planes: the global economy, which is understood as the plane of the macro-processes shaping the challenges and opportunities confronting rural Wales; and the local plane of connections between communities within rural Wales. The crucial element linking the two planes is *place*.

Responding to Globalization: Toward Place-Based Rural Development?

Responses to the economic development challenges facing rural Wales have been pulled away from the previous national planning paradigm in two directions. On the one hand, the economic potential of rural Wales is increasingly conditioned by globalization, such that economic actors within the region increasingly look not only to national markets but also to international markets. Yet, on the other hand, in seeking to gain competitive advantage in these markets, regional economic actors have re-emphasized their embeddedness in place and have increasingly sought to distinguish and add value to their products by valorizing place-based resources, local culture, and heritage.

Individual entrepreneurs have built up new businesses selling products to international markets, but they have done so in a way that is very much place-centred. Examples include the marketing of various distinctive local foodstuffs, clothing companies, and craft producers, but one of the most prominent commodities to receive this treatment is bottled spring water. The best-known Welsh brand of spring water, Ty Nant, was launched at the Savoy Hotel in London in 1989. In the space of less than two decades, production has expanded to close to 50 million bottles a year, 60% of which are exported. Ty Nant water, with its distinctive blue bottle, has been featured in Hollywood films and US television series including *Sex and the City*, *Friends*, and *The OC*. However, the company website emphasizes the source of the water and its "humble origins in the unspoilt countryside of mid Wales," telling the story of the discovery of the spring near the village of Bethania by a water diviner in 1976, and featuring photographs of the site (Ty Nant, 2008).

Llanllyr Source water was first bottled commercially in 1999, from a spring less than 10 km from the Ty Nant spring. It has not achieved the same volume of sales as Ty Nant, but has similarly secured an international reputation and market, positioning itself as a premium brand. As the company website boasts, "In Las Vegas and Hong Kong and many places in between restaurants and hotels now make llanllyr SOURCE spring water their number one choice" (Llanllyr Water, 2007). Moreover, like Ty Nant, the brand image of Llanllyr Source is at least in part based on its originating from a specific identified place in rural Wales. Thus, the company website describes at length the history of the site, claiming:

> We know that people in our small unspoilt valley in west Wales have been drinking the water here since at least the year 1180 when a nunnery was established here …but the known history of the site goes back to the 6th century so it's quite probable that even the nuns weren't the first people to enjoy the water! (Llanllyr Water, 2007)

Place and product are hence entwined in a mythology that extends to the present day, with the website similarly recounting the story of how the bottling plant was established as a venture in farm diversification responding to a fragile rural economy:

> But only 10 years ago all this was just a flicker of a dream as the family owners of the Llanllyr farm, whose ancestors first farmed the land almost 300 years ago, looked at how to cope with the region's declining agricultural income and the inevitable job losses involved. (Llanllyr Water, 2007)

Place has also been valorized through collective action as a means of refocusing the economy of whole towns or localities, with communities developing particular cultural or economic "niches" to establish a place brand and attract trade and visitors, often from outside (Woods *et al*., 2007). The best known "niche town" in rural Wales is Hay-on-Wye, the self-described "town of books" or "book capital of the world." A small town of 1,900 residents, Hay boasts over 30 second-hand bookshops stocking over 200,000 titles. Since 1988 it has hosted the annual Hay Literary Festival, attracting over 80,000 visitors from Britain and overseas. The global reach of the festival is reflected by the franchising of satellite festivals in Spain and Colombia, and by the profile of its speakers, including in recent years two former US presidents, Bill Clinton and Jimmy Carter, a former US vice president, Al Gore, and global literary figures such as John Updike, Margaret Atwood, Gore Vidal, and Salman Rushdie.

Other "niche towns" include Llangollen, which each year hosts the International Musical Eisteddfod, a cultural festival that draws 5,000 performers from 50 countries and audiences in excess of 50,000 to a town of 2,600 residents. As with Hay, the global reach of the festival is indicated by the profile of the performers that it has attracted, including Luciano Pavarotti, the Red Army Ensemble, and Ladysmith Black Mambazo. A slightly more offbeat strategy has been followed by Llanwrtyd Wells, a remote town of 600 residents that is a centre for outdoor pursuits, which has developed a number of distinctive events including the Man versus Horse Marathon and the World Bog Snorkelling Championship.

Initiatives such as those described above have tended to be initiated and driven by individual entrepreneurs, but in several cases they have also been supported by rural development programs and funding. The emphasis on endogenous, bottom-up development, which has prevailed in Welsh rural development policy since the 1980s, has encouraged local actors intent on regeneration to consider place as a resource and to find ways of valorizing place for economic gain (B. Edwards, 1998). This place-based approach formed the basis for a series of regeneration programs that have provided funding for economic development, including the European Union's LEADER programs, DBRW's Market Town Initiative, the WDA's Small Towns and Villages Initiative, and the Welsh Assembly Government's Rural Community Action program and Communities First program.

Ironically, while these initiatives are, in theory, designed to acknowledge local difference, permitting local actors to develop local solutions to locally identified problems, in practice they have frequently followed similar paths. They have all been founded on the principle of working in partnership, requiring collaboration between the public, private, and community sectors, and hence have conformed to fairly standard organizational forms and patterns of participation (B. Edwards *et al*., 2000; Derkzen *et al*., 2008). They have also often engaged in similar activities, commonly including improvements to the local environment, support for local festivals and events, and promotion of local heritage. For example, the Antur Cwm Taf a Tawe LEADER II group in Carmarthenshire developed a "Land of History and Legend" project to encourage tourism, producing and installing information boards to explain local heritage features; while Curiad Caron, the Market Town

Initiative delivery group in Tregaron, helped resurrect the local fair, produced a guidebook of local walks, and ran projects on local history (B. Edwards *et al.*, 2000). Some initiatives have developed projects that respond to the peripherality of their location, such as the Deudraeth 2000 Market Town Initiative in Penrhyndeudraeth, which sought to develop local IT provision. However, the spatially fragmented nature of place-based initiatives and the limited resources mean that they have limited capacity to address issues of accessibility and connectivity.

As such, the contribution of place-based initiatives to developing the next rural economy in Wales is open to question. There is no doubt that many small towns and rural communities have benefited from the funding channeled through such initiatives. They have seen improvements to local townscapes and environments, the provision or modification of community facilities, the revitalization of community events, and the enhanced promotion of the locality and its attractions to visitors. However, with funding attached to limited-term programs, many initiatives have struggled to sustain themselves beyond the original award period, and the activities they supported have also wilted over time.

Moreover, it might be argued that placed-based initiatives in rural Wales have been more successful at social development than economic development. They have helped provide a focal point for community action and, importantly, have formed a vehicle through which local residents have been able to reconsider and re-articulate the meaning of place in a globalizing countryside. Yet the number of actual jobs created has been limited, even in successful entrepreneurial ventures such as Ty Nant and Llanllyr Water. Meanwhile, behind the scenes, more jobs have arguably been created by ongoing "quiet" state intervention— business advice, start-up units, training schemes, and so on, as well as the expansion of public-sector employment by the development of public services and the relocation of government offices. The potential for major private-sector investment of the type likely to create hundreds or thousands of new jobs remains severely restricted by peripherality and poor accessibility. The space economy, it seems, still matters.

Conclusion

The political economies of rural place are being restructured and reconfigured in the emergent global countryside. The previous space economy, which dictated the political-economic trajectories of rural localities in terms of their accessibility from urban centres and peripherality to national cores, has corroded. Yet its passing marks not the annihilation of space, but the advent of a new space economy shaped by the uneven power-geometries of globalization. Some rural localities have been catapulted to the heart of new global networks as sites of global tourism, amenity migration, or commodity production. Others have been cast adrift, with established ties cut as production is relocated or trade lost in the face of global competition. For many rural regions, such as rural Wales, the impact has been less dramatic, but even here globalization is slowly changing the condition of the local political economy.

The shape of the next rural economy in regions such as rural Wales will depend on how well the region adjusts to the pressures of globalization, which in turn depends on how local actors seize the economic opportunities presented, counter the threats, and embrace the broadening of social and cultural horizons. The signs from regions such as rural Wales are positive, with social and economic entrepreneurs developing successful responses.

Significantly, these responses will frequently involve a reassertion of their rootedness in place and a trading on the distinctive cultural cachet of place. This process has been assisted by place-based regeneration initiatives focused on endogenous development and bottom-up action, which in turn reflect the new governmental mode of "governing through communities." Initiatives of this type provide a vehicle through which rural communities can reconsider and re-articulate the meaning of place in a globalizing countryside, but their economic impact in terms of business start-ups and job creation can be patchy. Place-based strategies mean places will be competing with each other as commodities, and only some will find a sustainable foothold in the marketplace. Success will be determined by a number of factors, including individual entrepreneurship, available capital, and marketing skills, but also accessibility and connectivity. Place, ultimately, cannot be divorced from space. The next rural economy will be shaped by both.

Acknowledgements

This chapter draws in part on research undertaken through the Wales Rural Observatory, funded by the Welsh Assembly Government, with research assistance from Graham Gardner and Catherine Walkley. It also draws on ideas discussed with the late Bill Edwards, whose expertise on rural Wales is greatly missed. I am grateful to Greg Halseth and the manuscript reviewer for their comments and suggestions.

References

BBC. (1999) The Laura Ashley story, BBC News website, news.bbc.co.uk/1/hi/wales/454434.stm. (accessed 21 June 2008).

Beacham Committee. (1964) *Depopulation in Mid-Wales*. HMSO, London.

Cheshire, L. (2006) *Governing Rural Development*. Ashgate, Aldershot, UK.

Cloke, P., Goodwin, M., and Milbourne, P. (1997) *Rural Wales: Community and Marginalization*. University of Wales Press, Cardiff.

Derkzen, P., Franklin, A., and Bock, B. (2008) Examining power struggles as a signifier of successful partnership working: A case study of partnership dynamics. *Journal of Rural Studies*, 24, 458–466.

Edwards, B. (1998) Charting the discourse of community action: Perspectives from practice in rural Wales. *Journal of Rural Studies* 14, 63–78.

Edwards, B., Goodwin, M., Pemberton, S., and Woods, M. (2000) *Partnership Working in Rural Regeneration*. Policy Press, Bristol, UK.

Edwards, J. (1985) Manufacturing in Wales: A spatial and sectoral analysis of recent changes in structure, 1975–1985. *Cambria* 12(2), 89–115.

Epp, R., and Whitson, D., eds. (2001) *Writing Off the Rural West*. University of Alberta Press, Edmonton.

Halfacree, K. (2007) Trial by space for a "radical rural": Introducing alternative localities, representations and lives. *Journal of Rural Studies* 23, 125–141.

Hartwell, S., Kitchen, L., Milbourne, P., and Morgan, S. (2007) *Population Change in Rural Wales: Social and Cultural Impacts*. Wales Rural Observatory, Cardiff.

Herbert-Cheshire, L. (2000) Contemporary strategies for rural community development in Australia: A governmentality perspective. *Journal of Rural Studies* 16(2), 203–215.

_____. (2003) Translating policy: Power and action in Australia's country towns. *Sociologia Ruralis* 43, 454–473.

Hooson, E., and Jenkins, G. (1965) *The Heartland: A Plan for Mid-Wales.* Liberal Publications Department, London.

Jones, N. (1993) *Living in Rural Wales.* Gomer Press, Llandysul, UK.

Kenyon, P., and Black, A. (2001) *Small Town Renewal: Overview and Case Studies.* Rural Industries Research and Development Corporation, Canberra.

Kitchen, L., and Milbourne, P. (2006) *Housing Need in Rural Wales: Towards Sustainable Solutions.* Wales Rural Observatory, Cardiff.

Llanllyr Water. (2007) Llanllyr Source website, www.llanllyrwater.com (accessed 21 June 2008).

Lovering, J. (1983) *Gwynedd—A County in Crisis* (Coleg Harlech Occasional Papers in Welsh Studies, No 2). Coleg Harlech, Harlech, UK.

Marsden, T., Murdoch, J., Lowe, P., Munton, R., and Flynn, A. (1993) *Constructing the Countryside.* UCL Press, London.

Massey, D. (2005) *For Space.* Sage, London.

Milbourne, P., and Hughes, R. (2005) *Poverty and Social Exclusion in Rural Wales.* Wales Rural Observatory, Cardiff.

Ray, C. (1997) Towards a theory of the dialectic of rural development. *Sociologia Ruralis* 37, 345–362.

Ty Nant. (2008) Ty Nant profile, www.ty-nant.com/profile.htm (accessed 21 June 2008).

Welsh Assembly Government. (2003) *People, Places, Futures: The Wales Spatial Plan.* Author, Cardiff.

Welsh Office. (1996) *A Working Countryside for Wales.* HMSO, London.

Williams, G. (1985) Recent social changes in Mid Wales. *Cambria* 12(2), 117–137.

Woods, M. (2005) *Contesting Rurality: Politics in the British Countryside.* Ashgate, Aldershot, UK.

_____. (2007) Engaging the global countryside: Globalization, hybridity and the reconstitution of rural place. *Progress in Human Geography* 31, 485–507.

Woods, M., and Watkin, S. (2008) *Central and Eastern European Migrant Workers in Rural Wales.* Wales Rural Observatory, Aberystwyth.

Woods, M., Edwards, B., and Walkley, C. (2007) *Small and Market Towns in Rural Wales and Their Hinterlands.* Wales Rural Observatory, Aberystwyth.

Chapter 14

Reviving Small Rural Towns in the Paris Periurban Fringes

Claire Aragau and Jean-Paul Charvet

In Europe, researchers and planners have traditionally held that periurbanism is not capable of creating new centralities. The former small towns that were quite numerous within the periurban areas, including the Paris periurban area, were considered to be increasingly dependent on central cities for job opportunities, and increasingly less capable of meeting their own needs for services. Improved transportation within periurban spaces is considered one of the main reasons for continuing urban sprawl, the declining independence of surrounding communities, and the increasing influence of urban centres on these rural-urban fringe areas. But in the case discussed in this chapter—which is, of course, a specific case—we demonstrate just the contrary (Aragau, 2007): that the addition of "space + place" planning strategies are contributing to the revival of two small rural towns—Montfort-l'Amaury and Houdan—located on the Paris periurban fringes (Aguilera *et al.*, 2006).

Impact studies dealing with highways have shown that they tend to increase the attractiveness of larger urban centres to the detriment of smaller towns located along the route. This is due to the time–distance reduction afforded by the highway system and the limited number of interchanges located along the routes. In this chapter we look at the impacts of a specific road system, the "expressway," which is different from a regular highway and offers a greater number of interchanges. In 2001, the "Nationale 12" (National Road 12) or N12 became an expressway between the cities of Bois-d'Arcy and Dreux, west of the Paris urban area (Fig.14.1). In the following sections we trace the impact of this system on the reconstructed territories of this area, which stretches from the Yvelines department to the Eure-et-Loir department.[1]

Methodology

When we study the changes that are generated by a new transportation infrastructure, we have to be very careful, as the traditional methodology for this type of study is often weak. "Effect" or impact analysis studies are attractive because they are relatively simple to understand. Most impact studies are built on a cost-advantage analysis, which takes into account and quantifies (often monetizing) the direct and indirect effects of new transportation infrastructure. Plassard, however, has shown that "the simplistic vision of cause and effect mechanisms cannot be used for studying the relationships between highways and regional development" (as cited in Offner, 1993, p. 235, our translation). Researchers generate misleading interpretations when they make hasty comparisons between "before" and "after" studies. According to Plassard, an impact study can be done on a natural environmental process, but not on a socio-economic one. So it is necessary to achieve a dynamic diagnosis: that is to say, the study should not be linear but, rather, dynamic, capturing the interactions between events. In this context, a systemic approach is best. It allows researchers to take into account factors at a given moment and thus avoid faulty conclusions based on problematic "before" and "after" comparisons. It is difficult and risky to compare two moments, when the political, economic, and sociological contexts may have individually and collectively evolved and transformed in important ways between the times the two "snapshots" were taken.

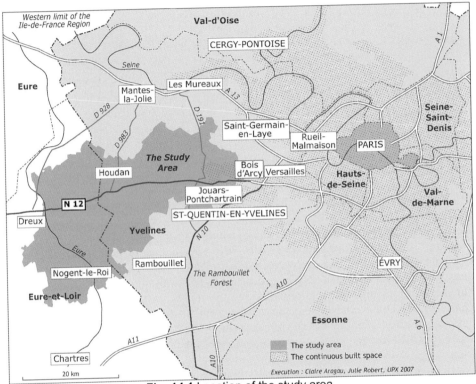

Fig. 14.1 Location of the study area.

For our study of the new expressway, we examine the N12's interactions with the region's commercial framework and with the development of specific areas of economic activity (*zones d'activités économiques*). This allows us to understand how "proximity territories" (*territoires de proximité*[2]) have been evolving around the small towns that are located close to the new expressway. According to the recent *Atlas rural et agricole de l'Ile-de-France* (Institut d'Aménagement et d'Urbanisme de la Région Ile-de-France, 2005), 84% of the French people believe that it is more pleasant to live in the countryside than in town. This percentage is similar for Ile-de-France inhabitants. If it were possible for them to make a choice, more than half the residents of Ile-de-France would prefer to live in the surrounding countryside. But after factoring in concerns regarding overall quality of life, it is clear that nearly half the residents (45%) consider access to services to be important or very important in their living environment. Accordingly, 28% say that they are unwilling to live too far from a town. They wish to benefit from the quality of life in the countryside and from the proximity to jobs, services, and leisure activities in town (Dubois-Taine and Chalas, 1997). The new expressway between Bois-d'Arcy and Dreux allows inhabitants in the region to benefit from better access to a major urban centre while also enjoying a preserved natural environment (Bryant and Charvet, 2003).

In the following sections, we will first present the area and the context in which this new transportation facility was established, describing the area it crosses and the selection of road choices. Then we will look at the integration of the new road into local development policies. At the end, we will describe the "life area" or "life basin" (*bassin de vie*) that is emerging and supported by this new expressway. To do this, we use the definition of "life basin" settled upon by the former DATAR (Délégation à l'Aménagement du Territoire et à l'Action Régionale), which underlines the geographical, social, economical, and cultural coherence of areas relying on homogeneous services and activities (Julien and Pougnard, 2004). Because the geographical coherence of a life basin is linked to the transportation network, the spatial framework (based on the level of access to intermediate-level services) that organizes the cultural, economic, and social coherence of a rural and small town area can be dramatically altered as a result of changes to transportation infrastructure (Charmes, 2005). This is why it is important that we study the impacts of the new expressway on the "life basin" of this part of the Paris periurban region.

Case Study: Spaces and Places

Between Town and Countryside on the Western Periurban Fringes of Paris

The case study area is located on the western periurban fringe of the Paris region, 40 to 80 kilometres from Paris, along a new express road (*voie express*) or expressway that follows the former route of the Nationale 12 (N12) leading from the Ile-de-France region to Brittany. This new expressway begins at the N12 and Nationale 10 (N10) interchange—that is to say, from the new town of Saint-Quentin-les-Yvelines—and extends to the town of Dreux. West of Dreux, the N12 serves the urban centres of Verneuil, Alençon, Rennes, and Brest in Brittany. The new expressway goes across the Yvelines and Eure-et-Loir departments, which belong, respectively, to the Ile-de-France Region and the Region Centre.

The study area is part of the Paris periurban fringe. The impact of changing transportation infrastructure is very important in the periurban fringe as it reorganizes the links between rural and small town locations and Paris and its closest suburbs. According to the new definitions of "rural" and "urban" recently adopted in France, the study area is considered by the French government's Statistics Services to be "periurban." In France, an "urban pole" is an urban unit with more than 5,000 jobs; a "periurban municipality" is a municipality that sends more than 40% of its resident working population toward an urban pole. However, according to the former, and still used, definitions of "urban" and "rural"— in which "rural" includes municipalities with fewer than 2,000 inhabitants and "urban" those with more than 2,000 inhabitants—the study area is largely rural: two-thirds of the municipalities have fewer than 1,000 inhabitants and one-third have fewer than 400. The people who are living in the area believe that they are living in a rural area and in the countryside (Institut d'Aménagement et d'Urbanisme de la Région Ile-de-France, 2005).

There are two small towns in the area, Houdan and Montfort-l'Amaury. In 2004, the town of Houdan had 4,000 inhabitants while Montfort-l'Amaury had 4,500. The population of the whole study area increased from 110,265 inhabitants in 1990 to 123,655 inhabitants in 1999, a population increase of 13,390 people (+ 12%) in ten years. This increase is still going on, albeit at a slower pace.

The case study is driven by the desire to know whether the road improvements will lead to either a growing urban influence in this rural region or to the creation of new "life basins" within the countryside. Research into urban influences focuses on Paris, the new town of Saint-Quentin-en-Yvelines, and a series of new urban sprawl or "dormitory suburb" areas. Interest in the formation of new "life basins" derives from their potential to create new labour markets and services areas. Within the Ile-de-France Region, the Schéma Directeur de la Région Ile-de-France (SDRIF), a regional planning document, presents among its planning goals the control of urban sprawl and the renewal of residential behaviours.[3] In the Region Centre, the planning situation appears to be less strong, but with similar goals.

The study area encompasses an east-west strip that includes the small market towns of Jouars-Pontchartrain, Thoiry, La Queue-les-Yvelines, Orgerus, and Bû, and the more important but small towns of Montfort-l'Amaury and Houdan (Fig. 14.2). The area is linked to Paris by railway (via Paris's Gare Montparnasse) and by the new expressway. The territorial organization of this space appears to be strongly linked to the new expressway.

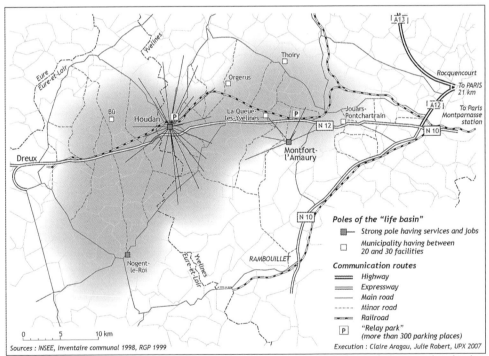

Fig. 14.2 The "life basin" and the expressway (Institut national de la statistique et des études économiques, 1999). Note: Facilities are amenities (shops, restaurants, post office) and relay parking lots are car parks where a lot of people park their cars before commuting by train each day to work.

Farmers and Residents

Around the small cities, the countryside consists of a combination of forests (covering large areas) and woods (covering smaller areas), the edges of which are attractive to new residential developments, and an agricultural landscape with very large fields, where cash grain farms are growing wheat, barley, maize, and rapeseed. There are few interactions between the farmers and the people who live in the area.

Farmers and residents, even if they are living in the same territory, often have very different concerns. For example, in order to protect one of the last green gateways to the urban area of Paris, a coalition of different associations, the majority of the population living in the area, and most of the local elected representatives asked the government to classify the Jouars Plain in accordance with a 1930 law dealing with protection of the natural environment. This classification would be aimed at preserving the agricultural and rural aspects of the region without placing too many or too heavy constraints on the people farming in the area. Even though different people may have had different perceptions of this 2,500 ha plain, at the beginning of the process there was general agreement on agriculture preservation. However, 50 area farmers, backed by the most important French farmers union, have recently taken the position that "protection" does not hold the same meaning for farmers as for village residents. From their perspective, classification in accordance with the 1930 law would lead to more constraints on building barns and other farm buildings, on plantings, and on other farm activities. They feel that they are adequately protected by the PLU (*Plans locaux d'urbanisme*, which are local planning documents drawn up at the municipal level) and by the SAFER (Société d'Aménagement Foncier et d'Equipement Rural, which has pre-emptive rights when agricultural land is sold).

While cash grain farmers have very few interactions with residents, the situation is different for vegetable growers. The example of the Chapellier family, which lives in Méré, a village close to Montfort-l'Amaury, illustrates this point. This family of vegetable growers is originally from Conflans-Sainte-Honorine, a small town located near the confluence of the Seine and Oise rivers. The Chapelliers came to Méré in 1985 for farmlands that are close to the railway station. They farm 12 ha, growing cereals on 9 ha and a large range of different vegetables, including potatoes, carrots, turnips, salads, cabbages, beans, leeks, and shallots, on the other 3 ha. In the past they sold their entire production in the central food market of Paris. But this market relocated to Rungis, near the Orly airport, and the Chapellier family is now selling its vegetables three times a week at the Conflans-Sainte-Honorine market, which is close to the case study area. The family benefits from a quality label that is also a label of origin: *Producteur de l'Ile-de-France* (Ile-de-France producer). In 2007, the Chapelliers opened a new market, close to an expressway interchange, in order to sell more vegetables directly to local consumers, some of whom are coming from Houdan in the west and Plaisir in the east. These direct links between farmers and consumers are not typical of the study area. Most of the time farmers and consumers ignore each other and live in separate worlds (Charvet, 2003; Charvet and Poulot, 2006).

The New Expressway and Municipal Policies

The New Expressway and New Proximities

The decision to transform the former N12 into an expressway followed a variety of proposals that first emerged in the 1970s when new periurban private housing estates were established in Beynes, Saint-Germain-de-la-Grange, and Jouars-Pontchartrain. At this time, most of the commuters were going to Paris or to municipalities close to Paris. Since the 1980s, however, commuting between different suburbs of Paris has become more and more common. This was the pattern followed by two-thirds of the Ile-de-France commuters in 1990, and it could be the case for three-quarters of them by 2015.

In the 1970s, the SDRIF was only looking at improving automobile traffic in the areas closest to Paris. At that time, nothing was planned to improve traffic conditions on the N12. At the end of the 1970s, however, studies showed for the first time an interest in building an expressway[4] between Bois-d'Arcy and Dreux. An expressway was suggested instead of a highway because there are more numerous access points on an expressway, and it is easier to navigate on an expressway than on a highway. It is also easier to maintain links with the former road network. The transformation to an expressway can be done step by step, and for this reason it is easier to secure the financing for construction. The main advantage of an expressway is that the links with the different local economies can be stronger as a result of the greater number of interchanges. Furthermore, in this particular case, the expressway improves the Ile-de-France Region's links with the Centre and Normandy regions. The 1994 SDRIF considered Houdan to be a "link town" (*ville trait-d'union*) between the Region Ile-de-France and the other regions. Houdan also serves the new town of Saint-Quentin-en-Yvelines, which recently became an important commercial, administrative, service, and university pole in the western part of the Paris area. One objective of expressway construction was to open more of the Paris area and its new towns to the other regions of the Parisian basin and to the regions that are closest to Paris. In the case under examination, there was also the objective of improving the roads leading to Brittany.

It took 20 years to complete the new expressway between Bois-d'Arcy and Dreux. It presents at least two advantages: first, people can drive faster (with a speed limit of 110 km/hour instead of 90 km/hour), with very few traffic jams thanks to the Jouars-Pontchartrain tunnel; second, it multiplies the number of access points for getting on or off the roadway, with ramps every two or three kilometres (Fig. 14.3). The expressway is different from the usual highway or motorway in other ways: it is toll free and does not generate the "tunnel effect." It remains well linked to the former branch road network thanks to the number of exits and to the improvement of these exits. Again, this leads to better accesses to the local towns (Dupuy, 2006). For a given constant driving time, the people are now living in an area with a larger range of different services (e.g., educational, medical), job opportunities, and leisure activities.

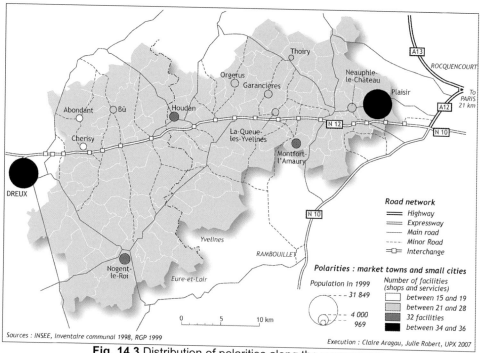

Fig. 14.3 Distribution of polarities along the expressway.

Different studies dealing with commuting, recently conducted by the Direction Régionale de l'Equipement of the Ile-de-France Region (the regional transportation directorate), have shown a variety of findings:

- Motorized trips are increasing in the region at a rate of 1% per year.
- The average length of time per trip is relatively constant over a 15-year period at about 29 minutes.
- It appears that improvements in the transportation network in the Ile-de-France Region have not reduced time per trip. Instead, they have increased the distance t ravelled per trip.
- The increase in trip distance enhances the choices available to regional residents for work, shopping, studying, and leisure activities.

The primary objective of commuters is to reduce travel time and increase access to activities, services, and employment. The new expressway succeeds in increasing accessibility to new locations across the region.

The mapping of potential travel times and distances provided a means to illustrate the range of accessibility improvements to the main small towns within the study area. Although there are methodological problems with this technique—for example, people do not necessarily choose the shortest distance when travelling—the two maps in Fig. 14.4 illustrate the range for a ten-minute drive from Plaisir, Houdan, and Montfort-l'Amaury before and after construction of the new expressway. Prior to 2001, the towns' areas of influence were, to a large extent, separate, with the exception of the links between Plaisir and Montfort-l'Amaury. Since 2001, the towns are far more interconnected. In France, a ten-minute drive is considered to be a standard threshold for trip surveys as these trips are mainly undertaken to buy food. Thanks to the new expressway, inhabitants from six additional municipalities may choose from two different poles that are within a ten-minute drive. New proximities to local "central places" have emerged since 2001 due to the expressway (Dureau and Levy, 2002).

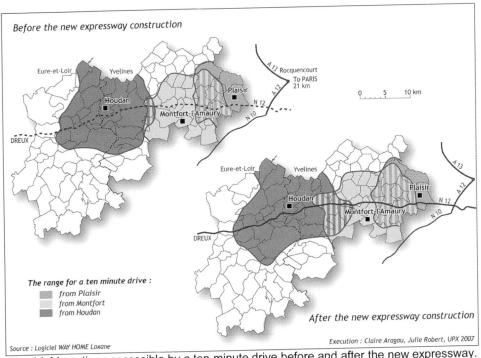

Fig. 14.4 Locations accessible by a ten-minute drive before and after the new expressway.

The New Expressway and Economic Dynamism

New areas of economic activity (*zones d'activités économiques*) are more often located along the expressway than along the former routes (Fig. 14.5). The occupancy rates of these new areas were generally lower before the expressway was completed, but these rates are rapidly increasing. The price for land close to the expressway appears to be double that of the local average. Prices also increase as you approach Paris. The more rapid access to Paris and Saint-Quentin-en-Yvelines is the primary explanation for the new "activity areas" in the Eure-et-Loir department, west of Houdan and the Ile-de-France Region. These areas are also providing new job opportunities, represented on the map by triangles and circles.

For the market towns, the economic indicators show a revitalization of the local economy. The number of small shopkeepers is still declining in some villages, but at a slower rate. In the small towns of Montfort-l'Amaury and Houdan, the number is increasing. These towns are benefiting from an important historical heritage dating from the Middle Ages and Renaissance. A feature of Montfort-l'Amaury is the two towers of Anne de Bretagne (from the 12th century). Houdan boasts the imposing "donjon de Houdan," a medieval fortified tower (also from the 12th century) that is very well preserved and can be seen from a great distance by visitors and tourists when they drive in the area. There is also the "Charnier" from the 16th and 17th centuries, a cemetery with galleries forming a cloister, which is located in the centre of Houdan, close to a number of ancient half-timbered houses. These historical legacies play an important role in the repositioning of the small towns as "central places."

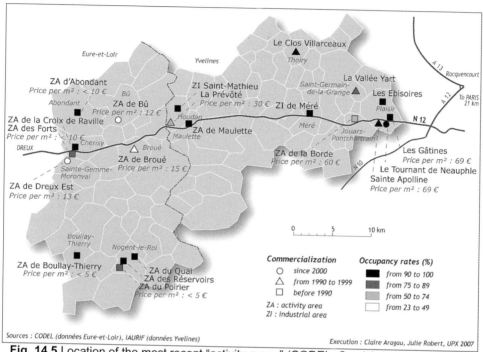

Fig. 14.5 Location of the most recent "activity areas" (CODEL, Comité de Développement conomique d'Eure-et-Loir. Institut d'Aménagement et d'Urbanisme de la Région Ile-de-France, 1999).

These attractive buildings could have remained as inanimate scenery. However, once they are linked to the economic dynamism of the towns, they contribute significantly to their overall attractiveness and economic potential in a variety of ways. The activity of a city centre is based mainly on trade activities, and these are jeopardized by the development of new market centres located on the peripheries of the towns. The evolution of food shops, particularly bread, pastry, and candy stores, constitutes a good indicator for measuring the attractiveness of a city centre. The same applies to the establishment of mini-markets (superettes). From 1993 to 2003, none of these shops closed in either Houdan or Montfort-l'Amaury. On the other hand, new shops were created or older shops underwent a change in ownership. Entrepreneurs created two new general food stores in Houdan during the last ten years, and one in Montfort-l'Amaury.

The Chambre de Commerce et d'Industrie (Chamber of Commerce and Industry) of Versailles suggested measures to safeguard and maintain city centres after conducting studies that identified the strengths and weaknesses of the local retail shops, street by street. It also proposed actions municipalities could take to improve their overall attractiveness and accessibility, including planning new parking lots and standardizing the opening hours for local shops. As these studies are quite costly, only the larger municipalities were able to afford them. In the end, the key factor for reviving trading activities in city centres appears to be the dynamism of consumer demand. In Houdan, eight shops and two real estate agencies were established in 2004. During the same year in Montfort-l'Amaury, seven new shops and three real estate agencies were created. In recent years, the number of bank agencies has remained constant in these two towns. These trends suggest a true viability and "sustainability" of small shops located in the centres of these two towns.

An important factor for explaining these recent changes is the high proportion of well-off people who are living in the periurban area west of Paris. They can afford higher prices for their houses, but also for the products and services they are purchasing in the area. To a large extent, this social dynamic contributes to the renewal and revival of the town centres. Images of quality are important for this social class. They are buying organic food, quality wines, and local crafts, and are willing to shop locally to support a local community that is not a "dormitory suburb." In Houdan and Montfort-l'Amaury, the house frontages in the town centres have been restored, a trend linked to the high purchasing power of the new residents.

In some of the villages, small retail food stores are popping up: 40 of them were created within the study area between 1993 and 2002. The pace of new store development is also increasing, with 30 of the stores being established between 1998 and 2002. The Versailles Chambre de Commerce et d'Industrie offers various aid programs for the development of new stores and activities in towns with fewer than 2,000 inhabitants (representing "rural" towns, according to the former French definition). These aid programs for economic development take the form of shopping and consumer studies, aids for accessing different subsidies, and assistance for finding new shopkeepers. The overall purpose is to propose a complete suite of studies for regional municipalities, conducted by a trade advisor from the Versailles Chambre de Commerce et d'Industrie. The studies take approximately six months to complete. The French government, the Conseil Régional de l'Ile-de-France, the Conseil Général des Yvelines (representing the Yvelines department), and local municipalities collaborate on these development studies. One of the reasons for the collaboration is that the studies are relatively costly to produce and will require partnerships between the contributors if they are to act on the study recommendations.

Municipal Policies

The Houdan and Montfort-l'Amaury populations have increased by more than 10% during the last decade. In an effort to accommodate this growth, the municipalities provided new services and infrastructure. They built new schools, child daycare centres, cultural centres, and sport centres. "Municipal communities" (*communautés de communes*) developed slowly in the Ile-de-France Region, beginning with Houdan. Surrounding communities then amalgamated with Houdan in January 1998 to create the municipal community "Communauté de communes du Pays houdanais" (which we can translate as "Houdan country"). To date, there are 32 municipal members of Communauté de communes du Pays houdanais: 27 of them are located in the Yvelines department and 5 within the Eure-et-Loir department. This organization is strengthening the position of "place" for Houdan as a structuring pole. The municipality is responsible for providing a wide range of benefits and services including community facilities, community amenities, economical development support, housing, transportation options, and landscape settings encompassing the dynamism of the Houdan area. The ability of Communauté de communes du Pays houdanais partners to access money from different institutional investors and subsidies from the Yvelines department (in some cases, up to 50% of the investments) constitutes evidence of the dynamism and capacity of Houdan.

A professional tax paid by local businesses is the main source of income for financing Communauté de communes du Pays houdanais policies and activities. In 2006, the municipal community signed a partnership agreement with the Versailles Chambre de Commerce et d'Industrie to develop a common policy for creating new jobs in the area. The partners carried out an economic and territorial diagnosis to identify priorities and the key economic players, diffusing training courses in relation to the needs of small local enterprises, improving relationships with customers, developing quality approaches, and facilitating experience exchanges between enterprises. This partnership with the Versailles Chambre de Commerce et d'Industrie relies on a broad approach for enhancing job creation and local economic development.

The unemployment rate in the Communauté de communes du Pays houdanais is one of the lowest in the Yvelines department; more jobs were created than lost in recent years. But this dynamism has to be consolidated. Elected representatives are looking for quality jobs and recognize that the types of enterprises that provide them are sensitive to the environmental and service quality in the area. The improvement of services and infrastructure became a priority in order to attract enterprises looking for competitiveness, quality of life, and visually attractive surroundings. In order to improve the transportation network, the Communauté de communes du Pays houdanais is studying financial plans for enhancing access to different services and facilities located in its territory. One of the plans involves using smaller buses that are more easily adapted to people's needs.

All of these changes contribute to the Houdan pole by improving its position as an attractive *place* within the region. The municipal community's collaboration with a large range of economic and administrative organizations and institutions serves to complement its positive *space* location on the western boundary of the Ile-de-France Region. This location is further improved by the new expressway, which creates and develops new links with the other spaces and places of the Parisian basin.

While the Houdan and Montfort-l'Amaury poles have their own areas of influence and are competing for different services, there is complementarity between the two poles for some services. In the case of health services, for example, the two town hospitals complement each other. A shared and reliable ambulance network has been developed. There is further cooperation on education. A high school, Lycée Jean Monnet, is located between Houdan and Montfort, along the expressway, in the municipality of La Queue-les-Yvelines. Other areas of complementarity include leisure activities. For example, the cinemas located in Montfort and Beynes have adopted different policies to attract different audiences (rather than being in direct competition by offering the same films). In this context, creation of the Communauté de communes du Pays houdanais is supporting new links and connections between the local towns and the villages that surround them.

Improvements in a Still-Dependent "Life Basin"

In 1999, the working population of the study area was 56,500, compared with approximately 35,300 jobs. As such, the area is still, to a large extent, dependent on jobs located in Paris or in the Paris urban area. However, the systemic model selected for this study helps to illustrate and explain how recent changes and improvements to the local economy are connected to changes in the transportation network. As is well known, the systemic approach offers a dynamic method by which to examine interactive phenomena; it highlights the interdependence between different elements without favouring one of them over others. The new expressway was the starting point for our analysis—in effect, it is a gateway for the analysis and serves as the linking element between each action and effect. In this context, the expressway is changing the relationship between space and place by enhancing accessibility across the entire periurban area.

The expressway provides technical features that guarantee traffic improvements, including better flows and higher speeds. This new road has directly improved the accesses to different spaces and services. For the populations coming from outside (mainly from Paris and its closest suburbs), the expressway facilitates their access to less expensive real estate, historic market towns, unique local services and heritage features, and the preserved rural environment. The image of the study area is a green one.

For the people who were living in the area before the N12 was upgraded to an expressway, this new transportation facility has improved accesses to new urban poles— that is to say, to activities and services formerly considered to be out of reach (Jaillet *et al.*, 2005). This new access is leading to new housing options. Considered together, greater access and housing opportunities are leading to the progressive emergence of a "life basin" within a periurban area. Thanks to the new expressway, the area became a larger real estate reserve, offering a preserved environment that is very different from the industrial Seine valley located just to the north. The area is attractive not only for new residents but also for enterprises looking for a particular brand image. This is particularly the case for companies developing new technologies.

These changes are also spurring retroactive effects. For example, many new residents are now actively trying to preserve the countryside environment of their new home (Sencébé, 2006). That said, some regulations are exploited for environmental and place-preservation purposes. For example, the "Barnier law" (an environmental protection law enacted in 1995) is being used to forbid building within a 75- to 100-metre strip along the main roads. Similarly, the PLU (Plans Locaux d'Urbanisme) often allocate quite large plots of land for building new houses in order to limit new development and to effectively close the area to newcomers. This policy clearly favours higher-income residents, but many elected representatives are justifying the large plots for reasons of environmental preservation and protection. With these planning actions, the expressway contributes to a process of favouring access for wealthier households (Desponds, 2006). As a result, socio-spatial segregation is increasing in the area (Berger, 2004). Mouillart summarizes the situation by arguing that "in order to preserve the areas where they are building, the well-off households agree to pay an 'entrance ticket': the higher the price for the ticket, the lower the risk of being located close to so-called 'undesirable' people" (Mouillart, 2006, p. 10, our translation). He concludes that "this is an expression of the famous 'club theory' used by select economists for explaining that the market is an exclusionary producer" (Mouillart, 2006, pp. 10–11, our translation).

The systemic model used in this study relies on the former DATAR's definition of "life basin." It underlines the geographical, social, economical, and cultural coherence of areas relying on homogeneous services and activities linked by the region's transportation network (Julien and Pougnard, 2004). The creation of the new expressway has resulted in dramatic changes in the "life basin." The establishment of eight new "activity areas" in the region since 1990 is bringing new jobs and people. Increased access is supporting new functions and shops in the market towns and a greater selection of service choices for rural residents. Development pressures may also be driving cultural and social change and may be supporting the development of spatial segregation and social class distinctions (Charmes, 2005). The expressway has affected the "life basins" of the area, and the situation is still evolving.

Conclusions

In spite of the nearness and weight of the Paris metropolitan area, it appears that, with accessibility improvements, small towns can develop a role and positive actions in territorial organization. As periurban people need proximity and human-scale territories, they appear to be able to build and grow "life basins" over time. The enhanced accessibility provided by the new expressway presents different advantages. First, it saves time for a given trip. Second, it provides the possibility of access, for a given driving time, to different urban centres (urban poles) in the region. And third, it generates new destination classifications in favour of proximity poles, to the detriment of more important regional poles located farther away.

In the specific case study, new developments in the local economy are linked to both space (to the traffic improvements arising from the new expressway) and place (to the different services, activities, and amenities created or improved for the local population). The new expressway was planned more than 25 years ago by a French government that was willing to improve the access to Brittany from Paris. The local investments by the Ile-de-France Region, the Yvelines department, and the local municipalities, particularly those of Montfort-l'Amaury and Houdan, are more recent. We did not find an appropriate and reliable methodology for pointing out, in this case, which of these planning phases, conceived and carried out at different times and on different spatial scales, was the most important for explaining the revival of the region. To date, they appear to have been working together, with some synergy between the different scales of planning activity. There appear to be very few studies dealing with expressways in France. But we hope that comparisons with other similar areas and cases in France, in Europe, and in other countries around the world will contribute to improving this body of research.

Notes

1. A department has two roles: it is an administrative unit and a local authority. There are 100 departments in France.
2. People living in "proximity territories" don't need to go a long way to find commodities, because the commodities are now available in the small towns. More than ten years ago, this was not the case. Residents living in the countryside had to drive farther because there were fewer services in the small towns.
3. Residential behaviours refer to changes that residents make to their way of life. These residents would rather shop in the proximity poles than places further away.
4. With an expressway, there are more access points than along a motorway. In France, there is an exit every 2 or 3 kilometres along an expressway and only every 20 kilometres along a motorway. The expressway is different from the usual highway or motorway in that it is toll free and does not generate the "tunnel effect".

References

Aguilera, A., Massot, M., and Proulhac, L. (2006) L'intégration du périurbain francilien à la métropole parisienne; Une mesure des flux quotidiens de personnes. In: Lanceneux, A., and

Boiteux-Orain, C. (eds.) *Paris et ses franges: Étalement urbain et polycentrisme.* Editions universitaires de Dijon, Dijon, 73-97.

Aragau, C. (2007) Aménagement d'une voie express et renouvellement urbain: Le cas de la N 12. PhD thesis. Université de Paris X, Nanterre.

Berger, M. (2004) *Les périurbains de Paris: De la ville dense à la métropole éclatée?* CNRS Éditions, Paris.

Bryant, C., and Charvet, J.-P. (2003) The peri-urban zone: The structure and dynamics of a strategic component of metropolitan regions. *Canadian Journal of Regional Science* 26(2/3), 231–250.

Charmes, E. (2005) *La vie périurbaine face à la menace des gated communities.* L'Harmattan, Paris.

Charvet, J.-P. (2003) Les conditions du maintien d'une agriculture vivante en Ile-de-France. *Canadian Journal of Regional Science* 26(2/3), 359–371.

Charvet, J.-P., and Poulot, M. (2006) Conserver des espaces ouverts dans la métropole éclatée: Le cas de l'Ile-de-France. In: Dorier-Aprill, E. (ed.) *Ville et environnement.* Sedes, Paris, 215–248.

Desponds, D. (2006) Spécialisations socio-résidentielles: Vers des divergences territoriales accrues dans le cadre du Val-d'Oise? *Hérodote, Ghettos américains, banlieues françaises* 122(3), 172–197.

Dubois-Taine, G., and Chalas, Y. (1997) *La ville émergente.* Éditions de l'Aube, La Tour d'Aigues.

Dupuy, G. (2006) *La dépendance à l'égard de l'automobile.* La Documentation française, PREDIT (Programme de recherche et d'innovation dans les transports terrestres), Paris.

Dureau, F. and Levy, J., eds. (2002) *L'accès à la ville: Les mobilités spatiales en questions.* L'Harmattan, Paris.

Institut d'Aménagement et d'Urbanisme de la Région Ile-de-France. (2005) *Atlas rural et agricole de l'Ile-de-France.* Author, Paris.

Institut national de la statistique et des études économiques. (1999) Inventaire communal 1998. INSEE, Paris.

Jaillet, M., Rougé, L., and Thouzellier, C. (2005) Vivre en maison individuelle en lotissement. In: Tapie, G. (ed.) *Maison individuelle, architecture, urbanite.* Editions de l'Aube, La Tour d'Aigues, 11–23

Julien, P., and Pougnard, J. (2004) *Les bassins de vie, au cœur de la vie des bourgs et petites villes.* INSEE Première, No. 953.

Moulliart, M. (2006) La crise du logement en France, pourquoi et pour qui? *Regards sur l'actualité* 320, 5–18.

Offner, J. (1993) Les effets structurants du transport: Mythe politique, mystification scientifique. *L'Espace géographique* 1993(3), 233–242.

Sencébé, Y. (2006) Mobilités quotidiennes et ancrages périurbains, attrait pour la campagne ou retrait de la ville? In: Bonnet, M., and Aubertel, P. (eds.) *La ville aux limites de la mobilité.* PUF, coll. Sciences Sociales et Sociétés, Paris, 153–160.

Chapter 15

When Rural–Urban Fringes Arise as Differentiated Place: the Socio-Economic Restructuring of Volvic Sources et Volcans, France

Salma Loudiyi

Within ongoing processes of socio-economic transformation, which cause a shift from a space-based economy to a place-based one, rural areas are undergoing a profound change in their economic structures, social formation, and governance. In this context, some rural–urban fringes are now emerging as attractive and accessible places, characterized by new forms of economic and residential development. As a consequence, they are also experiencing new forms of regulation. The challenges faced by rural–urban fringes are not unique and are similar in many European countries. Agriculture provides fewer and fewer jobs; in-migration increases urban pressure and strengthens the economic dependency of some peripheral rural areas as environmental pressures threaten local resources. In response to these challenges, rural–urban fringes have been exploring different planning strategies to increase their competitiveness and attractiveness.

In France, the reinforcement of inter-municipal cooperation has provided an opportunity to mobilize local actors around common objectives and take a stand on different strategies of adjustment. The processes of inter-municipal cooperation are the result of more than half a century of rural development policy. These processes allow local actors to implement place-based policies, developing contrasting strategies of adjustment and compromise in which culture, identity, environment, and community have come to be seen as new assets that can be developed to maintain place competitiveness. This institutional restructuring has been taking place in the context of a new paradigm of development: territorial development through a place-based approach. Applied to peripheral areas, inter-municipal cooperation favours collective action and can lead to different local strategies aimed at reaching a position of autonomy with respect to the urban core through the development of strategies aimed at differentiation.

In this chapter I present a case study of Volvic Sources et Volcans, a particular rural–urban fringe in the centre of France, which is located near the industrialized city of Clermont-Ferrand. (The case study is based on a survey of 18 elected officials that was carried out in November and December 2007.) The fringe area has been characterized for the last 20 years by its vulnerable agricultural economy and its dependence on Clermont-Ferrand. The reinforcement of inter-municipal cooperation since the 1990s provided the opportunity to devise and implement a development plan to attract activities and investments that would create a new image of environmental quality and a new conception of "rurality."

Institutional Restructuring to Facilitate Territorial Development

Rural areas have long been considered productive spaces, and post-war rural development policies, which promoted agriculture as a strategic sector, reinforced this image. However, since the mid-1970s, as profound social and economic changes have been occurring in French rural areas, new functions have been shaping social representations of the "rural." Residential functions have increased due to demographic growth in most rural areas following periurbanization or counterurbanization processes. Productive functions have shifted from agriculture-based activities to more diversified sources of employment, especially tertiary industry. Above all, open and accessible rural areas now represent a major tourist destination in France (35% to 40% of the market share) and have become more attractive because of the "nature" function they play within contemporary society. These profound changes can be encompassed by the concept of the multi-functionality of spaces (Van der Ploeg and Roep 2003, Aumond *et al.* 2006),[1] which implies a great heterogeneity of rural areas and leads to a wide range of issues that compromise their immediate future, especially in relation to rural–urban fringes.

One of the challenges rural–urban fringes face as a result of this multi-functionality is the negative impact of urban sprawl, particularly its increasing consumption of energy, land and soil. In France since 1994 there has been a 15% increase in urbanized lands, while population growth has been 5% (Institut français de l'environnement, 2005). On the fringes of mid-sized towns, the balance between town growth and the protection of agricultural and natural areas is a major issue. The national sustained-development strategy, for example, encourages better land management (e.g., reduced expansion of agricultural land consumption, land price management, and protection of cultural landscapes) in response to urban growth. Controlling urban sprawl, especially "leapfrog" urbanization, is crucial to the preservation of quality living environments and thus to the overall attractiveness of these rural–urban fringes. However, control and preservation depend on the capacity of local actors to manage these issues and set up adequate governance frameworks, and developing local capacity is the main challenge associated with urban pressures.

In France, the evolution of rural development policies has coincided with ongoing processes of socio-economic change occurring in rural areas. The change in emphasis from a space-based to a place-based approach to development is part of the whole process of rural restructuring. It has been accompanied by an institutional restructuring aimed at better managing the local challenges from a sustainable development perspective and by the emergence of a new paradigm of development: territorial development.[2] As a result, local actors have become more involved in constructing development strategies aimed at maintaining the competitiveness and attractiveness of a place.

Territorial Development: The New Paradigm of a Place-Based Approach to Development

In recent years in France, "territorial development" has become the paradigm shaping conceptions of community development. As explained by B. Jean (2008), the paradigm is based on assumptions that classical functional (and sectoral) approaches are no longer appropriate to drive development that is more socially and spatially harmonious. Instead, to understand how development arises in a specific place, we should consider both tangible (location, access to capital, and availability of resources) and intangible (social capital, capacity building, and the ability of local actors to construct shared local governance structures and processes) factors (Ray, 1999a). Consequently, we can define territorial development as "the enhancement of local actors' capacity to shape their own development dynamics" (Ray, 1999b, p. 259; Lardon *et al.*, 2001, p. 47). This definition implies three important dimensions (Angeon *et al.*, 2007). First, it implies that strong links exist between development dynamics and the local specificities of shared places. Second, it suggests that stakeholders are related and that the nature of their relationships influences decision making. Third, it implies there is a place where local initiatives and public policy can meet, where the actors should coherently construct their "territory." The territorial development paradigm is thus based on the consideration of territory as a specific place with its own features and contextual dynamics (e.g., different assets, resources, and stressors) and as a representation of social construction (B. Jean, 2008).

In turn, territorial development itself is based on social relationships, local partnerships, stakeholder strategies, coordination experiences, and learning processes that deeply influence community development and the nature of the differentiation strategies constructed and pursued at a particular place. In France, with the rise of the regional level of government and the European Union (EU) as major actors in the formation of rural policies, the local level has come to be seen as the efficient point from which to respond to uneven development. New considerations about territorial development and the importance of local participation in new governance structures (Marsden and Murdoch, 1998) go hand in hand with the belief that democracy plays a significant role in achieving development goals.

As did many countries from the mid-1980s onwards (Keating, 1997), France embarked on reforms that moved the country in the direction of decentralization and devolution of economic and social decision making and program management (Balme and Jouve, 1996). French decentralization gave new roles and functions to the "territorial collectivities" (i.e., the *région*, the *département*, and the local municipality or *commune*). *Régions* carry out economic decision making and development planning, while *communes*. with a greater autonomy, manage community matters, and *départements* handle social decision making. The transfer of functions occurred concurrently with fiscal measures that benefited the new levels of regulation, reinforcing local fiscal powers and providing financial compensation for functions transferred from the state level. Above all, the greater degree of autonomy accompanied an emphasis on non-hierarchical relationships between territorial collectivities.

At the same time, and through the second pillar of the EU's Common Agricultural Policy, the EU has promoted integrated operations through programs and broad-based zoning by objectives, all of which have been sustained by structural funds. The LEADER initiative, for example, sustained rural development projects that have—in some cases—played important roles in structuring partnerships between different stakeholders (Buller, 2000; Ray, 2000). As a result, these European initiatives have helped transform public intervention norms in relation to the logical structure of partnership building and development planning.

Institutional restructuring has recognized and accommodated local innovation and the importance of articulating different levels or scales of regulation. The shift in the nature, content, and administration of rural policies is illustrated by the rise of inter-municipal cooperation structures, a new institutional structure that promotes a place-based approach to development.

Inter-Municipal Cooperation as a New Institutional Structure for Territorial Development

Recent rural development policies in France have encouraged and reinforced territorial restructuring and cooperation between actors. The focus on place-based policies has been accompanied by a profound reform of the French institutional context. Decentralization, which was initially meant to shift the duties of the central state to the regional level, has been extended, since the mid-1990s, by the rise and recognition of additional, more efficient administrative frameworks: the inter-municipal cooperation structure. One of the requisites of these new structures is to promote development plans at a coherent territorial level. As a result, a 1999 law marked a new step in the institutional consolidation of *communes* in France by simplifying the complexity of earlier structures that managed sectoral activities. Three new structures were put in place: the *communauté de communes* (CC) for areas that are primarily rural and for *communes* with a total population of fewer than 50,000 inhabitants; *communauté d'agglomération* (CA) for areas with more than 50,000 inhabitants but fewer than 500,000; and *communauté urbaine* (CU) for areas with more than 500,000 inhabitants.

These three structures are differentiated by the functions transferred from the municipal level, the form of their fiscal association, and the population thresholds. The fiscal association inherent in these structures consists of granting taxation powers and then sharing the taxes collected. As Nevers (2002, p. 35) describes it,

> They vote the rate of the "taxe professionnelle" paid by firms, the most significant local tax. They can also vote additional taxes from three other local sources (two land taxes and the housing tax). This measure is intended to reduce the disparities of tax richness, related mainly to the "taxe professionnelle," and to reduce fiscal competition between communes in attracting new businesses.

Inter-municipal cooperation encourages the creation of municipal associations in order to achieve common objectives and come to grips with the significant fragmentation of municipalities (there are more than 36,000 in France). This cooperation enables local actors to coordinate their actions at the municipal level and to make them more consistent with the general plan at the inter-municipal level. Development plans are drawn up at the inter-municipal level to determine the general orientations of the actions to be taken. Moreover, most inter-municipal cooperation structures are integrated into a larger institutional structure, the *pays*, which links rural and urban areas. The *pays* provides a forum where local actors from different inter-municipal co-operation structures can have productive exchanges concerning the construction of development plans at the level of the *pays*, thereby ensuring the overall coherence of the policies developed within and between the inter-municipal cooperation structures.

The effort to create new institutional arrangements at the local level to define policy objectives, priorities, and strategies is related to the emergence of new governance frameworks. Through a procedural policy, the French state has drawn up intervention standards and rules that allow local actors to define their own objectives and means of action. The outcome is determined by a majority agreement of the municipalities involved. These new arrangements represent places of collective action and organization where social links can be strengthened and territorial coherence reinforced. Consequently, the construction of a shared vision of place depends on the abilities of local actors to identify common challenges, assets, and weaknesses. This represents the first informal step toward implementing a place-based policy, as well as the first step toward the social construction of a new territory. Thus, the determination of the geographic limits in which cooperation is managed goes hand in hand with specific local regulation and the definition of strategies of adjustment and differentiation. More than 90% of French municipalities (containing 85% of France's population) are involved in this process of cooperation, so it is considered to be a great success.

However, there remain large differences between the development plans of local actors and the content of the institutional structures. A first point of difference is the pattern of institutional structures in the rural–urban fringes. *Communautés de communes*, which are aimed at rural areas, make up 90% of the institutional cooperation structures. Considered to be the most flexible organizational form, the CC does not depend on a threshold of population (in contrast to the other two forms), and the devolution of new functions is not matched with shared fiscal revenues. In fact, while the *communautés d'agglomération* represent an opportunity to draw the urban core and its rural periphery together into a unique development plan, few rural–urban fringes have chosen this form to implement a development strategy. While 88% of the municipalities located in the rural–urban fringe are associated with similar municipalities through a CC, only 10% are associated through a CA.

A second point of difference concerns the varied strategies used by local actors to define the pattern of cooperation structures. Some French scholars (Y. Jean, 1999; Renard, 2000; Martin, 2001) have pointed out that rural–urban fringes are associated with each other because of a strong opposition to the urban core rather than by a willingness to work together. Fearing urban influence, rural–urban fringes try to preserve their identities and internal social balance and seek to protect their futures and identities by defining their own conditions and strategies for development.

The institutional restructuring resulting from the strategies of local actors in rural–urban fringes is oriented in each case toward a specific space-shared vision. The restructuring reveals the local stance, recognizing and representing local challenges and possible futures. Based on different strategies and actors' rationales, this stance reflects one of three main principles that guide the cooperation process (Loudiyi *et al.*, 2008). First, the process might be sustained by a dominant urban logic, with local actors acknowledging their dependence on the urban centre and profiting from the urban dynamics. Second, the process might follow an intermediate logic, with municipalities in the fringes drawing together around common points of reference related to their sense of similarity, which is in opposition to the urban core. In this case, they might use cooperation processes to preserve their own specificities and identities. Third, the cooperation process might add value to rural areas by helping them sustain their rural activities, reducing potential conflict between landowners and preserving their quality of life. These three principles do not, of course, describe the whole process, which is deeply tied to the social networks situated in the rural–urban fringes. Neither do they deal with the impact of external strategies. Rather, they provide a frame of reference we can use to grasp the way in which rural–urban fringes are restructuring. They also help to clarify different strategies of adjustment and differentiation.

Both the institutional and socio-economic restructuring of fringes involve specific development trajectories. Thus, by analysing each fringe's stance in relation to the urban centre as a sign of the shared representation of a new rurality and the nature of planning actions held in space, we can understand how differentiation processes occur and how they will influence the future of rural–urban fringes.

Volvic Sources et Volcans: From a Position of Autonomy to a Strategy of Differentiation

Volvic Source et Volcans (VSV) provides an example of one of the new institutional structures in practice. Located in the rural–urban fringe of Clermont-Ferrand, VSV has been created in opposition to the main city. This reflects local actors' desire to reduce urban dominance by implementing a rural-based development plan and vision. The restructuring also illustrates the need to develop a differentiation strategy to ensure that the new entity is visible to the urban centre. Hence, a vulnerable agricultural area that was strongly dependent on city employment and was under urban pressure that was transforming it both economically and socially is now emphasizing local assets and resources in order to reinforce its attractiveness and control its own destiny.

Spatial Configuration and Socio-Economic Features of Volvic Sources et Volcans

Volvic Sources et Volcans (Fig. 15.1) is an institutional territory that draws together six municipalities (Volvic, Châtel-Guyon, Sayat, Chanat-la-Mouteyre, Charbonnières-les-Varennes and St-Ours) northwest of Clermont-Ferrand. For many people, Clermont-Ferrand, a city of 150,000 inhabitants located in the centre of France, is well-known because of its strong tradition of industrial activities related to tire manufacturing. The international company Michelin has long dominated the economy of the city and its fringes, providing employment to the local population and a supplementary activity to farmers in the surrounding mountainous agricultural area.

VSV's perimeter overlaps three geographical entities linking plain and mountain. The countryside is recognized as a naturally preserved area because of the chain of volcanoes, water resources (mineral-water sources in Volvic and thermo-mineral sources in Châtel-Guyon), and forests (covering 46% of the total area, or 7005 ha). As Fel and Bouet (1983) point out, one of the most beautiful European volcanic regions is located near Clermont-Ferrand. The nature of the area's soils has long induced substantial water infiltration; it circulates deep underground and reappears at the periphery of lava flows as plentiful, pure, and filtrated water. The lack of surface water has been an obstacle to strong agricultural development. The lands were exploited through weak agro-pastoral activities (e.g., raising sheep, cultivating rye) until the mid-1970s. Then the agricultural system turned to rearing sheep for meat and breeding dairy cows, while forests, in the form of pine woods, hazel, and coniferous trees, gained ground. Nowadays, the territory is considered the recreation area of Clermont-Ferrand as well as the source of drinking water for a part of the city and its suburbs. Since the mid-1960s, the proximity of the city as well as the beauty of the place has attracted tourists and encouraged the construction of second homes that, from the mid-1980s, were increasingly transformed into middle-class residences (Loudiyi, 2003).

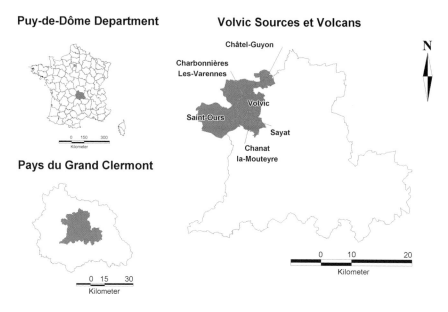

Fig. 15.1 Geographical situation of Volvic Sources et Volcans.

Following the reinforcement of inter-municipal cooperation in the mid-1990s, Volvic Source et Volcans was created at the end of 2002. It is an integral part of the Pays du Grand Clermont and the regional park of Volcans d'Auvergne. At the urban region level, it is one of the more populated territories (with a population of 15,000 and a population density of 98 people/ha) and provides more than 3,500 jobs. Two small towns are located at the east side of VSV: Volvic is known for the branded mineral water that is extracted locally by the Danone Company; Châtel-Guyon is recognized for its previously important thermal-springs activity, which is now in decline.

Through an ongoing process of in-migration since the end of the 1960s, VSV has experienced an urban demand from Clermont-Ferrand that has gradually transformed the whole countryside, both socially and economically. The population has risen by more than 60% since 1962, and some municipalities—those closest to the urban core—have seen their population increase twofold. VSV has turned into a residential countryside, and its economy, formerly based on vulnerable agricultural activity and some mineral-extraction activities, has been transformed. Since 1979 more than 65% of the farms have disappeared while the remaining ones have become concentrated in the more remote areas of the territory. In 2000, for example, 40% of the farms were in St-Ours.

The move away from agriculturally-based activities in VSV has been provoked, as elsewhere, not only by the crisis in agriculture but also by the rise of non-agricultural manufacturing and service industries. More than 560 service and commercial industries are located in the territory, providing opportunities for employment. The most important employers are Danone, which produces Volvic mineral water; Hermès, a well-known French brand that manufactures leather; and Vulcania, the European Park of Volcanism. About 26% of the residents work locally. However, the structural dependence on the urban centre remains, given that more than 73% of the employed residents commute daily to work outside their territory, mostly in Clermont-Ferrand. Consequently, the social structure has profoundly and rapidly changed. Today the importance of middle-class residents (46%) and retirees (20%) is strongly evident, while the traditional rural working class is declining (less than 5% in 1999, compared to 19% in 1975). VSV draws together a set of diversified material realities and can be characterized as a heterogeneous and multi-functional space with varied degrees of urban pressure, diversified agricultural and natural features, and a complex social structure.

Basic Institutional Governance of Volvic Sources et Volcans

The institutional restructuring of VSV was driven by the municipalities' shared sense of common identity as well as their desire to become more autonomous from the core city. The process of local coordination to set up coherent institutional geographic limits upon which to base the development plan took a complex path and depended on several factors related to local challenges and the urban governance structure.

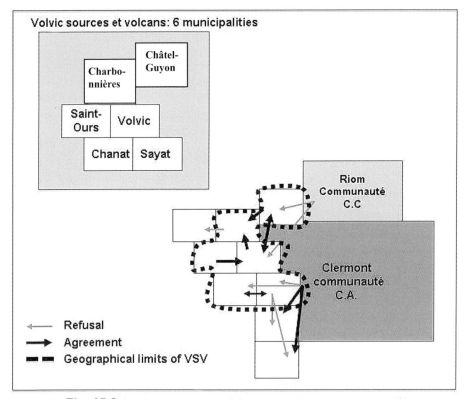

Fig. 15.2 Synthetic overview of the cooperation processes in VSV.

Around the mid-1990s, Riom—a small town north of Clermont-Ferrand—suggested to Volvic and Châtel-Guyon that they join together in an inter-municipal cooperation process, as Clermont-Ferrand had done with Sayat and Chanat-la-Mouteyre. However, the four peripheral municipalities refused to join an urban project. The marjor barrier was Volvic's and Châtel-Guyon's refusal to share tax income stemming from the presence of an international company (Danone at Volvic) and thermal tourist activities (casino at Châtel-Guyon). As the 1999 law reinforcing inter-municipal cooperation established the absolute necessity for spatial continuity, Volvic and Châtel-Guyon invited Charbonnières-les-Varennes to join with them to create an independent institutional structure on the periphery of Clermont-Ferrand. In the meantime, Sayat and Chanat-la-Mouteyre refused to join Clermont-Ferrand because they feared being "overwhelmed by the big city." After negotiations broke down, Sayat and Chanat joined with Volvic, Châtel-Guyon, and Charbonnières-les-Varennes. St-Ours has also chosen to take part in this institutional structure, although it had been engaged with another process for more than ten years, and it refuses to share taxes with lagging rural areas (Fig. 15.2).

Many factors explain the way in which the coordination of local actors has evolved in the region. First, alliances were based on a common refusal to join an urban organizational proposal and thus be part of an urban-centred perimeter. As a result, the strategies of the other peripheral municipalities determined the final geographic limits of VSV. Second, the financial argument has played a substantial role in defining the current result by convincing rich municipalities to work together. The argument for autonomy rests on municipalities' ability to attract and retain financial capital so they can achieve their own vision of the future. Financial taxes could be considered the prime cement of the territory. Third, when justifying their choices, local actors tended to advance their territorial identity (i.e., VSV as the greenbelt of Clermont-Ferrand), with the common ground being the mountains or a shared social space. Besides a deep determination to construct an inter-municipal cooperation organization on a human scale and preserve their natural environment, the municipalities also wished to carry more weight within the urban region (the Pays du Grand Clermont). Therefore, we can say that the final geographic perimeter is based on identified and perceived local challenges, but ever more so on social relationships developed between elected local officials over a long period of time. Such local alliances do not depend on actors sharing the same political party orientation, as is quite common in France, but rather on a strong tradition of working together and sharing similar objectives that became more relevant when placed in the context of institutional restructuring.

Planning Strategies and Differentiation Processes in Volvic Sources et Volcans

After the geographic perimeter has been defined, the functions transferred to the inter-municipal level are economic development and spatial planning and management. Two additional and optional functions may also be transferred: protection of the natural environment and establishment of housing and social environment policies. The functions are defined as broadly as possible to give local actors the opportunity to implement different development strategies in order to reach a position of greater autonomy in relation to the urban centre. Above all, the functions transferred involve local actors constructing or representing the identity of their territory. The development of this identity depends on the convergence of a common recognition of particular inter-municipal interests.

In Volvic Source et Volcans, the overall development plan is focused on economic development and environmental preservation and involves building an identity of a new rurality that is defined by natural resources and quality of life. As mentioned above, local actors consider their territory to be the greenbelt of Clermont-Ferrand. They tried to reconcile the new relationship between development and environment through discourses and actions on "quality of life," setting up planning strategies that would make their place visible and differentiated from the urban centre. They hoped to create a specific identity that would be recognized and appropriated by the local community and the outside world.

Four main planning strategies have been identified in VSV. These strategies, described below, are intended to build a development project directed by a new, modern, image of rurality that will attract additional population, reinforce economic centrality, preserve natural resources and, thus, construct a territorial identity.

Reinforcing Economic Development through "Territorial Resources"

VSV's economic development plan is based on traditional but declining thermal activities and the recent establishment of Vulcania, the European Park of Volcanism. Tourist activities are related to natural resource endowments (water, volcanoes), and local actors have attempted to structure the tourist flows as well as create a branded image of VSV. For example, Clair Matin, a large hotel with the capacity to accommodate more than 100 visitors, is being constructed in St-Ours. According to the mayor, who was interviewed for the 2007 survey, "We turn over a new leaf with Clair Matin. St-Ours was a peasant country. Today it doesn't exist anymore. Tourism has gained the upper hand" (*"C'est une page qui se tourne avec le projet de Clair Matin. Saint Ours était paysan. Maintenant ça n'existe plus, c'est le tourisme qui prend le dessus"*). Most of all, Vulcania is benefiting from promotion in the national media, and this specific infrastructure is making the whole territory more visible. In addition, the location of tourist activities is determined by local regulation, and stakeholders have tried to avoid conflicts between visitors and local users, such as woodsmen or hunters.

VSV is playing the role of a "branded" territory because of the international industries, such as Volvic/Danone and Hermès, located within its borders. These brands are "territorial resources," and local actors have appropriated them to promote the quality of the natural environment and the new idea of rurality, where industries can respect the environment. Following the same strategy, VSV is now investing to create a service pole by providing a health centre for residents as well as a new economic zone devoted to agricultural and tertiary services.

Attracting an Active and Young Population

The will to reinforce economic centrality in VSV converges with the local strategy to attract active and younger residents to keep their space alive with young people and to avoid uniform population aging. The extension of urbanization is a shared objective at the inter-municipal level. According to one of the local mayors, the densification solution is a way "to rationalize infrastructures, display a rural environment living...where people can meet and talk and know each other" (from the survey I conducted in 2007). Densification supports social cohesion as it helps to resolve some of the disorder of urban development.

There are large urban extension projects in VSV, usually involving agricultural lands. As the need for undeveloped land increases in rural–urban fringes, the price of agricultural land increases, and retired farmers often wish to receive the surplus value for their land. Elected officials, who control land administration and regulation, must balance local needs (for example, attracting additional population), agricultural landowners' strategies (selling land or passing it on to younger generations), and land preservation (a concern often defended by dwellers).

Preserving Environment and Landscapes

Promoting quality of life in VSV converges with the profound change occurring in social structure since the mid-1970s. The extension of urbanization is balanced by new demands concerning the living environment and protection of natural heritage. In VSV, environmental preservation goes hand in hand with planning greenbelts that separate the urban centre from the territory, as well as paying attention to landscapes (approaches, green spaces, panoramas). Greenbelts give a new image of rurality that relates more to an idea of preserved nature than to agricultural activities—even if the land use is often agricultural. The new rurality is an ideal of pure and tidy spaces. In the same way, efforts have been made to transform many wastelands into public gardens. Local actors consider landscape "the visiting card of the countryside" because dwellers and visitors "can observe the facial appearance of villages, the architectural value within green and natural surroundings" (Survey 2007). The aim of landscape management, therefore, is to produce a community life ideal that marks a difference from the outside world and supports a symbolic rural function.

As the place economy in VSV is strongly related to natural resources (especially water), local actors and Danone have pooled their efforts to preserve the water-spring area, controlling both urbanization and agricultural activities. This shows how local actors have tried to protect their competitive advantages by supporting tangible assets that enhance the area's attractiveness and symbolic image.

Constructing a Territorial Identity

Identity is often constructed through heritage conservation and/or the transformation and profiling of artifacts, which may be historical elements or local resources. In Volvic Sources et Volcans, the conservation of cultural heritage in the area includes the restoration of vernacular features such as crosses, fountains, troughs, and wash-houses, which remind us of both past agricultural activities (e.g., cattle breeding) and the main local resources (i.e., water and volcanic materials). Local actors often justify such preservation with remarks like "It symbolizes a past, a time that we try to preserve" ("*Ça symbolise une époque, un passé qu'on cherche à conserver*") or "We cannot abandon the fountains because water is life" ("*On n'abandonne pas les fontaines parce que l'eau c'est la vie*").

Some cultural heritage assets have also acquired new functions, as in the case of a water mill at Sayat, dating from the 17th century, which operated until 1950. A local association has managed the restoration, and the inter-municipal structure has helped to transform the water mill into a venue for art exhibitions to help draw the community together around cultural activities.

The most visible shared planning operations involve the display of heritage artifacts that are often located inside villages and on roundabouts. Every municipality has its own artifact "announcing" its local resources. These are symbolized by volcanoes, water mills, and fountains.

The territorial identity of Volvic Source et Volcans is summarized by the name local actors have chosen to describe their shared space. First, "Volvic" refers to the volcanic stones as well as to the mineral-water industries that are well-known overseas. Second, "Sources" reminds us that the territory has plenty of water and thus contains one of the most important elements of life. Third, "Volcans" evokes the natural environment and the unique and beautiful European volcanoes stretching throughout the territory. It is clear that local actors, following a differentiation strategy based on environmental quality, have relied on the national and international visibility of place-based industries to highlight different rediscovered local resources.

Discussion

The positioning of VSV for greater autonomy is based on a sense of shared identity that is totally constructed by local actors. It expresses the co-construction of a shared-space vision and refers to the common challenges facing local actors, who anticipate and create a better future for their community, in the process breaking away from uncontrolled urban dominance.

Actors meeting around a development plan and vision are what make the "territory" take form. Institutional structures define the places where actors may express their own development vision. In the case of France, decentralization processes and a territorial approach to public action (leading to institutional restructuring) have given elected officials the opportunity to set up a new local governance framework, which can be considered the first step for building local capacities. The "territory" is therefore the point where endogenous initiatives and state public action meet.

Some social interactions reinforce collective action as *organized proximity* (Gilly and Torre, 2000), which portrays different social interactions between stakeholders who share values, rules, and ways of thinking and acting. Organized proximity arises when actors belong to the same networks and share a similar space of reference. In the case study presented here, organized proximity allowed local actors to join each other in a development plan. *Social capital*, as a territorial resource, is valuable in developing a more autonomous position for a territory and is based in large part on trust and a long tradition of working together.

The development plan is based on the valuation of local resources and recognition of *place-specific resources*. Local resources represent merely the territory's potential and provide the means to create prosperity. The existence of a resource is then related to its valuation or invention and thus can be considered a territorial innovation. Territorial resources are fully constructed by local actors and become a specific feature of the shared space. Likewise, resource construction processes rest on the dynamic of local actors' cooperating and on their ability to reveal, enable, and qualify the resource. The construction of a territorial identity through local resources aims to fix a symbolic image and to reach an external and internal visibility through differentiation (i.e., to promote the territory as an entity and encourage the local commitment).

As Ray (1999b, p. 259) mentioned, "the aim of a territorial identity construction is to devise and put in place structures that enable the locality to mediate more effectively exogenous forces that, historically and temporaneously, have undermined the socio-economic well-being of locality." The achievement of place-specific resource construction rests on social appropriation by local communities and the establishment of a strategic territorial image.

In the case study presented, a specific range of actors, their interests, and their power relationships defined the governance framework. The institutional perimeter of VSV has been defined by a specific category of actors, elected officials, while the content of the development plan is the result of interaction with economic sectors, state representatives, and those same elected officials. There is no effective participation of other categories of stakeholders, such as residents, farmers, and associations or, more generally, civil society, which might have expressed other issues, stakes, and interests. The future of VSV is thus dependent on a great challenge that goes with the social appropriation of a wider community into the development plan. This social appropriation involves identification, participation, and mediation. It is also related to governance processes within the territory and how it could integrate *in itinere* new actors and new interests (Bryant, 2008) and deal with local conflicts and divergent strategies at the internal level. It assumes the importance of building capacities—not only of elected officials—given that various actors do not often have the same ability to express their interests and issues.

Territorial development as expressed by the case study in this chapter should confront additional challenges facing this territory. Central governments recognize the need for collective action (as a response to uneven development), and institutional restructuring provides the opportunity to gather local actors, improving their capacities to face external strategies and local issues. But, VSV should also confront how to articulate its actions and image with other levels of regulation (e.g., with the urban region). Strategic orientations of the development plan show that VSV is in a competitive position with respect to the main city rather than a cooperative one. This may be one of the most critical challenges to address, given that rural–urban solidarity should be defined according to a sustainable development perspective.

Notes

1. Multi-functionality of rural spaces refers to the ability of rural space to support several functions simultaneously, such as nature conservation, landscape protection, agricultural production, and residential development, among others.
2. The term "territorial development" is used in the French literature, while the English literature often refers to "endogenous development."

References

Angeon, V., Moquay, P., Lardon, S., Loudiyi, S., Pivot, J., and Caron, A. (2007) Le développement territorial: Principes et méthodes. In: Lardon, S., Moquay, P., and Poss, Y. (eds.) *Développement territorial et diagnostic prospectif: Réflexions autour du viaduc de Millau.* Éditions de l'Aube, La Tour d'Aigues, 27–48.

Aumond, A., Barthélemy, D., and Caron, P. (2006) Definitions, references and interpretations of the concept of multi-functionality in France. In: Caron, P., and Le Cotty, T. (eds.) *A Review of the Multi-Functionality and Their Evolution.* European Series on Multifunctionality 10. INRA-CEMAGREF-CIRAD, Paris, 5–39, www.inra.fr/sed/multifonction/cahiersMF.htm (accessed 30 September 2008).

Balme, R., and Jouve, B. (1996) Building the regional state: Europe and territorial organization in France. In: Hooghe, L. (ed.) *Cohesion Policy and European Integration: Building Multi-Level Governance.* Clarendon Press, Oxford, 219–255.

Bryant, C. (2008) Co-constructing rural communities in the 21st century: Challenges for central governments in working effectively with local and regional actors. Paper presented at Space to Place: The Next Rural Economies Workshop, Prince George, BC.

Buller, H. (2000) Re-creating rural territories: LEADER in France. *Sociologia Ruralis* 40(2), 190–199.

Fel, A., and Bouet, G. (1983) Le Massif central. In: *Atlas et géographie de la France moderne.* Flammarion, Paris, 340.

Gilly, J., and Torre, A. (2000) *Dynamiques de proximité*. L'Harmattan, Paris. Institut français de l'environnement. (2005) IFEN, www.ifen.fr (accessed 30 September 2008).

Institut Francais de l'environnement (2005) Les changements d'occupation des sols de 1990 à 2000: plus d'artificiel, moins de prairies et de bocages. *l'IFN*, N° 101, Mars 2005.

Jean, B. (2008) Rural development: The next territorial development paradigm. Paper presented at Space to Place: The Next Rural Economies Workshop, Prince George, BC.

Jean, Y., (1999) Les nouveaux territoires du Poitou-Charentes: Agglomérations, pays, intercommunalités. *Cahiers de l'IAAT* 3, 9–43.

Keating, M. (1997) The invention of regions: Territorial restructuring and political change in western Europe. *Environment and Planning C* 15(4), 383–398.

Lardon, S., Maurel, P., and Piveteau, V. (2001) *Représentations spatiales et développement territorial*. Hermès, Paris.

Loudiyi, S. (2003) Les hébergements touristiques dans les campagnes d'Auvergne: Contribution à l'analyse et à l'étude du tourisme en espace rural. PhD thesis, Université Blaise Pascal, Clermont-Ferrand, France.

Loudiyi, S., Lardon, S., and Lelli, L. (2008) Stratégies d'aménagement et gouvernance territoriale dans les périphéries d'agglomération. In: Loudiyi, S., Bryant, C., and Laurens, L. (eds.) *Territoires périurbains et gouvernance: Perspectives de recherche*. Laboratoire Dynamiques territoriales et développement durable, Université de Montréal, Montréal, 119–128.

Marsden, T., and Murdoch, J. (1998) The shifting nature of rural governance and community participation. *Journal of Rural Studies* 14(1), 1–4.

Martin, S. (2001) Autonomie périurbaine: La ville rejetée et enviée. In: Marcelpoil, E., and Faure, A. (eds.) *Espaces périurbains, environnement et intercommunalité en débats: Journées d'étude sur l'autonomie des territoires périurbains en Rhône-Alpes*. Cahiers de l'OIPRA 2, Grenoble, 17–19.

Nevers, J. (2002) Metropolitan government in Toulouse: From fragmentation to federalism. *GeoJournal* 58, 33–41.

Ray, C. (1999a.) Towards a meta-framework of endogenous development: Repertoires, paths, democracy and rights. *Sociologia Ruralis* 39(4), 521–537.

_____. (1999b.) Endogeneous development in the era of reflexive modernity. *Journal of Rural Studies* 15(3), 257–267.

_____. (2000) The EU Leader programme: Rural development laboratory. *Sociologia Ruralis* 40(2), 163–171.

Renard, J. (2000) Les espaces flous entre agglomérations et pays: L'exemple de la Loire-Atlantique. *Cahiers nantais* 53, 5–14.

Van der Ploeg, J., and Roep, D. (2003) Multi-functionality and rural development: The actual situation in Europe. In: Van Huylenbroeck, G., and Durand, G. (eds.) *Multifunctional Agriculture: A New Paradigm for European and Rural Development*. Ashgate, London, 37–54.

Chapter 16

Rural Development Strategies in Japan

Masatoshi Ouchi

In this chapter I will look back at the experiences of rural economic change in Japan and look forward to the future of Japan's rural economy, using five "izations," which together refer to five types of transformation within the postwar Japanese rural economy. First, I will review the historic development of the rural economy from the postwar period to the present through the stages of "urbanization," "globalization," and "localization." Second, I will explore further the "localization of the rural economy" by describing two subordinate types of localization: "channel-ization" and "place-ization." Finally, I will synthesize the discussion in a set of conclusions.

Conceptual Framework and the Japanese Experience

Urbanization, Globalization, and Localization

In this chapter, the urbanization process is understood to involve rural economies that are increasingly connected to, and bound up with, an urban economy. The strength of the urban economy is such that it can engulf and subsume surrounding rural economies. Once this occurs, there emerges one larger market of commodities, labour, land, housing, and so on. In this larger market, rural–urban relations are organized in a centre–periphery configuration, with the primary flow of benefits (jobs, commodities, etc.) moving from the rural to the urban economy. In this context, urbanization takes on a meaning over and above its more common definition (i.e., "growth of cities" or "expansion of an urban way of life"). That additional meaning emphasizes the market and changing relations within that market.

Globalization is understood in much the same way as urbanization. In the context of this chapter, the rural economy is being drawn into a relationship with the global economy. This provides opportunities for the rural economy by opening access to larger global markets, but it also has negative impacts by exposing the rural economy to low-cost competitors and redirecting benefits to core economies. The net result is that rural economies are pushed to the periphery. Today the Japanese rural economy is involved not only in the urban economy, but also in the global economy.

In contrast to these expanding markets, there has been a growing interest in the localization of the rural economy. In this case, localization is understood as focusing (or even shrinking) the rural economy to a "daily living area" or local market area. The concept stresses the delivery of local commodities to the local market. This sense differs distinctly from the usual definitions, which suggest moving commodities from the global to a local that still constitutes a part of the global marketplace, in which costs and prices are not locally determined.

The process of localization in the Japanese rural economy is complex. I use the terms "channel-ization" and "place-ization" to describe two distinct types of localization. Both terms reflect efforts within the rural economy to gain greater control and ownership of the local market, in spite of the pressures of urbanization and globalization. Localization is not defined here as an effort to make a closed system, such as a self-sufficient rural economy. Rather, it aims to create an open system with "gates." Channel-ization and place-ization differ in the strategies used to localize the rural economy. Channel-ization refers to movements "from the local"; place-ization refers to an increasing focus "to the local."

Japan's Postwar Rural Economy

I will now turn to the Japanese experience of rural economic change after World War II, tracing these changes through the three "izations" of urbanization, globalization, and localization.

The process of land reform between 1947 and 1950 provides the starting point for a discussion of the postwar rural economy in Japan. (For a detailed discussion of Japanese agriculture and rural economy, see Tweeten *et al.*, 1993; Apedaile *et al.*, 2004; and Odagiri and Jean, 2004.) After land reform, owner-farmers managed small holdings that averaged 0.9 ha in size. They worked their farmland with other family members and did not typically hire agricultural labourers. Their economic livelihood was derived almost entirely from full-time farming. Rice was a staple crop. A small village community consisting of 30 to 40 homogeneous farmers was their world.

The first changes were driven by the pressures of urbanization. High economic growth beginning in 1955 pulled rural youth into urban areas. Non-agricultural industries in urban areas needed increasing numbers of labourers and further promoted the urban concentration of people and economic activity. Later, urbanization creating growth in existing urban centres turned into urbanization of the countryside as manufacturing industries invaded rural areas and built factories there that required new, low-wage labour forces. The central and local governments helped industries move from concentrated urban areas into rural areas as part of a strategy to develop rural economies. While jobs were created, the profits from these urban industries in rural places still flowed to urban centres. The rural economy was transformed, developing a dual structure of agriculture and industry.

Urbanization and the dual economic structure divided homogeneous farmers into two types: full-time farmers and part-time farmers. Both types felt the growing influence of urban areas on the rural economy. A large number of part-time farmers emerged, becoming members of the urban-controlled industrial workforce. Those farmers who chose full-time farming felt market pressures to enlarge the scale of their operations and adopt an industrialized approach to production in order to be successful. They introduced new commercial products like fruits, vegetables, and livestock, which were marketed to increasingly affluent urban consumers. Urbanization changed rural areas differently according to their distance from the urban areas. Rural–urban relationships determined the type and strength of impacts on the rural economy.

The second set of changes that worked through the Japanese rural economy are associated with globalization. These changes increased following the Uruguay Round of GATT (General Agreement on Tariffs and Trade) negotiations in 1986 (for a detailed discussion, see Ouchi, 2005). As a result of these and other global economic agreements,

Japanese agricultural policy moved towards the greater liberalization of trade in farm products. The prices of agricultural products, previously protected by tariffs, were now set by the world market—a market that incorporated the Japanese agricultural market within its larger influence. Japanese farmers who produced for urban consumers faced decreasing prices for their agricultural products because lower-cost imports were entering the country. The farmers adapted to the pressures of globalization in two ways. Some continued to increase the size of their farm and the industrial organization of their farming activities. Others turned to the production of high-quality and niche products.

Another impact of globalization was related to wage rates. Some manufacturing industries, which had first come to rural Japan because of the low-wage labour force there, moved their factories to developing countries in search of lower-wage labour. The economic position of rural Japan in the global labour market changed the Japanese rural–urban relationship. Some corporations have maintained factories in rural Japan, but these are mainly for high-quality products.

Globalization affected both the agricultural and industrial elements of the rural economy by lowering prices of agricultural products and lowering wages in manufacturing industries. Both prices and wages are determined in global markets and are not affected by domestic factors.

The third wave of changes stemmed from movements to localize the rural economy, which emerged in the 1990s in response to the detrimental impacts of globalization and urbanization on rural Japan. Localization reorganized the economy with new resources, new forms of human capital, and new channels open to the outside world. This is "the next rural economy," the third stage of the rural economy in Japan. It is a mixture not only of localization but also of urbanization and globalization.

Beginning with its prototype structure immediately after World War II, the rural economy of Japan has passed through three stages of rural economic change: urbanization, globalization, and localization. The important feature is that all three stages continue to influence the rural economy, overlapping and interacting with each other. In other words, the rural economy of a place should be considered as the centre of three concentric circles (beginning with the centre) of local, national, and global influences. These three concentric circles, or markets, make up the rural economy of a place.

New Channels to the Urban Consumers: Channel-ization by the Individual

In this section, I will present two examples of localization in the next rural economy in Japan. The first concerns an example of "channel-ization" from the local; the second an example of "place-ization" to the local. The first is about new entrepreneurs in a mountainous area, Tsunan Town in Niigata Prefecture (Fig. 16.1), who opened new channels to urban consumers, bypassing the established agricultural cooperative (for a detailed description of Tsunan, see Yuda, 2005, 2007).[1] The second concerns a farmers' market at Uchiko Town in Ehime Prefecture.

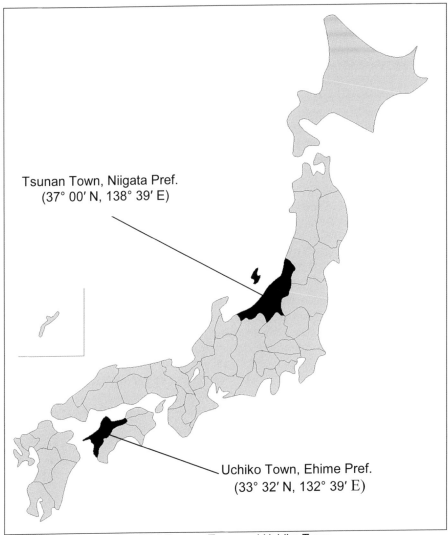

Fig. 16.1 Tsunan Town and Uchiko Town.

Background

Tsunan Town is 180 km north-northwest from Tokyo. As shown in Table 16.1, its population in 2005 numbered 11,719, a huge drop from 21,909 in 1955. But over those five decades, the number of residents who are 65 years old and over has been increasing. The youth have left Tsunan and the remaining population is aging in place.

    With the total population of Tsunan Town decreasing, the number of employed persons also dropped, from 10,882 in 1955 to 6,240 in 2005. Agriculture dominated the rural economy in Tsunan before the period of high economic growth in Japan. During that period, employed persons moved from agriculture into urban-based secondary and tertiary industries. While agriculture is still the main industry in Tsunan, it has declined, and other industries could not keep the excess labour force in the region.

Table 16.1 Population of Tsunan Town.

Year	1955		1980		2005	
	Population	%	Population	%	Population	%
Total population	21,909	100.0	13,841	100.0	11,719	100.0
65 years old and over	1,441	6.6	2,279	16.5	4,125	35.2
Total employed persons	10,882	100.0	8,054	100.0	6,240	100.0
Primary industry	7,877	72.4	3,588	44.5	1,728	27.7
Secondary industry	1,155	10.6	1,850	23.0	1,509	24.2
Tertiary industry	1,850	17.0	2,509	31.2	3,003	48.1

Source: Census of Population, 1955, 1980, 2005.

To counter job losses and out-migration from declining agricultural employment, Tsunan took an active role in attracting economic development. Through the 1960s, the town worked to develop a regional tourism industry by taking advantage of local hot-spring resorts and ski resorts. Tsunan is known for having the heaviest snowfall in Japan. Ski resorts were considered an opportunity to turn the otherwise annoying heavy snows into an economic asset. Two ski resorts remain, but they are not as busy as they once were. Many of the hot-spring resorts are still in business, but they also see fewer customers than they did in the past. When they were established, they brought a fresh sense to the rural scene, but they did not innovate and lost their appeal.

During the 1970s, Tsunan attracted new industries such as apparel and electronics manufacturers. These industries employed primarily rural women and temporarily raised the number of employed persons in the region. Some of these factories still operate; some have closed. The manufacturing and tourist industries have not succeeded in maintaining Tsunan's economy and have not prevented the population from shrinking.

Figure 16.2 and Table 16.2 present data on the present structure of Tsunan Town's population. They highlight three significant points. The first point is that after several attempts at development planning, Tsunan's population is an aged one. In 2005, the oldest cohorts (65 years and over) accounted for 35.2% of the total population. The single biggest five-year cohort was the one aged 75 to 79 years. This cohort has played an important role in Japanese rural society. Its members were born from 1926 to 1930 (before World War II), have been engaged in agriculture since the war, and are now retiring. In 2005, the biggest cohort active in agriculture was aged 70 to 74 years old (born from 1931 to 1934), but in 2000 the largest was the 1926–1930 cohort.

Second, the second largest five-year cohort was the one made up of 50 to 54 year olds born from 1951 to 1955 (after the war). They are the "next generation," mainly the sons and daughters of the 1926–1930 cohort. But they took a different career path from their parents and engaged in the secondary and tertiary industries that Tsunan Town invited from the outside. In this sense, Tsunan's developmental policy was successful in maintaining the population. However, the 1951–1955 cohort has played a similar role in almost all Japanese rural areas, so this is a general phenomenon, not specific to Tsunan or to actions taken there. This cohort was part of the "baby boomer" generation, which was born into the period of high economic growth in Japan. The eldest son would stay on the family farm and live with his parents. The other children pursued non-agricultural employment options in urban areas. The remaining members of the 1951–1955 cohort, obliged to stay with their parents, found jobs in commutable areas.

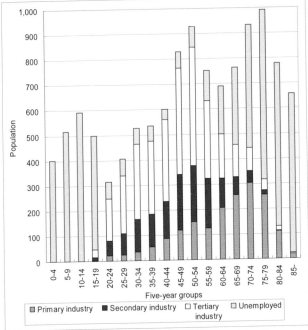

Fig. 16.2 Tsunan Town's population and employment by five-year cohorts (Census of Population, 2005).

Table 16.2 Tsunan Town's population and employment by five-year cohorts.

Five-year groups	Total Population	Employed				Unemployed
		Total	Primary Industry	Secondary Industry	Tertiary Industry	
			Population			
Total	11,719	6,242	1,771	1,466	3,005	5,477
0-4 yrs	402	0	0	0	0	402
5-9	517	0	0	0	0	517
10-14	593	0	0	0	0	593
15-19	500	45	3	13	29	455
20-24	314	248	22	59	167	66
25-29	406	339	24	85	230	67
30-34	528	465	34	131	300	63
35-39	535	474	55	129	290	61
40-44	601	560	86	149	325	41
45-49	828	764	120	220	424	64
50-54	928	846	151	224	471	82
55-59	753	631	126	197	308	122
60-64	689	499	206	117	176	190
65-69	764	456	255	73	128	308
70-74	933	443	304	48	91	490
75-79	992	317	255	18	44	675
80-84	778	131	110	3	18	647
85-	658	24	20	0	4	634

Source: Census of Population, 2005.

The third point is that there was no "next generation" peak after the 1951–1955 cohort. Surely we would expect to find a third peak of 10 to 14 year olds born in 1991 to 1995. But the members of this age group, who are currently students at elementary or junior high schools, will not form a third peak. Many of them are expected to leave Tsunan for higher education opportunities and jobs in metropolitan Japan. The family norm has been weakening, and the rural economy is not strong enough to provide this new generation with full employment. Development policy in Tsunan needs to focus on this next generation and provide it with job opportunities so as to stop youth out-migration and decreasing population.

Given the trends described above, Tsunan is planning to revitalize its rural economy with innovations in agriculture and agri-tourism (though agri-tourism has not yet met with success). The area seems to have abandoned the policy of trying to attract new industries from the urban areas. The fact that there is no longer a surplus pool of relatively cheap labour may have something to do with this change in strategy. The youth have gone and the remaining population is aged.

The main distribution channel for Tsunan agricultural products is JA Tsunan (Japan Agricultural Co-operative Tsunan), a cooperative that collects farmers' products and sends them to the vegetable and fruit markets in the metropolitan areas, where it then sells them to greengrocers. JA Tsunan, which was set up in 1966, is an amalgamation of six agricultural cooperatives from the Tsunan area. This amalgamation reflects the fact that Tsunan Town also started as an amalgamated municipality of six villages in 1955. JA Tsunan is the only general agricultural cooperative in the region. It is engaged in various activities that support local farmers, including marketing farm products, supplying production inputs, extending credit, underwriting mutual insurance, and providing farming guidance.

In 2008, the total number of JA Tsunan members was 3,332, which accounted for 28.4% of the 11,719 residents then living in Tsunan. There were 2,395 regular members and 937 associate members. (Regular members are required to be farmers, while associate members are not.) The number of farm families in Tsunan was 1,840. Thus, JA Tsunan counts all farmers and many ex-farmers as regular members. As a result of this participation, JA Tsunan has enormous influence in Tsunan. The marketing of farm products is a matter of vital importance to farmers and to the rural economy, and JA Tsunan has become a key local institution.

Sales through the agricultural cooperative occur under three rules: unconditional commission sale, joint account, and consignment of all products to the cooperative. These rules make it possible for the cooperative to plan its marketing strategy, collect large volumes of agricultural products, sell them profitably, and balance the members' books based on the use of an average selling price over the sales period. This fits very well into agricultural models of mass production and mass sale. The approach does, however, leave two minority groups dissatisfied. One group consists of very small-scale farmers, who produce little surplus and who may only engage in farming as a secondary economic activity. The other group includes the earnest (and entrepreneurial) farmers who produce excellent products and want to sell them at higher prices on their own. The agricultural cooperative tends to serve the majority of average farmers, but the aging of the farmer population is changing the relationship that has supported the cooperative to this point, as younger farmers begin to seek their own profit.

New Efforts

The next rural economy in Tsunan was started by entrepreneurs who cultivated various markets by themselves. I will describe three types of entrepreneurs. The first are new local traders, who collect and buy farmers' products and sell them directly to consumers, bypassing established markets and the JA Tsunan cooperative. At present, there are two independent traders working in the Tsunan area. One trader collects a wide variety of products in small quantities and sells them directly to supermarkets; the other collects a small variety of products in large quantities and sells them to intermediate wholesalers. The former buys products from small farmers; the latter from large farmers.

Despite these differences, the two traders share some similarities. They both employ a clear strategy to select and focus the producers, the products, and the markets. This is in contrast to the agricultural cooperative, which collects all products from its members and then sends those products to urban markets where there are many sellers and buyers. The two local traders both buy local agricultural products at their own risk, a practice that differs from the cooperative's method of collecting on consignment. The local traders buy products that are of good quality; they package those products and sell them directly to the buyers. Although they bypass the urban produce markets, the prices at which they buy and sell are based on those same markets' prices. As a result, these two local traders act as intermediaries between the farmers in Tsunan and urban consumers. As entrepreneurs, their first task is to market quality products and cultivate clients. Both were born in Tsunan, left there to join distribution businesses in metropolitan areas, returned to their hometown to take jobs, and, after retiring from them, became independent traders. As a result, they know Tsunan, urban consumers, and the best way to connect the two through agricultural product sales.

The second type of entrepreneur has emerged from the farmer population. These entrepreneurs specialize in a specific set of products and have established their own direct-marketing channels. For example, one farmer grows organic rice and vegetables and sells them to consumers directly and to upscale department stores. Another is a floriculturist who specializes in the Casa Blanca lily and delivers to consumers, major department stores, and specific flower markets.

The third type of entrepreneur has also emerged from the farmer population, in this case by shifting their emphasis from growing produce to processing agricultural products. For example, one farmer launched an operation to process tomato juice, while another processes pickled vegetables. The strategies of these farmer-processors are quite different. The former started to produce tomato juice at the request of his customers, who had asked him to wash tomatoes without synthetic detergent. The tomato juice received broad support from consumers and soon made him a full-time processor. Now he provides a very limited clientele with tomato juice, carrot juice, rice cake, rice porridge, jam, etc. He buys raw materials from about 100 farmers inside and outside Tsunan. The latter farmer-processor was supplying urban markets with wild vegetables when he began to process them so as to add value and profit potential to his farm operations. As his business grew, he began to source less-expensive raw produce from China. Today he uses different materials for different channels; the produce from China is used for ordinary souvenir stores outside the town, while domestic produce is used for local shops and mail-order sales.

Implications

These three types of entrepreneurs opened new doors to consumers. They did so in three unique ways: by being a local trader, by becoming a farmer-broker for specialized agricultural products, and by becoming an agricultural food processor. They have a relatively narrow access to the marketplace, and they focus on a limited set of clients, but their approach is markedly different from that of the agricultural cooperative, which makes volume sales into general produce markets. While these new entrepreneurs bypass the JA Tsunan cooperative, they are too small to replace it.

There are several reasons for the success to date of these new entrepreneurs. First, general nationwide improvements in transportation and communication systems allow the entrepreneurs to send their small volumes of goods to designated places in a cost-efficient, timely, and dependable manner. Telephones, faxes, and personal computers are indispensable business tools and are even more critical in rural areas where producers, entrepreneurs, and purchasers are separated by great distances and unable to meet regularly. Some entrepreneurs have their own website, where they advertise products and receive orders. There are minimal restrictions on the smooth and convenient flow of goods, money, and information as the national business and communications infrastructure eases the circulation of information and goods between the metropolitan regions and rural areas.

A second reason for the success of these new entrepreneurs involves their social ability to build good rural–urban relationships. The local traders' experiences working for various distributors, and living and working in metropolitan regions, have helped them as they set up their own businesses. The rice farmer and the juice processor, for example, expanded their sales by growing consumer support. They did so by increasing direct-to-consumer selling using the infrastructures noted above and their understanding of urban consumer demands.

Third, the entrepreneurs have worked out a new business model. They have "rebundled" rural agricultural products to go after niche markets, and they have reorganized farmers' networks in rural areas to collect agricultural products. They work closely with local farmers, encouraging them to improve quality and product focus, and sometimes even guiding the farmers in developing products. In addition, they have opened new channels of communication and shipping to the urban areas. Different channels, which transport a variety of different goods, diversify the range of agricultural products that can be economically grown in the region. Success has meant that "broader" channels now demand more products, which the entrepreneurs sometimes have to buy from farmers beyond the Tsunan region. These entrepreneurs are very much reorganizers of the rural economy.

Finally, we must situate our understanding of these new entrepreneurs in the fact that their businesses sprouted in the age of urbanization, globalization, and localization. Their actions reflect and reinforce each of these interdependent trends. They added new channels beside the established JA Tsunan agricultural cooperative, not replacing it. They buy raw materials mainly from local farmers but also from wider areas, even from China, as demands grow and change. They advertise their products as fresh and safe to the urban consumers—using place-name marketing to correspond to urban customers' mental images of a clean and natural rural Tsunan.

New Regional Market: Place-ization by the Collective

The second example of localization in Japan's next rural economy concerns a farmers' market at Uchiko Town in Ehime Prefecture, which is located in a mountainous area on Shikoku Island (see Fig. 16.1). The current municipality of Uchiko Town was established in 2005 when three towns—Uchiko, Oda, and Ikazaki—amalgamated. In this chapter, however, I will be referring to the Uchiko Town that existed before the amalgamation. (For a detailed description of Uchiko, see Uchiko tyosi hensan kai, 1995; Suzuki, 2000, 2006; Hujime, 2004, 2006; Noda, 2004; Shinohara, 2005; Shiraishi and Razaq, 2005a, 2005b; Uchiko Town, 2005.)

Background

Table 16.3 shows that Uchiko has a population structure similar to that of Tsunan Town. It had a population of 20,764 in 1955, decreasing to 10,559 in 2005 (Tsunan's population declined to 11,719 in 2005 from 21,909 in 1955). In both towns, the population declines were the result of young people leaving the area. The consequence is that both towns have a population that is aging in place. Elderly people (at least 65 years old) made up 31.4% of the local population of Uchiko in 2005, compared to 35.2% in Tsunan.

The number and distribution of employed people also shows a similar pattern of economic change. In 1955, the workforce in primary industry (mostly agriculture) in Uchiko was 6,546 people. This accounted for 66.0% of all employed persons. The number dropped dramatically to 1,415 (26.3%) in 2005. Tsunan also experienced a sharp reduction in the primary industry workforce, from 7,877 in 1955 to 1,728 in 2005 (decreasing from 72.4% to 27.7% of all employed persons). While agriculture in these two towns no longer holds the leading position in the regional economy that it once did, it remains an important contributor because there has been little diversification into new key industries.

Table 16.3 Population of old Uchiko Town.

Year	1955		1980		2005	
	Population	%	Population	%	Population	%
Total population	20,764	100.0	13,415	100.0	10,559	100.0
65 years old and over	1,442	6.9	1,968	14.7	3,311	31.4
Total employed persons	9,917	100.0	7,299	100.0	5,373	100.0
Primary industry	6,546	66.0	2,987	40.9	1,415	26.3
Secondary industry	1,268	12.8	1,871	25.6	1,390	25.9
Tertiary industry	2,103	21.2	2,441	33.4	2,562	47.7

Source: Census of Population, 1955, 1980, 2005.

The present population structure of Uchiko is also similar to that of Tsunan. Figure 16.3 closely resembles Fig. 16.2, and we can point out two peaks in total population: the 1926–1930 cohort of births and the 1951–1955 cohort. The former have been engaged mainly in agriculture and are retiring. The latter, children of the former cohort, now have jobs in secondary and tertiary industries. While the loss of an agricultural workforce is troubling, even more so is the fact that, with current patterns of youth out-migration, there is no "next" generation in the community to follow these two aging cohorts.

There is also a minor difference between the two towns. Although both of the towns have rapidly aging societies, Uchiko's population is younger than Tsunan's. In 2005, the percentage of children aged 14 and under was 15.1% in Uchiko, while in Tsunan it was 12.9%. Aside from this minor difference, they face similar demographic issues rooted in common regional economic problems.

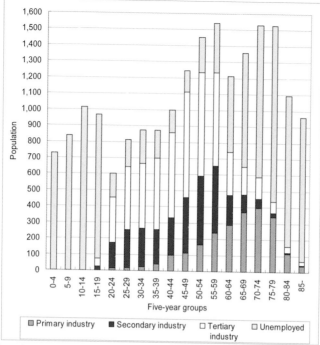

Fig. 16.3 Population and employment by five-year cohorts in new Uchiko Town, the amalgamation of old Uchiko, Oda, and Ikazaki (Census of Population, 2005).

Table 16.4 Population and employed persons by five-year cohorts in new Uchiko Town, the amalgamation of old Uchiko, Oda, and Ikazaki.

Five-year groups	Total Population	Employed				Unemployed
		Total	Primay Industry	Secondary Industry	Tertiary Industry	
		Population				
Total	17,042	9,625	2,259	2,677	4,689	7,417
0-4	727	0	0	0	0	727
5-9	837	0	0	0	0	837
10-14	1,012	0	0	0	0	1,012
15-19	967	75	0	26	49	892
20-24	602	455	13	161	281	147
25-29	812	645	19	233	393	167
30-34	873	665	26	239	400	208
35-39	872	701	42	214	445	171
40-44	997	858	97	235	526	139
45-49	1,246	1,112	112	345	655	134
50-54	1,454	1,234	164	426	644	220
55-59	1,540	1,234	238	416	580	306
60-64	1,212	742	290	186	266	470
65-69	1,359	652	369	108	175	707
70-74	1,528	589	397	56	136	939
75-79	1,527	437	340	25	72	1,090
80-84	1,093	160	112	6	42	933
85-	960	66	40	1	25	894

Source: Census of Population, 2005.

One of the strategies both towns used to revitalize the rural economy was tourism, but they each chose different ways to promote this industry. Tsunan exploited its natural resources/amenities and worked to develop and promote ski resorts. Uchiko paid more attention to local cultural resources and began a program to preserve historic buildings and streets. The town of Uchiko flourished from the 18th century to the early 20th century as a centre of Japanese vegetable-wax production (vegetable wax is rendered from a kind of sumac berry). The wealth of the manufacturers and merchants left a legacy of beautiful white-walled buildings. The town's historic preservation program started in the 1970s. Its success soon stimulated a parallel program in surrounding rural areas, where the aim was to preserve and restore rural landscape features such as water mills and old farmhouses. Through these efforts, Uchiko began attracting more and more tourists. Estimates suggest that as many as half a million tourists visit the town every year. Despite this growth, the tourism industry did not provide enough economic activity and opportunity to replace that which was lost in the declining agricultural sector.

New Efforts

Uchiko's farmers' market is called "Karari." The name was coined in an effort to encourage the image of a village where people enjoy fruits, flowers, herbs, and healthy processed agricultural products. ("Karari" is composed of three words—ka, which means "fruits, flowers, herbs, and processing"; ra, which means "enjoy"; and ri, "village.") This place-branding effort culminated in the start-up of a farmers' market, opening in 1997. The creation of the market, and the place-brand it embodies, happened only after deliberate and thoughtful preparation.

The planning and preparation process also served as a learning process for the community. Three parts of this learning process can be identified. First, in 1986 the community opened the Intellectual Rural School as a forum in which to consider the options for revitalizing agriculture in Uchiko. The school head was the mayor, students were citizens, and speakers were invited from outside the town to discuss issues like the branding of agricultural products, regional circulation of products, economic opportunities for rural women, and so on. This action brought new ideas to the community and stirred the "fixed thinking" of the citizens. The school is still open, which clearly shows the value of this exercise.

Second, in 1992 the local government developed a basic plan for agricultural renewal in Uchiko. The plan was centred on the concept of a "Fruit Park" and contained three goals: (1) to combine agriculture with the service industry, (2) to promote various forms of exchange between Uchiko and urban areas through such activities as agri-tourism, and (3) to develop a local agricultural information network. There were a couple of successful pioneers of the tourist farms/agri-tourism idea, and it was their success that gave the plan a more realistic base.

Third, in 1994 the town built an experimental shop and began preliminary exercises with a local farmers' market so as to learn how to sell agricultural products and manage the market. More than 70 local farmers participated, half of them women. This experimental shop was truly a learning exercise for all concerned. At first the farmers did not know how to line up or display products, how to mark prices, how to talk with customers, how to settle accounts, etc. They faced many challenges and worked to resolve each of them step by step.

In 1996 the town finally launched Uchiko's Karari farmers' market. It is managed by Uchiko Fresh Park Karari Inc., whose stock was owned initially by Uchiko Town, the

Uchiko Agricultural Cooperative, the Uchiko Forestry Association, the Uchiko Commerce and Industry Association, and the citizens of Uchiko. After 10 years of successful growth, Karari is considered one of the best models of a farmers' market in Japan.

Karari is not just a farmers' market but a complex of three parts; the market, processing facilities, and restaurants. In 2006 it was open every day, serving about 600,000 customers in a year. Annual sales of produce and products are now worth more than 670 million Yen. The farmers' market sells produce that is supplied by 430 local area farmers. The market accounts for about 70% of all Karari sales. While it is clearly Karari's main activity, the complex would not be successful without the two other activities.

There are three processing facilities in Karari. One is for making sherbet, another is for baking breads, and the third is for ham and sausage production. In 2006 they sold more than 100 million Yen worth of products. Key to the sales success is the place-marketing of these products as "grown in Uchiko."

Two restaurants at Karari also attract guests. In 2006 they sold more than 76 million Yen worth of meals.

As well as being able to buy agricultural products, local processed foods, and meals, guests also have the chance to participate in rural experiences, events, and festivals arranged by members of Karari. These special events add to the ongoing opportunity to meet and mingle with the area's farmers. For Karari members, this interaction gives them a chance to see themselves from the point of view of those outside the rural town. Thus, Karari is a place for farmers and consumers to meet one another.

Farmers are involved in Karari as stockholders, members of committees, employees, and suppliers of agricultural products. It is important to point out the vital roles played by rural women and the elderly. These two groups are the main providers of agricultural products to the market. They typically grow a wide variety of agricultural products but do so in small quantities. This small-scale production matched the small scale of the farmers' market through its early years. Originally, many of these market suppliers grew for family consumption only. Once the market was in place, they were able to expand their family-focused production and bring that additional production to the market. As a result, they welcomed the market because now they had the chance to earn some additional money for the household. The additional money helped improve their social status, as women and elderly farmers often did not have enough money to spend freely.

In contrast to women and elderly farmers, those active in large-scale farming, as well as many young farmers, were hesitant to participate in the farmers' market in the early years. Instead, they preferred to stay with established patterns of trading into big markets in the metropolitan areas. The growing number of customers coming to Karari has since attracted some of these other farmers to participate as well.

Agricultural suppliers are connected to the farmers' market by an information network called Karari-Net. Every morning, farmers bring in products, each with a bar-code seal attached. The bar code links to electronic data that show the product's name and price, the producer's name, and his or her phone number. The bar code is processed by a point-of-sale system, which tells farmers how many of their products have been sold each hour while the market is open. In this way, farmers are able to manage their inventories and stock in real time, and if some of their products sell out, they can bring in more to meet customer demand. The producer's name and phone number on the bar-code seal also confirm the farmer's link to, and responsibility for, the product. Some customers, recognizing the producer's name, will buy their products specifically. In 2005, the farmers' market added a fifth information element, traceability of pesticides and fertilizers, on each bar-code seal as it continues to enhance the quality of the agricultural products and the Karari place-brand.

The number of customers to Karari has been growing each year. There are now more than 800,000 visitors to Uchiko annually, including 600,000 customers at Karari. They come mainly from the urban areas of Matsuyama City, the capital of Ehime Prefecture, which is located just 40 km northeast of Uchiko. The Matsuyama City urban area has a population of 500,000 people. Some of the customers are from other small cities around Uchiko. But many visitors to Karari do not come only to buy agricultural products. Karari is a part of their tour, which may include the preserved historic buildings and streets, tourist farms, and farmer's inns that were developed as part of the earlier tourism strategy. In Uchiko, it is the combination of tourism development and support work, as well as the innovation of the Karari market, that has generated successful rural development.

Implications

We can draw some lessons from the Uchiko example, such as the importance of deliberate preparation, attention to opportunities/roles for women and the elderly, information technology, and local social capital. But in this section I would like to discuss how this case illustrates the process of moving from a space-based to a place-based approach to rural development. The keyword is "place-ization,"[2] which I coined to mean "to make 'a place in a space' 'the place in the space.'"

Uchiko has been made a marginalized place in Japan by the processes of urbanization and globalization. It is only one of many rural areas suffering under the effects of urbanization and globalization. But the place "Uchiko" has been reconstructed by citizens, who combined several forms of activities into a total place-branded image of Uchiko. Karari is not only a farmers' market; it also has processing facilities and restaurants. Furthermore, Karari is set within a specific surrounding landscape where heritage preservation both protects and codifies the rural imagination for urban visitors. It is thus a constructed image of the place that invites visitors, who are actually living in the space around Uchiko. The place-based approach refers to "the place in the space" as a whole. And the development of Uchiko deserves to be remembered as the process of moving Uchiko from being "a place in a space" to being "the place in the space."

Conclusions

Since the end of World War II, the Japanese rural economy has experienced three "stages" of urbanization, globalization, and localization. As a result of urbanization, the youth in rural areas flowed to urban areas seeking high wages and a different kind of lifestyle. Globalization brought impacts such as lower prices for agricultural products and lower wages for manufacturing industries. Urbanization and globalization forced Japanese rural areas, especially mountainous ones, to the social and economic periphery of Japan. These two external pressures marginalized rural and mountainous regions, and changed the rural–urban spatial configuration. Rural regions faced increased competition from Japanese urban areas and from foreign countries. Farmers expanded to a mass-production model in order to achieve efficiency.

But marginalization was not the end. Localization is an effort to revitalize rural economies in spite of the processes of urbanization and globalization. Thus, the next rural economy in Japan is set within a complex of urbanization, globalization, and localization. Localization was initiated by marginalized people in marginalized areas. Mass production was maintained by large farms, whose managers were male. They marketed a limited range of agricultural products in large quantities for metropolitan consumers through a long-established agent, the agricultural cooperative. In contrast, localization started with three types of marginalized people: entrepreneurs, rural women, and the elderly. The last two groups enhanced their family-scale agricultural production and grew a wider range of products in smaller volumes than did the large farms. The challenge was to organize and connect these groups with new consumers, which was resolved by the entrepreneurs.

As the process of localization developed, there were two types of beneficial devices: new channels to urban consumers (what I call "channel-ization from the local") and a new regional market ("place-ization to the local"). Channel-ization was advanced mainly by the individual entrepreneurs, place-ization by collective efforts. Channel-ization is a new way to connect to urban markets, and place-ization is a new opportunity for urban spending to come to the rural area. It is important to point out that both of them depend on highly advanced transportation and communication systems. Such mechanisms and infrastructure were critical for connecting not only the rural and the urban, but also the farmers' market and the farmers. Technology also played a major role in supporting the place-marketing of rural areas by confirming the responsibility of farmers for their products. Transportation and communication deliver not only products and information, but also trust and safety.

If marginalized people are to design new devices and use highly advanced systems, they need knowledge and learning.[3] The entrepreneurs in Tsunan drew upon their practical experiences in the distribution industry and their knowledge of how to connect rural producers and urban consumers. In Uchiko, the Intellectual Rural School taught women and the elderly how to sell products and participate in planning the agriculture of the town and the farmers' market. Uchiko is a learning community in a knowledge economy.

Finally, localization develops within processes of urbanization and globalization. Localization of the rural economy does not support the whole rural economy in the region, because the local market is limited. It is obvious that the volume of sales by channel-ization and place-ization is limited. The rural economy needs to be supported by urbanization and globalization. But localization has a distinctive feature, different from urbanization and globalization. It can involve a variety of people, from entrepreneurs to women and the elderly, and inspire a sense of "the place" in people. It is an indispensable core of the next rural economy in an age of urbanization and globalization.

Notes

1. The idea of "bypassing the establishment" came from Furuseth (2008). He indicated that "Separate from Chamber of Commerce establishment" was one of the "Functional Elements of Entrepreneurial and Business Development" in place-making.
2. Place-ization overlaps place-making (Furuseth 2008), but it stresses an effort to make "a place in a space" "the place in the space." It is a way of remaking a place up to the place.
3. The recognition of the importance of learning in localization came from comments by Bill Reimer and Greg Halseth.

References

Apedaile, L., Nakagawa, M., and Bollman, R. (2004) Sensitivity of rural enterprises to globalization and trade liberalization: A Japan/Canada comparison. In: Halseth, G., and Halseth, R. (eds.) *Building for Success: Exploration of Rural Community and Rural Development.* Rural Development Institute, Brandon University, Brandon, MB, 137–170.

Furuseth, O. (2008) A new rural North Carolina: Latino place-making and community engagement. Paper presented at Space to Place: The Next Rural Economies Workshop, Prince George, BC.

Halseth, G., and Halseth, R., eds. (2004) *Building for Success: Exploration of Rural Community and Rural Development*. Rural Development Institute, Brandon University, Brandon, MB.

Hujime, S. (2004) Regional revitalization and direct marketing of farm products in Uchiko Town. *Ehime University Bulletin of the Faculty of Law and Letters, Humanities* 17, 1–39.

_____. (2006) Comparative analysis of farmers markets in terms of community revitalization. *Ehime University Journal of the Society of Letters and Human Science* 8, 31–50.

Noda, H. (2004) *"Karari" Realized Women's Dream*. Venet, Tokyo.

Odagiri, T., and Jean, B. (2004) The roles of local governments for revitalization of rural areas in Japan and Canada. In: Halseth, G., and Halseth, R. (eds.) *Building for Success: Exploration of Rural Community and Rural Development*. Rural Development Institute, Brandon University, Brandon, MB, 363–392.

Ouchi, M. (2005) *Social Change in Post-war Rural Japan*. Norin Toukei Kyokai, Tokyo.

Shinohara, S. (2005) Revitalization of a mountain village by practical use of local resources and direct sales of agricultural products: A case study of Uchiko-cho in Ehime Prefecture. *Matsuyama University Review* 17(5), 147–179.

Shiraishi, M., and Razaq, A. (2005a) The role of farmers markets and discussion groups in developing agricultural marketing system in Uchiko Town of Ehime Prefecture, Japan. *Journal of Applied Sciences* 5(4), 753–760.

_____. (2005b) The role of information technology in the management of Karari farmers market at Ehime Prefecture, Japan. *Journal of Applied Sciences* 5(4), 787–793.

Suzuki, S. (2000) Community development in Ehime. *Matsuyama University Review* 12(5), 97–119.

_____. (2006) Regional development and tourism policy in Uchiko Town. *Matsuyama University Review* 18(1), 41–65.

Tweeten, L., Dishon, C., Chern, W., Imamura, N., and Morishima, M. (1993) *Japanese and American Agriculture Tradition and Progress in Conflict*. Westview Press, Boulder, CO.

Uchiko Town. (2005) Uchiko Fresh Park Karari, www.town.uchiko.ehime.jp/sightseeing/kankou_kar ari.php (accessed 13 June 2008).

Uchiko tyosi hensan kai. (1995) *A History of Uchiko Town*. Uchiko-tyo, Uchiko.

Yuda, K. (2005) Reorganization of rural economy in mountainous regions: A case study of important roles of entrepreneurs. *Journal of Rural Economics* 2005(special), 46–53.

_____. (2007) Types of privatization of public tourist facilities in mountainous areas: A study on Niigata in Tunan Town. *Journal of Rural Economics* 2007(special), 196–203.

Chapter 17

Heroes, Hope, and Resource Development in Canada's Periphery: Lessons from Newfoundland and Labrador

Kelly Vodden

> There is still reason for hope in Newfoundland and Labrador. You can take that hope to the bank.
>
> —Premier Danny Williams (CBC News, 17 October 2006)

Whether defined by economic, socio-political, or locational criteria, the province of Newfoundland and Labrador is a periphery within Canada and the world. It lies on North America's eastern-most edge, a land of rock, bog, and spruce, lakes, rivers, and the rugged shores of the Atlantic Ocean, where pack ice and icebergs bring late springs and short growing seasons. Newfoundlanders and Labradorians are known to say they have salt water in their blood. Their lifestyles, past and present, are tied to the ocean and captured in countless stories, songs, and traditions.

Economically, Newfoundland and Labrador has consistently been an underprivileged province within the Canadian federation: incidence of low income, unemployment, and reliance on social transfers are the highest among all Canadian provinces (Sorensen *et al.*, 2005). Accounting for over 8% of employment, dependency on primary sectors is conservatively twice the Canadian average (Statistics Canada, 2008). Despite a 1992 northern cod fishery moratorium, referred to as "the largest single layoff in Canadian history" (Dunne, 2003, p. 20), primary industry employment remains largely rural and fisheries based. Health, education, social assistance, and public administration sectors provide an additional 30% of all jobs, supported by government transfers and increasingly natural resource revenues (Government of Newfoundland and Labrador, 2008a, 2008b). Despite growing fiscal dependence on mining, oil, and gas, the sector constitutes just 2% of employment, and oil development benefits are concentrated in the capital region (House, 2006).

From a political economy perspective, the notion of a periphery implies uneven power relations between core and outlying region(s). These relationships are aptly illustrated by the nested peripheries of Newfoundland and Labrador. The prolific waters of Newfoundland and Labrador's continental shelf are home to the once-abundant northern cod and 22 whale species, both of which drew European colonial and economic powers to her shores beginning in the second millennium (Environment Canada, n.d.). The province was the last to be brought, reluctantly, into the Canadian Confederation in 1949, despite

223

endemic poverty and the promise of a social "safety net." After a vigorous campaign by first premier Joseph "Joey" Smallwood, the decision to join Canada came through a narrow majority (Francis *et al.*, 1996). Federal–provincial tensions have persisted, fuelled by geographic isolation, nationalist sentiments, and a perception of the province as the "poor cousin" within the federation (Marshall, 2008).

While signs of decline had long been reported, and many inshore fish harvesters and scientists anticipated the cod collapse, the 1992 announcement of the northern cod moratorium represented a significant blow to the psyche and the social, cultural, and economic well-being of the province and its rural residents (Ommer, 2007). Change has been a constant in the lives of Newfoundlanders and Labradorians, but the social-ecological transition of the past two decades is arguably unprecedented. In the midst of a recent period of economic growth, circumstances look much different today than in the 1990s or pre-moratorium eras. Drawing from a series of research projects, including the major collaborative research initiative Coasts Under Stress and an ongoing three-year project called Rural–Urban Interactions in Newfoundland and Labrador: Understanding and Managing Functional Regions, this chapter explores current population, economic, and policy trajectories and how they vary at local, regional, and provincial scales. Development approaches capable of sustaining rural Newfoundland and Labrador into the future are also considered, including examples of provincial policies and the local efforts of four island communities. The critical role of attitudes, particularly optimism and hope, and key actors at multiple levels are highlighted, along with positive and negative implications of dependency on both natural resources and popular charismatic leaders or "heroes."

Population Change

With a land mass of 405,720 km^2 and a population just over 500,000, Newfoundland and Labrador has the lowest population density among Canada's provinces. Trends such as population aging, natural population decline, and out-migration as residents leave in search of employment, especially high-paying jobs in the provinces of Ontario and Alberta, are particularly dominant in small communities of less than 1,000 residents. Reversing a 16-year trend, in-migration exceeded out-migration, and population increased during the last two quarters of 2007 (Government of Newfoundland and Labrador, 2008a). Growth is concentrated in the capital region and along the Trans-Canada Highway. Completed in 1965, the highway across the island resulted in a shift from water- to land-based transportation. Corresponding shifts in demographics, social and economic activity are still playing themselves out, leaving coastal outports struggling to cope with the cumulative impacts of these and many other changes.

Table 17.1 uses the Statistics Canada categories Census Metropolitan Areas (CMA) and Census Agglomerations (CA) to define "urban" areas and shows that the majority of Newfoundland Labrador's population still resides in rural and small-town regions. However, the province's highly traditional rural economy and culture is "rapidly urbanizing and interacting with mainstream norms" (Childs *et al.*, 2007, p. 1). In 2001, for the first time, most residents lived in a community of 5,000 or more, a category that includes only 16 of the province's 282 municipalities (Dunn, 2003; Municipalities Newfoundland and Labrador, 2005).

Table 17.1 Settlement and population change.

	2006 Pop.	Pop. Density (per km^2)	2001–2006 (% change)	% of pop. in a CMA or CA (2006)
Canada	31,612,897	3.5	5.4	81.1
NL	505,469	1.4	−1.5	45.9

Source: Statistics Canada, 2007a.

The Economy after Confederation: Fisheries, Megaprojects, and Resource Development

Former premier Joey Smallwood was an instrumental figure in the province's post-Confederation development. His regime encouraged industrial development, foreign-owned and export-oriented forestry and mining, and fisheries modernization through frozen-fish processing and loans and subsidies for larger vessels. Coupled with a growing fleet of international factory-freezer trawlers offshore, these policies contributed to the near exhaustion of groundfish species and the small-scale fishery that had been the foundation of the provincial economy (Wright, 2001). As the fishery faltered and Smallwood's modernization agenda was implemented, efforts were made to relocate outport residents to growth centres. Although relocation was already underway in many communities, the program was divisive in others because it forced residents to make a decision that was shaped by financial incentives and, in cases where a united community decision was required by government, by peer pressure from friends and neighbours. This experience left an enduring impression in the province's collective memory (Woodrow, 1996). Approximately 50% of an estimated 1,300 pre-resettlement communities remain. With the introduction of the 200-mile Exclusive Economic Zone and a brief period of optimism, fisheries employment more than doubled from 1975 to 1980, but after centuries of exploitation, the northern cod faced ecological collapse (Hamilton and Butler, 2001). Today, high-value shellfish have become the mainstay of a fishery that now exceeds $1 billion in annual seafood production value (Government of Newfoundland and Labrador, 2008a). While seafood-processing employment has fallen by more than 50% since 1990, many rural areas of the province continue to be fishery dependent. For many, seasonal employment (and unemployment) has become a way of life. Cutbacks in both the federal Employment Insurance program and government services have been "a double hit to the rural economy" (House, 2006), which is supplemented by relatively strong voluntary and informal sectors. Although threatened, studies suggest that self-provision activities (such as hunting, fishing, and wood cutting), barter, and unrecorded cash exchanges comprise as much as 42% of part-time fish harvester incomes (Hamilton and Butler, 2001).

The 1979 discovery of a vast offshore oil and natural gas field alongside the important Grand Banks fishery launched provincial and federal negotiations over the development of this valuable resource. The 1985 Atlantic Accord ensured employment and spinoff benefits (House, 1985). In 2007, after ten years of operation, oil production valued at $10.3 billion represented 35% of provincial gross domestic product (GDP). Bolstered by strong world commodity prices, petroleum refining and mineral shipments generated an additional $6.9 billion and the province led national real GDP growth. Continued natural resource-based growth in oil, minerals, and hydroelectric industries is expected (Government of Newfoundland and Labrador, 2008a). Other key sectors include manufacturing, construction, tourism, and ocean technology. Self-employment is most prevalent in rural and small-town communities (Sorensen *et al.*, 2005), where small manufacturing firms and a largely rural non-profit sector are important contributors (Stirling, 2007; Community Services Council of Newfoundland and Labrador, 2004).

Improved economic indicators have translated into a sense of optimism not experienced since the late 1970s and perhaps in the province's history (Table 17.2). Yet this newfound prosperity masks underlying issues such as resource depletion, continued staples dependence, inequitable wealth distribution, and labour shortages in the midst of high unemployment. Residents of rural and small-town Newfoundland and Labrador fall behind their urban counterparts in economic well-being, educational attainment, access to health care, and housing. Significant and growing inequalities also exist within rural and small towns, often exacerbated by fisheries and transition policies. Increasingly, labour shortages linked to low wages, inability to compete in national labour markets and lack of remaining workers with appropriate skills are reported (Morrissey, 2007). Inequities and demographic and labour-force changes represent significant challenges for current and future leaders.

Table 17.2 Economic change in Newfoundland and Labrador.

Late 1990s/early 2000s	2007/2008
16.7% unemployment (2000)	13.6% unemployment (2007)
GDP 14.1 billion (2000)	27 billion GDP (2007, unadjusted)
$913 million deficit (2004)	$1.4 billion surplus (2007–2008)
$11.9 billion debt (2005)	$10.3 billion debt (2007)
$1,040 million in equalization payments (1998-99)	$16–18 million in equalization entitlements projected (2008–2009)
Sense of loss and uncertainty	Sense of optimism and hope

Sources: Janigan, 1998; Statistics Canada, 2004; Government of Newfoundland and Labrador 2002, 2004, 2005, 2008a, 2008b.

Politics of the Periphery and Policy from Above

Merchants, clergy members, teachers, and union representatives dominated early politics in rural Newfoundland and Labrador. Limited by time, money, influence, and literacy, others played little role and local institutions were scarce (Baker and Pitt, 1988). In part a form of resistance to Smallwood's resettlement policy, a system of local governance began to develop in the 1950s. Committees formed to address issues of basic infrastructure such as roads and water, evolving into rural development associations and municipal governments. Together they created an organizational foundation for "bottom-up" development, engaging citizens and building leadership and administrative capacity (Greenwood, 1991; Royal Commission on Employment and Unemployment, 1986). Despite these developments, the influence of local institutions was, and continues to be, limited by a conservative, clientelistic, and highly centralized political and bureaucratic culture that favours development strategies based on industrialization and resource megaprojects (House, 1992; Close, 2007).

Savoie (1992) suggests that personalities shape Canadian development policy and federal–provincial relations. Newfoundland and Labrador's political history is full of colourful and dominant personalities. The province's population, marginalized and disempowered by economic circumstances, has, in a vicious circle, often turned to top-down leadership. Provincial leaders, from Smallwood to current premier Daniel "Danny"

Williams, have been portrayed in a hero-like fashion. Smallwood remained virtually unchallenged for 23 years, bringing the province into Confederation and providing related federally funded financial supports. This welcome relief for outport residents earned the premier saint-like worship in many rural areas but also resulted in a dependency on government support (Doran, 1999). Under what Smallwood himself referred to as a "democratic dictatorship," a policy agenda characterized by modernization, resettlement, resource giveaways, failed industrial projects, and federal transfers took its toll (Webb, 2001). The province's second premier, Frank Moores, responded by supporting rural development. Federally, however, a top-down approach remained popular, and many residents continued to pin their hopes on federal and, particularly, provincial, politicians.

Gezelius (2007, p. 417) describes a pattern of political distrust undoubtedly strengthened by and for some rooted in the Smallwood era: citizens have "little faith in their ability to influence government decisions." Residents and development practitioners describe a conflicted relationship with authority—respectful and dependent on the one hand and scornful of outside interference on the other. Residents are often closely connected with their politicians. Political favours and vote buying through project funding, natural resource allocations, and fish-plant licences contribute to today's social-ecological circumstances.

The province's history supports the general pattern of resource harvest and depletion observed generally in Canadian resource economies by authors such as Innis (1933) and Clapp (1998). Through a combination of structure and agency, ecosystem protection has been relegated to a low priority (Vodden, 2008). Leaders focus on the role of outside interests in the problems of the province, gaining acclaim for taking a strong stand in defending the periphery against centres of power (Tomblin, 2002). Williams, for example, negotiated an equity stake in the oil industry, engaged in public confrontations with Prime Minister Harper over oil revenue and equalization commitments, and took on former Beatle Paul McCartney on US television to defend the province's seal hunt and rural way of life. With approval ratings as high as 82% (CBC, 2008) and with 44 of 48 seats (Marland, 2007), Williams boasts of "a mandate to seize control of our own destiny" (CBC, 2006). In a speech to the Economic Club of Toronto in 2007, he quoted Napoleon—"leaders are dealers in hope"—and stated that his goal was "to launch our province on the road to hope and prosperity." Williams's popularity suggests residents are eager to buy in to this message. Without greater emphasis on bottom-up local development, however, dependency on transfers from Ottawa may be reduced, but rural dependency on the province's oil-rich economic and political core in St. John's is likely to increase.

The 1990s was a decade of renewed attention to rural development and attempts to scale up local efforts. Small-scale rural development had received limited encouragement and lacked resources, expertise, and political clout. Rural development associations had been undermined by their use as delivery mechanisms for short-term job creation programs and by concerns that they were not sufficiently proactive or representative. A 1986 Royal Commission suggested that the impact of developments such as offshore oil are best managed in partnership with regions, and expansion in major industries is best balanced with greater participation and long-term employment creation through regional and community development initiatives. However, enhanced skills and information were required at the local level (Royal Commission on Employment and Unemployment, 1986). As a result, 20 new Regional Economic Development Boards were created under Premier Clyde Wells, overlaid on more than 50 existing multi-community rural/regional development associations (RDAs). As with RDAs in the 1950s and 1960s, initiation and implementation of the Regional Economic Development Board system was influenced by personality, policy, and relationships between these two interconnected arenas (House, 1992).

Several other new development structures have since been put in place, including a Rural Secretariat under the Williams government. Facilitated by nine government-appointed Regional Councils and planners, the Secretariat is tasked with working toward an integrated approach to social, economic, cultural, and ecological well-being (Government of Newfoundland and Labrador, 2006a).

Yet the feeling remains that genuine commitment to rural development is weak. The Regional Councils have limited resources, are focused on information sharing and long-term planning, and are centrally controlled. Williams's support for the Regional Economic Development Boards is unclear. Both the boards and councils operate at a broader scale than the largely self-determined community groups represented by the RDAs and have mandates to plan and facilitate but not to implement local development. Despite increasing capacity in the municipal sector and the expectation that local agencies, including remaining RDAs, will help develop and then implement regional plans, for the most part these organizations lack the financial and human resources to fully engage in development activities.

While no comprehensive provincial strategy for rural development exists, many of the Williams government's largely top-down policy measures provide social and economic benefits for rural communities. For example, the governments of Canada and Newfoundland and Labrador launched the Fishing Industry Renewal Initiative in 2006, which led to measures for addressing inadequacies in fisheries science and impediments to the transfer of fishing enterprises within fishing families. In the face of labour shortages, a new Office of Immigration was established and the minimum wage increased. A Poverty Reduction Strategy and the Office of the Volunteer and Non-Profit Sector have been created, along with programs to support arts and culture, important components of rural revitalization efforts.

At the same time, grassroots organizations, local governments, regional boards, and provincial associations are creating their own innovative development strategies, partnerships, and networks, including rescaling initiatives that often parallel rather than connect to provincial efforts. Recognizing that economic flows such as journey-to-work and shopping patterns cross their boundaries (Fig. 17.1), Regional Economic Development Boards collaborate on planning and projects. Municipal governments are sharing services with others (see also Loudiyi, Chapter 15 this volume), and in some cases are forming new municipal structures. For many small communities, regional cooperation and even new regional forms of local government are considered necessary to ensure services are provided as populations and local tax bases decrease. As a result, the provincial municipal association has established a Community Cooperation Resource Centre to foster and facilitate cross-community collaboration.

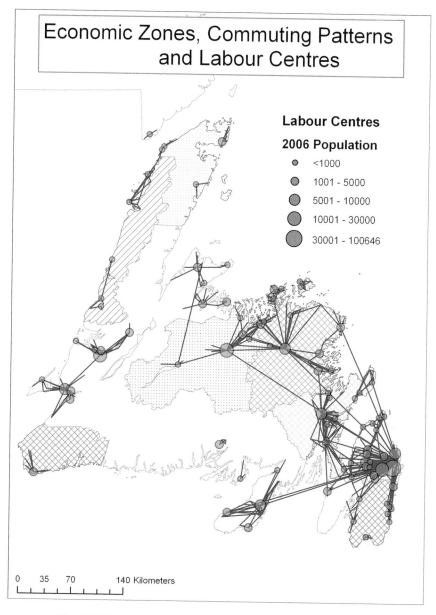

Fig. 17.1 Cross-boundary labour flows (Simms and Ward, 2009).

In 2008, the Newfoundland and Labrador Federation of Labour launched a series of Sharing the Wealth forums across the province aimed at revisiting the current model of regional development and addressing new social and economic challenges. The forums have provided a much needed opportunity for public discussion on how best to invest resource royalty revenues. A related background paper suggests that traditional development approaches have been insufficient and should be combined with "more holistic community and place-based approaches and initiatives that involve the local community and citizens and that help build on local assets and resources" (Goldenburg,

2008, p. ii). Examples of four community-based approaches to local development, described briefly below, illustrate the challenge and promise of place-based development within this provincial context.

A Tale of Four Island Communities

A comparison of four island communities in Regional Economic Zone 14 (Kittiwake zone), located on the northeast coast of the island of Newfoundland, demonstrates the diverse ways in which rural communities have adapted to change in the past and are struggling to shape their futures. The zone has a population of 47,225 people (in 2006) living in approximately 119 communities (Bennett, 2008). Six of these communities, including the urban centre of Gander, have more than 2,000 residents and make-up nearly 50% of the population.

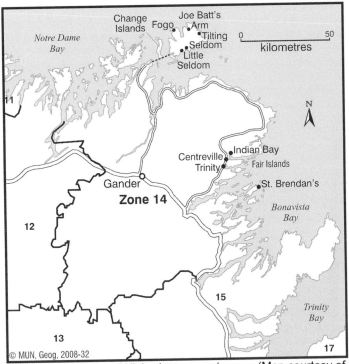

Fig. 17.2 Island communities of Kittiwake economic zone (Map courtesy of Memorial University of Newfoundland, Department of Geography, 2008).

Island communities are a particularly appropriate focus for studying community resilience and adaptation given exacerbated challenges of survival posed by their isolated geography. Most communities occupying the hundreds of small islands off the coast of Newfoundland and Labrador have been relocated over time. However, the people of three occupied islands within the Kittiwake zone, accessible only by ferry, have resisted relocation pressures. Part of the North Atlantic fishing grounds, all three were settled by European immigrants in the 17th and 18th centuries. They include the community of St. Brendan's on Cottel's Island in central Bonavista Bay, Fogo Island and Change Islands in

Notre Dame Bay. The circumstances and development strategies of these three islands are contrasted with Fair Islands, a group of Bonavista Bay islands resettled in the 1960s (Fig. 17.2).

Falling by 19%, St. Brendan's experienced the largest population decline of all Kittiwake communities from 2001 to 2006 (Table 17.3). Through the late 1800s and early 1900s, the island's fish harvesters along with others in the region, made their living from the migratory fishery of the Labrador coast in schooners that they built, owned, and sailed. This primary income source was combined with subsistence activities and a spring seal hunt. After joining Confederation, Smallwood encouraged harvesters to "burn your boats," promising "two jobs for every man" in new industries (R. Rogers, former Fair Island resident, 2008, personal communication). Government policy favouring the offshore fishery, low prices, technological change, and, later, poor catches ended the migratory Labrador fishery. Many St. Brendan's fish harvesters returned to fishing species such as cod, capelin, and lobster in local waters and later crab and turbot further offshore.

Table 17.3 Community population and economic indicators.

	Pop. (2006)	Pop. change (2001–2006)	Pop. change (1991–2001)	Unemployment (May 2006) [a]	% in primary	Per cap. income ($, 2004)
St. Brendan's	200	–19%	–34%	31%	44%	20,900
Fogo Island	2,700	–12%	–22%	20% [b]	26% [c]	17,300
Change Islands	300	–18%	–31%	39%	16%	15,300
CWT (Fair Islands)	1,130	–2%	–22%	45%	8%	15,500
NL	505,469	–1.5%	–10%	19%	8%	20,600

Sources: Statistics Canada (2008; 2007b); Government of Newfoundland and Labrador, (2006b).
Notes: (a) Percentage of the labour force unemployed in the week (Sunday to Saturday) prior to Census Day (16 May 2006).
(b) Ranging from 14% to 50% unemployment among Fogo Island communities.
(c) Ranging from 9% to 29% primary sector dependence among Fogo Island communities.

Today, an estimated 30 to 40 men and women remain involved in the fishing industry in the face of uncertainty associated with fish stocks, global markets, and fisheries policy (Government of Newfoundland and Labrador, 2006b; Statistics Canada, 2007b). A ferry, school, and shops also provide employment, which together afford a relatively high average income. Others travel afar for seagoing or construction jobs and return in off seasons, but the fishery remains a mainstay of the community. Despite growth in tourism and seasonal summer-home occupation on nearby Eastport Peninsula, the community has remained fishery focused. Harvesters such as St. Brendan's native Bill Broderick, a fifth-generation fisherman, have promoted the interests of the inshore fishery through provincial and national organizations, such as the Fish, Food and Allied Workers Union and Canadian Council of Professional Fish Harvesters (Fish, Food and Allied Workers Union, 2005;

Canadian Council of Professional Fish Harvesters, 1998). A former resident explains, "there is always the hope that the fish will return" (Broderick, 1999). Others are less optimistic, "waiting to see what kind of package the government will offer us" to move (St. Brendan's resident, 2006, personal communication).

Fogo Island is home to four incorporated municipalities and three unincorporated areas, each made up of what would have been a larger number of communities in earlier times. The largest is the town of Joe Batt's Arm–Barr'd Islands–Shoal Bay (778 inhabitants in 2006), followed by Fogo, Seldom–Little Seldom, and Tilting. Between 2001 and 2006, the island lost approximately 12% of its residents. Besides the fishery, local residents are employed in public services, tourism, retail, and commercial services. Douglas (2007, p. 2) notes that the efforts of Fogo Islanders to sustain their communities have been "recorded as celebrated case studies in community activism and courageous self-reliance and endogenous innovation," including "vigorous resistance to forced re-settlement in the 1960s, the formation of a local cooperative sector, the creation of its own RDA in the 1970s, and several other 'bootstrap' initiatives."

In 1996, local governments established the first Regional Council in the province to provide waste collection, recreation, and other island-wide services. Fogo Island Co-op began to pursue secondary fish processing, and tourism infrastructure was developed. In 2006/2007, local leaders initiated an island-wide socio-economic development plan, joining with neighbouring Change Islands, with whom they share a ferry service and other historic connections, to draw up "a blueprint for future development" (Kittiwake Economic Development Corporation, 2008, p. 4). At the same time, municipal leaders began a review of island governance, recognizing the need for new approaches. New initiatives in tourism and health-care provision have been launched, which have also been extended to the Change Islands. Change Islands, once a hub of the Labrador schooner fleet and home to 1,300 people (vs. 300 today), has undertaken its own initiatives in tourism, medical wear manufacturing, and craft production, and has established a Newfoundland pony refuge, youth centre, and partnerships with outside entrepreneurs to keep the community's fish plant operating (Woodrow, 2006).

Both Fogo and Change islanders have reached out to provincial and federal governments, the provincial municipal association, and the Regional Economic Development Board for support. They have sought business partnerships in areas such as tourism marketing and promotion with the urban centre of Gander, recognizing their interdependence within the larger region. Douglas (2007) suggests that this emergent case study establishes a case for endogenous, local, or bottom-up initiatives as a viable option, combined with a facilitative role for the state and a constructive role for intermediary organizations such as the municipal federation and Regional Economic Development Board.

Unlike the other islands, residents of Fair Islands, just north of St. Brendan's, decided to accept a resettlement offer from the Smallwood administration in 1961. The trend toward centralization and depopulation had already begun. Some islanders had moved, while others had left to work seasonally on "the mainland" (island of Newfoundland) in the woods industry, in domestic woodcutting and sawmilling, or in one of Smallwood's industrial projects. Residents decided the time had come to move their homes to nearby communities such as Centreville, Wareham, and Trinity. The Fair Islands were a cluster of islands occupied by at least five unique settlements. Most residents from the main island of Fair Island moved together to the new town of Centreville, where the provincial government had agreed to build new infrastructure for their arrival. Fair Islanders still engaged in the fishery moved their primary residences but continued to seasonally occupy subsequently constructed cabins on Fair Islands. Most turned to alternative occupations, returning to the islands only in the summer as a family vacation spot.

Seeking new forms of livelihood, industrious Fair Islanders created what is now a small-scale rural manufacturing cluster, with local firms producing fibreglass boats, steel and aluminum trailers, secondary wood products, cultured stone, niche-market fisheries products, and frozen berries. Many of these businesses have evolved from traditional industries. As a result, unlike the other three island communities, fisheries dependency has fallen below the provincial average. Other residents not involved in small-scale rural manufacturing or the fishery are engaged in long-distance commuting or seasonal work in Ontario, Alberta, or northern Canada, while still calling the now amalgamated community of Centreville–Wareham–Trinity, home. Some workers make the one-hour commute to the regional centre of Gander or travel to nearby fish-processing plants. Each year former residents return to Centreville–Wareham–Trinity to retire or young families come home to become the next generation of business owners. But after more than 40 years of resettlement, they continue to gather for summer weekends on their traditional island homes in the Atlantic.

The challenges of survival for each of these island communities are significant and the long-term success of their ongoing efforts uncertain. Local actors suggest that the communities are often stifled by red tape and rules from above and by limited resources for the implementation of plans and projects, a situation that is exacerbated by a declining volunteer and tax base, low levels of education, and other vulnerabilities. Each of these communities has pursued very different development paths. Fair Islanders accepted resettlement in the 1960s, while Fogo Island and Change Islands residents remain committed to maintaining their island communities. St. Brendan's has focused on the traditional fisheries sector, and residents exhibit a waiting-for-change attitude. Centreville–Wareham–Trinity has concentrated on small-scale manufacturing, coupled with amenity-based attraction of existing and former residents. Fogo and Change islands have emphasized partnerships, reorganization, fisheries diversification, and the attraction of tourists and seasonal residents. The outcomes of these strategies also differ, as do the leadership assets that have shaped them, such as union-organizing capacity in St. Brendan's, entrepreneurial risk taking in Fair Islands, or cooperative organizing on Fogo Island. Despite their diversity, the stories of these four island communities offer some common lessons, particularly when juxtaposed against a provincial regime that focuses on top-down, resource-based megaproject development.

Lessons for the Next Rural Economies

The popularity of Premier Williams and his message of hope has been both empowering and disempowering for rural Newfoundland and Labrador. Williams's leadership, coupled with new resource revenues, has delivered a much needed self-confidence boost among the general population and the business community, fuelling spending and investment and helping retain potential out-migrants. Strong leadership also provides the potential for significant change, particularly if that leadership is willing to entertain new ideas—whether from their own Executive Council Office, Ottawa, or community groups and citizens. However, Williams and others before him, particularly Smallwood, have been described as autocrats who monopolize power and are determined to set their own agenda for the future of the province (Webb, 2001). The negative implications of top-down leadership are highlighted by one long-time community leader who suggests hopefully that with strong federal and/or provincial leadership and policy support, local champions may no longer be a requirement for viable rural communities (Northeast coast community leader, 2008, personal communication). The island communities examined in this chapter have benefitted from government policy and program support, but their ongoing survival has been, and will continue to be, dependent on the hard work and commitment of many local leaders, and indeed on local "heroes."

The temptation for actors in the periphery to rely on the centre is strong—and dangerous. While a stronger commitment to rural development is needed at both provincial and federal levels, place-based development cannot be conducted through a centralized governance structure. Rural development attempts to intervene in complex social-ecological systems, which Anderson (2001) explains cannot be effectively governed from a single centre. Top-down and bottom-up leadership are needed within new forms of context-appropriate cooperation and organization. The communities examined, particularly Fogo Island and Change Islands, suggest that new and necessarily evolving regional structures can help facilitate multi-level planning *and* implementation with appropriate attention to communications, networking, and the local scale. Opportunities exist for new evolving spaces of relations, but their foundation and future directions are rooted in connection to place. Development, therefore, is both functional and territorial.

The challenge for Newfoundland and Labrador today is to not only reduce dependency on Ottawa or externally owned corporations, but also to recognize and address dependency and uneven development within the province and to create governance models that connect top-down (federal and provincial) and bottom-up efforts so that they better support one another (see Bryant, Chapter 11 this volume). This requires leadership from above that is willing to share responsibility and support local initiative along with willingness to take responsibility and increase self-reliance at the local level, building on a long tradition of resilience and survival in the face of adversity. Case studies demonstrate that this willingness is present but varied in rural Newfoundland and Labrador.

The livelihood and community adaptation strategies examined in this chapter further demonstrate the importance of a holistic, multi-pronged approach that seeks new opportunities both inside and outside traditional resource sectors and recognizes the importance of small business and the informal economy, which create more flexible rural economic systems better able to buffer changes in commodity-based resource economies. A range of natural resources and both large- and small-scale resource-based developments continue to be important to economies and ways of life in rural Newfoundland and Labrador. They require ongoing and greater attention to wise investment, ownership, and stewardship to continue into the future.

A strategic approach to labour force development is also required. Going away to work is a common livelihood strategy, a pattern that has existed since the province's inception. The return of long-distance commuters and retirees is closely linked to a strong commitment to (and love of) place, as is local entrepreneurship. If sense of place, positive attitude, and determination are as critical to rural development as the above case studies suggest, measures must be taken to foster and sustain such assets. Forming partnerships between communities so that leaders can support each other is but one example. Premier Williams's positive message can also contribute, as can measures to protect resource access and other aspects of the quality of life that draw and keep people home and motivate them to fight for the continued survival and well-being of their home places. As Beckley *et al.* (2002) and others suggest, more diverse indicators of well-being and community resilience are needed to reflect social, human capital, and rural quality-of-life advantages. In

Newfoundland and Labrador, these indicators include: (1) low crime, homicide, suicide, and self-reported stress levels; (2) high rates of home ownership, charitable giving and caring for one another; and (3) a unique culture (Statistics Canada, 2002, 2005; Hall *et al.*, 2006; Government of Newfoundland and Labrador, 2006b). Rural and small-town residents express a high level of satisfaction with their community despite the population loss and economic stress, valuing characteristics such as quietness, the people, small-town living, and proximity to nature (Ommer, 2007). Commonly used indicators mask these important factors.

The role of commitment to place, self-confidence, and positive attitude should not be underestimated, nor should the realities and magnitude of Newfoundland and Labrador's challenges. The majority of rural youth desire to leave their communities, often for work or education, despite their attachment to place (Palmer and Sinclair, 2000). Their ability to return is frequently impaired by a lack of economic opportunity. Creating a next rural economy that former residents and their families can come home to in this resource-dependent periphery will require leadership at multiple levels as well as more widespread institutional and societal adaptation.

Acknowledgements

The author acknowledges the Social Sciences and Humanities Research Council, Coasts Under Stress Project, Ocean Management Research Network, Simon Fraser University, Natural Resources Canada, and Municipalities Newfoundland and Labrador for their financial support of this research. Thanks are also due to those who provided constructive comments on earlier drafts and to the people of the Kittiwake coast for their inspiration, knowledge, and warm welcome.

References

Anderson, J. (2001) On the edge of chaos: Crafting adaptive collaborative management for biological diversity conservation in a pluralistic world. In: Buck, L., Geisler, C., Schelhas, J., and Wollenberg, E. (eds.) *Biological Diversity: Balancing Interests through Adaptive Collaborative Management*. CRC Press, Boca Raton, FL, 171–186.

Baker, M., and Pitt, J. (1988) The third tier: A historical overview of the development of local government in Newfoundland and Labrador. In: *Programme of the 38th Annual Convention of the Newfoundland and Labrador Federation of Municipalities, October 7-9, 1988*. Newfoundland and Labrador Federation of Municipalities, St. John's, NL, 39–43.

Beckley, T., Parkins, J., and Stedman, R. (2002) Indicators of forest-dependent community sustainability: The evolution of research. *Forestry Chronicle* 78(5), 626–636.

Bennett, J. (2008) Presentation at Centreville strategic economic plan consultation session,Centreville -Wareham-Trinity, NL.

Broderick M. (1999) From Helvick Head to Hescut Point: The St. Brendan's Irish, transcribed by R. Royle and R. Follett, www.rootsweb.ancestry.com/~cannf/bbcen_brendans.htm (accessed May 2008).

Canadian Council of Professional Fish Harvesters. (1998). Bringing fish harvester knowledge into fisheries science and management. *Creating New Wealth from the Sea* 3, www.ccpfh-ccpp.org/e_dbViewer.asp?cs=pubs&id=20 (accessed May 2008).

CBC News. (2006) In depth: Danny Williams, http://www.cbc.ca/news/background/williams_danny (accessed May 2008).

_____. (2008) Williams, PCs still dominate landscape, poll finds, www.cbc.ca/canada/Newfoundland -labrador/story/2008/03/07/...?ref=rss (accessed May 2008).

Childs, B., Van Herk, G., and Thorburn, J. (2007) The effects of urbanization and social orientation: Locally salient variables as indicators of linguistic change. Paper presented at NWAV 36, Philadelphia.

Clapp, R. (1998) The resource cycle in forestry and fishing. *Canadian Geographer* 42 (2), 129–144.

Close, D. (2007) The Newfoundland and Labrador strategic social plan: Governance misconceived and ill-applied. Paper presented at the annual meeting of the Midwest Political Science Association, Chicago.

Community Services Council of Newfoundland and Labrador. (2004) *The Nonprofit Sector as a Force for Sustainability and Renewal in Newfoundland and Labrador*. Prepared for the Government of Newfoundland and Labrador's Program Renewal.

Doran, Barbara (Writer/director). (1999) *Between Scoundrels and Saints: The Life and Times of Joey Smallwood* [Documentary film]. Morag Productions, St. John's, NL (available from National Film Board of Canada).

Douglas, D. (2007) *Fogo Island Local Government Development: A Case Study in Endogenous Rural Development*. Report for the Organization for Economic Co-operation and Development.

Dunn, C. (2003) Provincial mediation of federal–municipal relations in Newfoundland and Labrador. Paper presented at the Institute of Intergovernmental Relations Conference, Kingston, ON.

Dunne, E. (2003) *Final Report: Fish Processing Policy Review*. Department of Fisheries and Aquaculture, St. John's, NL.

Environment Canada. (n.d.) Ecozones of Canada—Northwest Atlantic marine, www.ec.gc.ca/soer-ree/English/Vignettes/Marine/nam/default.cfm (accessed May 2008).

Fish, Food and Allied Workers' Union. (2005) Union appoints inshore director. Press release, 15 September 2005, www.ffaw.nf.ca/NewsDetails.asp?id=149 (accessed 26 December 2008).

Francis, R., Jones, R., and Smith, D. (1996) *Destinies: Canadian History Since Confederation*. Holt, Rinehart and Winston/Harcourt, Toronto.

Gezelius, S. (2007) Three paths from law enforcement to compliance: Cases from the fisheries. *Human Organization* 66(4), 414–425.

Goldenburg, M. (2008) *A Review of Rural and Regional Development Policies and Programs*. Prepared for the Newfoundland and Labrador Federation of Labour.

Government of Newfoundland and Labrador. (2002) *The Economy 2002—Newfoundland and Labrador*. Economic Research and Analysis Division, St. John's, NL.

_____. (2004) *Highlights and Analysis: Consolidated Summary—Financial Statements Public Accounts, 31 March 2004*. Office of the Comptroller General, Department of Finance, St. John's, NL.

_____. (2005) *Highlights and Analysis: Consolidated Summary—Financial Statements Public Accounts, 31 March 2005*. Office of the Comptroller General, Department of Finance, St. John's, NL.

_____. (2006a) *Rural Secretariat Executive Council Annual Activity Report 2005-06*. Rural Secretariat, St. John's, NL.

_____. (2006b) Community accounts, www.communityaccounts.ca (accessed 4 October 2008).

_____. (2008a) *The Economy 2008—Newfoundland and Labrador*. Economic Research and Analysis Division, St. John's, NL.

_____. (2008b) *Estimates of the Program Expenditure and Revenue of the Consolidated Revenue Fund 2008-09*. Budgeting Division, Department of Finance, St. John's, NL.

Greenwood, R. (1991) The local state and economic development in peripheral regions: A comparative study of Newfoundland and Northern Norway. PhD thesis. University of Warwick, Coventry, UK.

Hall, M., Lasby, D., Gumulka, G., and Tryon, C. (2006) *Caring Canadians, Involved Canadians: Highlights from the 2004 Canada Survey of Giving, Volunteering and Participating*. Statistics Canada, Ottawa.

Hamilton, L., and Butler, M. (2001) Outport adaptations: Social indicators through Newfoundland's cod crisis. *Human Ecology Review* 8(2), 1–11.

House, J. (1985) *The Challenge of Oil: Newfoundland's Quest for Controlled Development*. ISER Books, St. John's, NL.

———. (1992) *Against the Tide: Battling for Economic Renewal in Newfoundland and Labrador*. University of Toronto Press, Toronto.

———. (2006) Oil, fish and social change in Newfoundland and Labrador: Lessons for British Columbia. Lecture to the Special Centre for Coastal Studies, Simon Fraser University, Burnaby, BC.

Innis, H. (1933) *Problems of Staple Production in Canada*. Ryerson, Toronto.

Janigan, M. (with B. Bergman). (1998) Provinces assess economic future. *Maclean's* 111(23), 26.

Kittiwake Economic Development Corporation (KEDC). (2008) Socio-economic plan for Fogo Island and Change Islands update. *KEDC Newsletter* 6(2), 4.

Marland, A. (2007) The 2007 provincial election in Newfoundland and Labrador. *Canadian Political Science Review* 1(2), 75–85.

Marshall, T. (2008) Get ready for "revolution between the ears": Marshall, www.cbc.ca/canada/new foundland-labrador/story/2008/04/29/revolution-ears.html (accessed 26 December 2008).

Morrissey, A. (2007) Newfoundland and Labrador unemployment rate 13.2%—National average 5.9%: A number for all seasons. *Telegram* (St. John's), 17 December, www.thetelegram.com/index.cfm?sid=90197&sc=79 (accessed 2 May 2008).

Municipalities Newfoundland and Labrador. (2005) *Strengthening Our Communities: President's Task Force on Municipal Sustainability Discussion Paper*. Author, St. John's, NL.

Ommer, R. (with the Coasts Under Stress Research Project Team). (2007) *Coasts under Stress: Understanding Restructuring and the Social-Ecological Health*. McGill-Queen's University Press, Montreal/Kingston, ON.

Palmer, C., and Sinclair, P. (2000) Expecting to leave: Attitudes to migration among high school students on the Great Northern Peninsula of Newfoundland. *Newfoundland Studies* 16(1), 30–46.

Royal Commission on Employment and Unemployment. (1986) *Building on Our Strengths: Final Report of the Royal Commission on Employment and Unemployment*. Author, St John's, NL.

Savoie, D. (1992) *Regional Economic Development: Canada's Search for Solutions*. University of Toronto Press, Toronto.

Simms, A., and Ward, J. (2009) "Rural-Urban Interaction: A Spatial and Temporal Analysis of Functional Areas in Newfoundland and Labrador." Unpublished manuscript, Memorial University of Newfoundland, St. John's.

Sorensen, M., and Aylward, J. (with R. Bollman, K. Humpage, J. Lambert, C. Binet, and J. Hannes). (2005) *National Rural Profile: A Ten-Year Census Analysis (1991-2001)*. Canada's Rural Partnership: Rural Research and Analysis, www.rural.gc.ca/research/profile/nat_e.phtml (accessed 4 October 2008).

Statistics Canada. (2002) Self-rated health, by sex, household population aged 12 and over, Canada, provinces, territories, health regions and peer groups, 2000/01, www.statcan.gc.ca/pub/82-221-x/01002/t/pdf/4196003-eng.pdf (accessed 4 October 2008).

———. (2004) Newfoundland and Labrador: The labour market in Newfoundland and Labrador continues to improve. In: *The Canadian Labour Market at a Glance 2003*. Author, Ottawa, 23.

———. (2005) General social survey: Criminal victimization, www.statcan.ca/Daily/English/051124/d051124b.htm (accessed 4 October 2008).

———. (2007a) Population and dwelling counts, for Canada, provinces and territories, 2006 and 2001 censuses, www12.statcan.ca/english/census06/data/popdwell/Table.cfm (accessed 4 October 2008).

———. (2007b) *2006 Community Profile* (Catalogue no. 92-591-XWE). Author, Ottawa.

———. (2008) CANSIM, table 282-0088, www40.statcan.ca/l01/cst01/labr67b.htm (accessed 4 October 2008).

Stirling, B. (2007) Canadian manufacturers and exporters—Newfoundland and Labrador Division. Presentation to the Local Action for Developing Regions Workshop, Grand Falls-Windsor, NL.

Tomblin, S. 2002. Newfoundland and Labrador at the crossroads: Reform or lack of reform in a new era? *Journal of Canadian Studies*, 37(1), 89–108.

Vodden, K. 2008. New spaces, ancient places: Collaborative governance and sustainable development on Canada's coasts. PhD thesis. Simon Fraser University, Burnaby, BC.

Webb, J. (2001) Provincial government: The Smallwood years, 1949–1972, www.heritage.nf.ca/law/prov_gov.html (accessed 4 October 2008).

Woodrow, M. (1996) Resistance to regulatory changes in the fishery: A study of selected communities of Bonavista North, Newfoundland. PhD Thesis. Université Laval, Montreal.

_____. (2006) *A Comparative Assessment of the Capacity of Canadian Rural Communities to Adapt to Uncertain Futures*. Draft Community Background Paper, Change Islands, NL.

Wright, M. (2001) *A Fishery for Modern Times: The State and the Industrialization of the Newfoundland Fishery, 1934–1968*. Oxford University Press, Don Mills, ON.

Chapter 18

Fly-in, Fly-out Resource Development: A New Regionalist Perspective on the Next Rural Economy

Sean Markey

Since the early 1980s, rural communities in Canada and in other industrialized countries have been adjusting to a period of rapid industrial restructuring and concomitant shifts in public policy. Whether these changes have created opportunity or crisis, the general trend has been a weakening of both industrial and government ties to community. The immediate postwar period of rural growth in Western countries was facilitated by, and regulated under, conditions of industrial responsibility toward community building and government policy oriented toward national equity. These industrial and governmental objectives have changed dramatically in favour of greater industrial flexibility, rural independence, and, as a by-product, increasing variability in the condition of rural places.

The dramatic shifts associated with restructuring (i.e., changes in the system of production) are most evident in the increasing use of fly-in/fly-out (FIFO) work camps for resource extraction. Under FIFO conditions of rural industry, the workplace is situated in a remote locale at a significant distance from the homes and communities of workers, thus requiring that workers fly/bus to a temporary living space for a set pattern of work days. The FIFO practice was used originally in the oil and gas sector, but is now being used in a variety of resource sectors, including mining, fishing, forestry, and hydroelectricity. The practice neatly captures and magnifies many of the opportunities and challenges associated with current trends in rural restructuring, and, as a result, it represents a dynamic conceptual leverage point from which to explore emerging rural development tensions and the implications of the new economy for rural and small-town places.

In this chapter, I will link FIFO with processes of rural restructuring and show the impacts and opportunities associated with these operations through a new regionalist lens. In isolation, FIFO appears to be the pinnacle of place-less development—completely flexible, isolated, and temporary. However, upon closer review, these operations have significant direct and indirect impacts at the local, regional, national, and even international level in terms of economic contribution or opportunity costs, social and cultural impact at community and personal levels, and environmental implications. A new regionalist perspective provides both theoretical and practical tools for assessing impact and for reconciling the place-less dimensions of FIFO with the place-based realities of rural and small-town economies.

I use secondary data from northern British Columbia, particularly the northwestern region of the province, to assess FIFO operational impacts and to reflect upon the potential contributions of a regionalist approach to mediating these impacts on a local scale. British Columbia is currently experiencing a boom in mining exploration and operational development; however, information on the specific dynamics associated with FIFO operations remains relatively thin. I begin the chapter with a more detailed look at FIFO; in the following sections I provide greater detail on the study area and discuss impacts and opportunities associated with FIFO from a new regionalist perspective.

Fly-in Fly-out: Origins and Dimensions

The term "long-distance commuting" was originally coined by Hobart (1979) to describe a situation where a workplace is located in a remote setting that is a significant distance from workers' homes. As a result, for a fixed number of days the company provides food and accommodation at the work site (Shrimpton and Storey, 1992). The specific nature of FIFO operations in terms of labour practices varies considerably according to job characteristics, location, and type. Common patterns of job residency identified in the literature include 7/7 (seven days on site and seven days at home), 14/7, 14/14, and 21/7.

Storey (2001a) indicates that the FIFO phenomenon was originally seen as a way to spread the effects of industrial activity throughout a specific rural region. Planners figured that economic benefits would flow to a variety of communities within a region that supplied workers and/or materials to FIFO operations. However, more recently the FIFO model has been reducing or eliminating direct economic linkages between industrial activity and surrounding communities for a couple of reasons. First, the FIFO system is increasingly being used when the work site may be directly adjacent to established communities. As Storey (2001b, p. 3) states, "this situation has become more common with the extended workday (ten to twelve hours) becoming the norm. In such circumstances even a one hour commute in each direction can mean a fourteen hour workday which has health, safety and productivity implications if sustained on a long-term basis." Second, FIFO operations may be sourcing and housing employees from communities that are thousands of kilometres away. For example, mining and oil and gas activity in British Columbia and Alberta relies heavily on an experienced workforce drawn from Newfoundland. As a result, potential benefits of this activity are increasingly "flying over" established adjacent or regionally proximate rural centres.

The fly-over effect is a concern given the loss of economic activity from FIFO operations and the "bust" of communities traditionally or potentially associated with industrial resource activity. Alternatively, from a resource "boom" perspective, communities adjacent to operations may struggle with infrastructure demands arising from increased industrial activity as businesses and new or temporary residents make growing demands on the town's social services and physical infrastructure like housing or sewerage and water systems. However, although the industrial activity represents economic growth potential, it is taking place within a policy vacuum and without sufficient structural linkages to either industry or senior government support (Costa, 2004). Communities are often left on their own without the financial resources to properly accommodate growth, given that the increase in economic activity is taking place beyond municipal taxation boundaries.

The boom and bust implications make the study of FIFO operations both theoretically and contextually complex. There are a variety of issue streams within the FIFO literature that help explain the rise of the FIFO phenomenon and its social and economic impacts.

First, the literature illuminates the origins of the phenomenon by tracing changes associated with government policy and industrial restructuring relative to the shift away from single-industry communities (Storey and Shrimpton, 1989; Shrimpton and Storey, 1992). In terms of policy changes, such factors as cost, lengthier approval processes, more stringent environmental assessment requirements, and an increasing absence of government from town development facilitated a preference for FIFO operations. Simply put, government support for the development of single-industry towns has waned. The model of new town development has proven to be expensive at both start-up and wind-down phases of such initiatives. For example, in the case of Tumbler Ridge, a town in northeastern British Columbia, the estimated total cost of townsite development exceeded $274 million, representing a per capita investment in the order of $45,700 (McGrath, 1986, p. 232). This scale of public investment is unlikely in a more fiscally conservative environment that seeks to facilitate investment.

Similarly, from an industrial perspective, economic restructuring processes have increased the demands for flexible production systems and decreased company linkages to and responsibility for communities (Hayter, 2000). Management costs associated with previous industry town development have become prohibitive in a highly competitive resource economy. Other cost drivers motivating the use of FIFO include improvements in transportation and communication (and associated cost reductions), lower rates of employee turnover and absenteeism observed in FIFO operations, and access to a larger supply of qualified workers. The combination of these drivers makes FIFO operationally easier and leaner from a corporate and government perspective (Shrimpton and Storey, 1992).

Second, social dimensions associated with FIFO operations (and home impacts) are prominent themes within the literature (Storey and Shrimpton, 1989). The work rotation system appears to contribute to increased levels of alcoholism and drug abuse, family violence, and parenting problems (Storey, 2001a). On the positive side, workers are drawn to, and have come to expect, metropolitan amenities, and the FIFO option creates a more likely scenario for dual-income opportunity with a home base in a larger rural or metropolitan setting. This dimension of FIFO research clearly outlines the tension between costs and benefits associated with the labour practice. Social dimensions also factor into considerations of overall regional benefits associated with FIFO operations.

Given the location of FIFO operations in more remote, rural settings, there has been an increasing amount of literature focused specifically on the interrelationships between FIFO operations and aboriginal communities (Hobart, 1979; Ritter, 2001; MiningWatch Canada, 2002; Bone, 2003; Kuyek and Coumans, 2003). Approximately 1,200 aboriginal communities are located within 200 km of producing mines in Canada. The aboriginal-impacts literature addresses issues of economic marginalization, employment and economic benefits, and cultural effects. This body of work is particularly relevant for northern British Columbia, where ongoing title and treaty issues dominate regional development discussions and give aboriginal communities considerable leverage in negotiations with resource industries.

The cumulative impact of the economic and political restructuring processes that are driving the use of FIFO means that the model is the dominant approach to new mine development (Costa, 2004). For example, in the Canadian North, there were no new mining towns built between 1982 and 1992, compared with the opening of 16 new FIFO operations (Shrimpton and Storey, 1992).

The advent of a neo-liberal-inspired policy agenda (which seeks to reduce the role of government and public investment), combined with the increasing demands of flexible production systems, has dramatically affected the economic characteristics of rural industry and rural communities. In political terms, a shift from an equity focus in the postwar period, which facilitated an interventionist approach by senior government in rural development, has faded in favour of withdrawn managerialism (Polèse, 1999). The enabling policy approach that accompanies this withdrawal is partly driven by demands for a greater degree of bottom-up participation (see Bryant, Chapter 11 this volume; Woods, Chapter 13 this volume). However, it is more directly rooted in and motivated by funding retrenchment from the complexities and investments of rural town development.

Economic restructuring affects rural communities in two fundamental ways. First, the demise of the Fordist compromise (a production agreement between labour, government, and industry), which facilitated large industrial development and high wages in rural areas during the postwar period, combined with the labour-shedding properties of technological advancement in all forms of production, has severely affected rural communities, which tend to be less economically diverse and more reliant on the resource sector (Hayter, 2000). Second, and ironically, just as governments have been withdrawing their commitments to rural community (re)investment, the nature of competitiveness in the new economy now demands high-quality services and infrastructure amenities. Kitson *et al.* (2004, p. 992) provide a straightforward definition of territorial competitiveness "as the success with which regions and cities compete with one another in some way—over market share or capital and workers." New approaches to competitiveness place an added burden on the capacity of communities and regions to construct a receptive and adaptive infrastructure environment (including physical, social, and human forms of infrastructure). From a rural perspective, communities have a limited capacity to respond to the amenity and other infrastructure demands of the new economy in terms of attracting and retaining a workforce accustomed to urban-style amenities, and also in terms of accommodating new modes of production and communication (Markey *et al.*, 2006). Communities' inability to meet new competitive standards contributes to fly-over effects that disassociate FIFO operations from surrounding communities and their economies.

Restructuring in Context: Northern British Columbia

Northern British Columbia comprises about 70% of the provincial land mass and contains approximately 10% of the provincial population. There is a single hub city of 70,000, Prince George. The small towns typically range from 5,000 to 20,000 people, while the rural areas are marked by small settlements of fewer than 1,000 people. The mountainous terrain limits the transportation network linking such places. The region is also culturally complex, containing 34 municipalities and more than 62 First Nations. A large share of the region's population lives in the rural countryside.

The economy of northern British Columbia is similar to other northern economies, being heavily dependent on forestry, mining, power generation, and tourism. There is also a robust second economy of public- and private-sector services, hunting, fishing, and trapping. Compared to the rest of the province, northern British Columbia has a more volatile pattern of population change, a younger population profile, and a relatively larger First Nations population.

The roots of the present economic and settlement landscape in northern British Columbia are found in two eras of development. First, through the 1950s and 1960s, the BC provincial government followed a coordinated public-policy approach based on a model of industrial resource development (Williston and Keller, 1997). This led to a 25- to 30-year period of rapid economic and community growth across the region (Halseth *et al.*, 2004). New communities and high-quality local infrastructure were the backbone of industrial centres using the province's rich resource base (Davis and Hutton, 1989; Horne and Penner, 1992).

Second, the period since the 1980s has seen considerable economic restructuring as described above (Barnes and Hayter, 1997; Barnes *et al.*, 2001; Halseth and Sullivan, 2002; Little, 2002). A recession in the early 1980s marked a fundamental shift in the Fordist compromise that linked industry and government with labour and, indirectly, with rural and northern communities. Layoffs and closures meant that the region began to lose population for the first time since World War II (Hutton, 2002). Hanlon and Halseth (2005) illustrate how the impacts of the restructuring process continued throughout and beyond the 1990s.

The general dynamics of the restructuring process in British Columbia are evident in the specifics of the mining sector. The industry experienced a recession crisis in the 1981–1987 period, resulting in significant structural change. A focus on reorienting productivity resulted in rationalization, cost reductions, and increased flexibility in production systems to better respond to global commodity prices and demands. A focus on labour productivity facilitated a shift in favour of FIFO operations. With FIFO, the mining sector found it less difficult to attract and retain workers. Shrimpton and Storey (1992) cite estimates of annual labour turnover in FIFO operations of approximately 5%, a reduction of 30% to 35% from the turnover in traditional operations.

The BC mining sector has experienced a considerable revival in recent years. Gross revenues in 2006 exceeded $8 billion, supporting 7,345 people in direct employment. Global demand for resources, combined with regulatory changes in the industry (e.g., tax incentives and easier access to land) are responsible for the growth (Government of British Columbia, 2005). Exploration expenses, a strong indicator of industry growth and confidence, mirror the revival in the sector. In 2006, the industry spent $265 million in exploration costs, compared with $27 million in 2000 (which was the lowest level since 1960) (PricewaterhouseCoopers, 2007). As of 2007, there were 24 mining projects undergoing environmental assessments or permit applications, with 10 coal, 11 metal, and 36 mineral quarries and mines (in addition to over 1,100 aggregate pits) in operation. At the time of writing, I am unable to confirm how many of these operations are FIFO—a knowledge gap that exists at the national level as well.

FIFO in Northwestern British Columbia

The regional study area of northwestern British Columbia (Fig. 18.1) contains a population of approximately 42,000 people in four municipalities and more than ten First Nations reserve communities. The region is composed of larger, more diversified communities located along Highway 16 (Terrace, Hazelton, Smithers, Telkwa, and Houston) and much smaller communities located along Highway 37 (Stewart, Iskut, Dease Lake, Telegraph Creek, and Good Hope Lake). The region in general displays a classic rural resource economic structure, with heavy income dependency on forestry (20%), mining (17%), and the public sector (27%); however, the diversity of communities makes for a complex regional research setting (Hutton, 2002).

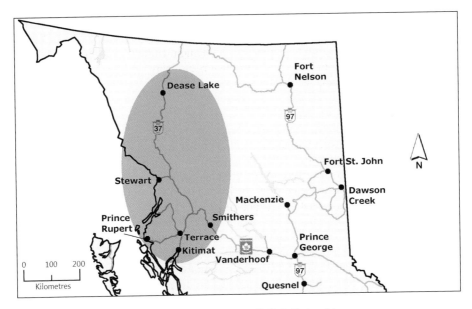

Fig. 18.1 Northwestern British Columbia.

There are three major mining sites currently in operation in the region:

- Eskay Creek: gold and silver; projected lifespan 1995–unknown (projected 2006, but still operational); employs 368 people; FIFO;
- Huckleberry: copper; projected lifespan 1996–2007; employs 283 people; FIFO with mostly local employees (123 km bus shuttle from Houston, BC);
- Kemess: mineral deposit; projected lifespan 1998–2007; employs 558 people; FIFO.

Three new mine operations are proposed for the region: Red Chris (copper-gold), Mount Klappan (anthracite coal), and Galore Creek (copper-gold). The future of these projects, with an estimated regional employment impact of over 935 people, is uncertain given the recent cancellation of a proposed power line along Highway 37. The $400-million transmission line was a joint project announced by the provincial government and Galore Creek's developers. Galore Creek was put on hold due to development costs, jeopardizing an initial $158-million investment in the line (Simpson, 2008). Other mine sites are also dependent on the status of the power line and at the time of writing were on hold.

The northwest's experience with FIFO operations reflects many of the economic and social trends documented in the literature. The economic impacts of FIFO operations depend on a variety of variables, including regional capacity, the regulatory environment, and operational standards and decisions. In the worst-case scenario, companies benefit from the resources of a particular region while giving little back to surrounding communities. This fly-over scenario is characterized by companies drawing their workforces exclusively from larger, distant centres, importing virtually all service functions, and forging no local business contracts (Storey, 2001a; Kuyek and Coumans, 2003). In these situations, FIFO operations contribute to regional population decline, which exacerbates the challenges rural communities face in supplying service and infrastructure support.

From a more positive perspective, FIFO operations may draw significant numbers of their labour force from surrounding communities, contribute taxes to local and regional governments, and work with local officials to implement a variety of community/regional benefit agreements. Community benefit arrangements may include a variety of terms (Gardner Pinfold, 2004; Markey, 2004), including:

- Employment quotas or targets
- Special training programs appropriate for local people
- Targets for local procurement of goods and services
- Support for local business development
- Support for women's employment and training, as appropriate
- Supportive work environment for distinctive local cultures
- Contributions to regional infrastructure.

In Canada, it is now common practice for developers to adopt an "adjacency principle," which gives workers and companies in communities closest to the site access to jobs and supply-and-service contracts if they are capable and competitive (Storey, 2001a). Despite this attention, however, there appears to be an absence of shared precedence or standards associated with local benefits. There may also be negative implications associated with plundering a local talent pool and hindering the capacity of communities to meet basic service functions.

In the northwest region, the direct regional employment associated with the three operating mines is approximately 493 people (G.E. Bridges, 2004). The mines hold a variety of local benefits contracts with surrounding communities, including transportation, road maintenance and snow clearing, and catering services. Indirectly, exploration and new development investment boost regional optimism, and infrastructure improvements, such as airport facilities to accommodate FIFO operations, have positive tourism and amenity migrant spinoffs. It is anticipated that the power line would also have a positive indirect economic impact on the region.

A substantial portion of the FIFO literature describes this type of operation's social impacts. Starting first with the negative trends, the separation and isolation common to FIFO operations are associated with harmful social behaviours that contribute to family breakups, violence, and increased abuse of alcohol and drugs by employees (Ritter, 2001; Storey, 2001a). In addition to these personal and family impacts, FIFO operations may drain capacity from surrounding communities and lead to lower levels of community engagement. Finally, while FIFO operations may provide an opportunity for aboriginal people to gain employment and retain elements of a lifestyle and culture associated with living within traditional territories, they might also erode aboriginal culture. FIFO operations provide high incomes (which may prove disruptive to more traditional communal practices), and their location adjacent to First Nations reserves can lead to concerns about negative exposure to outsiders with disposable income and no ties or sense of responsibility to local communities.

A variety of social impacts have been recorded in the northwest region. For one thing, the cycle of FIFO shift work puts pressure on the social and family dynamics of surrounding communities. While regional aboriginal communities suffer from substance-abuse issues tied to historical conditions of oppression, the income and displacement caused by FIFO operations may exacerbate these drug and alcohol problems. A socio-economic impact assessment carried out for the BC government documented a "non-stop party" when workers return to communities and revealed the pressures on mine "widows" when their partners leave for shift rotation (G.E. Bridges, 2004). In addition, while the mines have contributed local benefit agreements associated with contract labour, they reportedly do not contribute to community programs to ameliorate social problems, placing added stress on regional health and social programs that are already facing service pressures. As well, the socio-economic impact assessment (G.E. Bridges, 2004) described local concerns about youth leaving school early to access mining-related jobs. Finally, the report identified a "training gap": regional employees are able to handle service contracts and construction-related jobs, but operational and higher-paying jobs tend to go to out-of-region employees.

Mining in the northwestern region provides employment and business development experience for local communities and entrepreneurs. The cyclical nature of the sector and the ability of operations to fly in their own workforce and supplies do, however, contribute additional levels of uncertainty and, currently, unknown opportunity costs. The operations hold a relatively greater economic significance for the smaller and more remote communities located along Highway 37. G.E. Bridges and Associates (2004) noted that the economic impact of mine closure on the more diversified Highway 16 communities would be minimal, given the limited economic linkages that exist between the FIFO operations and these communities.

Socially, there are benefits associated with employment opportunities and increased income levels; however, the mines clearly create social challenges that are not being adequately addressed, and they strain the existing infrastructure of health and social services. Both the weak economic bonds and social pressures highlight a separation of industry from more entrenched and durable commitments to local communities in the region and expose infrastructure, service, and competitive challenges faced by rural regions that mirror overall restructuring trends.

Regionalism has experienced a revival in economic development and related research in a variety of areas specifically because of its capacity to address the challenges and shortcomings associated with restructuring processes at different scales. In the next section I will provide a brief orientation to the re-emergence of regionalism and apply specific regionalist themes to the particular challenges FIFO operations present to place-based development.

Impacts and Benefits: A New Regionalist Lens on FIFO

A number of researchers have summarized the major themes and drivers of a renewed interest in regionalism. Scott (2000) traces the conceptual lineage of the new regionalism through two distinct phases. First, researchers began to document impacts associated with the transition from Fordist to post-Fordist stages of industrialization—where regional disparities are distinctly highlighted. This focus is clearly seen in the recent research literature tracking changes and pressures in the BC resource economy. Second, Scott identifies how a rising interest in the forces and implications of globalization leads to a discussion of the role and function of the region as a distinct source of competitive advantage.

Barnes and Gertler (1999) summarize complementary ideas emerging in the literature surrounding the social and institutional relevance of regions. They identify two prominent research themes: first, that social economy/social capital relations represent an important factor in competitiveness; and second, that the erosion of regulatory power within nations places an extra burden of responsibility on regional institutions. This second theme envelops a more specific interest in questions of governance. Both of these themes resonate in a number of recent volumes by rural geographers interested in topics of community and economic development (Ramsey and Bryant, 2004; Essex *et al.*, 2005).

New regionalist research covers a variety of themes of particular relevance to FIFO operations. First, the transition from sectoral to territorial development is highlighted in new regionalism as a means for advancing and achieving a more holistic approach to place-based development (Scott, 2000; Terluin, 2003). There are two potential benefits to incorporating FIFO operations within the territorial perspective of a region. First, at a conceptual level, it allows regional decision makers and planners to view FIFO operations as part of the regional economy rather than as isolated activities. The absence of direct or formal industry–town linkages may reduce interaction and any sense of mutual responsibility, but regional economic planning can provide a foundation for re-linking FIFO operations in an integrated way to surrounding communities. Second, a territorial approach provides a potential framework with which to actualize and monitor local outcomes. Regionalizing community benefits will better enable planners to construct and maximize intended or potential regional spread effects of mining operations.

Second, new regionalist work is exploring the dynamics associated with pursuing place-based development within a competitive (rather than comparative) economic system (Kitson *et al.*, 2004; Turok, 2004). This theme underlines the challenges associated with place-based development in a rural, remote context dependent on industrial resource development. In a situation of comparative advantage, territories "produce those goods or services for which they have the greatest cost or efficiency advantage over others, or for which they have the least disadvantage" (Johnston *et al.*, 2000). This principle explains, in part, patterns of regional specialization (i.e., mining, forestry, fishing) across a resource periphery like British Columbia. By contrast, competitive advantage, although it is relatively poorly defined, refers to a complex array of interventions designed to enhance the productivity, social capital, or attractiveness of place for both labour and capital.

There are two potential benefits of adopting a competitive approach to mediate the impacts of FIFO operations within a region. First, Shrimpton (2005) indicates that in relation to FIFO operations, communities overestimate local capacity, overestimate the role of government, and misunderstand the dynamics of the industry. This is the result of communities applying traditional roles, established within a comparative framework, to a vastly restructured industrial and government setting. If communities understand the competitive demands of the sector (and the broader economy), they may be able to construct interventions to better engage the industry and capture, or retain, more local benefits (e.g., the capacity of communities and regional businesses to procure benefits). Examples of interventions include establishing sector-specific training programs, building housing stock, and creating other amenities in order to attract and retain a more versatile and diverse workforce. New regionalism provides a framework for investigating the challenges associated with regional service delivery and infrastructure development in the context of a less interventionist state and weak regionalist institutions (Polèse, 1999; Jones, 2001; MacKinnon, 2002). Second, pursuing a regional competitiveness strategy may help communities withstand the booms and busts commonly associated with the mining industry (particularly given the industry's capacity to quickly halt or restart operations as price and demand dictate). Competitive-oriented investments create a broader foundation for community readiness and flexibility to respond to both opportunity and economic crisis.

Finally, new regionalist research highlights the opportunities and challenges associated with a variety of territorial governance models. Through these governance arrangements, local actors and institutions have a chance to play more important decision-making roles (see Bryant, Chapter 11 this volume). This local voice emerges as a response to senior government withdrawal and also to legitimate concerns for bottom-up representation and control (Polèse, 1999). These new governance arrangements are relevant to FIFO operations as they indicate a regional capacity to mediate and negotiate impacts, including economic benefit agreements, which tend to be isolated agreements with individual communities, and also broader cultural and environmental issues. Regional governance may bring scale and regional collaboration to engagement with FIFO sites. It may also represent an asset for making strategic, shared investments between communities in a rural hinterland setting.

Conclusion

FIFO operations represent both an enticing and frightening prospect for the next rural economy. They challenge the very existence of rural communities based on a foundation of resource commodity dependency, potentially severing the industry–community bond that created and sustained many rural communities in the postwar era. In the northwestern region of British Columbia, FIFO sites appear to provide a complex series of benefits and challenges for surrounding communities. Select service and labour needs are met locally, producing the regional spread effect envisioned by early FIFO planners. However, because of local capacity limitations and industry's tendency to rely on the capacity and diversity of distant cities and towns, many benefits are leaking from the region. In addition, the disruptive nature of the shift rotations clearly places pressure on regional social dynamics.

New regionalism is open to critique concerning the stability and strength of regional institutions, the tendency toward elitism in the gap left by senior governments, and the challenges of operating in a more flexible, collaborative (rather than regulatory) environment (Lovering, 1999). However, in this chapter I hope I have provided some insight into how a regionalist approach might alleviate some of the variability and uncertainty associated with the impact of FIFO operations on surrounding rural communities. Specifically, a regional approach may facilitate better negotiation and coordination of community benefits as part of a broader strategy to ensure place benefits from an industrial activity that is essentially place-less.

The intense variability of the FIFO experience in the literature speaks to the relative resurgence of the phenomenon as a model for industrial resource development. Initial research in British Columbia indicates that FIFO operations exist in something of a policy vacuum that mirrors the uncertainties associated with operational activities at the local scale—for all actors. While our specific knowledge of the operations, their impacts, and the potential linkages to rural regions remains unclear, FIFO is a growing trend—in the mining sector and in other resource-related industries. New regionalism provides an appropriate and flexible framework with which to address many of these research gaps, returning and reorienting our understanding of the importance of place in the next rural economy.

References

Barnes, T., and Gertler, M., (1999) Preface. In: Barnes, T. and Gertler, M. (eds.) *The New Industrial Geography: Regions, Regulation and Institutions*. Routledge, New York, xv – xx.

Barnes, T., and Hayter, R. (1997) *Troubles in the Rainforest: British Columbia's Forest Economy in Transition* (Canadian Western Geographical Series, vol. 33). Western Geographical Press, Victoria, BC.

Barnes, T., Hayter, R., and Hay, E. (2001) Stormy weather: Cyclones, Harold Innis, and Port Alberni, BC. *Environment and Planning A* 33, 2127–2147.

Bone, R. (2003) *The Geography of the Canadian North: Issues and Challenges.* Oxford University Press, New York.

Costa, S. (2004) *A Review of Long Distance Commuting: Implications for Northern Communities.* Canadian Institute of Mining, Edmonton, AB.

Davis, H., and Hutton, T. (1989) The two economies of British Columbia. *BC Studies* 82, 3–15.

Essex, S., Gilg, A., and Yarwood, R., Smithers, J., and Wilson, R., eds. (2005) *Rural Change and Sustainability: Agriculture, the Environment and Communities.* CABI Publishing, Wallingford, UK.

Gardner Pinfold. (2004) *Review of Community and Socioeconomic Implications of Potential Offshore Oil and Gas in the Queen Charlotte Basin.* University of Northern British Columbia, Prince George.

G.E. Bridges & Associates Inc. and Robinson Consulting & Associates. (2004) *Northwest BC Mining Projects: Socio Economic Impact Assessment.* Prepared for Economic Analysis Branch, BC Ministry of Small Business and Economic Development, Victoria, BC.

Government of British Columbia. (2005) Ministry of Energy and Mines. *British Columbia Mining Plan.* Author, Victoria, BC.

Halseth, G., and Sullivan, L. (2002) *Building Community in an Instant Town: A Social Geography of Mackenzie and Tumbler Ridge, British Columbia.* UNBC Press, Prince George.

Halseth, G., Straussfogel, D., Parsons, S., and Wishart, A. (2004) Regional economic shifts in BC: Speculation from recent demographic evidence. *Canadian Journal of Regional Science* 27, 317–352.

Hanlon, N., and Halseth, G. (2005) The greying of resource communities in northern British Columbia: Implications for health care delivery in already-underserviced communities. *Canadian Geographer* 49(1), 1–24.

Hayter, R. (2000) *Flexible Crossroads: The Restructuring of British Columbia's Forest Economy.* UBC Press, Vancouver.

Hobart, C. (1979) Commuting work in the Canadian north: Some effects on native people. In: *Proceedings: Conference on Air Commuting and Northern Development.* Institute of Northern Studies, University of Saskatchewan, Saskatoon, 1–38.

Horne, G., and Penner, B. (1992) *British Columbia Community Employment Dependencies.* Planning & Statistics Division and Ministry of Finance & Corporate Relations, Victoria, BC.

Hutton, T. (2002) *British Columbia at the Crossroads.* BC Progress Board, Vancouver.

Johnston, R., Gregory, D., and Smith, D. (1994) *The Dictionary of Human Geography.* Blackwell, Oxford.

Johnston, R., Gregory, D., Pratt, G., and Watts, M. (2000) *The Dictionary of Human Geography.* Blackwell, Oxford.

Jones, M. (2001) The rise of the region state in economic governance: "Partnerships for prosperity" or new scales of state power? *Environment and Planning A* 33(7), 1185–1211.

Kitson, M., Martin, R., and Tyler, P. (2004) Regional competitiveness: An elusive yet key concept? *Regional Studies,* 38(9), 991–999.

Kuyek, J., and Coumans, K. (2003) *No Rock Unturned: Revitalizing the Economies of Mining Dependent Communities.* MiningWatch Canada, Ottawa.

Little, B. (2002) B.C.'s decades of genteel decline. *Globe and Mail,* 20 April, B1, B4.

Lovering, J. (1999) Theory led by policy: The inadequacies of the "new regionalism." *International Journal of Urban and Regional Research* 23, 379–385.

MacKinnon, D. (2002) Rural governance and local involvement: Assessing state–community relations in the Scottish Highlands. *Journal of Rural Studies* 18, 307–324.

Markey, S. (2004) Local benefits from land use and resource extraction. In: Clogg, J., Hoberg, G., and O'Carroll, A. (eds.) *Policy and Institutional Analysis for Implementation of the Ecosystem-Based Management Framework.* Coast Information Team, Vancouver, 67–83.

Markey, S., Halseth, G., and Manson, D. (2006) The struggle to compete: From comparative to competitive advantage in northern British Columbia. *International Planning Studies* 11(1), 19–39.

McGrath, S. (1986) Tumbler Ridge: An assessment of the local government method of resource community development. *Impact Assessment Bulletin* 4(1–2), 211–236.

MiningWatch Canada and the Assembly of First Nations. (2002) *After the Mine: Healing Our Lands and Nations*. MiningWatch Canada, Ottawa.

Polèse, M. (1999) From regional development to local development: On the life, death, and rebirth(?) of regional science as a policy relevant science. *Canadian Journal of Regional Science* 22(3), 299–314.

PricewaterhouseCoopers. (2007) *Opportunity: The Mining Industry in British Columbia. 2006.* Author, Vancouver.

Ramsey, D., and Bryant. C., eds. (2004) *The Structure and Dynamics of Rural Territories: Geographical Perspectives*. Rural Development Institute, Brandon University, Brandon, MB.

Ritter, A. (2001) Canada: From fly-in, fly-out to mining metropolis. In: McMahon, G., and Remy, F. (eds.) *Large Mines and the Community: Socioeconomic and Environmental Effects in Latin America, Canada, and Spain*. International Development Research Centre, Ottawa, 223–260.

Scott, A. (2000) Economic geography: The great half-century. In: Clark, G., Feldman, P., and Gertler, M. (eds.) *The Oxford Handbook of Economic Geography*. Oxford University Press, Oxford, 18–44.

Shrimpton, M. (2005) *Are You Positive? Striking a Balance in Addressing Socio-economic Impacts*. Jacques Whitford, St. John's, NL.

Shrimpton, M., and Storey, K. (1992) Fly-in mining and the future of the Canadian north. In: Bray, M., and Thomson, A. (eds.) *At the End of the Shift: Mines and Single-Industry Towns in Northern Ontario*. Dundurn Press, Toronto, 187–208.

Simpson, S. (2008) Coalition wants power line project revived. *Vancouver Sun*, 17 April, C2.

Storey, K. (2001a) Fly-in/fly-out and fly-over: Mining and regional development in Western Australia. *Australian Geographer* 32(2), 133–148.

_____. (2001b) Commuter Mining: A Bibliography. Unpublished report prepared for the Department of Geography, Memorial University, St. John's, NL.

Storey, K., and Shrimpton, M. (1989) *Impacts on Labour of Long-Distance Commuting Employment in the Canadian Mining Industry*. Memorial University, St. John's, NL.

Terluin, I. (2003) Differences in economic development in rural regions of advanced countries: An overview and critical analysis of theories. *Journal of Rural Studies* 19, 327–344.

Turok, I. (2004) Cities, regions and competitiveness. *Regional Studies* 38(9), 1069–1083.

Williston, E., and Keller, B. (1997) *Forests, Power and Policy: The Legacy of Ray Williston*. Caitlin Press, Prince George.

Chapter 19

Understanding and Transforming a Staples-based Economy: Place-based Development in Northern British Columbia, Canada

Greg Halseth

The territory that is now British Columbia has a long history with trade. For millennia, long-distance trading relationships sustained First Nations people as they traded for products not available locally. The post-World War II expansion of industrial forestry into the interior and north of the province was similarly based on long-distance trading relationships to encourage social and economic well-being. Success in these trading relationships was founded on the identification of goods and materials desired by other trade partners. Capitalizing on identified comparative advantages required overcoming the challenge of distance, or space, in connecting commodity-producing regions with markets. At the beginning of the 21st century, the commodity-based resource economies of northern British Columbia are being buffeted by changing global trading relations and must find new and creative ways to adapt.

In this chapter, I explore the foundations of a staples-based resource economy in northern British Columbia and the challenges that post-1980 economic restructuring is posing. After outlining these background issues, I will examine some of the current opportunities within a global economic context in which the unique attributes of place are becoming more important both as economic inputs and as commodities themselves. The basic argument is that renewal of northern British Columbia's economic foundations requires a concerted and coordinated public policy, private investment, and community-driven approach. Older foundations built on a space-based economy need to be rebuilt, and new foundations that are designed to capitalize on place-based competitive advantages must be constructed.

Background

First Nations Trade Networks

Since time immemorial, First Nations living in what is now British Columbia have traded to support themselves and their quality of life. It is important to recognize that before European contact, this region was a fully occupied and organized economic and political landscape, home to numerous aboriginal language groups, which held traditional territories, formed economic and political alliances, and engaged in international trade and diplomatic relations.

The ecosystems of British Columbia are highly varied, and each First Nation developed social and economic systems intimately linked to the ecosystems of its traditional territories. One consequence of such rich ecosystems was that trade networks could make available a wide array of goods and products, and First Nations could obtain valuable commodities not otherwise available locally. Although important trading goods included a large number of items, three main types have been identified: ornamentation, high-status foods (for ceremonial or social purposes), and high-grade materials for items such as weapons and tools. Only goods that could survive long and sometimes rough transport were suited to early First Nations trade.

First Nations trade networks worked at both regional and continental scales. For example, a regional-scale trade network might have involved oolichan grease. The oolichan is a tiny smelt-like fish that spawns in coastal estuaries each spring and was a welcome source of fresh food at the end of winter. Grease rendered from the oolichan was prized for its caloric value and was traded widely across British Columbia. More robust materials could survive the longer distances of continental-scale trade networks. For example, chemical signatures have identified that volcanic glass from Mount Edziza in the far northwest corner of British Columbia found its way into what is now the southern United States and Central America.

Impact of the Fur Trade

The long and well-established trading tradition of the First Nations of northern British Columbia meant that the activities of early European fur traders could easily be incorporated into expanded trade networks and relationships. Bartering common local goods for more scarce and valued goods was common practice in both economic systems. Within a short period of time, European fur-trade houses dominated northern British Columbia's trading landscape, and instead of trading a wide range of goods for needed materials or foods, First Nations soon focused on trading furs for credits they could use at Hudson's Bay Company trading posts and storehouses. So important was this relationship that Hudson's Bay Company trading posts and storehouses remained the economic centres for a number of small communities in northern British Columbia even into the early 1950s.

Industrial Resource Development after 1950

At the start of the 1950s, British Columbia's economy was in difficult circumstances. Its resource-sector industries were relatively small and undercapitalized, and its industrial service and support sector was underdeveloped. In addition, there were few major roads across northern and interior British Columbia, and the economic fortune of the province fluctuated depending on global demands and prices for its limited range of commodity exports. In the lexicon of Canadian federalism, British Columbia was a "have-not" province that depended on transfer payments from the federal government to sustain its basic services. But the immediate postwar period was one of awakening industrial giants, and British Columbia held many of the key inputs for rapidly growing industrial regions. A postwar reconstruction committee set up by the provincial government recommended that British Columbia build a robust economy based on its role as a supplier of basic commodity resources to the world's manufacturing regions (Government of British Columbia, 1943).

The province could capitalize on its abundance of natural resources and the resulting comparative advantage as the model to take its long-standing staples-based economy into the industrial age (Marchak, 1983; Barnes and Hayter, 1994; Hayter and Barnes, 1997; Marchak *et al.* 1999).

The election of W.A.C. Bennett's Social Credit Party in 1952 provided the impetus for implementing this model of industrial resource development. Under W.A.C. Bennett's direction, the post-World War II period was characterized by clear policy goals aimed at "province building" (Williston and Keller, 1997). As was happening elsewhere in Canada (Himelfarb, 1977), British Columbia's resource endowment was considered to be a foundation for provincial prosperity.

During the first decade of its 22-year reign, the Bennett government orchestrated a complex and highly interconnected public policy agenda to support its goals. Those goals, which were built on an industrial-resource foundation, sought to achieve three outcomes: (1) bring stability and certainty to the provincial budget through resource royalties; (2) support the creation of a vibrant global trade, finance, and administrative centre in the metropolitan Vancouver–Victoria region; and (3) generate as much wealth and GDP as possible from British Columbia's "minimally processed" raw materials. The latter would be accomplished by requiring local processing to create economic opportunity in British Columbia's many rural and small-town communities. By way of illustration, Halseth *et al.* (forthcoming) describe the coordinated public policy changes needed to support a pulp-and-paper industry in the interior of British Columbia:

> The Province facilitated access to raw material by reorganizing timber supply areas on a massive scale and creating new tenures, such as the "pulpwood harvesting areas." This new production required transportation options to different markets, and so the government-owned BC Rail (then the Pacific Great Eastern Railway) line was completed north of Quesnel into the Peace River region, and the regional highways system was completed and upgraded to handle logging and product traffic. Pulp mills also required power, a need supported by the construction of hydroelectric power dams and reservoirs on the Columbia and Peace river systems. These hydroelectric facilities then needed extensive power transmission and distribution systems. Pulp mills also required large supplies of oil for their boiler operations, facilitated by rights allocations to the oil reserves in BC's Peace River region and the development of a distribution system of pipelines. Finally, worker retention in small places was supported by a complete reorganization by the Province of the school and health-care systems, as well as extensive public-sector investments in local quality-of-life services.

As a result of these changes in public policy, British Columbia was able to use a comparative-advantage approach to build economic wealth from its natural resources. This period of growth was, therefore, firmly rooted in the ascendancy of a "space-based" approach to rural and regional development. The fundamental principle of comparative advantage involves the ability of territories to "produce those goods or services for which they have the greatest cost or efficiency advantage over others, or for which they have the least disadvantage." (Johnston *et al.*, 2000, p. 102) This principle helps to explain patterns of regional specialization, such as mining, forestry, and fishing, that occurred across British Columbia's resource periphery. The province's abundant resources were marketed into the expanding industrial regions of the world, with special emphasis on exports to the United States.

The comparative-advantage approach was challenged only by the costs of transporting goods over long distances. To address these costs, as suggested by Johnston above, British Columbia's resource regions needed to be connected to markets and ports. Within the regions themselves, investments were needed to attract and retain the workforce to support the new resource industries. In recognition of the synergy between worker satisfaction and the economic success of industry, the planner for the province's prototypical "instant" town of Kitimat wrote in the opening to his townsite master plan:

> The purpose of Kitimat is the industrial success of the plant. That success will depend on the degree that workers are content, that they like living in Kitimat. Unless the town can attract and hold industrial workers, there will be continuous turnover and difficulty. … The workers must find Kitimat more than temporarily acceptable. They must be enthusiastic about it as a particularly fine place in which to live and bring up their families. It must become the place they want as homeland, the town they are going to make their own. (Stein, 1952, p. 3)

The success of W.A.C. Bennett's industrial resource policy was perhaps without compare in Canada. From approximately 1950 to 1980, the province enjoyed continuous economic success as the supplier of critical raw materials to the industrial nations of the world. New towns and new industries attracted young workers, and good and stable jobs prompted many to start families. Such regional development attracted services and other economic activity. For 30 years, every region across the province experienced growth (Halseth *et al.*, 2004).

Restructuring since 1980

Since 1980, however, the resource economy of rural and small-town British Columbia has been under pressure. The deep economic recession of the early 1980s focused new attention on British Columbia in the global economy. As described by Hayter and Barnes (1997), the early 1980s marked a fundamental shift for British Columbia's resource industries. The pace of change that spawned an era of restructuring within the global economy also led to significant transformations in British Columbia's resource industries.

There is, of course, considerable debate about the course and the effects of globalization. As noted above, there is some validity to the argument that British Columbia's resource economy has been immersed in wider trading alliances and networks for millennia. When academic debate turns to the more recent implications of global economic change, there is a wide range of opinions. For some, little has changed; for others, everything has changed. I will examine several threads from this debate, beginning first with Harvey (1990), who argues that the fundamentals of capitalism remain unchanged: There is still a need for profit and accumulation to drive the system. Harvey argues that what has changed is the speed of transactions, which have increased dramatically, and the treatment of information, images, and signs as commodities. Hayter and Barnes (1997) maintain that British Columbia's resource industries have adjusted the organization of production in response to their ongoing need for profit in the increasingly competitive commodity-trading markets. In this case, it is the transition from "Fordism" to "flexible production" that marks the organizational shift.

Following Harvey, what is new in the global economy? To start, we know that it is more connected and complex than in the past. This connectivity accelerates an already fast-paced system as actions in one part of the world have almost instantaneous effects on economies in other parts of the world. An implication of this connectivity and fast pace is that "change" is much more the norm than it was in the past. If we achieve a workable regional development solution today, we know that, starting tomorrow, we will have to begin developing the next new workable solution. For British Columbia's resource industries, we know that the economic booms come faster (e.g., the recent demand for metals driven by the appetite of the Chinese economy) and the busts will also come sooner and will go deeper (e.g., the present crisis in the dimension lumber sector of the BC forest industry). Finally, new industry is global in its organization and orientation. Not only will regions have to compete to get new economic activity, but they will also have to compete to get a share of the jobs and services that might in the past have been assumed to come with such activity.

This competition in a more open global marketplace underscores a shift in the relative value of comparative advantage and competitive advantage. In the past, British Columbia's resource abundance allowed a comparative-advantage approach to be successful. However, in today's more connected global economy there are many regions that have similar resources—and the resource endowments in some regions may even be superior (e.g., there may be faster-growing tress with the same properties as BC timber for structural lumber production)—while at the same time having lower wages, less stringent environmental and labour regulations, and lower tax regimes. The shift to competitive advantage means that new issues are central to regional and economic development. Instead of focusing simply on raw commodities, regions and places must consider their mix of values, commodities, and economies. In this competitive environment, attention to amenities and unique local assets are driving opportunity. Dawe (2004) demonstrates nicely this change from comparative to competitive advantage in her study of "place branding" in the Orkney Islands. To be successful in this transition, places and regions need to know which assets they value and how they may want to develop those assets; they need to be creative in understanding their assets and their aspirations.

For British Columbia, the recession in the early 1980s marked a fundamental shift in the Fordist compromise that linked industry and government with labour and, indirectly, with rural and northern communities. Layoffs and closures meant that the region began to lose population for the first time since World War II (Hutton, 2002; Hanlon and Halseth, 2005). Limited action by both industry and government means that, 28 years later, there has been little change in the relative vulnerability of rural and small-town economies across northern British Columbia.

Change within Resource Industries

The pressures of economic restructuring have generated considerable change within British Columbia's resource industries, notably in changing modes of production and increasing concentration of ownership. Hayter (2000) describes a range of pressures driving this restructuring, including environmental debates, consumer demands for more specialized products, continuing demands for low-cost products, increasing relative labour costs, and increasing competition from low-cost global competitors. In British Columbia, restructuring has accelerated as a result of an ongoing trade dispute with the United States over softwood lumber, ideological shifts in resource policies by successive provincial governments (Hayter, 2003), and the recent rise in value of the Canadian dollar relative to the US dollar. As a consequence, resource companies are aggressively implementing a more "flexible" style of production. This often involves operating larger plants with increased levels of technology and fewer employees so as to keep per-unit production costs low and production flexibility high (Hoekstra, 2004).

Reducing costs has been the watchword for resource industries threatened by low-cost production regions. In terms of processing efficiency, companies have made aggressive investments in "super mills"—continuing the older practice of substituting capital for labour. However, the rising costs of energy and the increased distances raw logs must travel to reach these super mills suggest that the drive to larger and larger economies of scale may have tipped into "diseconomies of scale."

Resource companies have taken other actions, such as introducing flexible labour contracts to reduce the number of employees, spinning off tasks previously performed by employees to independent contractors who are hired only when needed, and using the bidding process for contract jobs as another opportunity to reduce operating costs. A recent trend in the BC forest sector has been to focus on a company's "core business," which means getting rid of "non-core" production lines or subsidiary companies. While this might bring short-term benefits for investors, it clearly also introduces more risk to the long-term investor by narrowing companies' foundations and making them increasingly vulnerable to disruption of their single commodity sales into single markets. Concentration on core business is also a blow to decades of public policy efforts to encourage the forestry sector to diversify into value-added products.

Finally, international capital is able to invest globally, and companies active in British Columbia's forest economy are themselves investing in low-cost production regions. United States-based Weyerhaeuser has substantial investments in places like Bolivia, while Canadian-based companies like West Fraser Timber and Canfor have invested, respectively, in the southern United States and Indonesia. The story of Schefferville, Quebec, is instructive here. For years, the Iron Ore Company of Canada took the profits from its Canadian operations and invested them in new mines in South America, eventually closing its Schefferville operations, not because the ore had run out, but for the profit advantage of operating in a lower-cost production region (Bradbury and St. Martin, 1983).

Towns and communities that thrived under the high-employment regimes of resource industry production from the 1950s to the 1980s have experienced considerable change and uncertainty (Halseth and Sullivan, 2002). In many places, the outcome has been job losses, which are particularly difficult because the dominant benefit remaining in resource-producing regions is the wages paid to local workers. Public policy supports that created the industrial resource model have not yet responded with a new vision based on the value of place and the need for a competitive development approach.

Provincial Government's Dependence on Resource Revenues

The province's rich resource endowment has been the basis for intensive industrial development since 1950, with little industrial diversification beyond raw commodity processing. As argued by Halseth (2005), successive provincial governments, regardless of political orientation, have adjusted policy to allow large resource companies to remain competitive and export oriented. This has continued in spite of massive restructuring in resource industries since 1980 that has led to job losses and mill closures. Successive governments have used public policy to support industrial capital (and, to a degree, organized labour) in order to maintain provincial tax revenue. The province's dependence on resource revenues cannot be overstated. For example, the current government is perpetuating the provincial reliance on "resource revenues at all costs" (Government of

British Columbia, 2003, 2004) with policies that loosen government regulations and allow larger firms enhanced freedom and the potential for greater profitability. The government also allowed expanded raw log exports in order to maintain provincial revenues during the softwood lumber dispute with the United States. Finally, the government's willingness to allow exploration for coalbed methane in the northeast corner of the province and its push to lift a moratorium on oil and gas development on the northwest coast are driven by the need to replace proportionally dwindling tax revenues from fishing and forestry as the provincial population continues to grow.

Approaching British Columbia's Next Rural Economy

Having examined these foundations of the provincial economy, I will now explore aspects of the next rural economy across northern British Columbia. This exploration builds on the notions of being more competitive in the global economy and of recognizing the ascendancy of "place" as a focal point for understanding our assets and opportunities. These first two points underscore a third, which is the need to renew a vision for participating in the global economy. I conclude the chapter with a look at the need to compete for both opportunity and talent.

Competing in the Global Economy

The concept of competitive advantage remains both pliable and poorly understood (Turok, 2004). Kitson *et al.* (2004, p. 992) define territorial competitiveness "as the success with which regions and cities compete with one another in some way—over market share or capital and workers." Malecki (2004) adds that regional competitiveness is multi dimensional, mixing traditional factors of infrastructure with more ethereal factors like amenities and social capital.

Older approaches to regional competitiveness tended to focus on simplistic booster techniques such as tax incentives, grants, and similar supports to attract investment and development. These approaches have not disappeared, and incidents of communities undercutting one another, offering greater enticements for fewer benefits to the community, may have increased as the impacts of restructuring make all places more vulnerable to the mobility of capital and workers. However, newer conceptualizations of regional competitiveness focus on processes of learning, innovation, and positive place attraction (Malecki, 2004), and the new regionalism literature has identified a number of variables associated with this updated understanding of competitiveness (Cook *et al.*, 2005; Iyer *et al.*, 2005; MacKinnon *et al.*, 2002; Amin, 1999; Scott, 1998; Storper, 1997). Kresl (1995) and MacLeod (2001) identify traditional factors like infrastructure, production, location, economic structure, and amenities, as well as more qualitative competitive variables, including social capital, innovation, and institutions. Just as the public-sector investments of the 1950s put in place the factors needed to support a comparative-advantage economy, so too will public policy have a role to play in equipping rural and small-town places to compete in the new economy.

"Place" in the Global Economy

In the previous section, I argue that places need to develop a different set of assets in order to succeed in an economy based on competitive advantage. In order to develop our place-based assets, we need to understand the changing relationship between space and place in the new global economy. In his analysis of the changing nature and forms of capitalism, Harvey (1990) argues that as the cost of moving goods and information decreases, the issue of space becomes less important. If, as a result, capital is increasingly free to locate "anywhere," then it is the small differences between places that will emerge as increasingly important. For rural and small-town places in northern British Columbia, the question becomes: If capital can locate anywhere, why would it locate in your community? How can northern British Columbia become equipped to exercise place-based advantages and meet development opportunities or challenges on its own terms?

Renewing our Vision

In an attempt to answer these questions, the Community Development Institute at the University of Northern British Columbia undertook an extensive consultation with communities and economic interests across northern British Columbia. The purpose of the research project was to explore options and opinions respecting a Northern BC Economic Vision and Strategy (www.unbc.ca/cdi).

As reported in Halseth *et al.* (2007), the economic transition in northern British Columbia was understood as involving a process of moving "from northern strength to northern strength." Those individuals consulted were adamant that economic development not only had to focus on creating jobs for northerners, but also had to be done in ways that respected the people, the environment, and the quality of life that defines a northern lifestyle. This view captures important aspects of a place-based approach. If the place is to bear the costs of development, it must also receive more of the benefits than was the case in the past. More of the wealth generated in northern British Columbia needs to stay in the region rather than going to "Victoria" (the provincial capital) to be recirculated to northern communities later through provincial government programs. A central and enduring notion of place is replacing a more transitory notion of space that characterized earlier approaches to resource development.

This expanded notion of place is also an inclusive one. When asked about the criteria that should be used to evaluate development proposals, people in northern British Columbia clearly identified four "bottom lines." These included the three recognized in common discourse—community, economy, and environment—to which northern British Columbians added the notion of culture. This addition is an explicit recognition of the First Nations and settler cultures that have collectively come to make northern British Columbia their homes. A vision for the future of northern places is one that includes all northern peoples. This means that, beyond the important questions of treaty settlement (the first priority in the Northern BC Economic Vision and Strategy), and a "new relationship" with BC First Nations, the entire provincial government approach to development needs to change. The days when northern communities and northern people were "consulted" in time-limited processes, mandated by law, that allowed them no substantive input to the approval process or outcome must give way to new approaches that take the form of local economic and policy partnerships.

To achieve success under these parameters requires a more complete understanding of local assets and their values in today's global economy. When viewed through the lens of a place-based approach, the natural *and* community resources of northern British Columbia are of high value. The value of natural resources has long been understood, but it is only now that people are beginning to recognize that a rural and small-town lifestyle is itself a valuable and saleable commodity. Using these high-value resources means that economic transition involves moving from resource dependence to a diversified economy that is grounded in resources but also includes manufacturing and other options. To achieve this end, we need to re-bundle our competitive assets in new and innovative ways. This will be a challenge as many assets and economic interests remain aligned with the old comparative-advantage economies. For example, provincial government demands for immediate resource revenues are now met through the sale of various forms of "lease" or "tenure" rights—an approach that will restrict the creative search for alternative and viable economic options and leave British Columbia stuck in an outdated comparative-advantage economy.

The process of moving from a comparative- to a competitive-advantage economy will require a set of strategic investments. The first of these should target the physical infrastructure of northern British Columbia and will include renovating and upgrading remnants of the older economy such as roads, rail lines, airports, and the power grid. It is difficult to compete in the 21st-century economy with an infrastructure base designed and built for the mid-20th century. Investment must also target the necessary infrastructure of the new economy, including Internet, courier, and container services of the "just-in-time" economy. In simple terms, "communications" is the tool for success in the global economy, and the lack of private-sector action to provide these services across northern British Columbia identifies them as a key area for public policy and investment.

There needs to be a concerted effort to address human capacity building. The recent economic boom in northern British Columbia highlighted the lack of skilled tradespeople available in the province, and there was a scramble to update training efforts/options to produce the needed workers. This skills gap is appearing across the economy as sector after sector finds itself short of trained workers. Even in those sectors that have a workforce presently in place, the nature of the work is changing to such a degree that workers need wholesale retraining to remain competitive. For example, what will our next forest economy look like, and what must we do now to equip its workforce with the skills and training needed to succeed?

The community capacity of northern British Columbia needs attention, particularly the voluntary sector and those facets of the community that support a superior quality of life. The long history of service cuts across northern British Columbia must be reversed. Instead of supporting the budget-cutting goals of centralized bureaucracies, we must apply technology creatively and break down administrative "silos" in order to deliver more effective and coordinated packages of services that sustain people in northern British Columbia's communities. Only with these tools will northern communities be able to compete for economic activity and people.

The economic and business infrastructure of northern places also needs assistance. When the region depended on large resource industries, many jobs were readily available. In a place-based economy, however, it is likely that small and medium-sized businesses will be the norm, and the owners, managers, and staff of these businesses will require training and assistance if they are to run them successfully.

During the 1950s and 1960s, government support for infrastructure (both physical and economic), capacity building, and services was seen as an investment for the future. Indeed, those investments have continued to pay dividends to the province ever since.

Unfortunately, in today's political climate, such actions are more likely to be seen as expenses, and lamentably costly ones. Only if this kind of thinking changes will the supports for a place-based economy be realized.

Finally, to be competitive in the global economy one needs to have a modicum of scale. For rural and small-town places this means it is imperative they work collectively as regions. Failure to do so will mean that every aspect of economic activity will be more difficult, whether it is advocating for suitable policy or having an impact on the marketplace. Scaling up in the global economy also entails establishing strategic alliances and knowledge relationships, which might involve access to technical knowledge, to shipping or trading networks and expertise, to marketing and market research, as well as to product development and innovations research.

Competing for Opportunity and Talent

To be competitive in the global economy not only involves the broad foundational supports noted above but also means competing for the talent that will be needed to ensure opportunities can be taken. This competition for talent first received attention in Florida's (2002) work on the "creative class," which identified a new type of economic driver in urban economies (similar in ways to Harvey's argument that images and signs are themselves commodities). To take advantage of these new types of economic opportunity, places had to attract workers for the creative economy. Achieving the right mix of educated workers and new economic drivers emerged as one of the keys to successful engagement in the knowledge-based global economy. The rural and regional development research literature has identified how this same process applies to non-metropolitan places as well.

If this is the case, then rural and small-town places need to "get into the game" of attracting and retaining talent. To do this, rural communities need to know something about this new workforce. For one thing, they will be able to exercise considerable bargaining power. Because they will be a relatively small workforce, they will be in demand. As a result, they will be able to go where they want, demand what they want. These demands will include matters beyond salary rates—they are certain that there will be a good salary, but they are looking for quality of life. This includes living in a clean environment, having access to a reasonable level of services, having a safe and healthy place in which to raise a family, achieving a balance in their work/life relationships, and enjoying a strong sense of community while still maintaining global connectivity. In many debates, these types of attributes are the very definition of rural and small-town places. Attention to these place-based characteristics can ground new economic initiatives.

The transition to the new global economy will involve mobilizing place-based competitive assets. The recruitment and retention of a creative-economy workforce requires the same actions. As a result, rural and small-town places are well positioned in this transformation. Place-based competitive assets include social networks and lifestyles that foster commitment to place, ready access to a diversity of resource wealth, possession of high-value natural and environmental amenities, relatively untapped local economies, embedded regional connectivity, and an affordable cost of living for households and enterprises relative to metropolitan regions.

Closing

The contemporary economy of northern British Columbia was built on a long history of trading relationships. The rapid postwar expansion of industrial forestry across the northern regions of the province married the notion of comparative advantage in natural resources with opportunities for long-distance trading relationships to build social and economic well-being. As noted, however, British Columbia's commodity-based resource industries are being buffeted by changing global trading relations such that a new vision and set of associated investments will be needed to re-create the foundations of success. In this chapter, I have explored how the foundations of a staples-based resource economy were established in northern British Columbia and how the post-1980 period of economic restructuring is posing significant challenges. I outlined how some of the current opportunities embedded within a global economy speak to the attributes of place as new forms of inputs but also as commodities unto themselves. To mobilize place-based attributes, however, will require concerted and coordinated public policies, private investments, and community leadership. The older space-based economy needs to be renovated and made more flexible in order to capitalize on place-based competitive advantages.

References

Amin, A. (1999) An institutionalist perspective on regional economic development. *International Journal of Urban and Regional Research* 23(2), 365–378.

Barnes, T., and Hayter, R. (1994) Economic restructuring, local development and resource towns: Forest communities in coastal British Columbia. *Canadian Journal of Regional Science* 17(3), 289–310.

Bradbury, J., and St-Martin, I. (1983) Winding down in a Quebec mining town: A case study of Schefferville. *Canadian Geographer* 27, 128–144.

Cook, P., Clifton, N., and Oleaga, M. (2005) Social capital, firm embeddedness and regional development. *Regional Studies* 39(8), 1065–1077.

Dawe, S. (2004) Placing trust and trusting place: Creating competitive advantage in peripheral rural areas. In: Halseth, G., and Halseth, R. (eds.) *Building for Success: Exploration of Rural Community and Rural Development*. Rural Development Institute, Brandon University, Brandon, MB, 223–250.

Florida, R. (2002) *The Rise of the Creative Class and How It's Transforming Work, Leisure, Community and Everyday Life*. Basic Books, New York.

Government of British Columbia. (1943) *Interim Report of the Post-war Rehabilitation Council*. Author, Victoria, BC.

_____. (2003) *The B.C. Heartlands Economic Strategy—A Plan to Revitalize Our Entire Province*. Queen's Printer, Victoria, BC.

_____. (2004) *Rebuilding the Heartlands—What we've accomplished together*. Queen's Printer, Victoria, BC.

Halseth, G. (2005) Resource town transition: Debates after closure. In: Essex, S., Gilg, A., Yarwood, R., Smithers, J., and Wilson, R. (eds.) *Rural Change and Sustainability: Agriculture, the Environment and Communities*. CABI Publishing, Wallingford, UK, 326–342.

Halseth, G., and Sullivan, L. (2002) *Building Community in an Instant Town: A Social Geography of Mackenzie and Tumbler Ridge, British Columbia*. UNBC Press, Prince George.

Halseth, G., Straussfogel, D., Parsons, S., and Wishart, A. (2004) Regional economic shifts in BC: Speculation from recent demographic evidence. *Canadian Journal of Regional Science* 27, 317–352.

Halseth, G., Manson, D., Markey, S., Lax, L., and Buttar, O. (2007) The connected north: Findings from the northern BC economic vision and strategy project. *Journal of Rural and Community Development* 2(1), 1–27.

Halseth, G., Markey, S., and Manson, D. (Forthcoming) *Renewal: The Next Rural Economy in Northern BC*. UBC Press, Vancouver.

Hanlon, N., and Halseth, G. (2005) The greying of resource communities in northern BC: Implications for health care delivery in already under-serviced communities. *Canadian Geographer* 49(1), 1–24.

Harvey, D. (1990) *The Condition of Postmodernity: An Enquiry into the Origins of Cultural Change*. Blackwell, Oxford.

Hayter, R. (2000) *Flexible Crossroads: The Restructuring of British Columbia's Forest Economy*. UBC Press, Vancouver.

_____. (2003) "The war in the woods": Post-Fordist restructuring, globalization, and the contested remapping of British Columbia's forest economy. *Annals of the Association of American Geographers* 93(3), 706–729.

Hayter, R., and Barnes, T. (1997) The restructuring of British Columbia's coastal forest sector: Flexibility perspectives. In: Barnes, T., and Hayter, R. (eds.) *Trouble in the Rainforest: British Columbia's Forest Economy in Transition* (Canadian Western Geographical Series, vol. 33). Western Geographical Press, Victoria, BC, 181–203.

Himelfarb, A. (1977) *The Social Characteristics of One-Industry Towns in Canada: A Background Report* (Royal Commission on Corporate Concentration, Study No. 30). Queen's Printer, Ottawa.

Hoekstra, G. (2004) World's largest sawmill opens. *Prince George Citizen*, 10 February, 1.

Hutton, T. (2002) *British Columbia at the Crossroads*. BC Progress Board, Vancouver.

Iyer, S., Kitson, M., and Toh, B. (2005) Social capital, economic growth and regional development. *Regional Studies* 39(8), 1015–1040.

Johnston, R., Gregory, D., Pratt, G., and Watts, M. (2000) *The Dictionary of Human Geography*, 4th ed. Blackwell, Oxford.

Kitson, M., Martin, R., and Tyler, P. (2004) Regional competitiveness: An elusive yet key concept. *Regional Studies* 38(9), 991–999.

Kresl, P. (1995) The determinants of urban competitiveness: A survey. In: Gappert, G., and Kresl, P. (eds.) *North American Cities and the Global Economy*. Sage, Thousand Oaks, CA, 45–68.

MacKinnon, D., Cumbers, A., and Chapman, K. (2002) Learning, innovation and regional development: A critical appraisal of recent debates. *Progress in Human Geography* 26, 293–311.

MacLeod, G. (2001) Beyond soft institutionalism: Accumulation, regulation, and their geographical fixes. *Environment and Planning A* 33(7), 1145–1167.

Malecki, E. (2004) Jockeying for position: What it means and why it matters to regional development policy when places compete. *Regional Studies* 38(9), 1101–1120.

Marchak, P. (1983) *Green Gold: The Forest Industry in British Columbia*. UBC Press, Vancouver.

Marchak, P., Aycock, S., and Herbert, D. (1999) *Falldown: Forest Policy in British Columbia*. David Suzuki Foundation and Ecotrust Canada, Vancouver.

Scott, A. (1998) *Regions and the World Economy*. Oxford University Press, Oxford.

Stein, C. (1952) Planning objectives. Reprinted in *Kitimat Townsite 1962 Report*. District of Kitimat, Kitimat, BC.

Storper, M. (1997) *The Regional World: Territorial Development in a Global Economy*. Guilford, New York.

Turok, I. (2004) Cities, regions and competitiveness. *Regional Studies* 38(9), 1069–1083.

Williston, E., and Keller, B. (1997) *Forests, Power and Policy: The Legacy of Ray Williston*. Caitlin Press, Prince George.

Chapter 20

Space to Place: Bridging the Gap

Bill Reimer

The title of our original workshop "From Space to Place – the next rural economies" not only identifies the characters in our story (space, place, and the future), but it gives away the plot as well. It indicates that we are giving precedence to "place" over "space" in our analysis of rural futures. The value of the story, therefore, is in the details—particularly the elaboration of the characters and their significance for the cases considered.

The value is also in the insights the story offers for policy and action at all levels: local, regional, national, and international. What can we learn from this research that will help us make more appropriate plans for the future and identify the actions which are most likely to produce the outcomes desired? These are demanding questions, especially given the complexity and changeability of current economic and social conditions, but they must be continually asked and answered, since inaction is an answer in itself.

In this chapter I will attempt to answer these questions by focusing on the implications of a place-based approach for analysis, policy development, strategic action, and research. Drawing upon the discussions and insights of the other chapters, I will outline a framework for thinking about possible futures for rural areas, then use it to consider how policy makers and rural citizens might position themselves for these futures—starting from the places in which they live. Finally, I will identify several research directions that are suggested by the analysis and the rich descriptive and analytical material found throughout this book.

A Framework for Community Change

We find it useful to think about community change processes and choices using a systems perspective that focuses on places, communities, regions, or networks as somewhat integrated systems. This is particularly attractive because it provides a way to integrate space- and place-based perspectives, highlight the ways in which choices are made, and appropriately represent the complex ways in which all elements of the system interact. Outcomes of the choices are themselves part of the ongoing process of system adaptation and change (Fig. 20.1). This framework can also be used for the analysis of multiple levels since individual, regional, or national levels can be substituted for communities in the figure.

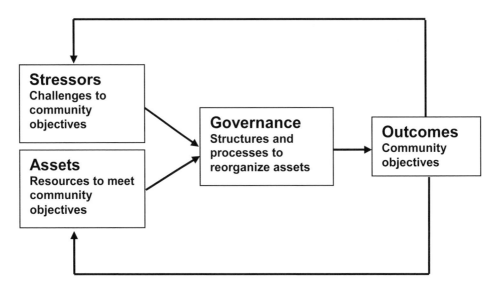

Fig. 20.1 Community and regional systems (adapted from Alasia *et al.*, 2008).

Using this framework, outcomes are considered to be the result of three sets of factors. The first set includes the stressors that affect the place, region, or other unit of analysis. These stressors can be a wide range of things, both "good" and "bad," but they are generally the many events, crises, and trends that affect the fate of communities or regions. In the literature, they are often discussed from a space-based point of view, which emphasizes the general over the specific. In line with the objectives for this book, we will focus on the trends that are likely to significantly affect rural places into the future.

The second set of factors refers to the assets of the community, region, network, or system being considered. These can be the natural resources, amenities, and/or the financial, human, and social characteristics of the region or community—the things that can be mobilized to deal with the stressors. The difference between a stressor and an asset is not hard and fast. Stressors can become assets and vice versa. But as we shall see, we prefer to treat them as separate at this point and conceptualize this interdependence as part of the overall dynamic of the system. The location-specific nature and structure of assets mean that they are usually discussed in the context of place-based orientations.

The third set of factors affecting the outcomes is the governance arrangements and actions that facilitate the reorganization and mobilization of assets in new ways to meet the challenges of the stressors—with any luck producing the anticipated outcomes for the community. These factors are addressed by most of the chapters in this book, either in terms of the limitations of current governance arrangements (see Cawley, Harrington, Markey, Ramsey, Woods) or in terms of the innovations that have emerged in response to local challenges (see Bryant, Che, Loudiyi, Vodden).

This framework is relevant for analysing a wide variety of outcomes—economic, social, political, and cultural. Our focus on rural communities and regions means that our primary concern is with outcomes of relevance to these places, but the framework can be used to consider outcomes at many other levels as well, from individual to national.

Since this is a dynamic system, outcomes can become stressors or assets in the future, either directly or indirectly. For example, reorganizing the Miramichi economy in New

Brunswick as an animation cluster produced new entrepreneurial outcomes, but these in turn created demands for services to facilitate the integration of new employees (Bruce, Chapter 10 this volume). Initiatives to encourage greater use of the countryside in the United Kingdom have often been successful, but they have, in turn, exacerbated stressful relations with local proprietors over land rights (Storey, Chapter 12 this volume). In general, the organization of the Canadian and Australian economies for a global staples market has been successful for national balances of trade but has created new stresses on populations, local services, and the natural resources themselves (Argent *et al.*, Halseth, Ramsey, Chapters 2, 19, 9 this volume).

The framework described here directs our attention to the following types of questions:

- What are the key stressors that rural places are likely to face in the near and distant future?
- What are the assets they can use to position themselves for those futures?
- How can rural places and people best organize themselves for the future?

Using the insights and examples from this book we will illustrate some of the answers that might be considered—to aid researchers, community activists, and policy makers as they face the challenges of their specific places.

Key Stressors and Assets

Our first question asks us to identify the key stressors that are likely to affect rural communities in the future. As discussed above, these stressors will be formulated in terms that are general and broad, with the analysis of future possibilities rooted in space-focused research. Urbanization, for example, is a stressor that appears explicitly or implicitly in all the chapters. It is assumed to affect all rural areas and is likely to continue into the future. In Canada, it has been a basic feature of society since the 1940s, and there are few signs that it will diminish.

Representations of urbanization have usually been articulated and developed within a discourse regarding the diminishing importance of rural areas in Canada and the sad tale of rural out-migration. This discourse is supported by general statistics confirming the rapid growth of urban centres in comparison to rural areas—a consistent, space-based form of analysis. By taking a place-based perspective, we can understand urbanization in a different way—one that highlights the dynamics of the framework we identified above.

From the perspective of place, urbanization is much more than just a negative stressor for rural places, especially if we see how the general trend (urbanization) manifests as different types of stressors in different types of places. Urbanization does not always mean rural decline, as demonstrated in the Canadian context by those rural areas in strong Metropolitan Influenced Zones (MIZ) and some of the boom towns in more remote locations (Fig. 20.2). This means that urbanization-related stressors affecting growing places will be substantially different from those in areas that are declining or showing little growth. For growing rural areas, this is a story of in-migration, housing pressure, service pressure, and conflicting values about the relative importance of economic growth, the environment, and lifestyle, to name only a few issues (see Argent *et al.*, Bryant, Aragau and Charvet, Gayler, Loudiyi, Chapters 2, 11, 14, 6, 15). For low- or no-growth areas, the stressors take the form of falling incomes, a decreasing pool of volunteers, and often an aging population (see Argent *et al.*, Bruce, Cawley, Harrington, Markey, Walford, Chapters 2, 10, 7, 3, 18, 5).

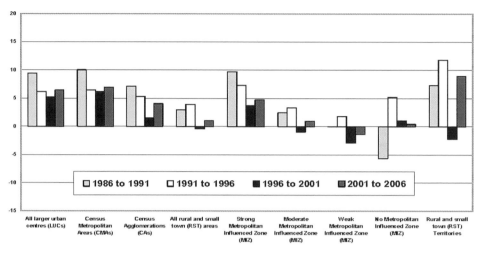

Larger urban centres (LUCs)   **Rural and small town (RST) areas**

Fig. 20.2 Percentage change in total population by Metropolitan Influenced Zones and time periods (Bollman and Clemenson, 2008).[1]

In both cases, the assets and opportunities are different. Growth areas have access to markets, services, enterprises, and governance structures that are largely missing from low- or no-growth areas. If we are working from a place-based point of view, we should resist the typical desire to periodically redefine areas as rural or urban based on density or commuting flows and instead follow a fixed set of boundaries over time. If we take the 1991 Canadian census subdivision (CSD) as our identification of place, for example, and then view the process of urbanization from the perspective of someone in one of those rural places, we see the type of differentiation outlined above. From this perspective, 2,439 (43%) rural CSDs across Canada faced the stress of population growth over the period 1991 to 2001; about 3,271 (57%) faced steady or declining populations during the same time. Of course, many of them have lost their rural status in the process, according to Statistics Canada, but this is only indirectly relevant to us from a place-based point of view.

From that perspective—as Lovering (1999) implies—we see a very different set of rural stressors, assets, and opportunities. Metro-adjacent rural areas make a significant contribution to urban places through the supply of land, amenities, and lifestyle options. The massive suburban growth, which we point to as evidence of rural decline, now becomes a sign of the growth and significance of rural places. The challenge for rural-growth places is to manage that growth and ensure it does not result in the loss of the assets they contain—open spaces, relatively cheap land, natural amenities, and access to services (which are some of the reasons why people are moving there in the first place).

Several chapters provide examples of places where managed rural growth is occurring (Gayler in the rural countryside outside Toronto, Canada; Loudiyi in France; Markey in northern Canada; Walford in Wales), and we all know of additional examples where existing social and physical infrastructure are used to sustain a walking and cycling neighbourhood, green spaces are maintained, low-density housing is provided in an environmentally and financially sustainable fashion, public transportation offers quick and cheap access to high-density areas, and commercial developments are established without billboards and neon signs. Growing places need to anticipate these stressors, consider the outcomes they want, and mobilize the necessary resources to ensure those outcomes—a governance issue to which we will return.

On the other hand, many rural communities and regions show little or negative growth in the face of urbanization. This usually occurs where distance or lack of transportation infrastructure block access to a sizeable centre of growth. Several chapters are clearly about these more isolated areas (Argent *et al.* in rural Australia; Bruce in Miramichi, New Brunswick; Cawley in several lagging regions in Ireland; Che in Michigan's fruit belt; Halseth in northern British Columbia; Harrington in the High Plains of the United States; Markey in fly-in/fly-out locations across northern Canada; Ouchi in Japan; and Vodden in rural Newfoundland). In these places, urbanization is most often seen as a liability that draws out populations, services, and capital. There often appears to be little that can or should be done in the face of these general stressors.

Taking a place-based approach, however, reveals options that are often overlooked. From this perspective, each place becomes unique in its history, assets, liabilities, and organization. Just as the constellation of general processes and trends has converged to contribute to this uniqueness, so may the place reorganize those assets in ways that modify the usual impacts of the general trends. Several chapters in this book highlight such examples (see Argent *et al.*, Loudiyi, Ouchi, Ramsey, Vodden), just as other examples can be found in the research literature (Halseth and Sullivan, 2002; Pierce and Dale, 1999; Rogers and Jones, 2006). By doing so, the authors and researchers challenge policy options that rely on space-based analysis alone.

As with urbanization, most of the other stressors affecting rural communities can be reconsidered in the light of a place-based approach. Since these stressors are likely to continue into the future—at least in Canada, if not in most countries in the world—they serve as a background for the consideration of future options for both rural and urban regions. The following are some of the most important stressors:

- The substitution of machines for labour is likely to continue as the value of human time increases relative to the value of technology (Bollman, 2007). As industries become more productive and price-competitive, they will require fewer workers, so turning to commodity production alone is likely to undermine population growth.
- The economy will continue to be global. This means that both competitors and markets are worldwide. It also means that our economies will continue to be highly dependent on transportation of goods and people, so they will be vulnerable to the price of energy and significant changes in our transportation technology.
- Knowledge will continue to be critical. This includes knowledge of global markets, knowledge about using the new technologies, and generally learning how to understand and anticipate the future. As we learn more about the interdependencies of our economies, societies, and environment, and as we struggle to understand the complexity, the importance of knowledge will grow.
- The environment, climate, and sustainability will increase in importance. Rural areas are particularly vulnerable to the effects of climate change because of their heavy reliance on natural resources and the weather. Urban areas will feel those effects because of their dependence on rural areas.

- Immigration will continue to be a necessity for Canada into the future, as it has been in the past. Since we are no longer reproducing ourselves, we will depend on newcomers for much of our labour and innovation. Rural areas will be particularly affected as their traditional cultural homogeneity is challenged to integrate different customs and perspectives.

The challenge for rural places is to find or create the assets that will help them deal with these stressors and their varied manifestations at the local level. In some cases this means making use of assets that were overlooked in the past, in some cases it means redefining the traditional assets in new ways, and in other cases it means creating the necessary assets through innovation and imagination. All cases involve considerable effort with respect to the third element of our framework: governance processes at multiple levels.

Governance

The issue of governance directly relates to our third question: How can rural places and people best organize themselves for the future? Several chapters in this book provide suggestions and examples in response to this question. Argent *et al.* and Vodden, for example, point out how focusing on the reorganization of local assets in innovative ways may be a more useful approach than trying to create new assets. Bruce explores how we might reorganize governance into regional clusters so we can redefine neighbouring communities as local assets for development rather than competitors and liabilities. Cawley reminds us that such reorganization should take place across sectors to maximize coordination and innovation opportunities. Bryant, Loudiyi, Markey, Ouchi, and Walford each provide additional examples of the ways in which this reorganization might take place.

But we are also warned that this regional approach is fraught with challenges. Storey shows us how relying on regional and local partnerships can produce new forms of social exclusion—either as a reflection of the partners' commitments or as a result of local capacities. Gayler illustrates how the changing power relations inherent in regional reorganization may threaten traditional alliances and undermine the collaboration necessary to make regional management work. Ramsey points out how the local, regional, and sectoral histories of places can significantly modify efforts to diversify for greater sustainability, and Harrington highlights the importance of environmental conditions that can challenge regional vulnerability.

Example: Governing across Communities

Details of the challenges presented by regional approaches in the Canadian context can be found in a comparison of Alberta and Quebec. The governments of both provinces champion a bottom-up approach and encourage local municipalities to engage in an expanded mandate over local decision making—moving beyond the maintenance of roads and water to include economic development and environmental stewardship. However, the institutional contexts of these two provinces are considerably different, reinforcing Loudiyi's point about the importance of institutions for defining "place."

During the early 1990s, Quebec established 86 *municipalités régionales de comté* (MRCs or regional county municipalities) and 18 *territoires équivalents à une MRC* (TEs or "territories equivalent to an MRC"). These boards provide county-level and some city-level venues where municipal officials can meet to debate and decide issues including social programs, territorial planning, economic development, and employment assistance. The emphasis is typically on regional development—across sectors and inclusive of social development. The MRCs and TEs are in turn grouped into 17 administrative regions responsible for the distribution of development funding and intra-level collaboration.

In Alberta, the approach was more laissez-faire in nature. As a result of several provincial initiatives, in 2000 the government established a mechanism by which municipalities could come together in regional economic development alliances (REDA). At present there are 14 REDAs throughout the province, in which over 250 communities are involved. These organizations are self-selected alliances of governments, businesses, and local institutions with the primary objective of economic development. The provincial government plays a supportive role, providing advice and financing based on proposals and business plans.

The results have been dramatically different at the local level. In Quebec there are many examples of regional initiatives tailored to local conditions that in turn provide a basis for second-order activities in small places. The initiatives are frequently broad-based—including economic, social, health, environmental, and cultural elements in independent or coordinated activities. Over the 20 or so years of their operation within this new regime, local municipalities have learned how to use the regional structures to voice their concerns, debate, negotiate, compromise, and collaborate with other municipalities. As well, they have learned to negotiate with the provincial government on behalf of their region and village or town.

In turn, the provincial government has discovered the value in subsidiarity. It now allocates responsibility to the regional boards for a wide range of economic and social policy and programs, and (most importantly) it shows its confidence in the decisions and accountability of the MRCs. This makes the governance of the province more efficient and more effective. This system of consultation has become even more elaborate with the recent emergence of regional roundtables, which are adapted to more issue-focused and regional-specific objectives.

In Alberta, the situation is different. The 14 REDAs involve about 75% of the province's municipalities. Many of them have ongoing projects, primarily focusing on growth, retaining businesses, marketing, identifying opportunities, and attracting investment (Government of Alberta, 2009a). Even the discussion of community development has a distinct focus on economic issues over social or environmental concerns (Government of Alberta, 2009b). Many municipalities, on the other hand, were unable to move beyond their protectionist traditions and reach agreements with their neighbours concerning the complex challenges they faced. They either denied that conflicts of interest existed or refused to discuss them in any but the most limited terms. In the end, the provincial government simply made decisions for these municipalities, pointing to the failure of regional collaboration, lack of accountability, and the pressure of time as a justification for top-down management.

Two lessons emerge from this comparison. First, the rhetoric of subsidiarity and collaboration must be critically assessed in terms of the results. Both provinces have remarkably similar articulations of their regional policy, but the implementation of those principles is very different. Second, a policy of bottom-up development can only work within a more general institutional context that supports it. Quebec established the regional boards with a broad mandate and sufficient resources to make them successful. Alberta created the opportunity for regional alliances to form, but granted them a relatively narrow focus and resources with conditions that matched that narrow focus.

It took Quebec's municipal representatives more than 20 years to learn how to use the MRCs—a period that was marked by conflict, mistrust, and failures. However, now we find that the MRCs and the regional roundtables offer critical assets for the municipalities, regions, and province. They provide venues in which the municipalities can express and negotiate their interests. These venues function well since the province has taken care to ensure that representatives of even the smallest places in the process are included, with little additional demand on local finances. For the regions, the MRCs and roundtables provide a forum where conflicts can be expressed, common interests identified, and collective action taken. Since the provincial government has come to respect those decisions and trust the accountability of the regional organizations, the MRCs and roundtables have also established a record of successfully acquiring the additional resources needed to implement their decisions. For the province, the MRCs and roundtables have taken on a considerable burden that formerly fell on the provincial government. Decisions emerging from the MRCs have proven to reflect the views of regional constituents in a reasonable manner, so the central government has felt comfortable leaving certain matters up to them. In addition, the regional bodies provide a convenient and sensitive source of information and intelligence for the province.

The particular form of regional government found in Quebec may not be satisfactory for all provinces, but the value of the principles remains. Local participation and influence are critical to reflect the unique circumstances of each location. At the same time, such bottom-up development needs an institutional context of strong regional governance to make it work. The inevitable conflicts of interest that emerge among municipalities require multiple venues for the expression, negotiation, and compromise that must take place before action is possible. Accountability and representation are necessary ingredients for establishing an adequate level of trust that will allow the system to work. All of this requires the development of a common language and understanding for collaboration.

Example: Governing across Understandings

It is especially challenging to find a common understanding for collaboration between formal government institutions and more informal community agencies and groups. Our formal systems of governance are primarily organized on the basis of generalized principles, policies, and regulations—essential ingredients of bureaucracies. To communicate effectively with such organizations, and to access the resources they control, it is necessary to represent oneself, one's community, or one's concerns in a manner that conforms to those principles and policies. In most cases, this means identifying oneself in terms of the appropriate role or objective that the organization will recognize. To access employment insurance, for example, I must have a social insurance number, be registered as a worker, and have suffered the loss of my job. Similarly, for a community to access funds for improvements to its sewerage system, it must represent itself in terms of the criteria appropriate to the relevant provincial regulations.

Such representations of individuals and communities are consistent with a space-based approach. Principles, policies, and regulations are formulated in terms of general characteristics; these characteristics are applicable to many different places and provide a common basis for comparison that is relatively ahistorical and generalizable. Expressing and negotiating unique local circumstances and needs, therefore, requires the capacity to reformulate those specific needs in terms of these general policies and regulations—a capacity most often reflected in the work of community development officers, lobbyists, and lawyers.

Place-based approaches, however, are more often reflected in a narrative style of representation and discourse. This approach emphasizes understanding and decision making on the basis of stories, unique social relations, and specific historical circumstances. From a narrative point of view, we cannot represent ourselves without including the story of our parents, our unique history, our friends, and our associates. In contrast, the bureaucratic or essentialist approach is about representing ourselves on the basis of roles, skills, or generalized characteristics. Both are critical ways of knowing and both are in a struggle for legitimacy—a struggle made most visible when it comes to our efforts for bottom-up governance.

Narrative ways of knowing and representation are closely related to an emphasis on "place." A dramatic illustration of this comes to us via the extensive work of Chandler and his colleagues in British Columbia (2003). In their work on adolescent suicide among aboriginal peoples, they discovered a strong relationship between suicide and the failure to recognize aboriginal culture. In those communities where the history and culture were celebrated, the suicide rate dropped dramatically (Fig. 20.3).

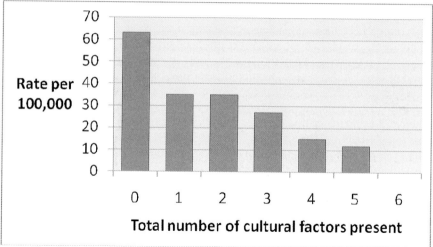

Fig. 20.3 Youth suicide rates by the number of cultural factors in the community, 1993–2000 (Chandler *et al.*, 2003, p. 43).

Their subsequent work has led them to argue the following case. First, a strong sense of identity and continuity is essential for healthy personal and social resiliency (and is an important mitigating factor against suicide). Second, identity and continuity are rooted in local events, relationships, and history—especially among narrative-based cultures. Third, undermining the legitimacy and credibility of local history and relationships has significant negative effects on the identity of those closely connected with it.

This research and supporting work among rural Quebec adolescents (Dagenais, 2007) suggest that place-based perspectives are important as more than simply a special focus of analysis for designing policy and research. They touch on a critical feature of our sense of self and humanity along with our ability to function in confidence and sympathy with others. The research also suggests that we need to aggressively seek to understand the nature of, and relationship between, narrative and essentialist approaches to the world. The disastrous policies of the Canadian federal government directed to the eradication of aboriginal culture, the elimination of cultural and ethnic traditions, and the relocation of communities make clear that the eradication of narrative for essentialist approaches is a questionable policy. Instead, we are much better off searching for new ways to integrate the strengths of narrative understandings with those of essentialist approaches in order to build new forms of governance that respect local places.

The Carcross/Tagish Nation in the Yukon provides an excellent example of one way this might occur. As a result of recent land and governance settlements, the Carcross/Tagish Nation—along with many aboriginal groups in British Columbia and other parts of Canada—are faced with the enormous challenge of organizing their economic, social, health, educational, political, and welfare institutions. They have responded with an innovative and promising approach that bodes well for the future of place-based governance (Carcross/Tagish First Nation, 2008).

Each of their policy documents begins with a study of stories—primarily oral stories told by their elders and recorded with a view to particular policy objectives. They started with family policy, compiling the stories and studying them in order to identify principles and themes that inform the Carcross/Tagish people's view of the role, importance, and nature of family in their culture. Out of these stories, they developed the positions, programs, and criteria that are necessary to merge with the more essentialist approach of Canada's government and judicial systems, producing a policy document to guide their institution building and their relations with other levels of government. The final act was to design a dance that represents the policy and its roots in the history and culture of the nation which developed it. So far, the territorial authorities have accepted this innovative approach to self-government—one that recognizes the people and places of Carcross, but which merges with the statutes and regulations of the broader government.

We include this example for two reasons. First, it illustrates some of the implications of our focus on place—implications that are likely to take us outside the comfort of our research and governance traditions and challenge us to entertain new forms of thinking and new forms of governance that are better adapted to the idiosyncrasies of place. Second, it inspires us to see how such exploration and transformation might be done—in this case learning from the people and cultures that we were so quick to discount and suppress. Many other experiments of this nature are taking place as we come to agreements with native peoples in British Columbia, in Nunavut, and across Canada.

Implications for Policy and Action

This brief survey identifies many questions that require further investigation. We can begin with those posed at the beginning of this chapter: What are the major stressors that rural places are likely to face in the future? In this book and elsewhere, we have answered this question with a relatively long list: urbanization, global competition, increasing importance of knowledge, climate change, and immigration, to name a few. But these chapters also illustrate how the characteristics of the place in which one lives will significantly alter the nature of those stressors—in some cases minimizing their impact; in others, increasing them significantly. Policies and programs must take those local conditions into account through research and the reorganization of governance.

Our second question asked: What are the assets that can be used to position local communities for the future? Our answers to this question reinforce the importance of "place" in the identification of assets (and liabilities). Each place will have its particular constellation of assets that may serve to mitigate or build upon the stressors. But we also have something to say about the things to consider when exploring potential local assets. Look broadly in that exploration. Consider social, natural, cultural, historical, formal, and informal assets as well as the usual economic, financial, land, and leadership ones. Remember as well that the successful use of assets is usually about recombining ones that are already in place rather than creating new ones. This is the message of Argent *et al.*, Bruce, Gayler, Markey, Ouchi, and Vodden.

Our third question—How can rural communities best position themselves for the future?—is intimately linked to the second and is also, of course, directly linked to identifying where people in each community would like to be in the future. In many ways, this question is the most difficult to answer—as reflected in the amount of attention devoted to it by the authors in this book. However, they provide some important insights regarding the potential directions to follow. First, they illustrate how good governance is inclusive, involving formal and informal organizations, local and regional groups, all relevant parties, and all relevant levels. Second, they show how good governance can be difficult. Storey, Ramsey, Loudiyi, and Gayler remind us that with multiple parties, there will be many conflicting interests, so we need to provide the venues for these differences of opinion to emerge, be debated, and be decided. Third, good governance needs imagination and flexibility. There are many ways to understand and manage the challenges we face, but the best responses often come from a new blending of them in place-appropriate ways (Argent *et al.*, Bruce, Gayler, Markey, Ouchi, and Vodden). Fourth, good governance needs a long-term vision. The example from Quebec provides an example of this principle, as does the Carcross approach. They both exemplify planning for generations, not just months or even years.

Finally, the chapters in this book reinforce the value of research as a tool for both space- and place-based approaches. Research has provided us with the ability to identify underlying processes of social change and the long-term trends associated with space-focused analysis of those changes. Research can also demonstrate the value of a place-based focus. This book shows how research can identify and interpret the anomalies in the general processes and trends, the many ways in which local communities and regions can reverse their fortunes, overcome deep-rooted trends and patterns, and create new opportunities for themselves and others through a focus on the special circumstances of their place. Redirecting our attention to the importance of place not only promises to advance our understanding of its role in rural change but also provides a more optimistic and inspiring view of rural communities. That optimism and inspiration are bound to produce the local action required for rural revitalization.

Note

1. For each five-year period, the data are tabulated within the (constant) boundaries applicable to the census year at the end of the five-year period. In 2006, Census Metropolitan Areas (CMAs) have a total population of 100,000 or more (with 50,000 or more in the urban core) and include all neighbouring towns and municipalities where 50% or more of the workforce commutes to the urban core. Census Agglomerations (CAs) have 10,000 or more in the urban core and include all neighbouring towns and municipalities where 50% or more of the workforce commutes to the urban core. Metropolitan Influenced Zones (MIZ) are assigned on the basis of the share of the workforce that commutes to any CMA or CA. In a strong MIZ, 30% or more commute; moderate MIZ, 5% to 29%; weak MIZ, 1% to 5%; no MIZ, no commuters.

References

Alasia, A., Bollman, R., Parkins, J., and Reimer, B. (2008) *An Index of Community Vulnerability: Conceptual Framework and Application to Population and Employment Changes, 1981 to 2001* (Catalogue No. 21-601-MIE No. 088). Statistics Canada, Ottawa.

Bollman, R. (2007) *Factors Driving Canada's Rural Economy, 1914 to 2006* (Catalogue No. 21-601-MIE No. 083). Statistics Canada, Ottawa.

Bollman, R., and Clemenson, H. (2008) Structure and change in Canada's rural demography: An update to 2006. *Rural and Small Town Canada Analysis Bulletin, 7,* 7.

Carcross/Tagish First Nation. (2008) *Traditional Beliefs and Practices.* Book One, *Our Place, Our Responsibilities,* www.ctfn.ca/ (accessed 20 September 2008).

Chandler, M., Lalonde, C., Sokol, B., and Hallett, D. (2003) *Personal Persistence, Identity Development, and Suicide: A Study of Native and Non-Native North American Adolescents* (Monographs of the Society for Research in Child Development 68(2), Series, No. 273). Blackwell, Malden, MA.

Dagenais, D. (2007) Le suicide comme meurte d'une identité. *Recherches sociographiques* 48(3), 139–160.

Government of Alberta. (2009a) Alberta's Regional Economic Development Alliances overview, www.albertacanada.com/documents/RD-RED_REDAOverview.pdf (accessed 21 March 2009).

_____. (2009b) Community economic development, http://www.albertacanada.com/regionaldev/12 16.html (accessed 21 March 2009).

Halseth, G., and Sullivan, L. (2002) *Building Community in an Instant Town: A Social Geography of Mackenzie and Tumbler Ridge, British Columbia.* UNBC Press, Prince George.

Lovering, J. (1999) Theory led by policy: The inadequacies of the 'new regionalism' (Illustrated from the case of Wales). *International Journal of Urban and Regional Research* 23(2), 379–395.

Pierce, J., and Dale, A. (1999) *Communities, Development, and Sustainability across Canada.* UBC Press, Vancouver.

Rogers, M., and Jones, D. (2006) *The Changing Nature of Australia's Country Towns.* Victorian Universities Regional Research Network Press, Ballarat, Australia.

Index